The Conduct of War

1789-1961

A STUDY OF THE IMPACT OF THE FRENCH, INDUSTRIAL, AND RUSSIAN REVOLUTIONS ON WAR AND ITS CONDUCT

by Major-General J. F. C. Fuller

Library of Congress Cataloging in Publication Data

Fuller, J. F. C. (John Frederick Charles), 1878-1966.
The conduct of war, 1789-1961: a study of the impact of the French, industrial, and Russian revolutions on war and its conduct / by J. F. C. Fuller. – 1st Da Capo Press ed.
p. cm.
Originally published: New Brunswick, N.J.: Rutgers University Press, 1961.
Includes index.
ISBN 0-306-80467-0
1. Military art and science – History. 2. Military history, Modern, I. Title.
U39.F82 1992 91-35633
537.009 – dc20 CIP

First Da Capo Press edition – 1992

This Da Capo Press paperback edition of *The Conduct of War* is an unabridged republication of the edition published in New Brunswick, New Jersey, in 1961.

Published by Da Capo Press
A Member of the Perseus Books Group
http://www.dacapopress.com

10 9 8 7 6 5

Manufactured in the United States of America

The first ground handful of nitre, sulphur and charcoal drove monk Schwartz's pestle through the ceiling: what will the last do?

T. CARLYLE

Contents

Preface

*

The conduct of war, like the practice of medicine, is an art, and because the aim of the physician and surgeon is to prevent, cure, or alleviate the diseases of the human body, so should the aim of the statesman and soldier be to prevent, cure, or alleviate the wars which inflict the international body. Unfortunately this has been little appreciated, and while in recent times the art of healing has been placed on a scientific footing, the conduct of war has remained in its alchemical stage; worse still, during the present century it has reverted to its barbaric form of destruction and slaughter.

Should the reader doubt this, let him look back on the two world wars. Should he be content with their conduct, this book is not for him. Should he not be, then he cannot fail to see that instead of being curative they were baneful. The cure has been worse than the disease: an entire epoch has been upheaved and submerged as if by a global Krakatoa. Empires have vanished, Europe has been torn asunder, Germany divided, and revolution stalks the world. Today, fear of annihilation grips every heart; no longer are there any signs of stability, or feeling of security, and, as bad, no bonds of honour or even of common decency bind the nations together.

Europe has seen many wars; for a thousand years war has been the constant occupation of her turbulent peoples. Nevertheless, not one of them since the Thirty Years' War has been so catastrophic as the wars of the present century. Yet the reason is not to be sought in war itself, but in its conduct as related to the great revolutions since 1789: the decay of aristocracy and the advent of democracy, the developments of industry and capitalism, the emergence of the masses and of socialism, the progress of science and the advances in technology, the growth of populations and the popular press, the decay of religion and ever-advancing materialism. All these vast changes have recast civilization, and had their impacts on warfare been diagnosed, and the conduct of war shaped accordingly, there is no reason why the world of today should be in its present mess.

'The first, the grandest, the most decisive act of judgment which the Statesmen and General exercises is rightly to understand the War in which he engages, not to take it for something, to wish to make of it something, which by the nature of its relations it is impossible for it to be.'

So wrote Clausewitz 130 years ago, and had the statesmen and generals of the two world wars heeded these words, they could not have blundered as they did.

Not to take war for something 'which by the nature of its relations it is impossible for it to be' is a problem of history, of the impact of the changes in civilization on human conflict, and to examine these changes and trace their influence on the conduct of war is the thesis of this book. So far as I am aware, it is a subject which has never been examined deeply, and it is one so vast and so intricate that my study of it can be no other than an imperfect and a tentative one.

Because of this the book is in no sense a history of the wars fought since 1789, nor is their conduct viewed primarily from the military angle; instead from that of the pressure of political, economic and social developments upon it. To bring it within the scope of a volume of medium length, I have not attempted to examine all developments, and have selected those I believe to be the more important. Nor in the chapters which relate to individual wars have I attempted to discuss them in detail; instead I have chosen from them those phases which I consider best illustrate their conduct and more frequently their misconduct.

The most important chapter is the one on Clausewitz, the father of modern war, and instead of attempting to condense his theories, I have quoted liberally from his *On War* for two reasons: because he was the first and remains one of the few who grasped that war 'belongs to the province of social life'; and because, although I have met many soldiers, politicians and others who have quoted or criticized his theories, I have come across only three or four who had carefully studied his great work. One of them was the late Colonel F. N. Maude, the editor of the second edition of *On War,* who over fifty years ago introduced Clausewitz to me. Of course there must be many others; nevertheless, none of them would seem to have been among those who were responsible for the conduct of the last world war on the part of the Western Allies, otherwise they could not have made such a ghastly hash of it.

I have also quoted freely from other writers, notably from the works of Marshal Foch, Lenin and Hitler, and albeit this may be somewhat tedious for the reader, I am certain it is more profitable to let these men speak for themselves than to attempt to paraphrase their theories.

As concerns the Industrial Revolution, throughout I have considered it as a single event from its hazy inception to the present day, and have not, as some writers have recently done, split it into two; one revolution up to the introduction of nuclear energy and the development of automation, and the other since their advent.

Other points I would mention for the guidance of the reader are:

Throughout the period under review, wars may be sorted into two categories; those with limited and those with unlimited political aims, and it is the first and not the second which have been profitable to the victor.

Never in war shackle yourself to the absolute. Never bind yourself with irrevocable compacts or decisions. Like a game of chance, war has no predetermined end. Throughout, action should always be adapted to circumstances, and circumstances are always fluid.

Brutality in war seldom pays, this is a truism with few exceptions. Another is, never drive your enemy to despair, for although it may win you the war, it will almost certainly prolong it to your disadvantage.

Throughout the history of war it is noticeable how frequently enemies and friends change sides in rotation. Therefore, once you have knocked your enemy out, it is wise to set him on his feet again, because the chances are that you will need his assistance in the next conflict.

Finally, I would like to conclude with a suggestion. There

are many manuals on war, and although I am no great lover of official textbooks, when I had written this book it occurred to me that there was ample room for one which should head the list – namely on 'The Conduct of War'. It should be written for both statesmen and soldiers, and be made compulsory reading. With advantage it might be divided into two parts: 'How to Conduct a War' and 'How not to Conduct a War'; for the second part, as this book will show, there is a superabundance of raw materials.

December 1960 J. F. C. FULLER

CHAPTER I

The Limited Wars of the Absolute Kings

*

1 · The Thirty Years' War and the Italian Condottieri

The age of the absolute kings arose from the ashes of the Wars of Religion, which culminated in the Thirty Years' War (1618–1648), the latter half of which was a hideous conflict of hastily enrolled mercenaries, as often as not accompanied by hordes of starving people.[1] When, in 1648, the Peace of Westphalia put an end to the anarchy, Central Europe lay in ruins; 8,000,000 people are said to have perished, not counting some 350,000 killed in battle. In one district of Thuringia, of 1,717 houses in 19 villages only 627 survived; in Bohemia, of 35,000 villages no more than 6,000 were inhabitable, and the population had shrunk from 2,000,000 to 700,000. During the war cannibalism was not unknown, and the people were so sunk in superstition that, in 1625 and 1628, the Bishop of Würzburg is said to have burnt 9,000 persons for witchcraft, and, in 1640–1641, 1,000 were burnt in the Silesian principality of Neisse.

It was the revolting cruelty of this war which brought its bludgeonry into contrast with the more humane practice of war in Italy during the fifteenth century. In Florence, in Milan, and in other ducal principalities, in their factional contests their tyrants relied on highly trained, professional mercenaries hired out by their *condottieri*, or contractor captains. These soldiers fought solely for profit; one year they might sell their services to one prince and to his rival the next. For them war was a business as well as an art, in which the ransom of prisoners was

[1] Gindely (*History of the Thirty Years' War* (1884), Vol. II, p. 334) mentions an army of 38,000 fighting men followed by 127,000 women, children and followers.

more profitable than killing their employer's enemies. Because war was their trade, to prolong a war rather than end it was clearly to their advantage; hence the historian Guicciardini writes: 'They would spend the whole summer on the siege of a fortified place, so that wars were interminable, and campaigns ended with little or no loss of life';[1] and by the end of the fifteenth century such noted soldiers as the *condottieri* Paolo Vitelli and Prospero Colonna declared that 'wars are won rather by industry and cunning than by the actual clash of arms'.[2]

Of these soldiers Sir Charles Oman writes:

'The consequence of leaving the conduct of war in the hands of the great mercenary captains was that it came often to be waged as a mere tactical exercise or a game of chess, the aim being to manoeuvre the enemy into an impossible situation, and then capture him, rather than to exhaust him by a series of costly battles. It was even suspected that *condottieri*, like dishonest pugilists, sometimes settled beforehand that they would draw the game. Battles when they did occur were often very bloodless affairs . . . Machiavelli cites cases of general actions in which there were only two or three men-at-arms slain, though the prisoners were to be numbered by hundreds.'[3]

In these inter-mercenary struggles the notion of a foreign diplomacy began to take root, and a distinction between the might of the soldier and the rights of the citizen began to appear. Thus it came about that Italy served as a laboratory for the early diplomatists and jurists of the sixteenth and seventeenth centuries.

2 · *The Jurists and the Limitation of War*

The most noted of the jurists was Hugo Grotius (1583–1645) who during the Thirty Years' War opened an attack on the international anarchy and the destructiveness of unlimited war in his *De Jure Belli ac Pacis*, a textbook of international law, in which he recommended moderation in fighting,

[1] Cited in *The Cambridge Medieval History*, Vol. VIII, p. 656.

[2] Cited by F. L. Taylor in *The Art of War in Italy, 1494–1529* (1921) p. 11.

[3] *Cambridge Medieval History*, Vol. VIII, p. 656.

making conquests, in despoiling the enemy's country, and in dealing with his civil population. Immediately after the war, Thomas Hobbes (1588–1679) lay down in his *Leviathan* that 'it is a precept, or general rule of Reason, *That every man ought to endeavour Peace, as farre as he has hope of obtaining it; and when he cannot obtain it, that he may seek, and use, all helps, and advantages of Warre*'. The first he calls the 'Fundamentall Law of Nature; which is, *to seek Peace, and follow it.* The second, the summe of the Right of Nature; which is, *By all means we can, to defend ourselves.*'[1]

Neither he nor Grotius nor any jurist of the seventeenth and eighteenth centuries contended that war should be outlawed. They were wise enough to exclude so utopian a possibility, and instead to urge that its violence and destructiveness should be moderated, and what moderation demanded was discussed and codified at length by Emmerich de Vattel (1714–1767) in his *The Law of Nations*, published at Neuchâtel in 1758. In it he asks the question: Since all belligerents affirm the justice of their cause, who shall be judge between them? His answer is: Because there is no judge, recourse must be made to rules whereby warfare may be regulated. These rules he called 'the voluntary law of nations'.

'The first rule of that law', he wrote, 'is that *regular war, as to its effects, is to be accounted just on both sides*. This is absolutely necessary . . . if people wish to introduce any order, any regularity, into so violent an operation as that of arms, or to set any bounds to the calamities of which it is productive, and leave a door constantly open for the return of peace. It is even impossible to point out any other rule of conduct to be observed between nations, since they acknowledge no superior judge.

'Thus, the rights founded on the state of war, the lawfulness of its effects, the validity of the acquisition made by arms, do not, externally and between mankind, depend on the justice of the cause, but on the legality of the means in themselves, – that is, on everything requisite to constitute a *regular war*.'[2]

Of the methods proper to employ in war he writes:

[1] *Leviathan*, Part I, Chap. XIV.
[2] *The Law of Nations* (trans. Joseph Chitty, 1834), pp. 381–2.

'All damage done to the enemy unnecessarily, every act of hostility which does not tend to procure victory and bring the war to a conclusion, is a licentiousness condemned by the law of nature.

'But this licentiousness is unavoidably suffered to pass with impunity, and, to a certain degree, tolerated, between nation and nation. How then shall we, in particular cases, determine with precision, to what lengths it was necessary to carry hostilities in order to bring the war to a happy conclusion? And even if the point could be exactly ascertained, nations acknowledge no common judge: each forms her own judgment of the conduct she is to pursue in fulfilling her duties. If you once open a door for continual accusation of outrageous excess in hostilities, you will only augment the number of complaints, and influence the minds of the contending parties with increasing animosity: fresh injuries will be perpetually springing up; and the sword will never be sheathed till one of the parties be utterly destroyed. The whole, therefore, should, between nation and nation, be confined to general rules, independent of circumstances, and sure and easy in the application. Now the rules cannot answer this description, unless they teach us to view things in an absolute sense, – to consider them in themselves and in their own nature.'[1]

Therefore moderation is the keynote, and nothing must be done to hinder a return to peace, of which Vattel says:

'A treaty of peace can be no more than a compromise. Were the rules of strict and rigid justice to be observed in it, so that each party should precisely receive every thing to which he has a just title, it would be impossible ever to make a peace. First, with regard to the very subject which occasioned the war, one of the parties would be under a necessity of ackowledging himself in the wrong, and condemning his own unjust pretensions; which he will hardly do, unless reduced to the last extremity. But if he owns the injustice of his cause, he must at the same time condemn every measure he has pursued in support of it: he must restore what he has unjustly taken, must reimburse the expenses of the war, and repair damages. And how can a just estimate of all the damages be formed? What

[1] Ibid., p. 369.

price can be set on all the blood that has been shed, the loss of such a number of citizens, and the ruin of families? Nor is this all. Strict justice would further demand that the author of an unjust war should suffer a penalty proportionate to the injuries for which he owes satisfaction, and such as might ensure the future safety of him whom he has attacked. How shall the nature of that penalty be determined, and the degree of it precisely regulated? In fine, even he who had justice on his side may have transgressed the bounds of justifiable self-defence, and been guilty of improper excesses in the prosecution of the war whose object was originally lawful: here then are so many wrongs, of which strict justice would demand reparation. He may have made conquests and taken booty beyond the value of his claim. Who shall make an exact calculation, a just estimate of this? Since, therefore, it would be dreadful to perpetuate the war, or to pursue it to the utter ruin of one of the parties, – and since however just the cause in which we are engaged, we must at length turn our thoughts towards the restoration of peace, and ought to direct all our measures to the attainment of that salutary object, – no other expedient remains than that of coming to a compromise respecting all claims and grievances on both sides, and putting an end to all disputes, by a convention as fair and equitable as circumstances will admit of. In such convention no decision is pronounced on the original cause of the war, or on those controversies to which the various acts of hostility might give rise; nor is either of the parties condemned as unjust, – a condemnation of which few princes would submit; – but, a simple agreement is formed, which determines what equivalent each party shall receive in extinction of all his pretensions.'[1]

Further: because 'The effect of the treaty of peace is to put an end to the war, and to abolish the subject of it';[2] therefore, 'If an unjust and rapacious conqueror subdues a nation, and forces her to accept hard, ignominious, and insupportable conditions, necessity obliges her to submit: but this apparent tranquillity is not a peace; it is an oppression which she endures only so long as she wants the means of shaking it off,

[1] Ibid., pp. 437–8.
[2] Ibid., p. 438.

and against which men of spirit rise on the first favourable opportunity.'[1]

3 · *The Armies of the Absolute Kings*

Whatever the jurists might propose would have been of little avail had not papal authority been drastically curtailed by the Reformation. Previously to it, the anointed king was looked upon as the accredited vicar of God for all secular purposes within his realm; subsequently to it, in Protestant States he became so for religious purposes also, and in Catholic countries monarchs ceased to admit that their coronation by an archbishop was anything other than the consecration of their titles. When in 1661 Louis XIV took over personal rule in France he assumed the power and rights of an absolute monarch. His theory of life was theocratic; as God's vice-regent he was possessed of divine infallibility, and he and his court became the model copied by all continental kingdoms. In brief, politically a return was made to the rule of the Italian despots.

There was, however, one great difference between the fifteenth century despots and the seventeenth and eighteenth century kings – a military one. While the power of the former resided in their professional mercenaries, the latter based their power on professional standing armies, and although the origin of the standing army is to be traced back to the formation of the *compagnies de l'ordonnance du roi* by Charles VII of France in 1445–1448, it was not until the old Spanish army was, in 1643, defeated at Rocroi by the Great Condé, that the French army – soon to be reorganized by Louvois – set the fashion for all standing armies for over a century. Unlike the earlier type, these new standing armies were permanently kept on a war footing, and were exclusively at the disposal of their respective sovereigns. Of them, in his *International Law*, Oppenheim writes:

'. . . the evolution of the laws and usages of war could not have taken place at all, but for the institution of standing armies. . . . The humanizing of the practice of war would have been impossible without [their] discipline; . . . and without them the important distinction between members of armed forces and private individuals could not have arisen.'[2]

[1] Ibid., p. 445. [2] Fourth Edition (1926), Vol. II, p. 136.

The separation of the soldier from the civilian was largely due to the horror of the barbarities the latter had suffered in the Thirty Years' War. Further, the exhaustion in population, in resources and in the wealth of every country in Central Europe had been so great that the new standing armies had to be limited in size; also the indifferent state of communications and agriculture restricted the growth of large ones.[1] In every country the army took the form of a disciplined body of long service troops, set apart from the civil population, and rigorously restricted as to its conduct in peace and war.

4 · *Limited Warfare*

In the opening sentence of his *Reveries*[2] Marshal Saxe, one of the most successful generals of the eighteenth century, writes: 'Troops are raised either by voluntary engagement, or by capitulation [contract]; sometimes too by compulsion, but most commonly by artifice . . . such as that of secretly putting money into a man's pocket, and afterwards challenging him for a soldier', which he reprobates. The men were recruited largely from the dregs of society, and in consequence discipline was ferocious. According to Frederick the Great, since honour meant nothing to them, 'They must be made to fear their officers more than danger', and that 'the slightest loosening of discipline would lead to barbarization'.[3]

Whether it would have done so may be disputed, but what cannot be is that brutal discipline went far to limit tactics to

[1] Marshal Saxe considered the ideal size of an army to be 46,000 men – 34,000 foot and 12,000 horse – say, 50,000 with gunners, etc.

[2] Posthumously published in French and English in 1757. In spite of Carlyle's stricture – 'a strange military farrago' – it is the work of a highly imaginative and unconventional soldier. Maurice Count de Saxe (1696–1750) was a natural son of Augustus Elector of Saxony (later Augustus II of Poland) and Countess Aurora Königsmark. He was present, under Eugène, at the sieges of Tournai and Mons and battle of Malplaquet in 1709; in 1712 served under Peter the Great; in 1715 took part in the siege of Stralsund; served against the Turks in 1717, and in 1734 under Marshal Berwick in Spain. In 1741 he surprised and took Prague and was promoted Marshal of France. In 1745 he defeated the Duke of Cumberland at Fontenoy; in 1747 won the battles of Rocoux and Lauffeldt, and in 1748 captured Maestricht.

[3] Cited in *Makers of Modern Strategy*, edit. Edward Mead Earle (1943), p. 55.

close order operations – those carried out under the eyes of the officers – because the only escape from the lash was desertion. In the eighteenth century it became so prevalent that Frederick drew up elaborate rules to prevent it: night marches were to be avoided, men detailed to forage or sent to bathe had to be accompanied by officers, and pursuits were seldom to be made, because in the confusion men would escape. Other limiting factors were the high cost of standing armies coupled with the scarcity of money, and the high casualties in the battles of this period, when volleys were frequently delivered at from thirty to fifty paces distant. Although Saxe writes: 'I have seen whole vollies fired [at close range] without even killing 4 men',[1] possibly the reason was that on occasions a tacit agreement existed between the opposing lines to fire over each other's heads, because normally casualties were appalling. Colonel Nickerson quotes that at Malplaquet one authority estimates the losses of the Allies at thirty-three per cent, and another at twenty-two, and that fifteen to twenty per cent, was common during the Seven Years' War (1755–1763). At Torgau (1760) Frederick lost thirty per cent, and at Zorndorf (1758) the Russians fifty per cent, 'a world's record for a field army during a single day's fighting in which the defeated side is neither crushed nor unresistingly massacred.'[2]

This readily explains why battles were avoided and manoeuvring became the fashion. Another reason was the change in the system of subsistence. Because pillage was prohibited, armies had to be rationed by supply columns, which in their turn demanded the introduction of magazines fed from the home base, or by purchase of local products on cash payment. Normally magazines were established in fortresses or fortified towns, hence the prevalence of sieges to obtain possession of them. The chief disadvantage of the magazine system was that, if an army were to be adequately supplied, it limited its advance to seven marches from the nearest fortress, and two days from the nearest field bakery. Only when the supply system broke down was enforced requisitioning resorted to. So completely was civil life divorced from war that, in his *A Senti-*

[1] Op. cit., p. 20.
[2] *The Horde Army 1793–1939*, Hoffman Nickerson (1940), p. 59.

mental Journey through France and Italy, Laurence Sterne relates that during the Seven Years' War he left London for Paris with so much precipitation that 'it never entered my mind that we were at war with France', and that on his arrival at Dover it suddenly occurred to him he was without a passport. However, this did not impede his journey, and when he arrived at Versailles, the Duke of Choiseul, French Foreign Minister, had one sent to him. In Paris he was cheered by his French admirers, and at Frontignac was invited to theatricals by the English colony.[1]

The strategy resorted to was one of attrition, not of annihilation; to exhaust the enemy, not to kill him, and normally its aim was to strike at the enemy's line of supply and his fortresses, not at his army. As early as 1677, the Earl of Orrery observes that 'we make War more like Foxes than Lyons; and you will have twenty Sieges for one Battel.'[2] And some twenty years later Daniel Defoe writes: 'Now it is frequent to have armies of fifty thousand men of a side stand at bay within view of one another, and spend a whole campaign in dodging, or, as it is genteely called, observing one another, and then march off into winter quarters.'[3] At the siege of Pizzighetone, in 1793, we are offered a perfect example of a 'limited' siege. A truce had been arranged, and we read:

'A bridge thrown over the breach afforded a communication between the besiegers and the besieged: tables were spread in every quarter, and the officers entertained one another by turns: within and without, under tents and arbours, there was nothing but balls, entertainments and concerts. All the people of the environs flocked there on foot, on horseback, and in carriages: provisions arrived from every quarter, abundance was seen in a moment, and there was no want of stage doctors and tumblers. It was a charming fair, a delightful rendezvous.'[4]

In all these drawn-out operations of the limited warfare era, attrition was the key principle. Because money was seldom plentiful, and standing armies, unlike militias, had to be paid

[1] York edition (1904), pp. 231–93.

[2] *A Treatise on the Art of War, etc.* (1677), p. 15.

[3] *The Earlier Life and Chief Earlier Works of Daniel Defoe,* Henry Morley (1889), p. 135.

[4] *Memoirs of Goldoni,* (trans. John Black, 1814), Vol. I, p. 207.

all the year round, it was obvious to the enlightened soldiers of this age that to exhaust the enemy's treasury was as potent a means of winning a war, and normally at smaller loss to oneself, than to attempt to destroy his army in battle. Money, not blood, was the deciding factor, and when through constant manoeuvring, which demanded high skill and sure judgment, the enemy's treasury began to run dry, rather than face bankruptcy he foreclosed with his opponent in a negotiated peace. This, in other words, is what Marshal Saxe has to say on the subject of a battle:

'Although I have dwelt so much upon the subject of general engagements, yet I am far from approving of them in practice, especially at the commencement of a war; yet I am persuaded that an able General might avoid them, and yet carry on the war as long as he pleased. Nothing reduces an enemy so much as that method of conduct, or is productive of so many advantages.'[1]

Modern critics, and notably Marshal Foch, have assumed that he was altogether opposed to fighting battles, and have ridiculed him for holding what to them is such an unwarlike view; an error, due either to their failure to read his *Reveries*, or, in order to support their contentions, to omit the rest of the paragraph.

The victor of Fontenoy, Rocoux and Lauffeldt appreciated as fully as did Frederick and Foch the value of battle; he concludes his paragraph as follows:

'Nevertheless, I would not be understood to say, that an opportunity to bring on a general action, in which you have all imaginable reason to expect the victory, ought to be neglected: but only to insinuate, that it is possible to make war, without trusting anything to accident; which is the highest point of skill and perfection, within the province of a General. If then, circumstances are so much in your favour, as to induce you to come to an engagement, it is necessary, in the next place, that you should know how to reap the profits of the victory, which is to follow; and, above all things, that you should not content yourself, with being master of the field of battle only, according to the custom which prevails at present.

[1] Op. cit., pp. 163–4.

The maxim, that it is most prudent to suffer a defeated army to make its retreat, is very religiously observed; but it is nevertheless founded upon a false principle: for you ought, on the contrary, to prosecute your victory, and to pursue the enemy to the utmost of your power: his retreat, which before perhaps was so regular and well conducted, will presently be converted into a confirmed rout.'[1]

During this era, in spite of its manoeuvres and sieges, many great battles were fought, and at least eight of them were decisive ones. Also it produced many great generals, to mention but a few: Vauban, Turenne, Eugène, Marlborough, Charles XII, Villars, Saxe, Frederick and Suvarov.

The comments of Sir John Fortescue upon eighteenth century warfare are worth recording:

'The object of a campaign in those days', he writes, 'was not necessarily to seek out an enemy and beat him. There were two alternatives prescribed by the best authorities, namely, to fight at an advantage or to subsist comfortably. Comfortable subsistence meant at its best subsistence at the enemy's expense. A campaign wherein an army lived on the enemy's country . . . was eminently successful, even though not a shot was fired. To force an enemy to consume his own supplies was much, to compel him to supply his opponents was more, to take up winter-quarters in his territory was very much more. Thus to enter an enemy's borders and keep him marching backwards and forwards for weeks without giving him a chance of striking a blow, was in itself no small success, and success of a kind which galled inferior generals, such as William of Orange, to desperation and so to disaster.'[2]

And of this rational, and therefore unemotional, system of war Guglielmo Ferrero's conclusion is:

'Restricted warfare was one of the loftiest achievements of the eighteenth century. It belongs to a class of hot-house plants which can only thrive in an aristocratic and qualitative civilisation. We are no longer capable of it. It is one of the fine things we have lost as a result of the French Revolution.'[3]

[1] Op. cit., p. 164.
[2] *A History of the British Army* (1899), Vol. I, p. 355.
[3] *Peace and War* (1933), pp. 63–64.

CHAPTER II

The Rebirth of Unlimited War

*

1 · Rousseau and the French Revolution

When in 1782 Edward Gibbon (1737–1794) was engaged on the fourth volume of his history, so serene did the political horizon appear to him that, in order to strike a contrast between the fall of the Roman Empire in the West and Europe of his day, he wrote:

'. . . a philosopher may be permitted to enlarge his views, and to consider Europe as one great republic, whose various inhabitants have attained almost the same level of politeness and cultivation. The balance of power will continue to fluctuate, and the prosperity of our own or the neighbouring kingdoms may be alternately exalted or depressed; but these partial events cannot essentially injure our general state of happiness, the system of arts, and laws, and manners, which so advantageously distinguish, above the rest of mankind, the Europeans and their colonies. . . . In peace, the progress of knowledge and industry is accelerated by the emulation of so many active rivals: in war, the European forces are exercised by temperate and undecisive contests.'[1]

Nevertheless, beyond the unruffled sky the most devastating political typhoon since the Reformation was brewing, and its coming was conjectured by the Comte de Guibert (1737–1794) who, eight years earlier, in his *Essai général de tactique* considered that wars of punctilious courtesies, of bloodless manoeuvres and honourable surrenders were only superficially cheap because they led to no grand political solution. In their place he proposed a very different kind of conflict.

'But let us suppose', he wrote, 'that a vigorous people were to arise in Europe: a people of genius, of resources and of political understanding: a people who united with these sterling

[1] *The History of the Decline and Fall of the Roman Empire*, Edward Gibbon (edit. J. B. Bury, 1925), Vol. IV, pp. 176, 178.

virtues and with a national militia a fixed plan of aggrandizement, and never lost sight of it: a people who knows how to make war cheaply and sustain itself on its victories. Such a people would not be compelled to limit its fighting by financial calculations. One would see this people subjugate its neighbours, and overthrow our feeble constitutions, like the north wind bends the frail reeds.'[1]

Twelve years earlier still – that is, in 1762 – the typhoon which was to overwhelm an epoch, and today is still bending the 'frail reeds', in embryo lay in the pages of Jean Jacques Rousseau's (1712–1778) *The Social Contract.* It was to be named ' e mocracy', the basis of which – that all men are equal – was also the basis of Christianity; and although, since times immemorial, moralists and philosophers had emphasised it, and never more so than during the first half of the eighteenth century, it was not until Rousseau's glowing phrase – 'Man is born free, and everywhere he is in chains' – lit the fuse of the bomb of the Age of Reason that an explosion became inevitable.

In his earlier work, *Discourse on the Origin of Inequality,* published in 1753, Rousseau held that in the state of nature man had been a noble savage.[2] Now, in his *Social Contract,* he exalted him to the position of an abstract being unrelated to place, time and circumstances. He opens his argument by asking the question: Why is it that man who is born free is everywhere enslaved? His answer is: Because the only legitimate government by natural (divine) right is the rule of the popular majority. The Contract, he writes, was: '. . . each of us puts in common his person and his whole power under the supreme direction of the general will . . . each giving himself to all, gives himself to nobody';[3] and should an individual refuse to do so, he must be forced by the majority to obey the general will, or, as he says, 'forced to be free'. By creating the myth that the sovereign will of the people is always right he endowed

[1] *Oeuvres Militaires de Guibert* (1803), Vol. I, p. 16.

[2] In an after-dinner conversation with Roederer, on 11th January 1803, Bonaparte said: 'I have been especially disgusted with Rousseau since I have seen the East. Savage man is a dog.' (*Oeuvres de Roederer*, 1854, Vol. III, p. 461.)

[3] *The Social Contract*, Bk. I, Chap. VI.

the nation-state with a quasi-divine sanction, and provided democratic revolutionaries with their most powerful weapon. Although he held that the organic idea of the State was hostile to organized Christianity, because the latter separates politics from religion, and thereby destroyed the unity of the State, he was aware that organized religion was a social necessity. In the place of Christianity he proposed a purely civil profession of faith, the articles of which the sovereign people would determine 'not exactly as dogmas of religion, but as *sentiments of sociability*, without which it is impossible to be a good citizen or a faithful subject.'[1]

Although his assumption that popular majorities are always able to discern the general interest and are willing to pursue it is patently a fallacious one,[2] it flattered the popular imagination and unthinkingly was accepted as an article of faith. Thus the jinni of popular absolutism was released from the monarchial brass bottle, to oust the absolutism of kings, to rebuild the tower of Babel, and to transform the auction-room of war into a slaughter-house.

In justice to Rousseau, it should be borne in mind that he drew his ideal from the classical city states, and held that popular majority rule was only workable in a country of limited size and population; he never suggested that it should be applied to so large a one as France.

When summing up his chapter on 'Philosophy of the Revolution', Mr P. F. Willert writes:

'The Revolution was an attempt to apply in practice the principle of individual freedom: a negative principle, mainly valuable as an instrument to overthrow restrictions, which have lost their use and meaning and have become injurious.[3] But it is remarkable that this negative principle was embraced

[1] Ibid., Bk. IV, Chap. VIII.

[2] Benjamin Franklin (1706–1790) was of the same opinion. He wrote: '. . . the judgement of a whole people, expecially of a free people is looked upon as infallible' (see Lord Acton's *Lectures on the French Revolution* (1932), pp. 21–22).

[3] Over 2,000 years before, Isocrates had said much the same thing to Philip of Macedon in his *Philippus:* 'Promise them [the Ionic cities] freedom, and scatter the word broadcast in Asia, which, falling on the soil of Hellas, has broken up our empire as well as that of the Lacedaemonians.' (*The Orations of Isocrates*, trans. J. H. Freese, Vol. I.)

with the fervour of a religious faith. The great work done by the philosophers was the part they took in exciting this fervour; and it was because there is little that is original in their teaching that it was received with enthusiasm.'[1]

On 14th July 1789, the rabble of Paris stormed the Bastille and massacred its garrison, and when the news was brought to Louis XVI he exclaimed: 'This is a revolt.' To which the Duke of Liaucourt replied: 'No, Sire, it is a revolution.'[2] And when the news of Louis' arrest at Varennes, on 21st June 1791, which put an end to his escape from France, reached Leopold II (1790–1792), Emperor of Austria, he declared that the arrest compromised the honour of all sovereigns, and he urged William II of Prussia (1786–1797) to rescue Louis and his queen, Marie Antoinette – Leopold's sister. The outcome was that, on 20th April 1792, France declared war on Austria, a war which, with one brief interlude, was to last until 1815. Two years before its declaration, on 20th May 1790, in the French National Assembly Mirabeau had predicted with remarkable clairvoyance what type of war it would be:

'je vous demande à vous-mêmes: sera-t-on mieux assuré de n'avoir que des guerres justes, équitables, si l'on délégue exclusivement à une assemblée de 700 personnes l'exercice du droit de faire la guerre? Avez-vous prévu jusqu'où les mouvements passionés, jusqu'où l'exaltation du courage et d'une fausse dignité pourroient porter et justifier l'imprudence . . . ? Pendant qu'un des membres proposera de délibérer, on demandera la guerre à grands cris; vous verrez autour de vous une armée de citoyens. Vous ne serez pas trompés par des ministres; ne le serez-vous jamais par vous-mêmes? . . . Voyez les peuples libres: c'est par des guerres plus ambitieuses, plus barbares qu'ils se sont toujours distingués. Voyez les assemblées politiques: c'est toujours sous le charme de la passion qu'elles ont décrété la guerre.'[3]

2 · *Conscription a Return to Barbarism*

France was lamentably unprepared for war: her treasury was

[1] *The Cambridge Modern History* (1904), Vol. VIII, pp. 34–35.

[2] Cited by Thomas Carlyle in *The French Revolution*, Bk. V, Chap. VII.

[3] Cited by Arnold J. Toynbee in *A Study of History* (1939), Vol. IV, p. 150.

bankrupt, her army chaotic, and her people hysterical. Her sole assets were that the bulk of her soldiers were too raw to fight in accordance with the rules which governed the 'sport of kings', and sufficiently intelligent to devise more practical ones of their own. Also, the Revolution had many admirers in neighbouring countries: in England Charles James Fox welcomed it and even condoned its crimes; in Germany its supporters were numerous, and the doctrine of the freedom of man was enthusiastically welcomed in the Netherlands, whose people were eager to cast off Austrian rule.

The first trial between the two forms of war, the now antiquated limited and the still embryonic unlimited, took place at Valmy on 20th September 1792, when the Prussians, under Charles William Frederick Duke of Brunswick, faced the French, under Charles François Dumouriez. Brunswick was a nephew of Frederick the Great, a highly cultured pedant, whose reputation was largely founded on his 1787 campaign in Holland, which was so completely bloodless that, in the eyes of his contemporaries, he was held to be the greatest soldier in Europe. Dumouriez, the son of a commissary of the French royal army, believed himself to be such; he was possessed of a fanatical audacity, and of principles he had but one – opportunism. When the two met, Brunswick so completely manoeuvred Dumouriez out of his position in the Argonne that, when the battle was fought, both armies faced their respective bases. There was practically no fighting, only a mutual cannonade of considerable intensity, toward the end of which, and as the Prussians were about to assault the ridge of Valmy, Brunswick suddenly summoned a council of war and pronounced the one and only decision he made during the campaign: it was '*Hier schlagen wir nicht*' ('We do not fight here'). After which he encamped his army, and, on the night of 30th September, skilfully withdrew from the last of the all but bloodless battlefields.

On the evening of 20th September, Goethe, who was present with the Prussians at the battle, turned to his dejected companions, and in reply to a question from one of them said: 'From this place and from this day forth commences a new era in the world's history, and you can all say that you were present at its birth.'[1] A hundred years later Marshal Foch summed up the influence of the cannonade in these words: 'The wars of Kings were at an end; the wars of peoples were beginning.'[2]

On 21st January 1793, as Carlyle puts it, 'the axe clanks down, and a King's Life is shorn away.' It is the life of Louis XVI; whereupon Danton cries: 'The coalised Kings threaten us; we hurl at their feet, as a gage of battle, the Head of a King.'[3] But where were the soldiers to follow up this grim challenge? They were so few that, a month later, the Convention decreed a compulsory levy of 500,000 men. Thereupon la Vendée burst into insurrection, and the Republic set out to march to Liberty over the corpses of her subjects.[4] This was the first step taken toward conscription – the return to tribal warfare.

Primitive tribes are armed hordes, in which every man is a warrior, and because the entire tribe engages in war, warfare is total. But since man abandoned the life of a hunter and of a nomad, with few exceptions, in the agricultural civilization which supplanted the barbaric, a distinction was made between the warrior and the food-producer – the non-combatant. In the classical city states, fully qualified citizens alone were enrolled in the city militias; in feudal times, the knights and their retainers when called to arms constituted but a minute fraction of the total population, and, as already mentioned, in the age of the absolute kings the civil population was altogether excluded from war. This differentiation was now abolished, and a return was made to the armed horde, this time on a national footing.

It was not a new idea, and it should not be confused with the one which underlay the old national levies, such as the Anglo-Saxon fyrd, which were only called out in time of war,

[1] Goethe's *Campaign in France in the Year 1792* (trans. Robert Farie, 1859), p. 31.

[2] Foch's *The Principles of War* (trans. Hilaire Belloc, 1918), p. 29.

[3] *The French Revolution*, Bk. II, Chap. VIII.

[4] General Westermann in La Vendée reported: 'I have crushed the children under the hoofs of the horses, massacred the women . . . who . . . will breed no more brigands. I have not a single prisoner with which to reproach myself. I have wiped out all. . . . The roads are strewn with corpses. . . . We take no prisoners: it would be necessary to feed them with the bread of Liberty' (cited in *The Armed Horde 1793–1939*, p. 91).

while conscript armies were standing armies. It is uncertain whether Machiavelli was the first to suggest the idea, but it is known that he composed the memorandum on the basis of which was promulgated the *Ordinanza* of 1506, the law which established obligatory military service between the ages of 18 and 30 in Florence. Later, Francis Bacon condemned the idea, and in his essay 'On Unity in Religion', he held it to be 'a thing monstrous to put it [the temporal sword] into the hands of the common people.' But in the eighteenth century, as previously mentioned, Guibert championed the idea, and so did Marshal Saxe who, when he referred to the raising of troops in his *Reveries*, asked the question: 'Would it not be better to establish a law, obliging men of all conditions of life, to serve their King and country for the space of 5 years?' and went on to expatiate on its application and advantages. But it was not until 23rd August 1793, that by a decree of the Convention the *levée en masse* was placed on a total footing. Article I of this law reads:

'From this moment until that in which our enemies shall have been driven from the territory of the Republic, all Frenchmen are permanently requisitioned for service in the armies.

'The young men shall fight; the married men shall forge weapons and transport supplies; the women will make tents and clothes and will serve in the hospitals; the children will make up old linen into lint; the old men will have themselves carried into the public squares to rouse the courage of the fighting men, to preach the unity of the Republic and hatred against Kings.

'The public buildings shall be turned into barracks, the public squares into munition factories, the earthern floors of cellars shall be treated with lye to extract saltpetre.

'All firearms of suitable calibre shall be turned over to the troops: the interior shall be policed with shotguns and with cold steel.

'All saddle horses shall be seized for the cavalry; all draft horses not employed in cultivation will draw the artillery and supply wagons.'[1]

[1] *Réimpression de l'Ancien Moniteur depuis la Réunion des Etats Généraux jusqu'au Consulat*, 25th August 1793 (Paris 1840–1845), Vol.

'This article', writes Toynbee, 'so deeply thrilled the deputies that they begged the rapporteur to recite it twice over; and each time it was cheered to the echo by men who sincerely believed that they were liberating themselves from Tyranny!'[2] And Colonel F. N. Maude, in his article on 'Conscription' in the eleventh edition of the *Encyclopaedia Britannica*, comments on it thus: 'There is perhaps no law in the statute-books of any nation which has exercised and is destined in the future to exercise a more far reaching influence on the future of humanity than this little known French act.'

From August that year onward, not only was war to become more and more unlimited, but finally total. In the fourth decade of the twentieth century life was held so cheaply that the massacre of civilian populations on wholesale lines became as accepted a strategical aim as battles were in previous wars. In 150 years conscription had led the world back to tribal barbarism.

3 · *The Changes due to Conscription*

Democracy made all men equal in theory, but it was conscription which did so in fact, and Condorcet must have sensed this when, in his *Esquisses d'un tableau historique des progrès de l'esprit humain*, he connected the rise of infantry with the rise of democracy. It would have been more correct had he reversed the sequence, because the musket made the infantryman, and the infantryman made the democrat: power to kill and, therefore, to enforce equality at the bayonet point was the essence of the question. Hence, one man one musket became one man one vote, until votes and muskets were to be reckoned in millions. This led to the greatest political and military transformation the world had as yet seen, which, as cited by Foch, was noted by Clausewitz as follows:

XVII, p. 478. '*Que voulez-vous?*' asks Barère in his report on this requisition of all Frenchmen, '*Un contingent . . . ? Le contingent de la France pour sa liberté comprend toute sa population, toute son industrie, tous ses travaux, tout son génie. . . . Publions une grand vérité: la liberté est devenue créancière de tous les citoyens: les uns lui doivent leur industrie, les autres leur fortune, ceux-ci leurs conseils, ceux-là leurs bras; tous lui doivent le sang qui coule dans leurs veines*' (cited in *A Study of History*, Vol. IV, p. 151).

[2] Ibid., Vol. IV, p. 151.

'By the strength and energy of its principles, by the enthusiasm with which it enraptured the people, the French Revolution had thrown *the whole weight of that people and all its forces* into the scale which had hitherto nothing but the weight of a *limited army* and of the *limited* (*regular*) *revenues* of the State.

'Paying little heed to the calculation of political alliances whereby cabinets anxiously weighed war or alliance, a calculation which weakened the force of the State and subordinated the brutal element of fighting to the reserves of diplomacy, the French army went haughtily forward through the countries and saw, to its own surprise and to that of its opponents, how superior are the natural force of a State and a great and simple motive to the artificial diplomatic assemblage in which these States stood mutually involved.

'The prodigious action of the French Revolution is certainly less due to the use of new military methods, than to a wholly transformed political and administrative system, to the character of the government, to the state of the nation, etc . . . that the other governments did not know how to appreciate those new conditions, that they tried to meet by ordinary means a display of overwhelming forces, this was the source of all their political errors.'

Foch's comment on this is:

'Truly enough, a new era had begun, the era of national wars, of wars which were to assume a maddening pace (*aux allures déchaînées*); for those wars were destined to throw into the fight all the resources of the nation; they were to set themselves the goal, not a dynastic interest, not of the conquest or possession of a province, but the defence or the propagation of philosophical ideas in the first place, next of the principles of independence, of unity, of immaterial advantages of various kinds. Lastly they staked upon the issue the interests and fortune of every individual private. Hence the rising of passions, that is elements of force, hitherto in the main unused.'[1]

To stimulate the thousands of recruits who poured into the

[1] *The Principles of War*, pp. 29–30. Foch does not give the source of his Clausewitz quotation; as it is not to be found in his *On War*, it must belong to another of his books.

depôts, reliance was placed on what today is called 'propaganda'. For the first time, on 25th April 1792, Rouget de Lisle's 'Marseillaise', the most soul-stirring of all war hymns, was sung in France, to intoxicate the multitudes. No step was left untaken by the demagogues to excite the pugnacity of the soldiers and foster hatred of their enemies. 'Without hate', writes George Sylvester Viereck, 'there can be no propaganda. Give me something to hate, and I guarantee to organize a powerful propaganda campaign anywhere within twenty-four hours.'[1] Hate governed France, hence warfare became interminable.

Propaganda unleashed the beast in man, and was called by a French Royalist, Mallet du Pan, a 'hellish tactic, . . . worthy of the monsters who had invented it . . . fifty thousand savage beasts, foaming at the mouth with rage and yelling like cannibals, hurl themselves at top speed upon soldiers whose courage has been excited by no passion.'[2]

Conscription changed the basis of warfare. Hitherto soldiers had been costly, now they were cheap; battles had been avoided, now they were sought, and however heavy were the losses, they could rapidly be made good by the muster-roll. Without conscription Napoleon's policy of conquest would have been impossible; in 1805, at Schönbrunn, he boasted to Metternich that he could afford to expend 30,000 men a month – men were now as cheap as dirt.

The armed hordes demanded a radical change in military administration and logistics. Hitherto armies had used tents; they had marched in long unbroken columns of route; had methodically concentrated before delivering battle, and had relied on supply columns, field bakeries, bread convoys, and magazines for their rations and forage. All this was either swept away or drastically modified. Tents vanished, and with them hundreds of wagons in which they were transported; instead, men bivouacked. The long, slow-moving columns of route were split up into compact divisional columns of all arms – miniature armies; this enabled concentration to be made during battle as well as before battle. Transport columns were

[1] *Spreading Germs of Hate* (1931), p. 16.
[2] Cited in *The Armed Horde*, p. 91.

cut to the bone, and compulsory requisitioning, which frequently meant plundering the countryside, was substituted for methodical rationing. These changes, which cut down the transport wagons and animals by thousands, added enormously to both the strategic and tactical mobility of the Revolutionary armies, and although increase in the distances of their marches and bivouacking in the open led to a higher human wastage than had the old and more comfortable system, conscription could readily make it good.

Conscription had yet another and very important influence on war. Because soldiers were recruited from all classes of society, on an average they were more intelligent than the men of the old royal armies, although not so highly disciplined. Not trained to carry out the mechanical evolutions of the period, they rapidly devised tactics which fitted their pugnacity and *élan*. Volley firing was either given up or largely supplemented by aimed deliberate fire; loose order was added to close order, and battalions of *tirailleurs* were raised, whose task it was to precede and prepare the way of the assault columns. The skirmishers were, says Sir Robert Wilson, 'as sharpsighted as ferrets and as active as squirrels.'[1] And the Duke of York's aide-de-camp wrote: 'No mobbed fox was ever more put to it to make his escape than we were, being at times nearly surrounded.'[2] Of the conscripts, a Prussian officer said: 'In the woods, when the soldiers break rank and have no drill movements to carry out, but only to fire under the cover of the trees, they are not only equal but superior to us. Our men, accustomed to fight shoulder to shoulder in the open field, found it more difficult to adopt that seeming disorder which was yet necessary if they were not to be targets for the enemy.'[3]

In spite of these overwhelming strategical and tactical advantages over the old royal armies, the conscript armies of the Revolution had one crucial defect which, politically, annulled one and all of them. This was the difficulty for a conscripted nation – that is, a nation in arms – a nation fed on violent

[1] *Life of Sir Robert Wilson*, H. Randolph (1862), Vol. I, p. 86.
[2] *Journals and Correspondence of Sir Henry Calvert* (1853), p. 220.
[3] Cited in *Les Guerres de la Révolution*, A. Chuquet, Vol. II, p. 96.

propaganda, to make an enduring peace. The peace treaties wrung from the vanquished were generally so unreasonable that they were no more than precarious armistices; the losers only signed them through duress, and with the full intention of repudiating them at the first opportunity.

'At the roots of this type of war, the war *aux allures déchaînées*', writes Ferrero, 'which the Revolution and the Empire thrust upon Europe, lies the psychological error of imagining that tremendous and crushing victories assist one to secure peace, whereas they really make it more difficult or even impossible to secure. This error is the key to the whole history of the Revolution, the Empire, and the nineteenth century up to our present confusions.'[1]

4 · *Democracy and Tribal Morality*

In Europe, with the exception of the Wars of Religion, which are near akin, wars *aux allures déchaînées* have been democratic conflicts, which derived their *élan* from the 'general will'. To quote Professor A. E. Freeman, the incessant wars between the democratic city-states of Classical Greece carried with them 'havoc and devastation', and 'every kind of wanton ravage'.[2] And, according to Sir Charles Oman, in the mediaeval wars of the democratic Swiss we find 'an appalling ferocity, and a cynical disregard for the rights of all neighbours . . . [they] were distinguished for their deliberate and cold-blooded cruelty.'[3] The behaviour of the democratic armies of the French Revolution – as exemplified by Westermann's conduct in La Vendée – was no whit different. Therefore it is strange to find that Professor Arnold Toynbee is at a loss to understand why democracy which emerged from the French Revolution, not merely failed to work against war 'but . . . positively put its "drive" into War.' How is this to be explained? 'And how is it possible', he asks, '*a priori*, for Democracy to act as an anti-social force? For Democracy "breathes the spirit of the Gospels . . . and its motive-force is Love".'[4]

[1] *Peace and War*, p. 127.

[2] *Historical Essays, Second Series* (1875), pp. 173–4.

[3] *The Art of War in the Middle Ages* (1924), Vol. II, p. 253.

[4] *A Study of History*, Vol. IV, pp. 156–7. The citation is from Henri Bergson's *Les Deux Sources de la Morale et de la Religion*.

This is as great a myth as Rousseau's 'noble savage', and as long as it persists, and democracy is held to be a peace-loving institution, no rational answer can be given to Toynbee's question. Nevertheless, the question is a valid one, because the understanding of the problem of war is wrapped up in its correct answer, and until it is correctly answered, there is little possiblity of moderating war, and absolutely none of eliminating it.

The answer is not to be discovered in abstract speculations but in human nature; of which Herbert Spencer once said: 'I believe you might as reasonably expect to understand the nature of an adult man by watching him for an hour (being in ignorance of his antecedents) as to suppose that you can fathom humanity by studying the last few thousand years of its evolution.'[1]

In 1892–1893, after half a century of work, Spencer completed his vast System of Philosophy with two volumes on *The Principles of Ethics*. In his studies of evolution he had hoped to find a code which placed human conduct (ethics) on a scientific footing. Instead, he discovered that evolution, as seen to work in human communities, spoke with two voices, each enunciating a separate code. He called the one the 'Code of Amity', and the other the 'Code of Enmity'. Of them he wrote:

Rude tribes and . . . civilized societies . . . have had continually to carry on an external self-defence and internal co-operation – external antagonism and internal friendship. Hence their members have acquired two different sets of sentiments and ideas, adjusted to these two kinds of activity.'[2]

'A life of constant external enmity generates a code in which aggression, conquest, and revenge, are inculcated, while peaceful occupations are reprobated. Conversely a life of settled internal amity generates a code inculcating the virtues conducing to a harmonious co-operation – justice, honesty, veracity, regard for each other's claims.'[3]

[1] *Life and Letters of Herbert Spencer*, D. Duncan (1908), p. 62.

[2] *The Principles of Ethics* (1892), Vol. I, p. 322. See also *Essays on Human Evolution*, Sir Arthur Keith (1946), pp. 104–5.

[3] Ibid., Vol. I, p. 471.

'As the ethics of enmity and the ethics of amity [arising] in each society in response to external and internal conditions respectively, have to be simultaneously entertained, there is formed an assemblage of utterly inconsistent sentiments and ideas.'[1] There thus comes 'to be two classes of duties and virtues, condemned and approved in similar ways, but one of which [code of Amity] is associated with ethical conceptions, and the other [code of Enmity] not.'[2]

Man is therefore acted upon by a double set of impulses: those supplied by nature which are inbred and have become instinctive, and those acquired by the pressure of his social environment. That the tribe may survive, tribal man must be willing to sacrifice himself in battle, and that the tribe may maintain its cohesion, he must submit himself to its taboos. Davie points out that the relation of tribes to one another is one of isolation, suspicion and hostility; but within the tribe the common interest against every other tribe compels its members to unite for self-preservation. That thus a distinction arises between one's own tribe – the 'in-group' – and other tribes – the 'out-group'; that between the members of the first peace and co-operation are essential, and that their inbred sentiment toward all outsiders is one of hatred and hostility. These two relations are correlative, and to reinforce his argument he quotes from Sumner's *Folkways*:

'The exigencies of war with outsiders are what make peace inside, lest internal discord should weaken the in-group for war. The exigencies also make government and law in the in-group, in order to prevent quarrels and enforce discipline. Thus war and peace have reacted on each other, and developed each other, one within the group, the other in the inter-group relations. The closer the neighbours, the stronger they are, the intenser the warfare, and then the intenser is the internal organization and discipline of each.'[3]

Thus it arises that there are two sets of morals – of mores – one for the in-group, and the other for the out-group, and

[1] Ibid., Vol. I, p. 316.
[2] Ibid., Vol. I, p. 324.
[3] *The Evolution of War. A Study of the Rôle in Early Societies*, Maurice R. Davie, (1929), p. 16; and *Folkways*, W. G. Sumner, (1906), p. 12.

both arise from the same interests. 'Against outsiders it is meritorious to kill, plunder, practise blood revenge and steal women . . .', whereas the opposite holds good for the in-group.[1]

This, in various contexts, has been know for centuries. For instance: Xenophon makes Cyrus object to his father's advice that a general must prove himself to be an arch-plotter, a cheat, a thief, and a robber, so that he may overreach his opponent at every turn. When Cyrus objects that this is contrary to the lessons he had been taught on how to behave, his father replies: 'Those lessons were for friends and fellow citizens, and for them they stand good; but for your enemies – do you not remember that you were taught to do much harm.'[2] Plato in his *Republic* makes Polemarchus reply to Socrates' question 'What is justice?' – 'Justice is helping friends and harming enemies.'[3] Hobbes in his *Leviathan* states: 'Force, and Fraud, are in warre the two Cardinall vertues',[4] which implies that in peacetime they are two cardinal vices. And David Hume in his *Essays and Treatises* writes: In war 'we recall our sense of justice and sympathy and permit injustice and enmity to take their place.'[5] A glance through almost any newspaper published during the First and Second World Wars will convince the most sceptical reader that this is still so.

The most dangerous foes of primitive man were those of his own species. Today man is man's only foe, and *homo homini lupus* is as true as it was half a million years ago. War and the chase still make their old appeal; this is why instinctively every small boy loves a gun, and every adult is thrilled by a murder.

War to the men of the Stone Age was not the business of a selected few, it was the occupation of every adult male, and it is still so, with the addition of numerous women. In savage warfare, the aim was to kill all enemy males and abduct the women and children. This has been improved upon by the invention of weapons which make discrimination between the victims impossible – slaughter is now on total lines.

[1] Davie, op. cit., p. 17.
[2] *Cyropaedia*, I, VI, 27–28.
[3] I, 334.
[4] Part I, Chap. XIII.
[5] Edit. 1772, Vol. II, p. 273.

Man as he is can only be explained by man as he was, and never by man as we would like him to be – the wishful thought of the pacifist. He is the product of the thousands upon thousands of generations of savage and bloodthirsty progenitors, who have bequeathed to him his instincts. Fear, the most potent of all, is the sentinel of barbarous and civilized man alike; it remains the oldest of protective mechanisms, and becomes manifested in every child before the end of its third month.[1] Extermination was the greatest dread of the tribal mind, and in no previous age has so great a dread of it possessed man's mind as in the present one.

Toynbee's question is now answered. The motive force of democracy is not love of others, it is the hate of all outside the tribe, faction, party or nation. The 'general will' predicates total war, and hate is the most puissant of recruiters.

[1] *This Human Nature*, Charles Duff (1917), p. 41.

CHAPTER III

Napoleonic Warfare

*

1 · Napoleon Bonaparte

Because the authority of a government, whatever be its character, is based on physical force,[1] the primary aim in a revolution is either to gain the support of or to disintegrate the military forces. In the first case, the revolution assumes the form of a *coup d'état*, and is seldom more than a limited confusion. In the second, it establishes an anarchy, and however fervently the people may support the revolutionary ideals, anarchy is the one thing they will not for long tolerate, and when it prevails they readily look for the man who will deliver them from it. When he appears, the normal sequel is for the energy generated by the anarchy to be directed outwardly in the form of a foreign war. This, in its turn, consolidates the people and normally leads to the establishment of a coercive regime which, with full military backing, takes the place of the original government.

Ten years before the storming of the Bastille in 1789, Guibert prophetically had written:

'A man will arise, perhaps one who hitherto was lost in the obscurity of the crowd; a man who has not made his name either by speech or writing; a man who in silence has meditated; a man who perhaps did not know his own talents, who can only become aware of them when called upon to exercise them; one who has studied very little. That man will seize hold of opinions, of opportunity, of fortune, and will say to the great man of theories what the practical architect, who addressed the Athenians, said to the oratorical architect: "All that my rival tells you, I will carry out." '[2]

[1] As Napoleon says: 'Without an Army . . . there is neither political independence nor civil liberty' (*Correspondance de Napoléon Ier* (1858–1869), III, No. 1800).

[2] *Oeuvres de Guibert* (1803), Vol. IV, p. 74.

Such a man was Napoleon Bonaparte (1769–1821) who, on the 13th of *Vendémaire*, Year 4 (5th October 1795), with his 'whiff of grapeshot' became apparent to all Paris. 'There was an eye to see in this man, a soul to dare and do. He rose naturally to be the King. All men saw that he *was* such.'[1]

He was the supreme egoist and architect, the entirely isolated and self-centred man who relied on himself alone and centralized everything. Méneval says of him: 'He took not only the initiative in thought, but also attended personally to the detail of every piece of business . . . his genius, superhuman in its activity, carried him away; he felt he possessed the *means* and the *time* to manage everything . . . in reality it was he who did everything.'[2]

Caulaincourt, the most illuminating of his memorialists, says much the same, but even more penetratingly: 'He spared neither pain, care nor trouble to arrive at his end', he writes, 'and this applied as much to little things as to great. He was, one might say, totally given over to his object. He always applied all his means, all his faculties, all his attention to the action or discussion of the moment. Into everything he put passion. Hence the enormous advantage he had over his adversaries, for few people are entirely absorbed by one thought or one action at one moment.'[3]

He was a man completely wrapped in his destiny, and he makes mention of this when, in 1812, he set out on the road to Moscow: 'I feel myself driven towards an end that I do not know. As soon as I shall have reached it, as soon as I shall become unnecessary, an atom will suffice to shatter me. Till then, not all the forces of mankind can do anything against me.'[4]

Apparent to his age, his task was to conquer, hidden from it and from himself, it was to create. In the destruction of an

[1] T. Carlyle in 'The Hero as King', *Heroes and Hero-Worship*.

[2] *Mémoires pour servir a l'Histoire de Napoléon Ier* (1894), Vol. III, pp. 50–51.

[3] *Memoirs of General de Caulaincourt Duke of Vicenza* (English trans. 1925), Vol. I, p. 93.

[4] Cited by Oswald Spengler in *The Decline of the West* (1925). Vol. I, p. 144. Oliver Cromwell made a similar remark; he said: why he mounted so high was because he did not know what was ordained for him.

Age he begot an Epoch, or, as Spengler puts it: 'Napoleon's life was an immense toil, not for himself, not for France, but for the Future.'[1]

The wars Napoleon waged were wars of conquest on the grand scale, and they had no precedent since the days of Charlemagne, with whom he was wont to compare himself.

In his first campaign in Italy (1796–1797) his aim was to seek out his enemy and destroy him in battle. This, and that he violated neutral territory, lived on the country, made war self-supporting by exactions and plunder, and pressed home his victories with relentless pursuits, shocked his contemporaries, who looked upon these unmannerly operations, not as legitimate acts of war, but as the incursions of a barbarian. This revulsion, not to say horror, is typified in the cartoons of the period; in one by Cruikshank, dated 14th April 1797, the French army is depicted as a dragon vomiting forth smoke, fire and guns, on whose back is seated a grotesque and forbidding figure wearing a Phrygian cap inscribed 'Buonaparte', before whom an army and two generals are in full retreat.[2] It grimly portrays the protagonist of the era of unlimited warfare.

2 · *The Elements of Napoleonic Warfare*

The elements to be considered here as the more typical of Napoleonic warfare are: (1) Unity of Command; (2) Generalship and Soldiership; and (3) Napoleon's System of Planning.

Unity of command he held to be 'the first necessity in war',[3] and it should be borne in mind that in its full sense it is only possible when political and military direction are in the hands of a single man, as they were in Napoleon's after he became First Consul in January, 1800. This full unity is not obtained when, as is normal in war, political decisions are divorced from military actions. This was the case under the Directory, and because Napoleon was aware of it, when he took over command of the Army of Italy he defined what unity of command entailed. On 19th January 1796, he wrote to the

[1] Ibid., Vol. I, p. 363.

[2] *Napoleon in Caricature* 1795–1821, A. M. Broadley (1911), Vol. I, pp. 99–100.

[3] *Corresp.*, XXXI, p. 418.

Directors: 'The government must have entire confidence in its general; allow him great latitude, and only provide him with the aim he should attain.'[1] Which, granted the aim to be a rational one, is a full definition. On military singleness of command he wrote: 'In military operations, I only consult myself; in diplomatic, I consult everybody';[2] and of his 1796 campaign: 'I made this campaign without consulting anyone; I should have accomplished nothing worthwhile had I been compelled to reconcile my actions with those of another.'[3]

As far as circumstances permit, unity of command demands the assembly of *all* available forces under a *single* general in the *main* theatre of operations, and a common tendency of an ignorant or a weak government is to scatter its forces in order to cover all vital points. In 1806, this was the course taken by Joseph Bonaparte King of Naples; to whom, on 7th June, Napoleon caustically wrote: 'If you intend to protect all points in your kingdom, there will not be sufficient troops in all France.'[4]

Unity of command was the foundation of Napoleon's many victorious campaigns and, strangely – as later we shall see – it became an element in his eventual downfall. Nevertheless, his maxims: 'In war men are nothing, it is the one man who is all',[5] and 'One bad general [in command] . . . is worth two good ones',[6] remain as true today as when they were first uttered.

What he expected of his generals and soldiers may be discovered from what he wrote and said on generalship and soldiership.

As regards the first: 'The essential quality of a general is resolution.'[7] 'A general should never paint pictures [of a situation]; his intelligence should be as clear as the lens of a telescope.'[8] 'A general who has to see things through the eyes of others will never be able to command an army as it should

[1] Ibid., I, No. 83. [2] Ibid., I, No. 399. [3] Ibid., I, No. 420.
[4] Ibid., XII, No. 10329. [5] Ibid., XVII, No. 14283.
[6] Ibid., XXIX, p. 107.
[7] *Sainte-Hélène Journal inédit* (1815–1818), General Gourgaud, (edit. 1899)),Vol. II, p. 423.
[8] *Napoléon en Exil, ou l'écho de Sainte-Hélène* (1822), B. E. O'Meara, vol. II, p. 248,

be commanded.'[1] 'Success in war depends on *coup d'oeil*, and on sensing the psychological moment in battle. At Austerlitz, had I attacked six hours earlier, I should have been lost.'[2] 'It is will, character and audacity that have made me what I am.'[3] And conversely: 'An army of lions led by a stag will never be an army of lions.'[4]

As regards his men, he never failed to stimulate their vanity, and increase their credulity at the expense of their fears and to the profit of their confidence, and thereby convert a prudent and cautious creature into a warrior – a man who is willing to sacrifice his life for a cause he frequently does not understand. 'All men who value life more than the glory of the nation and the esteem of their comrades', he said, 'should not be members of the French army.'[5] His appeal to them was not through their pockets; 'Bravery', he wrote, 'cannot be bought with money.'[6] Instead, he appealed to their sense of glory: 'When in the fire of battle I rode down the ranks and shouted: "Unfurl the standards! The moment has at length come!" it made the French soldier leap into action.'[7] And 'The 32nd Brigade would have died for me, because after Lonato I wrote: "The 32nd was there, I was calm." The power of words on men is astonishing.'[8] 'In Italy we were always one against three, but the men had confidence in me. Moral force more so than numbers decides victory';[9] and 'It is not the number of troops that gives strength to an army, it is their loyalty and good humour.'[10] He was so sure that personal touch between officers and men was the secret of successful leadership that in an Order of the Day we read: 'A battalion commander should not rest until he has become acquainted with every detail; after six months in command he should even know the names and abilities of all the officers and men of his

[1] O'Meara (English edit., 1822), Vol. II, p. 377.
[2] *Mémorial de Sainte-Hélène*, Comte de Las Cases (1823), Vol. II, p. 210.
[3] *Corresp.*, X, No. 8832.
[4] Ibid., XXX, p. 176.
[5] Ibid., I, No. 925.
[6] Ibid., IX, No. 7527.
[7] Ibid., XXXI, p. 416.
[8] Gourgaud, Vol. II, p. 109.
[9] Ibid., Vol. II, p. 119.
[10] *Lettres Inédites de Napoléon Ier*, Leon Lecestre (1897), No. 155.

battalion.'[1] The health of his men deeply concerned him: 'Sickness is the most dangerous of enemies',[2] he wrote, and 'It would be better to fight the most bloody of battles than to place the troops in an unhealthy locality.'[3] Of his men in general he said: 'If courage is the first quality of the soldier, perseverance is the second.'[4] And when in St. Helena Madame de Montholon asked him which were the best troops? 'Madame', he replied, 'those who win battles.'[5]

Napoleon's success as a planner of campaigns derived directly from his position as autocrat, which empowered him to combine in his own person the political and strategical conduct of war. This advantage, coupled with his single-mindedness and enormous industry, enabled him to transfuse his genius into his plans, at times so much so that they were quite beyond the comprehension of his generals. As the war lengthened and his problems grew more complex, the lack of comprehending subordinates became increasingly dangerous, and especially so during the Leipzig and Waterloo campaigns, when his brilliant manoeuvres were botched by the stupidity of his marshals. This is why, when at St. Helena, he said: 'If I had had a man like Turenne to second me in my campaigns, I should have been master of the world.'[6]

To him the planning of a campaign was an exacting work of art, as the following citations show: 'At the moment when war is declared, there are so many things to be done that it is wise to have looked a few years ahead . . .'[7] 'I am accustomed to think out three or four months in advance what I should do, and I base my calculations on the worst [situation] . . .'[8] 'Nothing is gained in war except by calculation . . .'[9] 'It is my habit to take so many precautions, that nothing is left to chance.'[10] 'It is only when plans are deeply thought out that one succeeds in war.'[11]

[1] *Correspondance inédite de Napoléon Ier, conservée aux Archives de la Guerre*, Ernest Picard et Louis Tuetey (1912), No. 247.
[2] *Corresp.*, XI, No. 9105.
[3] Ibid., XXII, No. 18041.
[4] Ibid., VII, No. 4855.
[5] Las Cases, Vol. VI, p. 85.
[6] Gourgaud, Vol. II, p. 135.
[7] *Corresp.*, X, No. 8075.
[8] Ibid., XIII, No. 10810.
[9] Ibid., XII, No. 10325.
[10] Ibid., XVI, No. 13652.
[11] Ibid., XVII, No. 14307.

The secret of all this was divulged by him to Roederer when he said to him:

'If I appear to be always ready to reply to everything, it is because, before undertaking anything, I have meditated for a long time – I have foreseen what might happen. It is not a spirit which suddenly reveals to me what I have to say or do in a circumstance unexpected by others – it is reflexion, meditation.'[1]

Napoleon entered upon each of his campaigns with a precisely premeditated plan which admitted of variations, each of which corresponded with an hypothesis he had made on his enemy's probable and possible movements. The plan was what he intended to do, and the variations covered the modifications he might have to make in it. Once the plan was activated, his problem became one of exploration. The current use of exploratory cavalry was to seek out the enemy's forces and report back on them. But, because Napoleon was more concerned with his own plan than his enemy's positions, and because normally they had changed by the time the cavalry reports were received, the object of his system of exploration – which included spies, agents, letters seized in post offices, etc. – was to confirm or eliminate his hypotheses. Therefore his cavalry, agents, etc., were directed in predetermined directions to elucidate doubtful points, knowledge of which was essential in order to confirm or eliminate an hypothesis. Thus, by reducing uncertainty to a minimum, by either eliminating or confirming his hypotheses, he not only simplified his own plan, but at the same time uncovered his enemy's. To discover what his enemy intended, more so than what his positions were, was the aim of Napoleonic exploration.

3 · *The Principles of Napoleonic Warfare*

Although Napoleon frequently wrote or talked about principles of war, nowhere does he enumerate them. Once he said in the hearing of Saint-Cyr: 'If one day I can find the time, I will write a book in which I will describe the principles of war in so precise a manner that they will be at the disposal of all

[1] Cited by Colonel Vachée in *Napoleon at Work* (English trans. 1914), p.7.

soldiers, so that war can be learnt as easily as a science.'[1] Unfortunately he never did so; nevertheless, a study of his campaigns reveals: (1) His invariable reliance on the offensive; (2) his trust in speed to economize time, and (3) to effect strategic surprisals; (4) his insistence on concentrating superiority of force on the battlefield, particularly at the decisive point of attack; and (5) his carefully thought out protective system.

OFFENSIVE. Of the offensive he said: 'I think like Frederick, one should always be the first to attack';[2] and 'It is a very great mistake to allow oneself to be attacked.'[3] 'Make war offensively', he said, 'like Alexander, Hannibal, Caesar, Gustavus-Adolphus, Turenne, Eugène and Frederick . . . model yourself on them, it is the sole means to become a great captain and fathom the secrets of the art.'[4]

But, unlike Charles XII, he was no foolhardy general. 'At the opening of a campaign', he said, 'one should carefully consider whether to advance or not, but once one has assumed the offensive it should be pushed to the last extremity.'[5] Again: 'Once one has decided to invade a country, one must not be afraid to deliver battle, and should seek out the enemy everywhere to fight him.'[6]

Although he did not invent the pursuit, it may be said that he systematized it, because he riveted it to the battle and made it an essential feature in his tactics. On 17th October, 1805, in the Ulm campaign, he sent the following message to Murat: 'I congratulate you on the success you have gained. But no rest; pursue the enemy with your sword in his back, and cut all communications.'[7] Nevertheless, because a sustained pursuit is one of the most difficult of operations, only four of his fully succeeded: at Rivoli (1797), at Austerlitz (1805), at Jena (1806), and at Echmühl (1809).

MOBILITY. 'Rapidity', writes Commandant Colin, 'is an

[1] *Mémoires pour servir à l'Histoire Militaire sous la Directoire, le Consulat et l'Empire*, Maréchal Gouvion Saint-Cyr (1831), Vol. IV, p. 149.

[2] Gourgaud, Vol. II, p. 336.

[3] *Corresp.*, XXVII, No. 21428.

[4] Ibid., XXXI, p. 418.

[5] Ibid., XXXII, p. 209.

[6] Gourgaud, Vol. I, p. 327.

[7] *Corresp.*, XI, No. 9080.

essential and primordial factor in Napoleonic war', and to reinforce this statement he quotes what the Comte de Dervieu has to say on this subject in his *La Conception de la Victoire chez les grands Généraux:*

'Movement is the soul of Napoleonic war, just as the decisive battle forms its means. Bonaparte makes his troops move with a calculated rapidity. . . . Multiply themselves by speed . . . make up for numbers by the quickness of marches, are maxims continually on his lips. "Marches", said he, "are war . . . aptitude for war is aptitude for movement . . . victory is to the armies which manoeuvre." '[1]

Two sayings of Napoleon reinforce this: 'In the art of war, as in mechanics, time is the grand element between weight and force.'[2] And 'The loss of time is irreparable in war; reasons alleged for it were always bad, because operations only fail through delays.'[3] Unfortunately for him, the delays of two of his subordinate generals, the one at Leipzig and the other at Ligny, went far to lose him the first of these battles and render the second indecisive. On the other hand, in the Ulm campaign his men said: 'The Emperor has discovered a new way of waging war, he makes use of our legs instead of our bayonets.'[4]

SUPRISE. Other than the unexpected concentration of his forces on the battlefield, Napoleon's surprises were seldom tactical ones, nearly all were strategic, and notably so at the battles of Marengo (1800), Ulm (1805) and Jena (1806); also in the first phase of the Waterloo campaign. 'Strategy', he wrote to Stein on 7th January, 1814, 'is the art of making use of time and space. I am less chary of the latter than the former. Space we can recover, lost time never.'

CONCENTRATION. For the decisive battle, Napoleon cut down all subsidiary operations in order to concentrate the greatest possible numbers. Colin quotes him as saying: 'The army must be assembled and the greatest force possible concentrated on the battlefield.'[5]

There is an important difference here between the meaning

[1] *The Transformations of War* (English edition, 1912), p. 254.
[2] *Corresp.*, XVIII, No. 14707. [3] Ibid., XII, No. 9997.
[4] Ibid., XI, No. 9392. [5] *The Transformations of War*, p. 243.

of 'assembled' and 'concentrated'. The former is explained in a letter Napoleon wrote to the King of Naples on 8th August, 1806: 'The art of disposing of troops is the art of war. Distribute your troops in such a way that, whatever the enemy does, you will be able to unite your forces within a few days.'[1] The assembly is the distribution of corps or divisions in the battle area, while concentration refers to the battlefield. On 14th February 1806, Napoleon wrote to his brother Joseph: 'Your army is too dispersed; it should always march in such a way that it is able to unite in a single day on the battlefield.'[2] The area of assembly, which includes the marching and resting columns, contracts as the enemy is approached, until all columns can be concentrated within a few hours. Because 'The first principle of war is that one should only engage in battle when all troops can be united on the battlefield',[3] and because, 'The art of generalship consists in, when actually inferior in numbers to the enemy, being superior to him on the battlefield',[4] it follows that an inferior force, if correctly assembled, will generally defeat a superior force that is not.

PROTECTION. From 16th September 1793, when as a penniless and unemployed captain, a sheer accident gave him command of the Jacobin artillery at the siege of Toulon, to 18th June 1815, when as Emperor of France, in the square of his 1st Grenadiers of the Guard, he retired from the field of Waterloo, never once did he engage in a purely defensive battle.

It is true that at Leipzig (1813), at la Rothière (1814), and at Arcis-sur-Aube (1814) he was driven to fight defensively; also it is true that, because of his inferiority, throughout his 1814 campaign he had to assume a strategical defensive; nevertheless, it consisted in a series of rapid marches and of furious attacks. Yet, notwithstanding his complete avoidance of the defensively planned battle, all his offensive operations were grounded on the protective principle. He defines it as follows: 'The whole art of war consists in a well reasoned and circumspect defensive, followed by rapid and audacious attack.'[5]

[1] *Corresp.*, XIII, No. 10629.
[2] Ibid., XII, No. 9808.
[3] Ibid., XXXII, p. 227.
[4] Gourgaud, Vol. II, p. 32.
[5] *Corresp.*, XIII, No. 10558.

This protective system was based on establishing in rear of his army a *place de campagne*, a fortress or a fortified town which could not be surprised, and in which the army magazines, park, hospitals, etc., were assembled: it was his base of operations. When the army moved forward from it, the object of its protective cavalry was to conceal his plan and the movements of the army, just as the object of his exploratory cavalry – already referred to – was to fathom the enemy's plan, so that he might modify his own. When forward movements could no longer be concealed by the protective cavalry curtain, as happened in the marches immediately preceding the battles of Jena and Echmühl, secrecy was sought in rapidity of movement.

Taken together, Napoleon's outlook on the defensive and offensive was a common-sense one. He said: 'Defensive warfare does not exclude the attack any more than offensive warfare excludes the defence';[1] 'that with mediocre troops one must shift much soil';[2] by which he meant, reinforce their confidence by entrenching them. This also applied to isolated detachments: 'It is a principle of war that all detached corps should entrench, and it is one of the first steps that one should take on the occupation of a position.'[3] But for an army it was otherwise, and as early as August, 1793 – that is, before he took command of the artillery at Toulon – in his well-known political pamphlet *Le Souper de Beaucaire*[4] he wrote: 'In the art of war it is an axiom that he who remains in his trenches will be beaten: experience and theory are in accord with this.' Static warfare was anathema to Napoleon.

4 · *The Defects of Napoleonic Warfare*

Napoleon's failure to achieve final victory, and through it a peace, not only profitable to France but also acceptable to her opponents, may be traced to three radical defects in his conduct of war. The first, a military one, was over-centalization of command; the second, a political one, was his unrealistic

[1] Ibid., XXXI, p. 347.
[2] Ibid., XIV, No. 12111.
[3] Ibid., V, No. 4083.
[4] Included in Panckoucke's *Oeuvres de Napoléon Bonaparte*, Vol. V.

policy; and his third, a grand-strategical one, that the means he relied upon to accomplish his policy could at best only lead to an armistice.

COMMAND. As regards the first, earlier in this chapter it was stated that, although his insistence on unifying command in his person led to a long succession of victories, ultimately it became an element in his downfall: how did this come about?

The answer is twofold: Firstly, as the war lengthened, it became so widespread, so complex, and the forces engaged in it so considerable that, without a well-organized General Staff, it was no longer possible for a single man – genius though he was – to manage it efficiently. Secondly, his enemies came gradually to understand that it was lack of unity between themselves which impeded the combination of their armies against him, and unless they did combine them they would continue to be defeated in detail. Ultimately, during the summer armistice which occurred in the middle of the Leipzig campaign, unity was established by the Treaty of Reichenbach, and, in accordance with one of its clauses, the Allied Powers – Russia, Austria, Prussia and Sweden – agreed that under no circumstances was any one of their armies to incur the risk of a single-handed encounter with Napoleon in person. Whichever army met him was at once to retire, until all forces in the field could be united against him. This drew the fangs of his offensive strategy.

Napoleon's Headquarters Staff comprised two unrelated departments: the Office of the Chief of Staff, and the General Staff. The first was under the direction of Marshal Berthier, Prince of Neuch^tel; it consisted of a secretariat and the Emperor's aides-de-camp – his liaison officers.[1] The second normally included three Assistant Chiefs of Staff, whose duties were analogous to those of a modern Quartermaster General, with a topographical section added.

'The staff', writes Colonel Vachée, 'in no way participated in the Emperor's intellectual work; it was never taken into

[1] Some were generals, others colonels, and some captains, employed on special missions or to carry orders to Napoleon's marshals on campaign or in battle. Some of the missions were extraordinary, see the one given to Baron Lejeune in February 1810, mentioned in his *Memoirs* (English edition, 1897), Vol. II, pp. 37–38.

his confidence; it had but to obey scrupulously. "Keep strictly to the orders which I give you; I alone know what I must do." Such were Berthier's orders.' And 'Berthier looked upon this effacement of his own personality as perfectly natural. "I am nothing in the army. I receive, in the Emperor's name, the reports of the marshals, and I sign these orders for him, but I am personally null" (Berthier to Soult, Osterode, March 1, 1807). "The Emperor, Monsieur le Maréchal, needs neither advice nor plans of campaign. No one knows his thought, and our duty is to obey" (Berthier to Ney, Warsaw, January 18 1807).'[1] To this Vachée adds: 'The Emperor himself said that the General Staff was the least necessary part of grand headquarters.'[2] As bad, the same cavalier treatment was meted out to his marshals.

The Duke of Fézensac's comment on this is:

'His orders had to be executed whatever the means of command. . . . This habit of undertaking everything with insufficient means, this determination not to recognize impossibilities, this boundless assurance of success, which in the beginning were the causes of our triumphs, in the end became fatal to us.'[3]

Some historians have held that the Emperor's lack of success in his later campaigns was due to ill-health or physical degeneracy; there is little to support this. The truth is, that it was his activity,[4] not his lethargy, which was as much the cause of his fall as of his rise, for it led him to believe that in his person he could combine the duties of commander-in-chief and chief of staff, and when skilled staff officers were needed they were not to be found. Caulaincourt informs us that in 1812 'The staff foresaw nothing, but on the other hand, as the Emperor wanted to do everything himself, and give every order, no one, not even the general staff, dared to assume the responsibility of giving the most trifling order.'[5] D'Odeleben says that in 1813 the staff was even less efficient than the year

[1] *Napoleon at Work* (English edition, 1914), p. 24. [2] Ibid., pp. 140–1.

[3] *Souvenirs Militaires de 1804 à 1814* (1863), pp. 118–9.

[4] For examples of it in 1812, see Caulaincourt's *Memoirs*, Vol. I, pp. 135, 141, and 245; and for 1813, see Baron d'Odeleben's *Relation Circonstanciée de la Campagne de 1813 en Saxe* (French edition, 1817), Vol. I, p. 224, etc.

[5] Op. cit., Vol. I, p. 155.

before, and that 'As a whole, the army in this campaign was a too complicated and imperfect machine to allow of co-ordination being established . . . the multiplicity of movements . . . gave place to difficulties which all the authority of Napoleon could not always surmount.'[1]

Napoleon's marshals had not been brought up to command, solely to obey, they were followers and not leaders, vassal princes, many of whom had been raised in rank for dynastic, political and personal reasons. After his fall and just before he left for Elba, Napoleon told Caulaincourt that:

'He found fault with himself for having made so much use of his marshals in these latter days, since they had become too rich, too much the *grands seigneurs*, and had grown war-weary. Things, according to him, would have been in a much better state if he had placed good generals of division, with their batons yet to win, in command.'[2]

There is truth in this, but it was his system of command more so than these defects which had emasculated them.

POLICY. Throughout, his dominant adversary was England who, by subsidizing her continental allies, raised coalition after coalition against him. The struggle with her was not one of right against wrong, but between two survival values that arose out of the early Industrial Revolution. To remain pro-perous and powerful, England had to export her manufactured goods; and to become prosperous, and thereby sustain her power, France had to protect her infant industries. As Metternich said: 'Everyone knew that England could not give way on this question [the maritime problem], which to her was a matter of life and death.'[3] And it was because Napoleon realized this that he devised what is known as his Continental System, the closing of all continental ports to English shipping, so that England's trade would be strangled and her credit undermined, without which she would be unable to raise enemies against him.[4]

'The power of the English', he said, '. . . rests only upon the monopoly they exercise over other nations, and can be maintained only by that. Why should they alone reap the benefits

[1] Op. cit., Vol. II, pp. 303–4.
[2] Caulaincourt, Vol. II, p. 10.
[3] Op. cit., Vol. II, pp. 363–4.
[4] Ibid., Vol. I, p. 531.

which millions of others could reap as well?'[1] And again: 'The good of that Europe which seems to envelop her with goodwill counts for nothing with the merchants of London. They would sacrifice every State in Europe, even the whole world, to further one of their speculations. If their debt were not so large they might be more reasonable. It is the necessity of paying this, of maintaining their credit, that drives them on...'[2]

In his struggle with England, he saw 'the basic solution of all the questions' that were 'agitating the world and even individuals.'[3] Therefore, as he told Caulaincourt, England was his sole enemy: 'He was working against England alone', and 'since their trade had ramifications everywhere he had to pursue them everywhere.'[4] It was out of this pursuit that his idea of universal empire arose. From a weapon with which to destroy England, the Continental System became an instrument whereby a new world conception would be realized – the vision of Europe united in concord.

When at St. Helena, he informed the world through Las Cases that his aim had been to unite the great European nations, hitherto 'divided and parcelled out by revolution and policy', into one confederation bound together by 'a unity of codes, principles, opinions, feelings and interests.' At its head, under the aegis of his empire, he dreamed of establishing a central assembly, modelled on 'the American Congress or the Amphictyons of Greece', to watch over the commonweal of 'the great European family.' Though this dream had been dissipated by his ruin, 'sooner or later', he said, 'it would be realized by the force of events. The impulse has been given, and I do not think that, since my fall and the destruction of my system, any grand equilibrium can possibly be established in Europe, except by the concentration and confederation of the principal nations. The sovereign who, in the first great conflict, shall sincerely embrace the cause of the people, will find himself at the head of all Europe, and may attempt whatever he pleases.'[5]

GRAND STRATEGY. A federated Europe was anathema to

[1] Ibid., Vol. I, p. 438.
[2] Ibid., Vol. I, p. 424.
[3] Ibid., Vol. I, p. 529.
[4] Ibid., Vol. I, p. 429.
[5] Las Cases (English edition, 1824), Vol. IV, Pt. VII, pp. 134–9.

England, because in face of it she could not survive as the dominant maritime power; therefore the clash between her and France was to the death; a struggle in which, no sooner had Napoleon destroyed one of her coalitions, than another arose from its ashes. To accomplish his aim, it was necessary to subjugate England without antagonizing the continental powers; for were they antagonized, they would the more readily coalesce with England. This is what his Continental System led to, because, not only did it deprive the continental nations of goods, which England alone could supply, but it involved one and all in his war with England. His grand strategy, therefore, was at fault; it was no more than a makeshift substitute for the fleet he had lost at Trafalgar in 1805.

Immediately after the battle of Jena, the Emperor initiated his continental blockade by his Berlin Decree, and England retaliated with an Order in Council which prohibited neutral trade with France and her allies. Thus an economic war was launched, and after the defeat of the Russians at Friedland, on 7th July 1807, Russia and Prussia agreed to take common action with France against England. With this success to his credit, Napoleon extended his blockade to Denmark, Portugal and Spain, and later to Holland. In March 1809, he placed his brother Joseph on the Spanish throne, and the result was the outbreak of the Peninsular War. War with Austria followed, and soon after her defeats at Echmühl and Wagram the Russian alliance with France began to weaken, and in 1810 Tzar Alexander allowed English merchantmen to enter Russian ports. The situation then deteriorated so rapidly that Napoleon remarked to Caulaincourt: 'War will occur in spite of me, in spite of the Emperor Alexander, in spite of the interests of France and the interests of Russia. I have so often seen this that it is my experience of the past which unveils the future to me. . . . It is all a scene of the opera and the English control the machinery.' When at St. Helena, he said to Las Cases: 'Russia was the last resource of England. The peace of the whole world rested with Russia. Alas! English gold proved more powerful than my plans.'

Napoleon's disastrous Russian campaign followed; in 1813 he was decisively defeated by Russia, Austria, Prussia and

Sweden at Leipzig, and on 11th April 1814, he abdicated his throne. Thus, both his policy and grand strategy utterly failed. So long as England was in the field, though he could overrun Europe, he could not bind Europe to his throne, because in conquering her he sold his birthright to her peoples.

In 1792, the spirit of French nationalism, awakened by the Revolution, became the soul of the French armies, and had this not been so there would never have been a Napoleon. Then, after Jena, he began to squander his heritage, and his exactions awoke, first in Spain, then in Austria, then in Prussia, and lastly in all Europe the selfsame spirit that had propelled his armies across that continent. In Spain, the Spanish guerrillas, as much so as Wellington's small army, pinned down scores of thousands of his troops; in 1809 Austria adopted conscription, and when on 13th March 1813, Prussia, in alliance with Russia, declared war on him, a *levée en masse* was forthwith proclaimed. Every man not acting in the regular army or *Landwehr* was to support the army by acting against the enemy's communications and rear. The people were to fight to the death and with every means in their power. The enemy was to be harassed, his supplies cut off and his stragglers massacred. No uniforms were to be worn, and on the enemy's approach, after all food stocks had been destroyed, and mills, bridges, and boats burnt, the villages were to be abandoned and refuge sought in the woods and hills. 'Such', writes Fain, 'are the new means that the . . . enemies of Napoleon propose to employ against him.'[1] It was to be a repetition of 1792.

Thus Napoleon, like a missionary – indeed he was one with cannon and sword – preached the gospel of the Nation in Arms throughout the length and breadth of Europe, and in time it became the military creed of all her troublesome peoples. Spiritually linked with this is what Stanislas Girardin, in his *Memoirs*, relates on Napoleon's visit to the tomb of Rousseau. In reply to a question of Girardin's he said: 'Well, the future will show whether it would not have been better for the repose of the world that neither I nor Rousseau had existed.'[2]

[1] *Manuscrit de Mil Huit Cent Treize*, Baron Fain (1824), Vol. I, p. 39. Fain was Secretary of Napoleon's Cabinet.

[2] Cited by John Holland Rose in his *The Life of Napoleon* (edit., 1913), Vol. I, p. 21.

CHAPTER IV

The Theories of Clausewitz

*

1 · *Karl von Clausewitz*

Karl von Clausewitz (1780–1831) was born at Burg, near Magdeburg, and was posted to the Prussian army as ensign in 1792. He served in the Rhine campaign of 1793–1794, and in 1801 entered the Berlin Military Academy, then under the direction of the noted Colonel von Scharnhorst. In 1806, as an aide-de-camp of Prince Augustus of Prussia, in the Jena campaign he was wounded and taken prisoner. In 1809 he assisted Scharnhorst in the reorganization of the Prussian army, and on the outbreak of the Russian campaign of 1812 he transferred to the Russian army. During the final stage of Napoleon's retreat from Moscow he negotiated the Convention of Tauroggen, which led to the War of Liberation. In the 1813 campaign he was appointed chief of staff to Count Wallmoden, and in 1815, as chief of staff to General Thielmann, he was present at the battles of Ligny and Wavre. In 1831 he died of cholera at Breslau.

From this brief biographical note it will be seen that throughout his military career he never held a command, and probably was unsuited for such. He was essentially a student of war, and after his death his collected works were published in ten volumes, the first three of which contain his masterwork *Vom Kriege* ('On War'), upon which he had been engaged for some twelve years; it was left unfinished and largely unrevised.

In a note discovered after his death among his papers, dated 10th July 1827, as well as another note, undated and apparently written later, he stated that only the first chapter of Book I was completed; that Books II to VII had yet to be revised, and that Book VIII, the final one, was 'merely a track, roughly cleared'. In the first of these notes he pointed out that in his final revision he intended to draw a clearer distinction between the two kinds of war he had in mind: those with a total aim, in which the overthrow of the enemy is sought, and those with a restricted aim, such as the readjustment of a frontier. Further, that throughout he intended to accentuate more than he had done that '*War is only a continuation of State policy by other means.*'

As the book stands – incomplete and unrevised – it is largely a jumble of essays, memoranda, and notes set together in no very precise form. It is prolix, repetitive, full of platitutdes and truisms, and in places contradictory and highly involved. It is not, as it is sometimes held to be, a study based on the Napoleonic wars. Instead it is a pseudo-philosophical exposition on war interlarded with valuable common-sense observations. Because Clausewitz lived in an age when philosophy was in fashion, it would appear that he assumed, on Kantian lines,[1] the existence of an architypal or absolute form of war, toward which all military operations should be directed. In brief, the ideal of the sum total of war, which in his mind he related to Kant's *Ding-an-sich* ('Thing-in-itself'). Whether this was so or not, it is clear that he looked upon his absolute concept of war as a yard-stick with which to measure all military activities. Again and again he resorts to it, gets completely confused with its measurements, and then abandons them for common sense. The reader of *On War* should bear this peculiarity in mind, otherwise he is likely to become as confused as Clausewitz often was, worse – misled.

As will be reverted to at the close of this chapter, in spite of his twenty years' experience of Napoleonic warfare, Clausewitz had but a vague understanding of it. Nevertheless, because of Napoleon's offensive principle, he foisted on to him his absolute concept, and thereby, not only misled many of his future students, but indirectly was largely responsible for the vast extension of unlimited warfare in the twentieth century. On the other hand, his penetrating analysis of the relationship of war and policy has never been excelled, and is even more

[1] According to Colonel J. J. Graham (the English translator of *On War*) Clausewitz was a pupil of Kiesewitter, who indoctrinated him in the philosophy of Kant 'in homoeopathic doses' (*On War*, Vol. I, p. xxxvii).

important today than when first expounded. Strange to relate, its lack of appreciation was an even more potent factor in the extension of unlimited war than his absolute concept.

Because of this, and because the bulk of *On War* is only remotely related to the higher conduct of war, and is now obsolete, the intention in this chapter is to restrict observations on Clausewitz's theories to those only which have influenced wars subsequent to his day.

2 · *What is War?*

Clausewitz likens war 'to a duel on an extensive scale' (I, p. 1),[1] and compares it with a struggle between two wrestlers. From this he infers that war 'is an act of violence intended to compel our opponent to fulfil our will' (I, p. 2) – violence is the means, and 'the compulsory submission of the enemy to our will is the ultimate *object*' (I, p. 2). Violence must be pushed 'to its utmost bounds' (I, p. 4), and 'the disarming or overthrow of the enemy must always be the aim of Warfare' (I, p. 5). He scoffs at the old idea of 'War without spilling blood', calls it 'a real business for Brahmins' (I, p. 287),[2] and considers that '. . . to introduce into the philosophy of War . . . a principle of moderation would be an absurdity' (I, p. 3). Therefore, he writes, 'Let us not hear of Generals who conquer without bloodshed' (I, p. 288).

This insistence on violence as an imperative has misled many of his disciples, who have accepted it in its absolute sense. Nevertheless, once he has freed himself from the toils of his philosophy, Clausewitz goes out of his way to explain that war is not made 'with an abstraction but with a reality' (I, p. 139); that 'the absolute . . . nowhere finds any sure base in the calculations in the Art of War', and that 'War in all branches of human activity [is] most like a gambling game' (I, p. 20). 'The Art of War', he writes 'has to deal with living

[1] References are to volumes and pages of the English edition of *On War*, revised by Colonel F. N. Maude and published in 1908.

[2] In I, p. 229 he writes '. . . in these feints, parades, half and quarter thrusts of former Wars, they find the aim of all theory, the supremacy of mind over matter, and modern Wars appear to them mere savage fisticuffs, from which nothing is to be learnt, and which must be regarded as mere retrograde steps towards barbarism.'

and with moral forces, the consequence of which is that it can never attain the absolute and positive. There is therefore everywhere a margin for the accidental, and just as much in the greatest things as in the smallest' (I, p. 21). That 'War is the province of danger' (I, p. 47), 'the province of uncertainty' (I, p. 48), and 'the province of chance. In no sphere of human activity is such a margin to be left for this intruder' (I, p. 49).

Further, 'If, adhering closely to the absolute, we try to avoid all difficulties by a stroke of the pen, and insist with logical strictness that in every case the extreme must be the object, and the utmost effort must be exerted in that direction, such a stroke of the pen would be a mere paper law, not by any means adapted to the real world' (I, p. 6); in which 'War belongs . . . to the province of social life. It is a conflict of great interests which is settled by bloodshed, and only in this is it different from others' (I, p. 121). Nevertheless, because, as will be seen in the following Section, Clausewitz uses the term 'absolute war' to denote Napoleonic warfare, as well as in its philosophical sense of a 'conflict of forces left to themselves, and obeying no other but their own inner laws' (I, p. 6), many of his followers were completely flummoxed and fell victims to his apotheosis of violence.

3 · Absolute and Real War

The subject of this Section is dealt with in Chapter II of Book VIII, in which Clausewitz first refers back to Chapter I of Book VIII, and points out that, although philosophically, there can be 'no other reality'[1] in war than 'the overthrow of the enemy', almost everywhere we find that this does not happen – why? We need not follow his involved answer, because the common-sense reply is, that one side or the other gives up fighting when it has had enough of it. But this is far

[1] On this question he refers the reader to Chapter XVI of Book III' 'On the Suspension of the Act of Warfare', in which the most exquisite philosophical nonsense is to be found – such as '. . . a suspension in the act of Warfare, strictly speaking, is in contradiction with the nature of the thing; because two Armies, being two incompatible elements, should destroy one another unremittingly. . . . What would be said of two wrestlers who remained clasped round each other for hours without making a movement?' (I, p. 225.)

too simple an answer for the philosophical Clausewitz, who goes on to ask: As this is undoubtedly so, is the absolute notion of war actually found in reality? His answer is 'yes', because we have 'seen real warfare make its appearance in . . . absolute completeness . . . in our own time. After a short introduction performed by the French Revolution', he continues, 'the impetuous Buonaparte quickly brought it to this point. Under him it was carried on without slackening for a moment until the enemy was prostrated' (III, p. 81).[1]

Next, Clausewitz asks: are we satisfied with this? Should war be of this kind, or of some other kind? and after another lengthy argument, which with profit may be skipped, the answer is: that in the theory of war as a whole 'the foremost place [must be given] to the absolute form of War', and 'that whoever wishes to learn something from theory', should 'accustom himself never to lose sight of it, to regard it as the natural measure of all his hopes and fears, in order to approach it *where he can, or where he must*' (III, p. 82).

4 · *War as an Instrument of Policy*

Clausewitz's outstanding contribution to military theory is his insistence on the relationship of war and policy. In 'all circumstances', he writes, 'War is to be regarded not as an independent thing, but as a political instrument; and it is only by taking this point of view that we can avoid finding ourselves in opposition to all military history. This is the only means of unlocking the great book and making it intelligible. Secondly, this view shows us how Wars must differ in character according to the nature of the motives and circumstances from which they proceed' (I, p. 25).

This observation is more fully elaborated in Sub-Section B of Chapter VI of Book VIII, of which the following is a summary.

Clausewitz opens his discussion by stating, although it is well known that war is called forth through the political inter-

[1] This shows clearly the confusion into which Clausewitz's concept of absolute war led him. In Book I, Chapter I, Sections 6–9, he proves that war can never be absolute; now he states that Bonaparte's system of war was one of 'absolute completeness'. What, presumably, he means is, as near the ideal as it is possible to get.

course of governments and nations, it is generally assumed that intercourse is broken off by war, 'and that a totally different state of things ensues, subject to no laws but its own.'

This is erroneous, because 'War is nothing but a continuation of political intercourse, with a mixture of other means.' He emphasizes the word 'mixture', so as to make it clear that political intercourse, though changed, does not cease, and that 'the chief lines on which events of the War progress . . . are only the general features of policy which run all through the War until peace takes place. . . . Is not War merely another kind of writing and language for political thoughts? It has certainly a grammar of its own, but its logic is not peculiar to itself.' Therefore 'War can never be separated from political intercourse', and should it be, then 'all the threads of the different relations are . . . broken, and we have before us a senseless thing without an object.'

After this, he indulges in a little philosophy, and then reverts to his subject.

'If War belongs to policy', he writes, 'it will naturally take its character from thence. If policy is grand and powerful, so also will be the War, and this may be carried to the point at which War attains to *its absolute form*. . . .'

It is 'Only through this kind of view War recovers unity; only by it can we see all Wars as things of *one* kind; and it is only through it that the judgment can obtain the true and perfect basis and point of view from which great plans may be traced out and determined upon. . . .'

'There is, upon the whole, nothing more important in life than to find out the right point of view from which things should be looked at and judged of, and then to keep that point; for we can only apprehend the mass of events in their unity from *one* standpoint; and it is only the keeping of one point of view that guards us from inconsistency.'

It is of paramount importance, he insists, always to keep in mind the main aim in war, not from either the soldier's point of view or that of the administrator or the politician, but from the point of view of policy, which should unite all interests. And in no circumstances can the Art of War be regarded as its preceptor, because policy represents the interests of the whole community. 'The subordination of the political point of view to the military would be contrary to common sense, for policy has declared the War; it is the intelligent faculty, War is only the instrument, and not the reverse. The subordination of the military point of view to the political is, therefore, the only thing which is possible.'

When it is recognized that war, other than an anarchy, should proceed from policy, 'plans come, as it were out of a cast', and conflicts between political and military interests are avoided. Should, however, policy make demands on the war which it cannot respond to, then policy is at fault. 'But if policy judges correctly the march of military events, it is entirely its affair to determine what are the events and the direction of events most favourable to the ultimate and great end of the War. In one word, the Art of War in its highest point of view is policy, but, no doubt, a policy which fights battles instead of writing notes.'

'It is only when policy promises itself a wrong effect from certain military means and measures . . . that it can exercise a prejudicial effect on War by the course it prescribes.' Also, should it not read correctly the nature of current events, its implementation may be disastrous. To illustrate this, Clausewitz turns to the French Revolution.

'If policy', he writes, 'had risen to a just appreciation of the forces which had sprung up in France, and of the new relations in the political state of Europe, it might have foreseen the consequences which must follow in respect to the great features of war, and it was only in this way that it could arrive at a correct view of the extent of the means required as well as of the best use to make of those means. We may therefore say, that the twenty years' victories of the Revolution are chiefly to be ascribed to the erroneous policy of Governments by which it was opposed.'

On the other hand, it was because the policy of the French Revolution called out other means and measures that France was enabled 'to conduct War with a degree of energy which could not have been thought of otherwise.'

'Therefore, the actual changes in the Art of War are a consequence of alterations in policy; and, so far from being an argument for the possible separation of the two, they are, on the contrary, very strong evidence of the intimacy of their connection.

'Therefore, once more: War is an instrument of policy; it must necessarily bear its character, it must measure with its scale: the conduct of War, in its great features, is therefore policy itself, which takes up the sword in place of the pen, but does not on that account cease to think according to its own laws.'

Of other observations on policy and war, which are not mere repetitions of items in the above, the following throw additional light on the subject:

'No war should be commenced . . . without first seeking a reply to the question, What is to be attained by and in the same' (III, p. 79).

'Theory demands, therefore, that at the commencement of every war its character and main outline shall be defined according to what the political conditions and relations lead us to anticipate as probable.' The first step should not be taken 'without thinking what may be the last' (III, p. 87).

'In order to ascertain the real scale of the means which we must put forth for War, we must think over the political object both on our own side and on the enemy's side; we must consider the power and position of the enemy's State as well as of our own, the character of his Government and of his people, and the capacities of both, and all that again on our own side, and the political connections of other States, and the effect which war will produce on those States' (III, p. 89).

5 · *Grand Strategy and the Centre of Gravity*

Because the essence of grand strategy is the subordination of strategy to policy, whatever policy may be, its fulfilment must be within the power of strategy to attain. Therefore, as Clausewitz says, 'the political object . . . must accommodate itself to [the] means', and at times this 'may involve modifications in the political objective'. Nevertheless, whatever modifications may be agreed, policy retains its 'prior right to consideration' (I, p. 23).

With reference to this interplay:

'. . . . the first, the grandest, and most decisive act of

judgment which the Statesman and General exercises is rightly to understand . . . the War in which he engages, not to take it for something, or to wish to make of it something, which by the nature of its relations it is impossible for it to be' (I, p. 25).

Clausewitz goes on to say:

'War is . . . not only chameleon-like in character, because it changes its colour in some degree in each particular case, but it is also, as a whole, in relation to the predominant tendencies which are in it, a wonderful trinity, composed of the original violence of its elements, hatred and animosity, which may be looked upon as blind instinct; of the play of probabilities and chance, which make it a free activity of the soul; and of the subordinate nature of a political instrument, by which it belongs purely to the reason.

'The first of these three phases concerns more the people; the second more the General and his Army; the third, more the Government' (I, pp. 25–26).

Further on, he writes:

'To conduct a whole War, or its great acts, which we call campaigns, to a successful termination, there must be an intimate knowledge of State policy in its higher relations. The conduct of a War and the policy of the State here coincide, and the General becomes at the same time the Statesman . . . but he must not cease to be the General. He takes into view all the relations of the State on the one hand; on the other, he must know exactly what he can do with the means at his disposal. . . . In this sense, Buonaparte was right when he said that many of the questions which come before a General for decision would make problems for a mathematical calculation not unworthy of the powers of Newton or Euler' (I, pp. 68–69).

Closely related with Clausewitz's conception of grand strategy is his theory of the centre of gravity, that point in the enemy's organism – military, political, social, etc. – at which, should he be defeated, or should he lose it, the whole structure of national power will collapse. It is one of the most important of Clausewitz's theories, because it governs the grand strategical aim of a war.

'To distinguish these "*centra gravitatis*" in the enemy's military power', he writes, 'to discern their spheres of action is . . . a supreme act of strategic judgment' (II, p. 355). And later, in volume III, he expands this as follows:

'Alexander had his centre of gravity in his Army, so had Gustavus Adolphus, Charles XII and Frederick the Great, and the career of any of one of them would soon have been brought to a close by the destruction of his fighting force: in States torn by internal dissensions, this centre generally lies in the capital; in small States dependent on greater ones, it lies generally in the Army of these Allies; in a confederacy, it lies in the unity of interests; in a national insurrection, in the person of the chief leader, and in public opinion; against these points the blow must be directed' (III, pp. 106–107). 'The centre of gravity of the French power lies in its military force and in Paris. To defeat the former in one or more battles, to take Paris and drive the wreck of the French across the Loire, must be the object of the Allies. The pit of the stomach of the French monarchy is between Paris and Brussels' (III, p. 171).

In a war against a coalition, such as Napoleon's conflict with England, Clausewitz shows remarkable insight.

'If two or more States combine against a third', he writes, 'that combination constitutes, in a political aspect, only *one* War. . . . We may, therefore, establish it as a principle, that if we can conquer all our enemies by conquering one of them, the defeat of that one must be the aim of the War, because in that one we hit the common centre of gravity of the whole War' (III, p. 108).

Napoleon was fully aware of this, and it was because he lacked naval power to win command of the English Channel and hit at England directly, that he relied on his Continental System to bankrupt her and render her impotent to raise coalitions against him.

6 · The Principles of War

Once the grand strategical aim is fixed, the next problem to consider is, what principles should govern the plan of war and its execution? Clausewitz mentions two, which he holds to be fundamental:

'The first is: to reduce the weight of the enemy's power into as few centres of gravity as possible, into one if it can be done;

again, to confine the attack against these centres of force to as few principal undertakings as possible, to one if possible; lastly, to keep all secondary undertakings as subordinate as possible. In a word, the first principle is, *to concentrate as much as possible.*

'The second principle runs thus – *to act as swiftly as possible;* therefore, to allow of no delay or detour without sufficient reason' (III, p. 141).

When combined, these principles bear close resemblance to Napoleon's maxim: 'In the art of war, as in mechanics, time is the grand element between weight and force.'

Besides these two principles, Clausewitz lays down a series of general principles, which he deduces from his three principal war objects, which are:

'(a) To conquer and destroy the enemy's armed force.

'(b) To get possession of the material elements of aggression . . . of the hostile Army.

'(c) To gain public opinion.'

To attain the first, the chief operation must be directed against the enemy's principal army, which must be beaten before the remaining two objects are tackled. In order to seize the material resources, operations should be directed against those points at which they are established – large towns, fortresses, etc. As regards the third, 'Public opinion is ultimately gained by great victories, and by the possession of the enemy's capital.'

Next, Clausewitz lays down the principles which should be followed in the attainment of these objects:

'(1) To employ *all* the forces which we can make available with the *utmost* energy. . . .

'(2) To concentrate our force as much as possible at the point where the decisive blows are to be struck. . . .

'(3) Not to lose time. . . . By rapidity many measures of the enemy are nipped in the bud, and public opinion is gained in our favour. . . . Surprise . . . is the most powerful element of victory. . . .'[1]

[1] Clausewitz also says that surprise 'lies at the foundation of all undertakings without exception'; that it is 'not only the means to the attainment of numerical superiority; but it is also to be regarded as a substantive principle in itself, on account of its moral effect;' and that 'secrecy and rapidity are the two factors in this product' (I, p. 199).

'(4) Lastly . . . to follow up the success we gain with the utmost energy. The pursuit . . . is the only means of gathering up the fruits of victory.

'The first of these principles is the foundation of the three others. . . .

'Due attention being paid to these principles, the form in which the operations are carried on is in the end of little consequence' (III, pp. 209–211).

Because the principles of war are so frequently referred to and so seldom defined by military writers, and because Clausewitz opens his study with the statement that 'War is nothing but a duel on an extensive scale', it is strange that he made no attempt to deduce his principles from this definition. Had he illustrated this simplest form of war by a fight between two pugilists, instead of a struggle between two wrestlers, he might have seen that throughout it each pugilist has to do four things – to think, to guard, to move and to hit.

Before the bout opens, each man must consider how best to knock his adversary out, and although, as the fight proceeds, he may be compelled to modify his tactics, he must never abandon his aim. At the start he must assume a defensive attitude until he has measured up his opponent. Next, he must move toward him under cover of his defence, and lastly, by foot-play, and still under cover of his defence, he must assume the offensive and attempt to knock him out. Thus we arrive at four primary principles: (1) The principle of the maintenance of the aim or object; (2) the principle of security of action; (3) the principle of mobility of action, and (4) the principle of the expenditure of offensive power.

Should the two pugilists be skilled, they will recognize the value of three accentuating principles. They will economize their strength, so as not to exhaust themselves prematurely; they will concentrate their blows against the decisive point selected, the left or right of their opponent's jaw, etc., and throughout will attempt to surprise him – that is, take him off guard, or do something he does not expect, or cannot prevent. Thus we arrive at: (5) The principle of economy of force; (6) the principle of concentration of force, and (7) the principle of surprise.

It will at once be recognized that these seven principles of war are akin to those deduced from Napoleonic warfare.

7 · The Defensive as the Stronger Form of War

When Clausewitz's insistence on war as 'an act of violence pushed to its utmost bounds' and his acceptance of Napoleonic warfare as proof of his theory of absolute war are borne in mind, it is puzzling that he should devote over a quarter of *On War* to the defensive, and to stress, time and again, that it is a stronger form of war than the offensive.

Before his theory is outlined, it is as well to consider two of his remarks on the offensive. The first occurs in Chapter IX of Book VIII, entitled 'The Destruction of the Enemy as the Object'. He writes 'that almost the only advantage which the offensive possesses is the effect of surprise at the opening of the scene. Suddenness and irrestible impetuosity are its strongest pinions; and when the object is the complete overthrow of the enemy, it can rarely dispense with them' (III, p. 153). In Chapter XV of Book III, 'Attack of a Theatre of War with the View to a Decision' – an all but identical title – he demolishes this:

'The first aim of the attack is victory. To all the advantages which the defender finds in the nature of his situation, the assailant can only oppose superior numbers. . . . Our object in this observation is to set aside those vague ideas of sudden attack and surprise which, in the attack, are generally assumed to be fertile sources of victory, and which yet, in reality, never occur except under special circumstances' (III, p. 31).

Should this be so, then the only possible deduction is, that the defensive *is* the stronger form of war.

His theory is as follows:

'What is the object of the defence? *To preserve.* To preserve is easier than to acquire [the object of the offence]; from which it follows . . . that . . . the defensive is easier than the offensive . . . but as the defensive has a negative object, that of *preserving*, and the offensive a positive object, that of *conquering*, and as the latter increases our means of carrying on the War, but preserving does not, therefore, in order to express ourselves distinctly, we must say, *that the defensive form of War is in itself stronger than the offensive. . . .*

'If the defensive is the stronger form of conducting War, but has a negative object, it follows of itself that we must only make use of it so long as our weakness compels us to do so, and that we must give up that form as soon as we feel strong enough to aim at the positive object' (II, pp. 134–136).

Clausewitz's defensive is, therefore, a delayed offensive, or what is sometimes called 'the defensive-offensive', in which the first phase is attrition and the second counter-attack. Or, as Clausewitz says: 'The defensive form of War is . . . no mere shield but a shield formed of blows delivered with skill' (II, p. 134); and again: '. . . a defensive, without an offensive return blow, cannot be conceived' (III, p. 3).

But it can be, because long before he had reached this conclusion, in Chapter II of Book I he had written:

'If then the negative purpose, that is the concentration of all the means into a state of pure resistance, affords a superiority in the contest, and if this advantage is sufficient to *balance* whatever superiority in numbers the adversary may have, then the mere *duration* of the contest will suffice gradually to bring the loss of force on the part of the adversary to a point at which the political object can no longer be an equivalent, a point at which, therefore, he must give up the contest' (I, pp. 34–35).

Whether this is meant to be a philosophical comment or a practical proposal is uncertain, but from its context it would appear to be the latter.

The trouble with Clausewitz is that his philosophical way of thinking – his habit of reducing operation to 'things-in-themselves' – constantly trips him up. Neither the defensive nor the offensive is inherently stronger or weaker; they are complementary operations, and which is the more suitable to an occasion depends on the circumstances which surround it. At times the offensive is the more so, as it was with Napoleon, because his genius coupled with his enemies' obsolescent ideas favoured it. At times the passive defence was profitable, as with Wellington at Torres Vedras; and at times, also with Wellington, it was the defensive-offensive which was correct, and in Spain he handled it in a masterly way. The foundations of all operations of war are not philosophy, they are common sense, as the seven principles of war so clearly show.

8 · The Decisive Battle

In Clausewitz's conception of the decisive, or great, battle there is no more nonsense about weaker and stronger forms of war, and he speaks with no uncertain voice.

'The combat is the real warlike activity, everything else is only its auxiliary' (I, p. 238).

'. . . the essence of War is conflict, and the [great] battle is the conflict of the main Armies, it is always to be regarded as the real centre of gravity of the War' (I, p. 270).

'. . . the direct destruction of the enemy's forces is everywhere predominant; we contend here for the overruling importance of the destructive principle and nothing else' (I, p. 241).

Numerical superiority is only one of the factors relied on to produce victory (I, p. 193). Others are the enveloping attack (II, p. 145); manoeuvre 'to turn or surround' (III, p. 11), and surprise (I, p. 262). These three additional means are 'only possible for the side which has the initiative' – the attacker (II, p. 145).

Rightly he points out that, although 'The battle is the bloodiest way of solution . . . it is not merely reciprocal slaughter, and its effect is more a killing of the enemy's courage than of the enemy's soldiers' (I, p. 286). Because 'loss of moral force is the chief cause of the decision . . . this loss continues to increase until it reaches its culminating-point at the close of the whole act' (I, p. 246). After which, 'the next question is . . . not about reorganizing [etc., etc.], but only of pursuit of fresh blows' (III, p. 155).

9 · The People's War

In Section (4) of Chapter II it was pointed out that the essential factor in primitive tribal warfare was concord between the members of the tribe, so that the maximum war effort might be directed outwardly. Normally the same holds good among civilized states, and during the era of absolute monarchies, in theory at least, the concord of civil populations became absolute, because they were altogether excluded from the ravages of war. But with the coming of the Napoleonic Wars (Clausewitz's absolute war), because Napoleon's aim was the the complete overthrow of his opponents, and because the French armies lived on their enemy's country, the civil population was at length roused against them,[1] and an inner front was added to the outer front, both of which the invader had to subdue. This additional front, as later will be referred to, eventually became as important and finally more important than the outer front – the traditional battleground of contending armies.

Clausewitz was one of the first to note the importance of this in the warfare of his day. He points out that, although the influence on war of a single inhabitant is barely perceptible, 'the *total influence* of the inhabitants of a country in war is anything but imperceptible. Everything goes on easier in our own country, provided it is not opposed by the general feeling of the population', and 'the spontaneous cooperation of the people . . . is in all cases most important' (II, p. 159).

Conversely, in an enemy country this applies to the invader, and to illustrate it Clausewitz turns to Spain, where '. . . the war, as regards its leading events, is chiefly a war carried on by the people themselves, we may see that we have here virtually a new power rather than a manifestation of increased cooperation on the part of the people' (II, p. 159). Indeed a foreseeing remark.

'According to our idea of a people's War', he writes, 'it should, like a kind of nebulous vapoury essence, never condense into a solid body; otherwise the enemy sends an adequate force against this core [and] crushes it.' It should be supported by small regular detachments, in order to encourage the inhabitants. They should not be too large, otherwise too many of the enemy's troops will be drawn toward them, and the inhabitants will leave it to the regular forces to fight it out. Also, the presence of large bodies of troops makes too great a demand on the resources of the people in provision of quarters, transport and contributions (II, pp. 346–347).

[1] See D'Odeleben's *Relation Circonstanciée de la Campagne de 1813 en Saxe* (French edition, 1817), Vol. I, p. 167.

His remarks on Russia are highly interesting, and never more so than today. Russia, he says, is a country which cannot be conquered by force of arms. 'Such a country can only be subdued by its own weakness, and by the effects of internal dissension. In order to strike these vulnerable points in its political existence, the country must be agitated to its very centre' (III, p. 159). In other words, Russia can only be conquered on her inner front. This means victory through revolution, and Clausewitz was probably the first to suggest this.

10 · Clausewitz's disregard of Napoleonic Warfare

When it is borne in mind that Clausewitz not only lived throughout the Napoleonic Wars, but also took part in the campaigns of 1806, 1812, 1813 and 1815, it is astonishing that he pays so little attention to Napoleon's generalship. Equally astonishing is it that, although he saw in Napoleon the greatest exponent of the offensive, and could write: 'Buonaparte hardly ever started upon a War without thinking of conquering his enemy at once in the first battle' (I, p. 289), he nevertheless held that the defensive was the stronger form of war. Again, it is astonishing that in his illuminating discussion on the centre of gravity he does not mention Napoleon's struggle against six English coalitions, and his ultimate failure to win his long series of wars because of his inability to 'hit the common centre of gravity of the whole war.'

Although he points out that 'Napoleon always showed great foresight in the provisions he made [to secure] the rear of his Army; and in that way, even in his boldest operations, he incurred less risk than might be imagined at first sight' (III, p. 221), he did not grasp the main reason for it. It was, in order to gain complete freedom of movement, to move away from his communications should he wish to: he was willing to accept their temporary loss as long as his base remained firm.

Instead of holding, as Clausewitz did, that 'there is no more imperative and no simpler law for strategy than to *keep the forces concentrated.* No portion is to be separated from the main body. . . . On this maxim we stand firm' (I, p. 208), Napoleon frequently sought to trap his enemy by dividing his army.

Instead of keeping it concentrated to cover his line of communications, as Clausewitz would have done, he split it into three or more widely spaced columns and formed what he called a *bataillon carrée* ('battalion square'), because they were distributed in diamond formation. Each column was sufficiently powerful to hold its own, should the enemy strike at it, until one or more of the remaining columns came to its support, while one or more manoeuvred against the enemy's flank. Whichever column first encountered the enemy became the advanced guard to the other columns.[1] That Clausewitz, who took part in the Jena campaign – its most notable example – was completely ignorant of this flexible method of concentration, as opposed to his own rigid method, is proved by his statement that, '. . . serious combats of advance guards which precede a battle are to be looked upon only as necessary evils' (I, p. 264).

But of all Clausewitz's blind shots, the blindest was that he never grasped that the true aim of war is peace and not victory; therefore that peace should be the ruling idea of policy, and victory only the means toward its achievement. Nowhere does he consider the influence of violence on eventual peace; actually the word 'peace' barely occurs half a dozen times in *On War*. In Napoleon he found the past-master of his theory of absolute war; yet to where did absolute war with its maximum of violence lead him? Not to the peace he aspired, but to St. Helena. Violence pushed to its utmost bounds ended in absolute failure. Better the advice of Montesquieu: 'That nations should do each other the most good during peacetime and the least harm during wartime without harming their true interests',[2] if peace is to be anything more than a temporary suspension of arms.

[1] For a full description of the *bataillon carrée* in the Jena campaign, see the author's *Decisive Battles of the Western World* (1955), Vol. II, pp. 423–6.

[2] Cited by Guglielmo Ferrero in *The Reconstruction of Europe, Talleyrand and the Congress of Vienna* (English edition, 1941), p. 38.

CHAPTER V

The Influences of the Industrial Revolution

*

1 · Impact of the Revolution on Civilization

Man's mind and emotions shape his culture – his religion, his ideals and his arts; his bodily activities fashion his civilization – his mode of living. Except for remnants of ancient hunting and pastoral societies hidden away in far-off lands, up to the eighteenth century of the Christian era world civilization had for millennia been based on agriculture. The bulk of mankind lived in villages, and the inhabitants of the towns and cities – the centres of culture – lived off the field lands which surrounded them; hence political and social power and status derived from those lands, their lords and lordlings ruled, their peasants and serfs toiled, and together with the townsfolk they formed a functional, organic society.

Then, suddenly, in the second half of the eighteenth century, like an unheralded typhoon, came steam-driven machinery, each single horse-power of which – so it has been estimated – could do the work of fifteen men. Thus the Industrial Revolution was born, and man emerged from his caterpillar stage, from his life on the surface of the soil, to rise, like a mechanized dragon, into a hitherto undreamt of industrial empyrean – a way of life so suddenly thrust on him that it could not fail to have cataclysmic impacts on peace and war.

It transcended all previous revolutions, including those of the great religious teachers, whose influence, however far-reaching, was limited in radius, and before the nineteenth century had run its course, the legions of the Industrial Revolution lorded the entire world, and claimed tribute from all its non-industrialized peoples. 'Mechanics', writes Lewis Mumford, 'became the new religion, and gave the world a new

Messiah: the machine;' or, at least, 'a new Moses that was to lead a barbarous humanity into the promised land.'[1]

Before this global revolution set in, the manufacture of commodities was predominantly carried on in the homes and small workshops of domestic workers, whose sole mechanical power was derived from wind and water. But when the factory began to challenge the domestic system, like a magnet coal drew the new-born industries towards it. This led to the rise of the Black Country in England, Clydeside in Scotland, the Ruhr in Germany, and the Lille area in France, with their conglomeration of great industrial towns, which steadily replaced agricultural civilization by urban, and when the cities became the centres of business, increasingly their cultural value declined. As early as 1804, William Blake prophetically engraved above the title of his Laocoon: 'Where any view of Money exists, Art cannot be carried on', and under it: 'Art Degraded, Imagination Denied, War Governed the Nations.'[2]

In a remarkably brief space of time, machines displaced hand labour; they conscripted the hand-workers and regimented them in factories, which Lewis Mumford compares to barracks.[3] In them mass production in big units was rendered possible, and they not only deprived the domestic workers of their jobs, but at the same time of their skills, because in mechanized manufacture the unskilled worker is the real worker, and the skilled craftsman is no more than his auxilliary, who prepares his work for him.

These radical changes in Western Civlization began to take root soon after James Watt (1736–1819), a Scottish instrument maker, in 1769 patented his improved steam engine, and, twelve years later, Matthew Boulton, a wealthy and far-sighted engineer, who had entered into partnership with Watt, wrote to him that 'The People of London, Birmingham, and Manchester are steam-mill mad.'[4] In 1818, Lord Cochrane (later

[1] *Technics and Civilization* (1934), pp. 45 and 58.

[2] *The Poetical Works of William Blake* (edit. Edwin J. Ellis, 1906), Vol. I, p. 433.

[3] He holds that 'The army is in fact the ideal form toward which a purely mechanized system of industry must tend' (Op. cit., p. 89).

[4] Cited in *European Civilization, its Origins and Development* (edit. Edward Eyre, 1937), Vol. V, p. 305.

tenth Earl of Dundonald), in a speech in the House of Commons said: In the late war England would have been brought 'to total ruin', but 'for the timely intervention of the use of machinery';[1] and in 1824, Stendhal wrote: 'What a change from 1785 to 1824! In the two thousand years of recorded history, so sharp a revolution in customs, ideas, and beliefs has perhaps never occurred before.'[2] By 1830, Great Britain had become 'the workshop of the world', as Napoleon had feared; yet, in spite of all his genius, he failed in his struggle against her commercial might, because, as Dundonald bore witness, although still in its cradle, the Machine had proved itself to be mightier than the Sword.

2 · *Impact of the Revolution on Society*

The most important social consequence of the Industrial Revolution was the emergence of a class of permanent wage-earners, the proletariat of the Socialist theorists. Permanent wage-earners were known in the domestic system, but as individuals and not as a class. They were not herded together; they could chat, sing and whistle as they liked, and because they were their own masters they were not badgered by foremen. Although the wages they earned were as low as those of the industrial workers, and their hours of work frequently longer, they were free human beings who possessed status, however humble, in the society of their day. While they belonged to a scattered fraternity, which prevented them from becoming class-conscious, the industrial workers were herded into the new mill villages and factory towns, which were entirely divorced from the ameliorating influence of any form of culture. They were condemned to live in insanitary houses amid sordid surroundings; their round of life was one of unremitting toil; their work was repetitive and monotonous, and they were subject to strict and frequently harsh factory discipline.

In the poverty of the worker lay one of the 'contradictions' of the capitalist system of that day. Mass production demands as its complement mass consumption, which in its turn demands sufficiency of purchasing power. The less money

[1] *The Autobiography of a Seaman* (edition 1800), p. 150.
[2] Cited in *War and Human Progress*, John U. Nef (1950), p. 290.

there is in circulation the less can be bought, and as the worker's wage was barely sufficient to keep him and his family alive, he was excluded from the market. Therefore, if the home market were to be enlarged, higher wages would have to be paid.

But in the early days of industrialization it was the foreign market that came first, and the competition between the factory owners was so violent that, in order to survive, they had to plough back the greater part of their profits into their businesses. To raise wages would have meant less profits, and less profits would have meant falling behind in the competitive race. This struggle is well described by Andrew Ure, the great apologist for Victorian capitalism.

'The present', he exclaimed in 1835, 'is distinguished from every preceding age by a universal ardour of enterprise in arts and manufactures. Nations, convinced at length that war is always a losing game, have converted their swords and muskets into factory implements, and now contend with each other in the bloodless but still formidable strife of trade. They no longer send troops to fight in distant fields, but fabrics to drive before them those of their old adversaries in arms, and to take possession of a foreign market. To impair the resources of a rival at home, by underselling his wares abroad, is the new belligerent system, in pursuance of which every nerve and sinew of the people are put upon the strain.'[1]

While the factories poured out goods for profit, in order to finance the pouring out of more goods wherewith to oust their rivals, the workers rotted in their slums, which became hotbeds of discontent and class-hatred, and the sight of others living in comfort and often in luxury aroused in them a sullen wrath against society. Thus, as industrialization spread, it created a class of malcontents in every industrialized country, a class increasingly antagonistic to the existing social order, the institutions of which, deriving as they did from the agricultural age, were not designed to give expression to the functions of an industrial one, or status to the industrial worker.

[1] The opening paragraph of his Preface to *The Philosophy of Manufactures: or An Exposition of the Scientific, Moral and Commercial Economy of the Factory System of Great Britain* (third edition, 1861), p. v.

3 · *Karl Marx and the Class Struggle*

Of the social reformers and revolutionaries brought into the field by the Industrial Revolution, historically the most important is Heinrich Karl Marx (1818–1883). Of Jewish parentage, he was born at Trèves on 5th May, 1818, and six years later his family adopted the Protestant faith. When he attained manhood he took to journalism, and, in 1842, became editor of the radical *Rheinische Zeitung* which, because of his violent sallies, was suppressed in 1843. Soon after he met Friedrich Engels (1820–1895), the son of a wealthy cotton spinner, who owned a factory near Manchester. Between them there sprang up a lifelong friendship, greatly to the advantage of Marx, because not only did Engels collaborate with him in many of his writings, but when he inherited his father's property he paid him an annuity of £350. Without it, Marx would have been reduced to a proletarian existence, which would not have suited him at all. In 1847, together they produced *The Communist Manifesto,* a violent declamation, which still remains the gospel of orthodox Communism. In 1849, on his expulsion from Prussia, Marx took up residence in London, where he spent the rest of his life, and wrote numerous works, including his monumental *Capital* which, like Clausewitz's *On War*, he never finished or revised. Its first volume appeared in 1867, and after Marx's death, on 14th March 1883, the remaining two volumes were arranged from his notes and edited by Engels; they were published in 1883–1885 and 1890–1894 respectively.

As a thinker Marx owed much to Hegel, from whom he adopted the Socratic dialectical system he had employed in his philosophy of history. It was a critical process of question and answer, the aim of which was to delve out contradictions in the subject under discussion. But while Socrates looked upon contradictions as obstacles to be surmounted, Hegel held that they were of essential value, because, so he maintained, it was only through opposition that progress toward truth could be made. His dialectical process was, therefore, one of thesis, which affirms a proposition; of antithesis, which denies it; and of synthesis, which embraces what is disclosed to be true in both. But once the synthesis replaces the thesis, it itself becomes a thesis to be faced with another antithesis; this leads to yet another synthesis, and so on, step by step, until Absolute Truth (God) is reached. In brief, a system that winnows the grain of truth from the chaff of falsehood.

Marx, as he himself said, inverted Hegel's dialectic. Instead of working upward toward the Absolute, he worked downward from what he held to be axiomatic – that the material world is the fundamental and only reality. He discarded idealism, and with the materialists he held that the world possessed an objective existence apart from man's perception of it, and that by means of the dialectical process it was possible to obtain a knowledge of the world which, although incomplete, would contain a core of absolute truth, and that this core would grow as the process progressed. Dialectical materialsm was, therefore, the only scientific method by which reality could be arrived at.

According to his interpretation of history, historical materialism is dialectical materialism applied to human relations within society.[1] In the preface of his *Contribution to the Critique of Political Economy*, he starts off by stating that the production of the means to support life is the principle that governs all human relations,[2] and next to it the exchange of all things produced; therefore the determinant of social change is to be found in the mode of production and exchange. Next, production entails two relationships; the first between man and his instruments of production ('productive forces'), and the second between men and men ('productive relations'), and when the first change so do the second.

At an early period of history, so his argument runs, certain members of society acquired control over the productive forces; this led to private ownership. Then the productive

[1] For a criticism of this see *The Materialist Conception of History: A Critical Analysis*, Karl Federn (English edition, 1939).

[2] In his speech at the graveside of Marx, Engels said that Marx 'discovered the simple fact, hitherto concealed by an overgrowth of ideology, that mankind must first of all eat and drink, have shelter and clothing, before it can pursue politics, science, religion, art, etc.' Apparently he overlooked the 'simple fact' that mankind has to breathe before he eats, etc; but this would not have fitted his economics. (See *The Illusion of an Epoch*, H. B. Acton (1955), p. 143.)

relations became those of two antagonistic classes, or, as Marx declares in *The Communist Manifesto*: 'The history of all hitherto existing society is the history of class struggles.'[1]

To show that this was so, he distinguished five economic forms of production, each of the last four of which, in accordance with the dialectical principle, is an advance upon its predecessor, because each in turn takes up whatever is of value in the preceding one once it has reached maturity. The first is the primitive form, in which means of production are socially owned;[2] the second is the antique or classical form, in which the slaveholder owns them; the third is the feudal form, in which the feudal lord owns the greater part of them;[3] and the fourth is the bourgeois form, in which the capitalist owns them, and although he does not own his workers, through fear and starvation they are compelled to work for him. Ultimately, when capitalism has reached maturity the fifth form comes into force; the proletariat appropriates the means of production,[4] and with the negation of the contradiction inherent in Capitalism, which is that the rich become richer and richer and the poor become poorer and poorer,[5] production reaches its fullest development.

Although Marx never clearly defined what he meant by 'class', as we see, he held that since primitive times there had invariably been two: one which controls the means of production and the other which does not. And we see also that the force which shapes the world is the clash of classes, and that it must inevitably lead to the dictatorship of the proletariat, when, with the transformation of Socialism into Communism,

[1] Centenary edition (1948), p. 13.

[2] Compare with Rousseau's 'noble savage'.

[3] This is a bad shot, because the feudal order was a military and not an economic one, and to suggest that it took over what was best in the classical means of production is historically absurd; its antithesis was not capitalism but gunpowder. The antithesis of the classical age – if it had one – was the barbarian invasions, whose 'productive forces' were conquest and robbery.

[4] 'The proletariat will use its political supremacy to wrest, by degrees, all capital from the bourgeoisie, to centralize all instruments of production in the hands of the State, i.e., of the proletariat organized as the ruling class; and to increase the total of productive forces as rapidly as possible' (*The Communist Manifesto*, p. 34).

[5] This is the opposite of what has occurred since 1848.

a classless and stateless society will be established. But nowhere does he seek to prove, as R. N. Carew Hunt points out, 'that the worker *is*, in fact, fitted for the role assigned him; nor does it occur to him that the negation of Capitalism may lead to the emergence of a wholly new class which is strictly speaking neither capitalist nor proletariat.'[1] Marx's insistence that the history of all hitherto existing society is the history of class struggles vitiated the dialectics of his intellectual followers – the Marxist intelligentsia – and led them to attribute to the proletariat qualities which, at best, were confined to themselves.

On this contradiction in Marx's dialectic Peter F. Drucker is highly illuminating:

'Perhaps the greatest fallacy of our age', he writes, 'is the myth of the masses which glorifies the amorphous, societyless, disintegrated crowd. Actually the masses are a product of social decomposition and rank poison.' The danger does not lie in their revolt, because revolt is 'still a form of participation in social life, if only a protest. . . . The danger of the masses lies precisely in this inability to participate. . . . Since they have no social status and function, society to them is nothing but a demoniac, irrational, incomprehensible threat . . . any legitimate authority appears to them as tyrannical and arbitrary. They are therefore always willing to follow an irrational appeal, or to submit to an arbitrary tyrant if only he promises a change. . . . Without beliefs, they can swallow anything provided it is not a social order. In other words, the masses must always fall prey to the demagogue or the tyrant who seeks power for power's sake. They can only be organized by force, in slavery and negation. . . . Any society which cannot prevent the development of masses is doomed.'[2]

In our examination of the theories of Clausewitz, it will be remembered that he was one of the earliest, if not the first, of military thinkers to recognize the importance of the impact of war on the civil population, and that the most important of its by-products was the creation of what we called the 'inner front'. Now a moment's thought will reveal that Marx's

[1] *The Theory and Practice of Communism* (1950), p. 39.
[2] *The Future of Industrial Man* (1943), p. 26.

insistence on class war leads to an identical conclusion, with one difference: while Clausewitz's inner front comes into existence only during wartime, Marx's inner front is a permanent one established during peacetime with the aim of overthrowing a government by revolution. Therefore the aims of revolution and absolute war are identical – the means alone differ.

This is no coincidence, because Engels, who had a first-class military brain, was a student of Clausewitz,[1] and his study of *On War* led him to realize that the clash of armies was only one of the means of waging war. According to Sigmund Newmann, both he and Marx were fully aware 'that modern warfare is of a fourfold nature – diplomatic, economic, psychological, and only as a last resort military. . . . They were fully aware that military campaigns could be lost before the first bullet was shot, that they would in fact be decided beforehand on the preliminary battlefronts of economic and psychological warfare. . . . To them war was fought with different means in different fields. In the words of the later militant syndicalist Georges Sorel, a general strike could become a "Napoleonic battle" . . . During the "promising" crisis of 1857, Engels wrote to Marx: "A continuing economic depression could be used by astute revolutionary strategy as a useful weapon for a chronic pressure . . . in order to warm up the people . . . just as a cavalry attack has greater *élan* if the horses first trot five hundred paces before coming within charging distance of the enemy." '[2]

These original speculations on the art of waging war, indirectly derived from Clausewitz, were destined two generations later to revolutionize the whole conduct of war. Class war was, indeed, a profound military problem, because the social health of a nation is the moral foundation of its military power.

[1] On 25th September 1857, Engels wrote to Marx: 'I am now reading Clausewitz, *On War*. A strange way of philosophizing but very good on the subject. To the question whether war should be called an art or a science, the answer given is that war is most like a trade [*On War*, Vol. I, p. 40]. Fighting is to war what cash payment is to trade, for however rarely it may be necessary for it actually to occur, everything is directed towards it, and eventually it must take place all the same and must be decisive' (*Makers of Modern Strategy*, p. 158)

[2] Ibid., p. 156.

4 · *Impact of the Revolution on Military Power*

Due to the inertia of armies and navies, their disregard of industry as the source of their power, and the reaction against war which followed the Napoleonic conflict, between the dates mentioned by Stendhal the impact of the Industrial Revolution on them was negligible; so much so that in 1824 they differed but slightly from what they had been in 1785. Nevertheless, a spirit of invention had been awakened, and here and there some enthusiast hit on an idea which years later weevilled its way through the military carapace.

In 1759, Cugnot, in France, bolted a steam boiler onto a wagon frame, and succeeded in making the first steam-driven road vehicle. His idea was that it would be useful in war; but during its first public trial he had the misfortune to knock down part of a wall; was cast into jail, and his experiment abandoned. Yet, should Mr Manchester be right, its value did not go unnoticed, because later 'Napoleon must have visualised the possibilities of Cugnot's machine for military purposes, for when the great general was selected a member of the French Institute, the subject was "The Automobile in War".'[1]

In 1783, the Montgolfier brothers built the first man-lifting balloon; it made its maiden flight on 15th October, and on 7th January, the following year, it crossed the English Channel. Its military possibilities were at once appreciated, and soon after the opening of the French Revolutionary Wars an aeronautic school was founded at Meudon, and four balloons were made for the Army of the North. One of them was used to reconnoitre the Austrian position just before the battle of Fleurus, on 16th June 1794.

The application of steam propulsion to ships was also experimented with at an early date, and the earliest steamboat would appear to have been constructed by James Rumsey, a Virginian, in 1775. Strangely enough, instead of making use of the paddle-wheel, which dated from Roman times, Rumsey's steamboat was driven by water-jet propulsion: a steam pump sucked in water at her bow and ejected it at her stern.

[1] 'The Forerunner of the Tank', H. H. Manchester, *The American Mechanist*, Vol. 49, No. 15.

These new powers of locomotion evoked the prophetic foresight of Dr. Erasmus Darwin who, in 1791, in a poem wrote:

> "*Soon shall thy arm, unconquer'd steam! afar*
> *Drag the slow barge, or drive the rapid car;*
> *Or on wide-waving wings expanded bear*
> *The flying chariot through the fields of air.*
> *Fair crews triumphant, leaning from above,*
> *Shall wave their flutt'ring kerchiefs as they move;*
> *Or warrior bands alarm the gaping crowd,*
> *And armies shrink beneath the shadowy cloud.*"[1]

Although these possibilities were not to begin to influence armies and fleets for well over half a century, there were a number of early inventions which were to add enormously to the destructive power of the cannon and the musket.

In the last quarter of the eighteenth century two new artillery projectiles were devised: in 1784, Lieutenant Henry Shrapnel's 'spherical case', as he called it, better known as the 'Shrapnel shell'; and during the siege of Gibraltar (1779–1783) Mercier's 'operative gun shell', a 5.5-inch mortar shell adapted to be fired from a 24-pounder. The first was not adopted by the British Ordnance Committee until 1803, and the second, which was destined to render obsolete the wooden battleship, not until 1822.

Two other inventions, the percussion cap and the cylindro-conoidal bullet, revolutionized infantry tactics. The first was impracticable before the discovery of fulminate of mercury in 1800 – an explosive which detonates on concussion. Seven years later, the Revd A. Forsyth patented a percussion priming powder composed of chlorate of potash, fulminate of mercury and powdered glass, and in 1816, among other claimants, Thomas Shaw of Philadelphia invented the copper percussion cap. Although it led to the introduction of the percussion-operated sporting gun, vastly reduced misfires, and, unlike the flintlock, could be fired in windy and rainy weather, so conservative was the British Ordnance Department that not until 1839 were flintlock muskets converted to the percussion prin-

[1] *The Poetry and Aesthetics of Erasmus Darwin*, James Venable Logan (1936), p. 117. Dr Erasmus Darwin was grandfather of Charles Darwin the naturalist.

ciple. Its superiority became immediately apparent; in 1841 'A company of Sepoys, armed with flintlock muskets, which would not go off in a heavy rain, were closely surrounded by some 1,000 Chinese and were in imminent peril, when two companies of marines, armed with percussion-cap muskets, were ordered up, and soon dispersed the enemy with great loss.'[1]

The cylindro-conoidal bullet was invented by Captain Norton of the British 34th Regiment in 1823. It had a hollow base, so that, when fired, the bullet would expand and seal the bore. The origin of his idea is an interesting one: when in Southern India, he examined the blow-pipe arrows used by the natives, and found that their base was formed of elastic locus pith, which by its expansion against the inner surface of the blow-pipe prevented the escape of air past it (windage).

In 1836, Mr Greener, a London gunsmith, improved on Norton's bullet by inserting a conoidal wooden plug into its base. Although both inventions were rejected by the Ordnance Department, the idea was taken up in France, and in 1849 M. Minié adopted Greener's design and produced the deadly Minié bullet. The British Government then paid Minié £20,000 for his patent, and Greener got £1,000 for having supplied him with the idea. In 1851 the Minié rifle was issued to the British army, and in the Kaffir War of 1852 it was discovered that 'at a range of from twelve to thirteen hundred yards small bodies of Kaffirs could be dispersed.'[2] These two inventions made the rifle the most deadly weapon of the century.

While other nations were wrangling over the merits and demerits of the flintlock and percussion cap muzzle-loaders, in 1841 Prussia took a bold step forward and issued to certain regiments the Dreyse breech-loading rifle, better known as the 'needle-gun', a bolt-operated weapon which fired a paper cartridge. Because of escape of gas at the breech, its range was considerably less than that of the Minié rifle; but it could fire seven shots a minute to the Minié two. Its main advantage

[1] 'Dispatch of Lieut.-General Lord Viscount Gough', *London Gazette*, 8th October 1841.

[2] *A History of the British Army*, J. W. Fortescue (1927), Vol. XII, p. 561. The idea of rifling was old and dated back to 1631. The main trouble was that the crude gunpowder used fouled the rifling after a few shots, and in consequence made loading difficult.

was, however, not rapidity of loading; it was that a breech-operated rifle can freely be loaded when the rifleman is lying down; this had a most demoralizing effect on the Austrians in 1866.[1]

On account of cost, the development of artillery was slower than that of the rifle, and although breech-loading and the rifling of cannon were as separate ideas old, it would seem that, when combined, they were first experimented with in England in 1745.[2] Next, exactly one hundred years later, an effective breech-loading 6.5-inch rifled gun was invented by Major Cavalli, a Sardinian officer, and a still more effective one by Baron Wahrendorff in 1846. Nevertheless, no country would face the cost of re-equipment. Then came the war in the Crimea (1853–1856), during which a number of cast-iron, muzzle-loading, smooth-bore 68-pounders and 8-inch guns were converted into rifled pieces on the Lanchester principle.[3] Because their greater range and accuracy made the bombardment of Sevastopol a 'very hideous thing', after the close of the war all the Powers set about to experiment with rifled breech-loading ordnance.

A weapon which was introduced in the early years of the Industrial Revolution, and which stands apart from both musket and cannon, was the war-rocket. It is the oldest of all explosively propelled projectiles, and in Asia dates from the thirteenth century. It was the rocket used by Tipu Sultan at the siege of Seringapatam in 1799 which attracted the attention of the British gunnery expert Colonel Sir William Congreve; he took it as his model and improved on it. He tells us that he made rockets of from two ounces – 'a species of self-motive musket ball' – to three hundredweights.[4] In 1806 they

[1] See *Military Reports*, Colonel Baron Stoffel, French Military Attaché in Prussia, 1866–1870 (English edition, 1872), p. 64. The breech-loading system dates from very early days. It was advocated for rifled cannon and muskets in 1742 by Benjamin Robins in his *New Principles of Gunnery*, a book studied by Napoleon.

[2] See *Tracts on Gunnery*, Benjamin Robins, p. 337.

[3] The rotation of the shell was achieved, not by grooves in the bore of the gun, but by the shape of the bore, which was oval, it twisted round the axis of the gun from the breech to the muzzle.

[4] *Congreve Rocket System as Compared with Artillery*, Maj.-General Sir W. Congreve, Bart., M.P., (1827), p. 39.

were first used at the siege of Boulogne, when, as Congreve writes: 'In less than ten minutes after the first discharge the town was discovered to be on fire.'[1] They were used at Walcheren and Copenhagen in 1807, at the battles of Leipzig and Waterloo, and at New Orleans in 1815. In the last, Major A. Lecarrière Latour writes: 'a cloud of rockets continued to fall in showers during the whole attack.'[2]

Of this weapon Congreve predicted: 'The rocket is, in truth, an arm by which the whole system of military tactics is destined to be changed.'[3] And Marshal Marmont considered that the rocket 'may become the first arm . . . must exercise an immense influence on the destinies of armies.'[4]

Besides the war-rocket, four other weapons, all ancient in idea, were either designed or suggested during this period; they are worth a mention, because in years to come they were to play havoc with fleets and armies.

In 1776, David Bushnell, an American, built the first submarine; her crew was one man, and during the War of Independence, but for an error of judgment on his part, he would probably have sunk the British warship *Eagle*. In 1801, Bushnell was followed by another American, Robert Fulton, a man of quite exceptional inventive genius, who built a 'plunging boat', called *Nautilus*, which in Brest harbour remained under water for half an hour. In 1812 Dundonald suggested the use of burning sulphur as an asphyxiant, and in 1855 he revived the idea, and urged its use against Sevastopol, but his proposal was rejected as too horrible to contemplate.

The remaining two weapons were steam operated. The first was the Perkins steam-gun, an account of a demonstration of which, attended by the Duke of Wellington, is to be found in *The Courier*, a London newspaper of December 9 1825. We are told that it discharged nearly 1,000 balls per minute, which penetrated a quarter-inch thick iron plate. In the editor's opinion, 'this wonderful specimen of human ingenuity and

[1] Ibid., p. 18.

[2] *Historical Memoir of the War in West Florida and Louisiana in 1814–15* (1816), p. 154.

[3] *Congreve Rocket System* etc., p. 42.

[4] Cited by Captain Boxer in his pamphlet on the *Congreve Rocket* (1860), pp. 65–66.

destructive power' heralded an era of universal peace, 'for how could any population supply the loss by such destructive instruments.' Its use would seem to have been revived during the Crimean War, in which another novel weapon was suggested. In 1855 James Cowan, a wealthy philanthropist, took out a patent for a steam-driven 'locomotive land battery fitted with scythes to mow down infantry.' It was a four-wheeled armoured vehicle armed with guns, and 'looked like a huge dish-cover on wheels.' It was rejected by Lord Palmerston as being too brutal for civilized warfare.[1]

In 1813, Robert Fulton built the first steam-propelled armoured ship, the *Fulton*. She was of twin-hull construction with a paddle-wheel between the hulls, and she was protected by a belt of timber fifty-eight inches in thickness. This monstrous vessel clearly showed that a more suitable system of propulsion and a less clumsy means of protection were needed. In 1836 the first was met by John Ericsson's successful application of the screw propeller, and the second by substituting iron for wood.

Strangely enough, the British Admiralty was opposed to the introduction of steamships, and when the Colonial Office asked the First Lord for a steam packet to convey mails from Malta to the Ionian Islands, the following reply was received: 'Their Lordships felt it their bounden duty to discourage, to the utmost of their ability, the employment of steam vessels, as they considered that the introduction of steam was calculated to strike a fatal blow at the naval supremacy of the Empire.'

Thus it came about that, when Great Britain became involved in the Crimean War, except for a few warships fitted with auxiliary engines, and a number of steam tugs, her entire fleet consisted of wooden sailing ships. What is so astonishing is that since 1822 the introduction of the shell gun had rendered the wooden ship so vulnerable as to deprive her of all fighting value. This was demonstrated at the battle of Sinope in November 1853, when a squadron of Turkish frigates was almost blown out of the water by the shell fire of the Russian

[1] See *The Tanks*, Captain B. H. Liddell Hart (1959), Vol. I, p. 13.
[2] Cited in the *Journal of the Royal United Service Institution* (1931), Vol. LXXV, No. 502, p. 258.

ships. The outcome was that Napoleon III at once ordered the construction of a flotilla of floating batteries protected by armour able to resist both solid shot and explosive shell. Their success was complete, and not only was the need to armour ships proved beyond doubt, but also that the introduction of armour would necessitate the introduction of more powerful ordnance. This led to the general adoption of rifled cannon, and soon after the war to the construction by France and Great Britain of the first two armoured warships, *La Gloire* and the *Warrior*.

The first locomotive was built by Richard Trevithick, an English engineer, in 1801; it was designed to work on colliery tramways, and did so with great success. In 1812 one of his locomotives was at work at the Wylan colliery, Newcastle, and George Stephenson (1781–1848), who at the time was engine-wright at the Killingworth colliery, was so impressed with it that he was authorized to construct a 'travelling engine' for a tramroad between the colliery and the shipping port. This he did, and it proved so profitable that he succeeded in persuading the projectors of the Stockton and Darlington railway, who contemplated using horses to draw their wagons, to turn to steam traction. They adopted his proposal, and on 27th September 1825, the first true railway came into existence. No other development of the Industrial Revolution had so profound an influence on the future of peace and war.

Although the locomotive was wholly of British origin, it is no coincidence that the nation which produced Clausewitz was the first to grasp the importance of the railway in war. Even before a rail had been laid in Prussia, civil thought turned to the military importance of railways. In 1833, F. W. Harkort pointed out that a railway between Cologne and Minden and another between Mainz and Wesel would add enormously to the defence of the Rhineland; and C. E. Pönitz urged the general building of railways, in order to protect Prussia against France, Austria and Russia. Simultaneously, Friedrich List (1789–1846), an economist of unique genius, pointed out that, from the position of a secondary military power, whose weakness lay in her central position between powerful potential enemies, Prussia could be raised by the railway into a formidable one. 'Germany could be made into a defensive bastion in the very heart of Europe. Speed of mobilization, the rapidity with which troops could be moved from the centre of the country to its periphery, and the other obvious advantages of "interior lines" of rail transport would be of greater relative advantage to Germany than to any other European country.'[1] List himself wrote: 'Every mile of railway which a neighbouring nation finishes sooner than we, each mile more of railway it possesses, gives it an advantage over us . . . it is just as little left in our hands to determine whether we shall make use of the new defensive weapons given to us by the march of progress, as it was left to our forefathers to determine whether they should shoulder the rifle instead of the bow and arrow.'[2]

In 1846, the year List died, the first extensive troop movements by rail was made by a Prussian army corps, 12,000 strong, with horses and guns to Cracow. This experimental move led to the Prussian General Staff making a comprehensive survey of the military value of railways. Next, during the revolutionary upheaval of 1848–1850, Prussia gained further experience in rail movements, and when, in 1849, Napoleon III intervened in the Italian War, the French made all possible use of railways. From then on the railway increasingly became the dominant factor in strategy, until the time came when it was possible to supply armies of millions of men in the field. It was George Stephenson more so than Napoleon or Clausewitz who was the father of the nation-in-arms.

In 1836 – twenty years before the conclusion of the period discussed in this chapter – Baron Jomini (1779–1869) wrote in his *Summary of the Art of War:*

'The new inventions of the last twenty years seem to threaten a great revolution in army organization, armament and tactics. . . .

'The means of destruction are approaching perfection with frightful rapidity. The Congreve rockets, the effect and direction of which it is said the Austrians can now regulate, – the shrapnel howitzers, which throw a stream of canister as far as

[1] *Makers of Modern Strategy*, p. 149.
[2] Ibid., cited in p. 150.

the range of a bullet, – the Perkins steam-guns, which vomit forth as many bullets as a battalion, – will multiply the chances of destruction, as though the hecatombs of Eylau, Borodino, Leipsic, and Waterloo were not sufficient to decimate the European races.

'If governments do not combine in a congress to proscribe these inventions of destruction, there will be no course left but to make the half of an army consist of cavalry with cuirasses, in order to capture with great rapidity these machines; and the infantry, even, will be obliged to resume its armor of the Middle Ages, without which a battalion will be destroyed before engaging the enemy.

'We may then see again the famous men-at-arms all covered with armor, and horses will require the same protection.'[1]

[1] American edition (1868), pp. 48-49.

CHAPTER VI

The American Civil War 1861-1865

*

1 · Impact of the Industrial Revolution on the United States

The American Civil War was the first great conflict of the steam age, and its origins were intimately related to the impact of the Industrial Revolution on what Marx calls the 'productive forces' prevalent in the youthful United States. This led to a change in 'productive relations', and ultimately to war between two variant economic societies – the inhabitants of the Northern States and those of the Southern. While the former were staunch democrats, mainly occupied in agriculture and commerce, the latter were an aristocratically-minded people, almost feudal in outlook, whose plantations were cultivated by slave labour.

Although during the War of Independence (1775–1783), or immediately after, the founding fathers of the Union reprobated slavery, when, in 1787, the Constitution was drafted, on the insistence of South Carolina and Georgia slavery was retained.[1] As things then stood, slavery was on the decline, and had the 'productive forces' remained as they were, the probability is that, within a generation or two, slavery would have withered away.

This was not to be, because four years after the ratification of the Constitution in 1788, suddenly there appeared an invention which was enormously to stimulate the cultivation of

[1] Slavery was abolished in the Northern States between 1777 and 1804; the first State to free its slaves was Vermont and the last New Jersey. Actually, this was of small advantage to the slaves themselves, because most of the Northern slaves were transferred to the Southern slave markets.

cotton in the Southern States. In 1792, Eli Whitney, an American, designed his 'saw gin' for separating cotton from the seed, and it made cotton so profitable that between 1815 and 1861 it became known as 'King of the Southern States'. Coincidentally this placed slave labour on a highly profitable footing, with the result that, instead of slaves being a drug on the market, their supply fell short of demand. Prior to the introduction of the saw gin, tobacco, more so than cotton, had been the staple crop of the South, but by 1820 the cotton crop had risen to 160 million pounds; ten years later it had doubled, in 1850 it passed the 1,000 million pounds mark, and in 1860 it stood at 2,300 million pounds. Concurrently, the price of a 'prime field hand' rose from about $500 in 1830 to about $1,800 in 1860, which shows how vital their supply had become to the prosperity of the South.

Meanwhile rapid economic changes were taking place in the Northern States. The two long trade embargoes, the first between 1807 and 1812, during the Napoleonic Wars, and the second between 1812 and 1815, in the war with England, had compelled the Northern States to rely on and extend their home industries. Thus it came about that, while in the South capital was represented by slaves, in the North it increasingly became represented by factories. By 1812 they were so firmly established that textile machinery made America independent of foreign importation of cotton fabrics. In 1840, there were 1,200 cotton factories in the United States, the majority in New England, and by 1860 their goods were reaching the remoter parts of the West.

The iron industry in Pennsylvania developed more slowly, and to protect it and other infant industries tariffs were introduced. Essential as they were to the Northern foundry and mill owners, the Southern planters did not directly benefit from them, and in South Carolina they were pronounced to be unconstitutional devices to tax the South for the benefit of the North. So violent became the dispute over tariffs that, in 1832, South Carolina declared the Tariff Act of 1824 – known as the 'Tariff of Abominations' – null and void. At length a compromise was agreed, and the first phase in the struggle for State rights terminated.

While this struggle was under way, a more intractable cause of dissension took root. In 1803, the immense region of Louisiana was purchased from France, and in 1819 Florida was purchased from Spain. These regions doubled the size of the United States, and when, in 1822, Mexico broke away from Spain, friction between her and the States led to the Texan War in 1836 and the Mexican War in 1846. These wars added to the United States territories as extensive as Louisiana – namely, the State of Texas, and the future States of New Mexico, Arizona, California, Nevada, Utah and part of Colorado.

These vast acquisitions of land, which bordered the Southern States, gave rise to the next bone of contention: Were the new territories eventually to become free or slave states? If the former, the North would dominate the Union; if the latter, then it would be the South. Not only did the Southern planters insist on the extension of slavery, but they urged that the federal law of 1807, which prohibited traffic in slaves, be repealed. For the North this was an impossible demand; not only might it lead to war with England,[1] but of a certainty it would render the democracy of the North contemptible in the eyes of the world.

It was not the existence of slavery in the Southern States which antagonized the North, it was its extension to the new regions; therefore, as long as their future status remained undecided, the quarrel continued, and it was approaching its climax when, in 1858, during the presidency of James Buchanan (1857–1861), a comparatively unknown man, Abraham Lincoln (1809–1865), appeared on the scene. In his contest for the senatorial seat of Illinois he poured no little common sense on the burning question, and won the ears of his fellow countrymen when he proclaimed:

' "A house divided against itself cannot stand." I believe this government cannot endure, permanently half-slave and half-free. I do not expect the Union to be dissolved – I do not

[1] In 1814, by the Peace of Ghent, Britain and the United States mutually bound themselves to do all in their power to extinguish the traffic in slaves; and by the Ashburn treaty of 1842, to reinforce this both agreed to maintain squadrons on the West Coast of Africa.

expect the house to fall – but I do expect it will cease to be divided. It will become all one thing, or all the other.'[1]

The now fast approaching crisis was hastened when, on 16th October 1859, John Brown, a fanatical Abolitionist, at the head of twenty-two followers, seized the arsenal at Harper's Ferry, Virginia; his aim was to set on foot a servile insurrection. This blew the quarrel into white heat, for although he was speedily hanged his purpose was massacre; therefore, Union or no Union, anti-slavery had to be fought to the death.

Thus matters stood when, on 6th November 1860, Lincoln was elected president. The verdict announced to the South that its dream of an extension of slavery was at an end. On 20th December, South Carolina passed an ordnance of secession; and by 1st February 1861, Georgia, Alabama, Mississippi, Florida, Louisiana and Texas had followed suit.[2] Their militias were called out; Federal forts and arsenals in the Southern States were occupied, and, on 4th February 1861, a provisional government, known as the Confederate States of America, with Jefferson Davis (1808–1889) as president, was set up at Montgomery, Alabama.

At length, on 12th April, the tension could no longer bear the strain. Contrary to instructions, in the morning twilight, and when none could see clearly what that historic day portended, the Confederates in Charleston bombarded Fort Sumter, and the thunder of their guns announced that the argument of a generation should be decided by the ordeal of war. A war, not between two antagonistic political parties, but a struggle to the death between two societies, each championing a different civilization. Or, as Stephen Benét concisely depicts it:

The pastoral rebellion of the earth
Against machines, against the Age of Steam.[3]

[1] Cited in *The Living Lincoln*, edit. M. Angle and Earl Schenck Miers (1955), p. 212.

[2] Between 17th April and 20th May, Virginia (less the Western half, which in 1863 became the State of West Virginia), Arkansas, Tennessee and North Carolina joined the Confederacy.

[3] *John Brown's Body* (English edition, 1929), p. 375.

2 · *The Character of the Civil War*

Because its aim was all-embracing, the war was to be absolute in character: Was the Union to be dissolved, or was it to be maintained? If the latter, then, either the Southern States must unconditionally submit to the Northern, or the Northern must unconditionally subdue the Southern. Therefore, because the South refused to submit, for the North it was to be a war in which there could be no compromise.

Like the total wars of the twentieth century, it was preceded by years of violent propaganda, which long before the war had obliterated all sense of moderation, and had awakened in the contending parties the primitive spirit of tribal fanaticism.[1]

Thus it came about, as Vattel had held, that 'If you once open a door for continual accusations of outrageous excess . . . the sword will never be sheathed till one of the parties is utterly destroyed.'[2]

From the standpoint of American Constitutional Law, Lincoln was none other than a dictator, and this he showed himself to be immediately the war opened, for without the sanction of Congress he proclaimed a blockade of the Southern ports, and simultaneously ordered the enrolment of 75,000 volunteers; also, on his own authority, he suspended the writ of *habeas corpus* in parts of Maryland. People suspected of disloyalty were imprisoned without trial; 'A loyal mayor of Baltimore, suspected of Southern sympathies, was arrested and confined in a fortress for over a year', and a Maryland judge 'who had charged a grand jury to inquire into illegal acts of government officials was set upon by soldiers when his court was in session, beaten and dragged bleeding from his bench, and imprisoned for six months.' These are exam-

[1] This is noted by N. Stephenson in his *Lincoln*. He writes that a new temper had formed throughout the land: 'a blend of all elements of violent feeling which war inevitably releases . . . the resurrection of that primitive bloodlust which lies dormant in every peaceful nation like a sleeping beast.' (Cited in *The Growth of the American Republic*, Samuel Eliot Morison and Henry Steel Commager (1942), Vol. I, p. 673.

[2] See *supra* Chapter I, p. 18.

ples of dictatorial acts cited by Morison and Commager.[1]

In the Confederacy, President Davis was, all but in name, also a dictator, and as arbitrary as Lincoln; but while Lincoln was very human and magnanimous, Davis was starched and egoistic, a man who would neither argue nor listen, and who could not tolerate either assistance or opposition. Nevertheless, even should personalities be set aside, the fact remains that absolute wars demand absolute leaders to fight them.

3 · The Strategical Problems

The Confederacy stretched from the Rio Grande del Norte to Chesapeake Bay, and from the Missouri River to the Gulf of Mexico, and vast expanses of it were virgin land. It was inhabited by from five to six million whites and three and a half million slaves, together less than half the population of the Northern States, and, except for the Tredegar Iron Works at Richmond, which could turn out a limited amount of ordnance and heavy castings, its industrial resources were nil. Cut off as the Confederates were from the Northern factories, they depended on Europe for all warlike stores and manufactured goods; these they reckoned to obtain by the barter of cotton.

Strategically, the Confederacy was divided by the Mississippi, the greatest of all thoroughfares from north to south, and the area east of it to the Atlantic, which constituted the main theatre of war, was split into two sub-theatres by the Appalachian or Alleghany Mountains, which, from the Potomac River in the north ran in a south-westerly direction to Chattanooga, on the Tennessee River, and thence into northern Alabama. In the eastern of these sub-theatres were located the opposing capitals, the Federal at Washington on the Potomac, and the Confederate at Richmond on the James River, about one hundred miles south of the former.

Because roads were mainly cart tracks, throughout the war

[1] Op. cit., Vol. I, pp. 699–700. In the summer of 1863, in reply to a thinly veiled censure passed on him at a public meeting in Albany, Lincoln defended himself by stating that 'arrests are made, not so much for what has been done, as for what probably would be done.' This is of the essence of dictatorship, because it places the head of government above the law. (For Lincoln's reply in full see *The Living Lincoln*, pp. 545–554.)

all considerable movements were made by rail and river. Of the railways in the Confederacy the most important were the two lateral ones, which ran from Richmond to the Mississippi; one by way of Chattanooga to Memphis, and the other by way of Atlanta to Vicksburg. Atlanta lay about one hundred miles south of Chattanooga, and both towns were linked by a railway which ran from Louisville in northern Kentucky to Savannah in Georgia, with a branch line to Charleston in South Carolina. Chattanooga and Atlanta were of the utmost importance to the Confederacy, for should they be lost, the two lateral railways would be cut and connection between the two sub-theatres severed.

Because the Confederates could not hope to conquer the Northern States, their problem was to resist conquest. In other words, to tire the Federals out, and force them to abandon the war. Its solution depended on how long their resources would hold out, and, in order to add to them, it was vital to maintain contact with Europe, which demanded that the main ports in the Confederacy should be kept open.

On the other hand, the Federals could only hope to conquer the Confederacy bit by bit, that is reduce it systematically, not only in size but also in resources, until it was unable to sustain its armies in the field. At the outset of the war this was realized by the Federal Commander-in-Chief, Lieutenant-General Winfield Scott (1786–1866), who appreciated the relationship between economic pressure and attack. His project was to seal up all Southern ports, and simultaneously form two powerful armies, one to move down the Mississippi and cut off the western half of the Confederacy from its eastern half, while the other threatened Richmond and pinned down the main Confederate forces in Virginia.

Of the Confederate ports, nine were linked to the interior by rail, and all of these, except Mobile, Charleston and Wilmington, were in Federal hands by April, 1862. Of the three which were not, Wilmington was of incalculable importance to the Confederacy, in fact it may be said to have been its mouth; nevertheless, it was not occupied by the Federals until 15th January 1865 – a first-rate blunder. Scott's other proposals were not adopted until late in the war; instead the main battles were fought to gain Richmond, and, until 1865, all were abortive.

When we turn to President Davis, we find he failed to appreciate that the only means open to him to prevent the conquest of the Confederacy were, while he husbanded its resources, to hold the Federals back. This demanded a defensive strategy, but instead he adopted an offensive one, and attempted at one and the same time to protect Richmond and drive the Federals out of the war by a series of battles aimed at the occupation of Washington. Yet both geography and communications indicated that early in the war the most effective way to protect Richmond was to base a powerful army on Chattanooga, and carry out a defensive-offensive campaign in Tennessee, while a less powerful army covered the capital. A vigorous campaign in Tennessee would almost certainly have drawn Federal forces out of Virginia to meet it, and simultaneously have directly protected the vital railway hub Chattanooga-Atlanta, as well as indirectly the important crossing of the Mississippi at Vicksburg. Although something like this was attempted in a muddled way, because the preservation of the Confederacy depended more on husbanding resources than on winning battles, to seek them in Virginia was to squander staying-power.

Not until the opening of 1863 was Scott's project fully[1] resorted to by General Ulysses S. Grant (1822–1885) who, on 30th January, opened his campaign against Vicksburg. On 4th July the fortress surrendered to him, and the result was that the western half of the Confederacy was severed from its eastern half. Next, by his victory at Chattanooga, on 24th–27th November, Grant opened the road to Atlanta, with the result that the Confederacy was virtually reduced to Virginia, the two Carolinas and Georgia. Lastly, while in the summer of 1864 Grant held the main Confederate army, under Robert E. Lee (1807–1870), around Richmond, General William T. Sherman (1820–1891) moved forward from Chattanooga, occupied Atlanta on 1st September, and from there marched

[1] New Orleans had been occupied by the Federals on 2nd May 1862, and from it in June and July two abortive attempts were made to take Vicksburg.

through Georgia and the Carolinas against Lee's rear. This dual campaign on exterior lines brought the Confederacy to collapse at Appottomax Court House on 9th April 1865.

4 · *Tactical Developments*

The tactical background of the war was more than extraordinary – it was unique. Before the outbreak of hostilities, the United States' regular army numbered some sixteen to seventeen thousand officers and men; of the latter the vast majority came from the Northern States, and a high percentage of the former from the Southern. The consequence was that, when the Southern States seceded, the bulk of the men remained loyal to the Union, and many of the officers, including most of the ablest, went over to the Confederacy. This would have left the Union army almost leaderless, had not there been at the time a number of experienced retired officers – McClellan, Grant and Sherman, to mention the more eminent – who could be recalled to active service. In short, while the Union got the body of the old army, the Confederates got the brains, and the result was that – certainly during the first half of the war – in strategical and tactical ability the Confederates outclassed the Federals.

At first both armies depended on voluntary enlistment, but as the war lengthened conscription was resorted to, by the Confederates in April 1862, and by the Federals a year later. During the war the Union called to the colours about forty-five per cent. of its military manhood, and the Confederacy, about ninety per cent. According to Colonel Thomas L. Livermore, the total enlistments in the Union army numbered 2,898,304, and in the Confederacy between 1,227,890 and 1,406,180.[1] These figures exceed anything previously recorded in history, and were not to be surpassed until 1914.

The tactical foreground was novel in the extreme, but at the time little appreciated. Although since the Napoleonic Wars improvements in fire-arms had revolutionized tactics, tactical theory remained Napoleonic, and although Clausewitz's *On War* is never mentioned, Jomini's *Summary of the*

[1] *Numbers and Losses in the Civil War* (edit. 1957), p. 63. There are several other estimates, but all vary and some considerably.

Art of War was to be found in many a knapsack. In Napoleon's day, the flintlock musket had an effective range of at most 100 yards, and as it was outranged by cannon firing grape or canister, the gun was the superior weapon. But in 1861 the musket had been superseded by the Minié rifle, which had an effective range of at least 500 yards, and as it outranged grape and canister fire, tactics underwent a profound change. The gun had to fall back behind the infantry, and became a support instead of an assault weapon, and the infantry fire-fight opened at 500 yards range, instead of 100. The results of this long-range fire-fighting were that the bayonet assault died out, individual good shooting was more effective than volley firing, and for full effectiveness it demanded individual initiative and collective loose order.

Two of the outstanding tactical characteristics of the war were: (1) The futility of frontal assaults, and (2) the demand for field entrenchments, and both were a consequence of the rifle bullet.

On every occasion, a frontal assault delivered against an unshaken enemy led to costly failure. Nevertheless, neither side learnt this lesson. At Fredericksburg, on 13th December 1862, the Federals, under Burnside, delivered a massed frontal assault on the Confederates, under Lee, and were ignominiously repulsed; at Gettysburg, on 3rd July 1863, Lee delivered a massed frontal assault on the Federals, under Meade, and was disastrously thrown back; and at Cold Harbor, on 3rd June 1864, Grant repeated the same blunder and with identical results.

Throughout the war, the spade increasingly became the complement of the rifle, until, in 1864, every battle fought between Grant and Lee in the Wilderness of Virginia was an entrenched one,[1] and when Grant neared Petersburg and Richmond, both sides became so extensively entrenched that siege warfare set in and lasted for nearly ten months. Even in Sherman's simultaneous advance on Atlanta, the mobility of his campaign was due, not only to his skill in manoeuvring

[1] Colonel Theodore Lyman writes: 'The great feature of this campaign is the extraordinary use made of earthworks' *Meade's Headquarters 1863–1865* (1922), p. 99.

his men, but also in his ability to manoeuvre their entrenchments with them.

A graphic picture is penned by Colonel Lyman of what a battle was like in this war:

'I had taken part', he writes, 'in two great battles, and heard the bullets whistle both days, and yet I had *scarcely seen a Rebel* save killed, wounded, or prisoners! I remember even line officers, who were at the battle of Chancellorsville, said: "Why, we never saw any Rebels where we were; only smoke and bushes, and lots of our men tumbling about"; and now I appreciate this most fully. The great art is to *conceal* men; for the moment they show, *bang, bang*, go a dozen cannon, the artillerists only too pleased to get a fair mark. Your typical "great white plain", with long lines advancing and manoeuvring, led on by generals in cocked hats and by bands of music, exist not for us. Here it is, as I said: "Left face – prime – forward!" – and then *wrang, wr-r-ang*, for three or four hours, or for all day, and the poor bleeding wounded streaming to the rear. That is a great battle in America.'[1]

It was the rifle bullet and the spade which made the defensive the stronger form of war, a fact also noted by Lyman: 'Put a man in a hole', he said, 'and a good battery on a hill behind him, and he will beat off three times his number, even if he is not a very good soldier.'[2] And Frank Wilkeson wrote: 'Before we left North Anna [May 1864] I discovered that our infantry were tired of charging earthworks. The ordinary enlisted man asserts that a good man behind an earthwork was equal to three good men outside it.'[3] And it should be remembered that this was in the days of the muzzle-loading rifle.

Other changes were that the cavalry charge died out, that the rifled cannon came more and more to the fore, and that the dethronement of the bayonet was complete. Of this weapon, wrote an eyewitness, General John B. Gordon: 'The bristling points and the glitter of the bayonets were fearful to look upon as they were levelled in front of a charging line; but

[1] Ibid., p. 101.
[2] Ibid., p. 224.
[3] *The Soldier in Battle, or Life in the Ranks of the Army of the Potomac* (1896), p. 99.

they were rarely reddened with blood. The day of the bayonet is passed.'[1] And Surgeon-Major G. Hart wrote that he saw few bayonet wounds 'except accidental ones... I think half-a-dozen would include all the wounds of this nature I ever dressed.[2]

The war fought by Grant and Lee, Sherman and Johnston and all the other generals was a war of rifle bullets and trenches, of slashings, abattis, and even of wire entanglements – an obstacle the Confederates called 'a devilish contrivance which none but a Yankee could devise', because at Drewry's Bluff, on 16th May 1864, they had been trapped in them and 'slaughtered like partridges.'[3] It was a war of astonishing modernity, of wooden wire-bound mortars, hand and winged grenades, rockets, and many forms of booby traps. Machine guns – Requa's and Gatling's – were introduced, and a breech-loading magazine rifle, the Spencer, adopted. Torpedoes, land mines, submarine mines, the field telegraph, and lamp and flag signalling, were tried out. Armoured trains were used; balloons were employed on both sides, and although the Confederates did not think much of them, they made one out of silk dresses, and to the sorrow of many a Southern belle it was speedily captured – 'the meanest trick of the war', so said General Taliaferro.[4] Explosive bullets are mentioned,[5] also a flame projector,[6] and in June 1864, General W. N. Pendleton asked the Chief Ordnance Officer at Richmond whether he could supply him with stink-shell which would give off 'offensive gasses', and cause 'suffocating effect'. The answer he got was 'stink-balls, none on hand; don't keep them; will make if ordered.'[7] Nor did modernity halt here, for warfare at sea was completely revolutionized by the ironclads *Merrimac* and the *Monitor*[8] in one day – 9th March 1862 – and the

[1] *Reminiscences of the Civil War* (1904), pp. 5–6.

[2] *Papers of the Military Historical Society of Massachusetts* (1913), Vol. XIII, p. 265.

[3] *Battles and Leaders of the Civil War* (1888), Vol. IV, p. 212.

[4] Ibid., Vol. II, p. 513.

[5] *Campaigns and Battles of the Army of Northern Virginia*, George Wise (1916), p. 190.

[6] *Meade's Headquarters*, p. 284.

[7] *The War of the Rebellion*, Vol. LXIX, pp. 888–9.

[8] For this historic engagement see *Battles and Leaders of the Civil War*, Vol. I, pp. 696–709.

wooden navies of the entire world rendered obsolete. 'A submarine was built by Horace L. Huntly at Mobile, twenty feet long, five deep and three and a half wide, which was propelled by a screw worked from the inside by seven or eight men.'[1] On 17th February 1864, she sank U.S.S. *Housatonic* off Charleston, and went down with her.

5 · *Moral Retrogression*

As the defensive gained in strength, the more stubborn and indecisive became the fighting, and the more the outcome of the war was prolonged, the intenser grew the hatred, until frustration awakened a spirit of vengeance in the hearts of the Federals against the entire population of the South. Until Grant and Sherman opened their dual campaign in 1864, with few exceptions, violence had been restricted to the outer front – that is to the armed forces of the Confederacy; but now it was also to be directed against the inner front, the civil population of the South – that is, against the moral and economic foundations of both the Confederate government and its army. This change in the direction of violence was stimulated – as in future wars it was increasingly to be – by the advancing materialistic civilization of the North.

Of Lee, Rhodes says that in all essential characteristics he resembled Washington;[2] therefore, he belonged to the eighteenth century – to the agricultural age of history. Sherman, and to a lesser extent Grant, Sheridan, and other Federal generals, belonged to the age of the Industrial Revolution, and their guiding principle was that of the machine which was fashioning them – namely, efficiency. And because efficiency is governed by a single law, that every means is justified by the end, no moral or spiritual conception, or traditional behaviour, can be tolerated should it stand in its way.

Sherman was the leading exponent of this return to barbarism. He broke away from the conventions of nineteenth century warfare, and waged war with steel as ruthlessly as Calvin had waged it with the word. After severe fighting, on

[1] *Papers of the Military Historical Society of Massachusetts*, Vol. XIV, pp. 450–3.

[2] *History of the United States* (1893–1906), Vol. III, p. 413.

1st September 1864, he took Atlanta, 'the gate city of the South', and bent on leaving no enemies behind him he evacuated the entire population. He explained in a letter to General Halleck, Chief of Staff at Washington: 'If the people raise a howl against my barbarity and cruelty, I will answer that war is war. . . . If they want peace they and their relatives must stop the war.'[1]

For the nineteenth century this was a new conception, because it meant that the deciding factor in war – the power to sue for peace – was transferrred from government to people, and that peace-making was a product of revolution. This was to carry the principle of democracy to its ultimate stage, and with it introduce the theory of the psychological attack – in essence Marxist warfare. Of Sherman, Major George W. Nichols, one of his aides-de-camp, says: 'He is a Democrat in the best sense of the word. There is nothing European about him. He is a striking type of our institutions.'[2]

Later, when Sherman set out on his famous march through Georgia, he made this new concept of war his guiding principle, and waged war against the people of the South as fully as against its armed forces.

Nothing like this march had been seen in the West since the maraudings of Tilly and Wallenstein in the Thirty Years' War. Southern guerillas, as Sherman notes, had shown and continued to show much brutality; but the atrocities they perpetrated were individual acts and not acts of policy. With some justification Jefferson Davis calls Sherman 'the Attila of the American Continent.'[3]

Terror was the basic factor in Sherman's policy, he openly says so. Here are three citations out of a considerable number:

'Untill we can repopulate Georgia, it is useless to occupy it; but the utter destruction of the roads, houses and people will

[1] *Personal Memoirs of General W. T. Sherman* (1957 edition), Vol. II, p. 111. On this, Sherman comments: 'I knew, of course, that such a measure would be strongly criticized, but made up my mind to do it, with the absolute certainty of its justice, and that time would sanction its wisdom.'

[2] *The Story of the Great March* (1865), p. 80.

[3] *The Rise and Fall of the Confederate Government* (1881), Vol. II, p. 279.

cripple their military resources . . . I can make the march, and make Georgia howl.'[1]

'Should I be forced to assault . . . I shall then feel justified in resorting to the harshest measures, and shall make little effort to restrain my army.'[2]

'We are not only fighting hostile armies, but a hostile people, and must make old and young, rich and poor, feel the hard hand of war. . . . The truth is the whole army is burning with an insatiable desire to wreak vengeance upon South Carolina. I almost tremble for her fate.'[3]

Sherman, like Nichols, believed that his army was 'God's instrument of justice.'[4] Hitchcock, another of Sherman's aides-de-camp, says much the same thing: 'It is war now that it may not be war *always*. God send us peace – but there is no peace save in *complete submission to the Government:* and this seems impossible save through the terrors of war.'[5] Also: 'Sherman is perfectly right – the only possible way to end this unhappy and dreadful conflict . . . is to make it *terrible beyond endurance*.'[6]

Although the soldiers were forbidden to enter civil dwellings or 'commit any trespass', because they were instructed to 'forage liberally' no attention whatever was paid to these prohibitions, and 'liberally' at once led to plunder and pillage. Hitchcock writes: 'Soldiers "foraged liberally" – took all her peanuts drying on roof of shed: and as we left the house, after riding some distance, saw her barn, old and rickety, on fire. . . .'[7] 'Yesterday we passed the plantations of a Mr Stubbs. The house, cotton gin, press, corn-ricks, stables, everything that could burn was in flames. . . . And wherever our army has passed, everything in the shape of a dog has been killed.'[8]

One result of this unrestricted foraging – really brigandage – was a lapse of discipline; the army became a rabble. Hitchcock

[1] *The War of the Rebellion, etc.*, Vol. LXXIX, p. 162.

[2] Ibid., Vol. LXXIX, p. 737.

[3] Ibid., Vol. XCII, p. 799.

[4] Nichols, op. cit., p. 101.

[5] *Marching with Sherman, Letters and Diaries of Henry Hitchcock* (1927), p. 53.

[6] Ibid., p. 35.

[7] Ibid., p. 82.

[8] Ibid., pp. 51–52.

jots down: 'Not so much shooting on the flanks today, but soldiers all the time "foraging" and straggling. To a novice there seems more of this than consistent with discipline.'[1]

Sherman himself was impotent to stop the wanton pillaging he had unloosed. Here are two instances:

'There', said Sherman, 'are the men who do this. Set as many guards as you please, they will slip in and set fire. That Court House was put out – no use – daresay whole town will burn . . . didn't order this, but can't be helped. I say *Jeff. Davis burnt them.*'[2]

'General advised V very kindly (in tone) to bring all he could of corn, wheat, etc. into *his house*, for safety from the soldiers.'[3]

What a confession of impotence!

On 21st December Savannah fell to Sherman's pillaging horde, now followed by thousands of plundering negroes. The next day he presented it as a Christmas gift to President Lincoln. Then the Carolinas were devastated. In Georgia Sherman estimates the damage done at $100,000,000 of which only $20,000,000 'inured to our advantage'; the remainder was 'simple waste and destruction.'[4]

This savagery was resented by many of Sherman's officers, notably Generals J. C. Davis, H. W. Slocum, J. R. Hawley and J. Kilpatrick, and Hitchcock himself considered it morally wrong.[5] Ropes, the historian, correctly points out that, 'military operations are not carried on for the purpose of inflicting punishment for political offences', and therefore, 'if Sherman purposely destroyed, or connived at the destruction of, property which was not needed for the supply of his army or of the enemy's army, he violated one of the fundamental canons of modern warfare; and . . . conducted war on obsolete and

[1] Ibid., p. 83.
[2] Ibid., p. 53.
[3] Ibid., p. 83.
[4] *The War of the Rebellion*, etc., Vol. XCII, p. 13. 'In nearly all his [Sherman's] dispatches after he had reached the sea, he gloated over the destruction of property' (Rhode's *History of the United States*, Vol. V, p. 22).
[5] Op. cit , pp. 86–7 and 92–3.

barbarous principles.' And he rightly points out that the depredations of Sherman's army as a punishment for political conduct had little influence on Grant's operations in Virginia.[1]

6 · *Results of the War*

One of the strangest things about Sherman is, that on the plinth of his statue at Washington are inscribed the noble words he once uttered: 'The legitimate object of war is a more perfect peace.' Yet, apparently, he could not see that plunder and arson are not legitimate means to attain it. Unfortunately, the ruthlessness he relied on was carried into the peace which followed the war.

On 14th April 1865, five days after Lee's surrender, President Lincoln was assassinated, and the trial of the alleged conspirators was to stand as the greatest travesty of justice for eighty years, when the theme, harped on by the Assistant Judge-Advocate at the trial, was again to be exploited. The theme was: 'The rebellion, in aid of which this conspiracy was formed and this great public crime committed, was . . . itself . . . a criminal conspiracy and gigantic assassination.'[2] Therefor the entire population of the South stood condemned.

Although the Civil War brought ruin to the South, and although its ills were aggravated by the vengeance of the years of reconstruction, to the North it brought victory and unprecedented prosperity.

'Never before', write Morison and Commager, 'had the American people exhibited greater vitality, never since has their vitality been accomplished by more reckless irresponsibility. To the generation that had saved the Union everything seemed possible: there were no worlds, except the worlds of the spirit, that could not be conquered. Men hurled themselves upon the continent with ruthless abandon as if to ravish it of its wealth.'[3]

The resources of the new empire were all but inexhaustible: iron, coal, oil, labour and individual energy abounded. Inventions flowed from drawing boards, goods from the factories,

[1] *Papers of the Military Historical Society of Massachusetts* (1895), Vol. 10, pp. 148–51.

[2] *Why was Lincoln Murdered?*, Otto Eisenschiml (1937), p. 245.

[3] Op. cit., Vol. II, p. 9.

and wheat from the fields, while hundreds of thousands of emigrants poured into the cities and over the plains.

Within less than two generations after the war ended, the United States had risen to be the greatest capitalist and the greatest industrial power in the world. Stephen Vincent Benét calls them 'The great metallic beast', and depicts their emergence from the titanic struggle of the Civil War in these tremendous lines:

> *"Out of John Brown's strong sinews the tall*
> *skyscrapers grow,*
> *Out of his heart the chanting buildings rise,*
> *Rivet and girder, motor and dynamo,*
> *Pillar of smoke by day and fire by night,*
> *The steel-faced cities reaching at the skies,*
> *The whole enormous and rotating cage*
> *Hung with hard jewels of electric light,*
> *Smoky with sorrow, black with splendor, dyed*
> *Whiter than damask for a crystal bride*
> *With metal suns, the engine-handed Age,*
> *The genie we have raised to rule the earth."*[1]

[1] Op. cit., p. 376.

CHAPTER VII

Moltke, Foch, and Bloch

*

1 · Field Marshal von Moltke

The need for an effective General Staff, the lack of which had so largely led to the ruin of the Napoleonic system, was first recognized by Prussia, and although its origins ante-date the battle of Jena, it was not until after 1806, when General Gerhard von Scharnhorst, as Minister of War, set out to reorganize the Prussian army that a true General Staff came into being. To assist him in this task, Scharnhorst added to the Ministry a special section, whose duties were to collate intelligence, concern itself with strategy and tactics, and prepare operations. To extend his control over the army, he posted staff officers to its formations.

In 1821, a change was made; the king took over supreme command of the army; the General Staff was separated from the War Ministry, and the Chief of the General Staff became the King's personal adviser. The administration of the army remained in the hands of the War Minister. Forty years later, when William I (1861–1888), a soldier by instinct and training, became King of Prussia, he set out to reorganize the army and create an effective force of 371,000 officers and men backed by a reserve of 126,000. Already, when regent, in 1857 he had appointed Count Helmuth von Moltke (1800–1891) Chief of the General Staff; next, in 1859, he selected Count Albrecht von Roon (1803–1879) as Minister of War; and lastly, in 1862, he made Otto von Bismarck (1815–1898) his Minister-President and Foreign Minister. These three men were destined to raise Prussia from a position of comparative insignificance to one of supremacy in Europe.

Moltke, though jealous of his authority, was an exceptionally humble man: he was highly cultured, and in every sense of the word a practical soldier. He looked upon war more as a business than as a science or an art, in which military force represented capital to be invested, and victory the dividend paid on it. He was a profound student of war, deeply versed in the methods of Napoleon and the theories of Clausewitz; but not a blind follower of them, because he related them to subsequent technical developments. From Napoleon he learnt that movement is the soul of war; therefore that railways would become the most important factor in strategy. From Clausewitz he learnt that statecraft and generalship are closely related, and in consequence he took a profound interest in politics and foreign affairs. He was one of the earliest to appreciate the defensive power of the muzzle-loading rifle, and from it he inferred that, except in holding operations, frontal attacks were likely to become too costly to be remunerative; therefore that victory should be sought through envelopment. He was a voluminous writer who, not only produced a large number of military histories, and a technical work on railways, but throughout his life he set down his problems on paper, analysed them, and rewrote them again and again until he was satisfied with their solutions.

His studies led him to appreciate that, because armies were growing larger and larger, deployments more and more extensive, and means of movement increasingly more rapid, command demanded decentralization. Further, because no plan of operations can with any certainty look beyond the initial clash of major forces, once it has occurred, it is incumbent on subordinate commanders to act on their own initiative, but in accordance with a common doctrine. Therefore, once battle was engaged, general directives should replace detailed orders. In this there was a risk of confusion arising, as it did on several occasions in 1870; but Moltke accepted it as the lesser of two evils, the greater was loss of time.

In 1860 he wrote a memoir on the deployment of the Prussian army in the event of a war with Austria, and although it is too long to quote at length, a few brief extracts from its opening paragraphs will give some idea of how Moltke thought out his problems.

'A war between Austria and Prussia would affect all the Powers of Europe; for a considerable success of the one or the other would end the present disintegrated condition of Germany . . . and found in the centre of Europe a united State, which would be equal or superior in power and influence to any of its neighbours.

'Among the great Powers, England necessarily required a strong ally upon the Continent. It would find none which would better correspond to all its interests than a united Germany, which can never claim the command of the sea. . . . Yet it is probable that England, clinging to the old order, would take the side of the party attacked in order to prevent a political remodelling of Europe, of which it must be admitted that the far-reaching consequences cannot in all their bearings be foreseen. . . . France least of all can wish . . . for an empire of the German nation, comprising 70,000,000 inhabitants, but from the conflict itself may hope for the very greatest advantages – the acquisition of Belgium, of the Rhenish Province, and perhaps of Holland; indeed, these advantages may be looked for almost with certainty if Prussia's principal forces are held fast upon the Elbe and Oder. . . .'

Russia, he continues, would probably take Prussia's side in order to gain Constantinople, which can only be prevented by Austria, and by none of the Maritime Powers.

'But for Prussia the help of Russia has always taken the two-fold disadvantage that it comes too late, and is too powerful. . . . The might of the Russian army will arrive at our frontier when we shall either have conquered, and therefore no longer require help, or shall have been defeated, and must pay dear for it with provinces. For Russia, if she comes in at the end of the campaign with a fresh army of 300,000 men is mistress of the situation, and has the chief share in deciding the limits up to which we may make the most of our success, or must submit to our misfortune.'[1]

This memoir is a masterpiece of logical reasoning, which during the following six years, as the political situation changed, was periodically brought up to date by Moltke.

Moltke's two wars, the Austro-Prussian of 1866 and the Franco-Prussian of 1870–1871, relaid the political foundations of Europe, and consequently were epoch-making. They created

[1] *Moltke's Projects for the Campaign of 1866 against Austria*, translated and prècised for the General Staff, War Office (London, 1907), pp. 4–6.

the German Empire and established it as the strategic hub of Europe; for England they evoked a challenging trade competitor; they debased the prestige of France, hitherto the leading continental power; and they weakened the Austro-Hungarian empire which, like a bastion, had for centuries protected eastern Europe against the encroachments of Turks and Slavs. The effects of some of these changes will become apparent later, here our observations must be restricted to the conduct of these two wars.

When compared with previous wars, their brevity is remarkable. The first war was won by Prussia in seven weeks, and although the second lasted five months, its outcome was decided by the battle of Sedan on 1st September 1870, in slightly less than seven weeks of the French declaration of war. The reasons for these rapid decisions were: the limited nature of both wars, the superiority of the Prussian General Staff, the speed of Prussian mobilization, and superior Prussian tactics.

Both wars were limited by their aims. In the Austro-Prussian Bismarck's policy was closely circumscribed. Because the existence of Austria as a great power was essential to Prussia's security, it was not to humiliate Austria, or to annex part of her homelands; it was to drive the Austrians out of Germany, and this the decisive battle of Sadowa (also called Königgrätz), fought on 3rd July 1866, succeeded in doing; furthermore, it went far to paralyse France. By the terms of the peace treaties which followed it, Prussia gained Hanover, Schleswig-Holstein, Hesse, Nassau and the free city of Frankfurt-am-Main; Saxony was left intact, and the States north of the Main were formed into a North German Confederation under Prussia, and those south of it into a separate Southern Union.

Again in the Franco-Prussian War, Bismarck's policy was equally clear-cut, it was to unite all Germany under the leadership of Prussia, and it was the determination of France to prevent this union which was the cause of the war, and not the dynastic question in Spain, which was no more than a pretext. Except for the cession by France of Alsace and German Lorraine with Metz, which popular clamour compelled

Bismarck to demand, neither of these wars was a war of conquest, let alone a war of annihilation. Once their limited aims were gained, both were terminated by moderate peace settlements. In character, they were totally different from the American Civil War; the main reason was that they were purely political conflicts, in no way influenced by economics or ideologies, which always awaken the beast in man.

In 1866 the Austrian army was held to be one of the best in Europe; its men were enlisted for seven years, its cavalry was highly trained, and its rifled field guns were superior to the Prussian; nevertheless, it was beaten in seven weeks. This was due, firstly to the inferiority of its General Staff, which Moltke had closely watched and found very indifferent in the 1864 Schleswig-Holstein War; and secondly, because its infantry were armed with the Lorenz muzzle-loading rifle which, although its range of fire was twice that of the Prussian breech-loading needle gun,[1] was completely outclassed by it. Against the massed Austrian formations its fire was devastating. At the battle of Nachod, six and a half Prussian battalions, by rifle fire alone, held back twenty-one Austrian battalions for two hours and inflicted five times their own losses on them. At Sadowa, although for the greater part of 3rd July the Austrians fought on the defensive with odds of five to three in their favour, they lost 18,000 in killed and wounded to the Prussian 9,000. Further, the quick and easy loading of the needle gun in the prone position had a demoralizing effect on the Austrian infantry, who had to stand up to load. An Austrian colonel said that in action his men felt themselves disarmed the greater part of the time, while the Prussians were always ready to fire.[2]

Based on his experiences of 1866, in 1869 Moltke issued his *Instructions for Commanders of Large Formations*, and in them he wrote:

'It is absolutely beyond all doubt that the man who shoots without stirring has the advantage of him who fires while advancing, that the one finds protection in the ground, whereas in it the other finds obstacles, and that, if to the most spirited

[1] The former was sighted to 1,000 meters, and the latter to 400.

[2] *Military Reports*, Colonel Stoffel (English edition, 1872), p. 64.

dash one opposes a quiet steadiness, it is fire effect, nowadays so powerful, which will determine the issue. If it is possible for us to occupy such a position that the enemy, for some political or military reason, or perhaps merely from national *amour propre*, will decide to attack it, it seems perfectly reasonable to utilize the advantages of the defensive at first before assuming the offensive.'[1]

The Sadowa campaign confirmed Moltke in his belief that the breech-loading rifle had made the defensive the stronger form of war, and that the decisive attack must be sought through envelopment. 'Little success', he wrote, 'can be expected from a mere frontal attack, but very likely a great deal of loss. We must therefore turn towards the flanks of the enemy's position.'[2]

In 1866 Moltke made the fullest use of the five railways at his disposal, and he based his plan largely on those the Austrians were likely to use. In 1870 he did the same, and a study of the French railways made it clear to him that the French would almost certainly assemble their forces about Metz and Strasbourg, which meant that they would be separated by the Vosges. On this he based his plan, and to conquer space by time, he relied on the rapidity of his mobilization of the army, coupled with the fullest use of the railways leading to the Rhine. Of his intention he says:

'But above all thc plan of war was based on the resolve to attack the enemy at once, wherever found, and keep the German forces so compact that a superior force could always be brought into the field. By whatever special means these plans were to be accomplished was left to the decision of the hour; the advance to the frontiers alone was pre-ordained in every detail.'[3]

The French plan was a bastard edition of the Jena campaign of 1806, with the third Napoleon instead of the first in command. Because the French Emperor knew that the Prussian

[1] Cited in *The Transformations of War*, Commandant J. Colin (1912), p. 33.

[2] Cited by Lieutenant-General von Caemmerer in *Developments of Strategical Science during the 19th Century* (English edition, 1905), p. 214.

[3] *The Franco-German War of 1870–71*, Field Marshal von Moltke (English edition, 1891), pp. 10–11.

army would outnumber his own, he decided on an *attaque brusquée* before mobilization was completed – few decisions could have been more disastrous. Fixed in his mind was the idea that a sudden attack eastward over the Rhine would force the South German States to desert Prussia, and would bring Austria and possibly also Italy to his support. Once he had forced neutrality upon the South Germans, his intention was to link up with Austria, and by way of Jena march on Berlin!

Even had this fantastic plan been in any way practicable, for success it demanded the most rapid mobilization, the most careful preparations, and the most exact timings; yet nothing was prepared, nothing was thought out. This was due to the unbelievable inefficiency of the French General Staff, a collection of young 'bloods' out of touch with the army, and elderly clerks overwhelmed with the minutiae of routine. So profoundly did Marshal Bazaine distrust his General Staff that he forbade its officers to appear on the battlefield, and instead of them he relied on his personal staff, as Napoleon I had done sixty years before. This inefficiency was inexcusable, because in February 1868, Baron Stoffel, the French military attaché in Berlin, had reported:

'But of all the elements of superiority which Prussia, in case war broke out, would possess, the greatest and most undeniable will be that she will obtain from the composition of her corps of staff officers . . . ours cannot be compared with it. . . . The composition of the Prussian staff will, in the next war, constitute the most formidable element of superiority in favour of the Prussian Army.'[1]

In 1870 the Prussians were faced with a breech-loading rifle, the French chassepot sighted to 1,200 meters. It was greatly superior to the Prussian needle-gun; but the French bronze muzzle-loading field guns were inferior to the Prussian iron breech-loaders, and the expert use the Prussians made of them more than compensated for the inferiority of their rifles. A weapon the French might have made better use of was Reffeye's *mitrailleuse*, a machine gun of twenty-five barrels, axis grouped and sighted to 1,200 metres, which could fire at

[1] *Military Reports*, pp. 48, 56.

the rate of 125 rounds a minute. In order to keep it a dead secret, it was not issued to the army until a few days before the outbreak of hostilities, and, according to Reffeye, it was then used 'in a perfectly idiotic fashion', which is not surprising as no troops had been trained to use it.

The French rifle tactics were based on long-range volley fire, so as to take full advantage of the superior range of the chassepot; next to dig in and await the enemy's approach, and lastly to overwhelm him with fire. Moltke met these tactics by assuming the tactical defensive-offensive: first, he held his enemy in front and next he attacked him in flank. Every tactical group from the company upwards was instructed to remain always on the offensive, so as to allow the French no breathing space: to hold by fire, attack by fire, manoeuvre under cover of fire, and outflank by fire; in short, never cease to fire until the battle was won.

Throughout the war neither side succeeded in taking a position by a frontal attack, nor did either side succeed in bringing troops in close order into the firing line. 'On both sides . . . the tactics of the drill ground and of peace manoeuvres were completely altered. . . . Bayonets were never crossed in the open field, and but seldom in village or wood fights.'[1]

The power of artillery came more and more to the fore. The French did not mass their guns, the Germans did, and notably at Gravelotte and Sedan. Sedan was the greatest artillery battle of the war; all the French attacks were brought to a standstill by gun fire, and most of them at 2,000 yards distance – that is, far outside effective rifle range. At Sedan a French officer, who was taken prisoner, described the Prussian offensive as 'five kilometers of artillery.'[2]

Cavalry steadily lost ground. Only one successful charge was made, that by General von Bredow's brigade at Vionville, and although the French were short of ammunition, the brigade lost half its horsemen. At Sedan General Gallifet

[1] *Tactical Deductions from the War of 1870–71*, Lieutenant-General A. von Boguslawski (English edition, 1872), pp. 79–80.

[2] Cited in *Decisive Battles since Waterloo, 1815–1887*, Thomas W. Knox (1887), p. 358.

attempted a most gallant charge at the head of the *Chasseurs d'Afrique;* but only to suffer 'So thorough a destruction by what may be called a single volley probably the oldest soldier now alive never witnessed.'[1] Nevertheless, although the cavalry assault was no longer a practical operation of war, for protective and reconnaissance duties cavalry remained of essential value, yet for such they were indifferently employed by both sides.

2 · *Marshal Ferdinand Foch*

When the time came to examine the causes of the defeat of the French army in the Franco-Prussian War, instead of looking for them in its all-round unpreparedness, French military analysts singled out the aggressive tactics of its opponents as the main one. And when in the next war, the Russo-Turkish of 1877–1878, the Turks, who fought on the defensive, were beaten, instead of relating their defeat to the many factors responsible for it, the analysts arrived at the conclusion that they were right about 1870, and in spite of the fact that the leading tactical lessons of the Russo-Turkish War were the defensive strength of entrenched riflemen and the crippling cost of attempting to storm entrenchments.

Any doubts the exponents of the offensive may still have had were, in 1880, dissipated by the publication of a book entitled *Études sur le Combat,* which at once became a classic. It was compiled from memoranda and notes found among the papers of a French infantry officer, Colonel Ardant du Picq, who had died of wounds within a month of the outbreak of the Franco-Prussian War. In brief, his theory was that success in battle is a question of morale, and should the morale of the attacker be superior to the morale of the defender, the attacker will win. The following extracts make his theory clear:

'In battle, two moral forces, even more so than two material forces, are in conflict. The stronger conquers. The victor has often lost . . . more men than the vanquished. . . . With equal or even inferior power of destruction, he will win who is determined to advance . . . [who] has the moral ascendency.

[1] *My Experiences of the War between France and Germany*, Archibald Forbes (1871), Vol. I, p. 236.

Moral effect inspires fear. Fear must be changed into terror in order to conquer. . . . The moral impulse lies in the perception by the enemy of the resolution which animates you. . . . Manoeuvres . . . are threats. He who appears most threatening wins.'[1]

Although there is much value in du Picq's book, especially his comments on classical warfare, he was a man totally carried away by his emotions. He failed to appreciate the moralizing effect of order on the defenders, and the demoralizing effect of disorder on the attackers. He entirely overlooked the moralizing effects of entrenchments, behind which men can fire at those who advance in the open against them. Nevertheless, the French school of the offensive took inspiration from him, and in the last decade of the nineteenth century it found its leading exponent in Lieutenant-Colonel Ferdinand Foch (1851–1929).

In 1894, Foch was appointed a professor at the *École de Guerre,* later he became its Commandant, and the lectures he gave his students were published in two books, *De la Conduit de la Guerre,* and *Des Principes de la Guerre;* they became the new testament of the French army.

Foch was an able soldier, and as a Marshal of France one of the few outstanding generals of World War I. Nevertheless, he was so carried away by his theory that the *offensive à outrance* could alone lead to victory, that he was blind to its contradictions.

In the first chapter of *The Principles of War,*[2] the later and the more important of his two books, he extols the theory of absolute war as practised by Napoleon and preached by Clausewitz (pp. 24–25). In this there is nothing to complain of, but his deep set prejudice of all other forms of war is noticeable in his unreasoned depreciation of what he calls the 'antiquated methods' of war which were upset by the French Emperor. He pours scorn on limited warfare, and among others castigates Marshal Saxe for having said: 'I am not in favour of giving battle; especially at the outset of a war. I am convinced that a clever general can wage war his *whole life*

[1] Seventh edition (1914), pp. 121–3.
[2] All references are to the English translation by Hilaire Belloc (1918).

without being compelled to do so' (p. 28). Whether by intention or oversight, these words are torn from their context, and misrepresent what Saxe actually had in mind.[1]

Once he has reduced to ridicule a method of warfare utterly repugnant to him, he sets out to prove that 'Any improvement of firearms is ultimately bound to add strength to the offensive. . . . Nothing is easier', he adds, 'than to give a mathematical demonstration of that truth.' It is worth quoting, if only to show how completely a rational man may be obssessed by an irrational theory:

'Suppose you launch 2 battalions against	1	
You then launch 2,000 men against	1,000	
With a rifle-fire of 1 shot a minute, 1,000 defenders will fire	1,000	bullets
With the same rifle, 2,000 assailants will fire	2,000	,,
Balance in favour of the attack	1,000	,,
With a rifle firing 10 shots a minute, 1,000 defenders will fire within 1 minute	10,000	,,
With the same rifle, 2,000 assailants will fire	20,000	,,
Balance	10,000	,,

'As you see, the material superiority of fire quickly increases in favour of the attack as a result of improved firearms. How much more quickly [here enters du Picq] will grow at the same time the ascendancy, the moral superiority of the assailant over the defender' (p. 32).

This is mathematical abracadabra. To mention one fact out of several, because 1,000 defenders lying prone will offer but one-eighth of the target of 2,000 assailants advancing, the assailants' hits must be reduced by seven-eighths; therefore the balance against the assailants will be 7,500 bullets, and not 10,000 in their favour.

[1] See above Chapter I, pp. 24-5, for Saxe's remark in full.

Once Clausewitz has been out-Clausewitzed, Foch sets out to out-du Picq du Picq. He quotes Joseph de Maistre[1] as saying: ' "A battle lost is a battle one thinks one has lost; for", he added, "a battle cannot be lost physically." Therefore, it can only be lost morally. But then, it is also morally that a battle is won, and we may extend the aphorism by saying: *A battle won, is a battle in which one will not confess oneself beaten*' (p. 286). This may be more or less true in an affray between men armed with broomsticks, but in a battle in which both sides are armed with magazine rifles it is nonsense, if only because, however high the assailants' morale may be, it does not render them bullet-proof.

Foch was right to impress on his students the importance of the offensive; but, when it is borne in mind that he was instructing the future leaders and staff officers of the French army, he was most unfortunately wrong to exalt it into a fetish.

It is a relief to turn from his exaggerated stressing of the offensive to his penetrating analysis (pp. 35–39) of the causes of war as he saw them at the opening of the present century.

With von der Goltz's remark, that 'Modern wars have become the nations' way of doing business', as his text, he sets out to show that they are commercial in origin, and in support of this he alleges:

By their victories of 1870–1871, the Germans not only assured for themselves a dominant position in Europe, but outlets for their industry and commerce. Also they secured from France 'most favoured nation treatment' as regards tariffs and trade, 'which shows well enough that a nation's wealth largely consists, nowadays, in drawing an income from its neighbour. . . . The German victories of 1870 have enriched the individual German. Every German has *a share in the profits*, and is directly interested *in the firm, in the constitution, in the victory. That is what now is meant by a people's war.*'

In the 1894 war with China, although by the terms of the treaty signed at Shimonoseki Japan secured meagre territorial concessions, the commercial advantages she gained were

[1] French diplomatist, 1754–1821. The quotation is from his *Soirèes de St. Petersburg.*

enormous. 'The guns of Wei-hai-wei and of the Jalu paved the way for a mercantile navy which would export, first to the Eastern seas, then to the Western, articles which Japan manufactured under conditions no longer possible in Europe.'

On a small scale, the Russo-Japanese War of 1904–1905 was a 'complete model of the nature of contemporary warfare; for war, to-day, is a commercial enterprise undertaken by the whole nation. It concerns the individual more directly than did war in the past, and therefore appeals much more to individual passions.'

'Further proofs: the Spanish-American War; our own last difficulties with the British over Fashoda. What were we all seeking? for commercial outlets to an industrial system which produces more than it can sell, and therefore is constantly smothered by competetion. What happens then? New markets are opened by force of arms.'

' "The Stock Exchange has acquired such an influence that it is able, in order to protect its interests, to launch armies into war" (von Moltke). Who was responsible for the Boer War? Certainly not the Queen of England, but the merchants of the City.'

'Such are the origins of modern war. Here is its moral: you must henceforth go to the very limit to find the aim of war. Since the vanquished party now never yields before it has been deprived of all means of reply, what you have to aim at is the destruction of those very means of reply. . . . It may be stated then, that such features as war already possessed at the beginning of the nineteenth century are still more marked at the end of the century: a national war; a war of numbers; a war violent and at quick march.'

What will this war of numbers and violence be like? Foch's answer is: it will be Napoleonic; therefore 'it is to the theory of *decision by arms* that war is now wholly returning; one can now apply no other. Instead of condemning Bonaparte's battles as acts less civilized than those of his predecessors, this theory considers them as the only efficient means; it seeks to repeat them by seeking the same sources of action as he had' (p. 42).

Both sides will take up arms 'for an idea, a principle – a

change of tariff, for instance: no matter what the end so that it be a policy to be attained', and both will 'back his political and financial theories by force.' The enemy 'will only renounce those theories when he has been deprived of the means of defending them. He will only confess himself beaten when he is no longer able to fight; that is, when his army shall have been materially and morally destroyed. Therefore modern war can only consider those arguments which lead to the destruction of that army: namely *battle, overthrow by force.*' What does this demand? 'To seek out the enemy's armies – the centre of the adversary's power – in order to beat and destroy them; to adopt, with this sole end in view, the direction and tactics which may lead to it in the quickest and safest way: such is the whole mental attitude of modern war' (p. 42).

Therefore for Foch, 'Tactical results are the only things that matter in war.... Where there is no battle, there is no award, nothing is accomplished.... *No strategy can henceforth prevail over that which aims at ensuring tactical results, victory by fighting*' (p. 43); and the 'synthesis we can deduce from history ... is characterised by three things: preparation; mass; impulsion' (p. 44).

When he has explained what he means by preparations; in brief, that they must forestall and out-distance those of the enemy, Foch returns to tactical action.

'In what does it consist?' he asks, and answers: 'There is but one means of treating with the adversary, namely to beat him, and therefore to overthrow him. Hence the idea of a *shock* composed of two terms: *mass* and *impulsion.*' Because in modern warfare mass absorbs 'all the physical and moral forces of the country, the same will be true of any tactical operation.... The greatest part of our forces, if not the whole, will be reserved as a *masse de choc*' (p. 45).

As regards *impulsion*, 'Tactics on the battle-field will be the *tactics of movement.* The last word of offensive or defensive fighting will be therefore: the troop in *movement* – that is, attacking.... The theory which aims at achieving the *strongest possible shock* prescribes to strategy as a primordial condition *to bring to the point of shock all* available troops.... Movement governs strategy. May we not stand and await that shock? Of course not. If we did not seek it, it might well either not occur at all, or occur under bad conditions; we might then fail to destroy the forces of the adversary, which is in war the only means of reaching our end. . . . Such is, the first law that governs the theory, a law from which no troop can ever escape and which has been expressed by the military formula: of all faults, one only is degrading, namely *inaction*' (p. 45).

In the concluding pages of *The Principles of War* (pp. 341–349), Foch discusses the 'Decisive Attack'. It is 'to fall on [the enemy] in *numbers* and *masses*: therein lies salvation', because 'numbers imply *moral superiority* in our favour', and create 'surprise in the enemy's ranks, as well as the conviction that he cannot resist.'

The battle is opened by an intense artillery bombardment; preliminary preparations may last for the greater part of the day, and during them the infantry assemble. The moment to act then arrives. 'In order to decide the enemy to retreat, we must *advance* upon him; in order to conquer the position. . . . Here begins . . . the action of infantry in masses. They march straight on to the goal . . . speeding up their pace in proportion as they come nearer.' When the mass reaches a point 600 to 800 yards distant from the enemy, it develops its maximum fire power. Then, writes Foch:

'The consideration of what fire one may oneself receive now becomes a secondary matter; the troops are on the move and must arrive; moreover, there is but one means to extenuate the effects of enemy fire: it is to develop a more violent fire oneself . . . another means consists in rapid advance. To march, and to march quickly, preceded by a hail of bullets; in proportion as the enemy is hard pressed, to bring forward more and more numerous troops, and, moreover, troops well in hand, such is the fundamental formula for the formations to be taken and tactics to be adopted.'

The supports then advance 'to push the first line on ahead', and finally the reserves come up to impart 'a last impulsion to the attacking force.' The charge is then sounded, and 'out of a cloud of dust or of smoke', suddenly appear the cavalry. 'They charge thence on anything that is still resisting among the enemy, or on enemy cavalry trying to charge on the attacking infantry, or on arriving enemy reserves as they come up.' When the cavalry are omitted, this is Gettysburg over again!

When we look back upon Foch's *offensive à outrance*, we sense Clausewitz throughout. Not the contemplative student of war, but a Clausewitz drunk on violence. We see also a tactically demented Napoleon, for whereas his battles were based on the weapons of his day – and weapons should always give shape to tactics – Foch ignores them. Step by step, with a few variations, he follows Napoleon in face of magazine rifles and quick-firing artillery as if they were the muskets and cannon of Jena and Friedland. More disastrous, his *offensives à outrance* and his battles *aux allures déchaînées* became the doctrine of the French army.

3 · Mr I. S. Bloch

Bloch was by birth a Polish Jew and by profession a Warsaw banker; he was also a pacifist of an unusual kind. His aim was not to eliminate or restrict war, instead it was to persuade the nations to realize that the ever-increasing power of firearms had, through their very deadliness, already eliminated war as a profitable political instrument. For him the cult of the offensive was an illusion, and in corroboration of this he set out to collect every possible fact which would support his contention. In 1897 he gave voice to it in an elaborate analysis of war in six volumes, a veritable *olla podrida* of statistics, graphs, calculations, and deductions; the book is entitled: *The War of the Future in its Technical, Economic and Political Relations*. In 1899 he won to his support the English journalist W. T. Stead, who brought out an English translation of the sixth volume, under the title *Is War Impossible*.[1] Fortunately for the reader, Stead added to it a long Preface based on conversations with Bloch, and as it summarizes all that remains of value in the volume, it is unnecessary to read further.

What is exceptional about Bloch's theory is that, although the facts it is based on are frequently erroneous and sometimes

[1] A reprint appeared in 1900 with title changed to *Modern Weapons and Modern War*. Also in 1900 unabridged translations of the six Russian volumes appeared in Germany and France.

ridiculous, his forecast of future war is uncannily accurate. One reason for this is that he was one of the very few of his generation who fully accepted that the defensive was increasingly becoming the stronger form of war; this led to his outlook on war being the very opposite to that of Foch.

With Clausewitz he held that war is a political instrument, but unlike so many of the military writers of his day, his systematic study of economics had led him to appreciate that, because civilization had since the days of Clausewitz passed out of the agricultural age and into the industrial one, war, as a political instrument, had been completely changed. In fact, in his opinion, it was now a negative instead of a positive instrument.

'What is the use', he said to Stead, 'of talking about the past when you are dealing with an altogether new set of considerations? Consider for a moment what nations were a hundred years ago and what they are to-day. In those days before railways, telegraphs, steamships, etc., were invented each nation was more or less a homogeneous, self-contained, self-sufficing unit. . . . All this is changed. . . . Every year the interdependence of nations upon each other for the necessaries of life is greater than it ever was before. . . . Hence the first thing that war would do would be to deprive the Powers that made it of all opportunity of benefiting by the products of the nations against whom they were fighting. . . .' And again: 'The soldier is going down and the economist is going up. There is no doubt of it. Humanity has progressed beyond the stage in which war can any longer be regarded as a possible Court of Appeal.' Therefore war between the great industrial Powers is nothing more than mutual suicide. The old conception of war as a business is absurd; today it is a mad kind of burglary – the plundering of one's own house.

Of modern weapons – the military expression of industrial civilization – he said: 'The outward and visible sign of the end of war was the introduction of the magazine rifle. . . . The soldier by natural evolution has so perfected the mechanism of slaughter that he has practically secured his own extinction.'

Bloch's forecast of modern war may, in his own words be summarized as follows:

'At first there will be increased slaughter – increased slaughter on so terrible a scale as to render it impossible to get troops to push the battle to a decisive issue. They will try to, thinking that they are fighting under the old conditions, and they will learn such a lesson that they will abandon the attempt for ever. Then, instead of war fought out to the bitter end in a series of decisive battles, we shall have as a substitute a long period of continually increasing strain upon the resources of the combatants. The war, instead of being a hand-to-hand contest, in which the combatants measure their physical and moral superiority, will become a kind of stalemate, in which neither army being willing to get at the other, both armies will be maintained in opposition to each other, threatening the other, but never being able to deliver a final and decisive attack. . . . That is the future of war – not fighting, but famine, not the slaying of men, but the bankruptcy of nations and the break-up of the whole social organization. . . . Everybody will be entrenched in the next war. It will be a great war of entrenchments. The spade will be as indispensable to a soldier as his rifle. . . . All wars will of necessity partake of the character of siege operations . . . soldiers may fight as they please; the ultimate decision is in the hand of famine. . . . Unless you have a supreme navy, it is not worth while having one at all, and a navy that is not supreme is only a hostage in the hands of the Power whose fleet is supreme.'

Bloch was of opinion that in a war between the Triple and the Dual Alliances 'there would be ten millions of men under arms', and that battle frontages would become so enormous that command would be impossible. That battles would grow longer and longer in duration, and more and more costly; a war would cost at least £4,000,000 a day should the five nations of the two Alliances partake in it. Cavalry he considered would be useless, the day of the bayonet past and gone, and artillery the dominant arm. The only noted soldier recorded to have troubled himself to criticize Bloch's views was old General Dragomirow, a veteran of the Russo-Turkish War. He condemned them because they failed to prove that the bayonet was still supreme.

CHAPTER VIII

The Roots of Armageddon

*

1 · The Overseas Expansion of Western Europe

After the Napoleonic Wars, the Industrial Revolution began to take root on the continent of Europe, first in Alsace, north-eastern France and Belgium, but in Germany and other countries it can hardly be said to have done so until the 1840's. Ten years later industrial expansion in Germany had become more rapid than in any other continental country, and after the Franco-Prussian War, the war indemnity of £200,000,000 received from France so greatly accelerated it that Germany was able to step forth on the road travelled by England over a century before, when the gold seized by Clive in Bengal went far to fertilize the British industrial revolution.

While German energy was concentrated on her industries, one of the most astonishing of phenomena in world history took shape. Certain European Powers, by now in various stages of industrialization, under the plea of spreading civilization among the heathen, set out to seek raw materials for their factories and markets for their goods in a scramble for colonies, first in Africa, and later in Southern Asia, the Pacific and China.

In 1870, except for Egypt, Tripoli, Tunisia and Algeria in the north, the Cape of Good Hope, the Orange Free State and the Transvaal in the south, and a number of scattered European settlements on the coasts of Africa, the map of that country was still almost a blank. Thirty years later, in 1900, except for Morocco, Tripoli, Abyssinia and Liberia, in all some 1,200,000 square miles in extent, the remaining 10,000,000 square miles of the continent had been parcelled out between Britain, France, Germany, Italy, Spain, Belgium and Portugal, although much of it was still unexplored.

As a whole, this partitioning does not concern us, but

certain items in it do, namely those which led to contentions between the colonizers.

In 1875, in order to secure the route to India, the British Prime Minister, Benjamin Disraeli, bought the Khedive's shares in the Suez Canal, a French project opened in 1869, the construction of which had been opposed by Lord Palmerston. Next, in 1877, Britain annexed the Transvaal and two years later conquered Zululand. Because this relieved the Boers of the Zulu menace, like the American colonists after 1763, safety at home led the Boers to seek independence, which, in 1881, they regained by defeating the British in the First Boer War, out of which was to sprout the second.

No sooner was this war at an end than the Arabi revolt broke out in Egypt, and Gambetta, then head of the French Government, invited Great Britain to discuss measures to secure the Khedive. But early in 1882 the Gambetta government fell, and the proposal was abandoned until June, when riots broke out in Alexandria. Britain then asked France to co-operate with her in restoring order, but de Freycinet, now in power, declined the request and so did Italy. In July the British bombarded Alexandria, and on 13th September Sir Garnet Wolseley crushed Arabi Pasha at Tel-el-Kebir. From Egypt the British were drawn into the Sudan, and in 1885 occurred the Gordon tragedy. The conquest of that vast country was then suspended because of the Penjeh crisis, which arose out of a boundary squabble between Great Britain and Russia in Turkistan, and it was not revived until 1898, when on 2nd September General Sir Herbert Kitchener's victory over the Sudanese at Omdurman led to the annexation of the Sudan.

In the meantime France had extended her power over the vast regions of the Sahara and, in 1881, occupied Tunisia, much to the annoyance of the Italians. In 1883 she proclaimed a protectorate in Madagascar, and two years later annexed Tongking, whereupon Britain occupied Upper Burma. In 1893, a dispute between the two countries occurred over Siam, which was only saved from being annexed by one side or the other because of their mutual jealousies. In 1898, another dispute between them arose over Fashoda, a post on the White

Nile, 600 miles above Khartum, which brought them to the verge of war, and left them at enmity until 1904.

Meanwhile, in 1884, Leopold II of Belgium acquired the enormously rich basin of the Congo, an area seventy-nine times the size of his own country. It aroused the envy of German merchants interested in Africa, and due to their pressure and the growing need for new regions to absorb Germany's increasing trade, Bismarck was at length convinced that the time had come to provide Germany with colonies. The result was that, in 1884, Germany occupied the coast of Angra Pequeña in South West Africa, Togoland, Cameroon, and part of New Guinea, to which, in 1885, the hinterland of Zanzibar was added, to become German East Africa. This led to tension with Great Britain, because German South-West Africa was adjacent to Cape Colony, and New Guinea to Australia. But as the recent British footing in Egypt had antagonized France, Great Britain was in no position to push her quarrel with Germany, and when Bismarck extended a friendly hand, Mr Gladstone grasped it and welcomed Germany as an ally in the labours of spreading civilization.

Toward the close of the century, a newcomer joined in the game of colonial snatch-and-grab – Japan. In 1894 she went to war with China, defeated her, and gained Formosa and the Liao-tung peninsula. This at once brought the European powers on the scene. For long Russia had been seeking an ice-free port as an outlet to Siberia, and her eyes had been fixed on the Liao-tung peninsula. Supported by France and Germany, Russia compelled Japan to relinquish it, and in reward obtained the right to carry the trans-Siberian railway, then under construction, over Chinese territory, while France was granted a rectification of her Mekong valley frontier.

While Russia and France were profiting by what they were pleased to call China's generosity, Germany received no reward, and, in 1897, she proceeded to help herself by occupying Kiao-chow Bay. Thereupon Russia demanded the lease of Port Arthur on the Liao-tung peninsula, a demand which China could not resist. To this Great Britain strongly objected, but on finding it a *fait accompli*, she swallowed her wrath and compelled China to lease to her Wei-hai-wei; whereupon

France obtained the lease of Kwang Cho Wan. In 1900 came the Boxer rebellion, the massacre of Europeans, the siege of the foreign legations in Pekin, and their relief by an international force. As things then stood, it looked as if China was to be the next country to be carved up.

Thus, by the close of the century, eight Western European powers – Britain, France, Germany, Italy, Spain, Portugal, Belgium and the Netherlands – together in extent slightly under 1,000,000 square miles, had within a generation added some 11,000,000 square miles of foreign territories to their homelands; an area three and half times the size of the United States, and rather more than one-fifth of the land surface of the globe! So extensive a conquest had no equal since the invasions of the Mongols in the thirteenth century, and no previous conquest had been so rapid and bloodless since the age of Alexander the Great. Like his, it was destined to be followed by the wars of its Diadochi.

2 · *Military Developments 1870–1903*

The period of Colonial expansion coincided with three major developments in weapon-power: the general adoption of the small-bore magazine rifle, firing smokeless powder; the perfection of the machine gun; and the introduction of quick-firing artillery.

By 1871, the single-shot breech-loading rifle had reached so high a standard of efficiency that the next step was to convert it into a repeating, or magazine, rifle. Although the idea was an old one, it was not fully practicable until the adoption of the all-metal cartridge case, which reduced jamming in the breech. The first European Power to introduce the magazine rifle was Germany who, in 1884, converted her 1871 pattern Mauser rifle to the magazine system; the magazine was of the tube type inserted in the fore-end under the barrel, it held eight cartridges. In 1885, France adopted a somewhat similar rifle, the Lebel, which fired smokeless powder – an enormous advantage. Next, in 1886, the Austrians introduced the Mannlicher with a box magazine in front of the trigger guard and below the entrance of the breech. And two years later the British adopted the .303 calibre Lee-Metford with a box magazine of eight cartridges, later increased to ten. By 1900 all armies had magazine rifles approximately of equal efficiency, and of calibres varying from .315 to .256; all were bolt operated, fired smokeless powder, and were sighted to 2,000 yards or metres.

Simultaneously with the development of the magazine rifle proceeded the development of the machine gun – another very old idea. Many types were experimented with and some adopted, such as the improved Gatling,[1] Nordenfeldt (1873), Hotchkiss (1875), Gardner (1876), Browning (1889) and Colt (1895). The crucial year in their development was 1884, when Hiram S. Maxim patented a one barrel gun which loaded and fired itself by the force of its recoil. The original model weighed 40 lb., was water cooled and belt fed, and 2,000 rounds could be fired from it in three minutes. It was adopted by the British army in 1889, and was destined to revolutionize infantry tactics.

The introduction of quick-firing artillery arose out of proposals made in 1891 by General Wille in Germany and Colonel Langlois in France. They held that increased rate of fire was impossible unless recoil on firing was absorbed. This led to much experimental work on shock absorption, and to the eventual introduction of a non-recoiling carriage, which permitted of a bullet-proof shield being attached to it to protect the gun crew. Until this improvement in artillery was introduced, the magazine rifle had been the dominant weapon, now it was challenged by the quick-firing gun, which not only outranged it and could be fired with almost equal rapidity, but could be rendered invisible by indirect laying.

The increasing growth in the size of armies raised the problem of their supply, and the first attempt to solve it was centred in the traction engine. Already in the Crimean War traction engines had been employed to haul trains of loaded wagons from the magazines at Balaclava to the front over tracts of country impassable for horsed vehicles. Again in the Franco-Prussian and the Russo-Turkish Wars they were so used, as well as for the haulage of heavy guns. Between 1872

[1] An excellent gun, first introduced toward the end of the American Civil War.

and the end of the century a number of experiments and trials with traction engines were carried out in England, France, Germany, Russia, Italy and Switzerland. In November, 1899, the British Government dispatched twenty-four to assist in the war in South Africa; others followed, including six armoured road trains, each of which consisted of an armoured traction engine and four armoured wagons; the armour was a quarter of an inch thick and could resist direct rifle fire at twenty yards. Both the engine-driver's cab and the wagons were loop-holed for rifle fire, and one idea was to use these armoured trains as self-contained mobile block-houses, which could move across the veld from point to point; but there is no record that they were so used.

This problem was, however, not to be solved by steam-power but by petroleum, the rapid production of which in the United States from 1859 on brought it more and more into commercial use,[1] and in 1876 led to the invention of the stationary gas engine[2] by Doctor N. A. Otto. Next, in 1885, Gottlieb Daimler devised an internal combustion motor using petroleum spirit, and fitted it to a bicycle:[3] such was the first step taken toward the production of the modern petrol driven road vehicle. Two years later MM. Panhard and Levessor secured the French patents from Daimler for the propulsion of road carriages. From then until 1894 little interest was shown in them; but that year the *Petit Journal* gave impetus to the French motor car industry by organizing a trial run of motor vehicles from Paris to Rouen. It aroused so much interest that in the following year a race was organized from Paris to Bordeaux and back, a distance of 744 miles, and the winner covered it at a mean speed of fifteen miles per hour. The next year, 1896, motor vehicles first took part in the French army manoeuvres, and three years later the first tactical motor vehicle, a four-wheeled cycle, equipped with a Maxim gun which could be fired from it through an armoured shield when in motion, was

[1] In 1859 2,000 barrels were produced; in 1869 – 4,215,000; and in 1879 – 19,914,146.

[2] In idea old. The first constructed would appear to be Christian Huygens' in 1680; it was worked by gunpower and air.

[3] Also in 1885, Butler in England propelled a tricycle by means of an internal combustion engine using benzoline vapour.

exhibited in England. Toward the end of the century propulsion by means of the internal combustion engine had so far advanced that, on 17th May 1900, Mr Arthur Balfour said in the House of Commons, he sometimes dreamed that in addition to railways and tramways, the future might see 'great highways constructed for rapid motor traffic, and confined to motor traffic.'[1]

But the greatest triumph of the new engine was yet to come. On 17th December 1903, at Kill Devil Hill, Kitty Hawk, North Carolina, Orville Wright in a power-driven aeroplane flew for twelve seconds, and thereby added a third dimension to war.

In the internal combustion engine lay hidden the greatest revolution in civil life and war since primitive man first tamed the horse. Its influence on civilization was so profound that, were it possible today by the wave of a magician's wand to abolish all motor vehicles, civil life would be brought to a complete standstill, and next to utter chaos. It made oil so essential a source of motive power that its acquisition became the most vital of political problems. Logistically and tactically it completely changed the organization of armies; it abolished horse transport, led to the introduction of armoured fighting vehicles, and in the skies opened a universal roadway for airborne supplies, artillery, and armies. Comparable with its influence on peace and war, only one other invention of this period challenged it – that was wireless telegraphy.

In 1887 it was first given theoretical form by Rudolf Hertz, who proved that under certain conditions an electrical spark creates an effect which is propagated into space as an electromagnetic wave. Other scientists investigated the problem, and between 1894 and 1896 Guglielmo Marconi concentrated his attention on the improvement of devices which could detect electromagnetic waves. He was so successful that, in 1899, during the British naval manoeuvres he transmitted a wireless message between two cruisers, and on 12th December 1901, he sent electromagenetic wave signals across the Atlantic from Cornwall to Newfoundland, a distance of 3,000 miles. Its in-

[1] *Mechanical Traction in War for Road Transport*, Lieut.-Col. Otfried Layriz (English edition, 1900), p. 96.

fluences on civil life and on naval strategy were enormous, and no wit less so on land and air warfare. Also it went far, if not to create psychological warfare, to give world-wide power to propaganda; to dement entire nations by transforming the spoken and written word into a weapon of war possessed of the velocity of light and in radius global. Further, it led to the development of the science of electronics.

In 1903, although the influences of these amazing changes lay behind the iron curtain of the future, that curtain was by no means altogether impenetrable. Nevertheless, it was so little penetrated by the minds of statesmen and soldiers that the conduct of future warfare was to be reduced to a game of chance – a blind gamble between players who moved their pieces in the dark on a totally novel kind of board.

3 · The Last of the Wars of Expansion

At the close of the nineteenth century and at the opening of the twentieth two small wars and one major one were fought; the Spanish–American War of 1898; the Anglo-Boer War of 1899–1902; and the Russo-Japanese War of 1904–1905. Beside their political importance, all three are of considerable tactical interest, because they were the first in which the new weapons were put to the test.

The dominant cause of the first of these wars was that, with the projected Panama Canal in mind, the United States was determined to oust Spain from the Caribbean Sea; a long-standing aim of successive administrations since the time of Jefferson, because it was feared that Cuba might fall into other European hands than those of Spain. A revolt of the Cubans in 1895, followed by severe repressive measures which involved American commercial interests, presented the United States with a pretext to intervene. Politically, the war was important, because it raised the United States from the position of a continental power to that of an inter-continental one; militarily it was a small affair. Its two naval battles were executions rather than contests, in them two Spanish squadrons, the one in Cavite Bay (Philippines) and the other off Santiago Bay (Cuba) were utterly destroyed at the cost of two American officers and six ratings slightly wounded in the one, and one man killed and one wounded in the other – a measure of the value of modern against obsolete warships. In the one major engagement on land, the battle of El Caney – San Juan Hill, the Americans, many of whose rifles and all of whose artillery fired black powder, at once found themselves at a serious disadvantage to the Spaniards whose powder was smokeless.[1] Once again the defensive power of earthworks was demonstrated. 'It may be said without exaggeration', writes Herbert H. Sargent, 'that one soldier behind the entrenchments of El Caney or on San Juan Hill was equal in fighting power to six or eight soldiers advancing to attack him.'[2]

One small incident is worth a mention, because it showed that chivalry was not altogether a thing of the past. When Naval Constructor Richmond P. Hobson most gallantly sank the American collier *Merrimac* in the narrow entrance of Santiago Harbour, the Spanish admiral, Cervera, set out in his steam launch and rescued him and his men from drowning. Later in the day, under flag of truce, he sent a message to Admiral Sampson, in command of the blockading squadron, 'extolling the bravery of the crew [of the *Merrimac*] in an unusual manner.'[3]

The Second Anglo-Boer War – the cause of which Marshal Foch so accurately gauged – was, as the German official historian described it: not merely a contest between the bullet and the bayonet, but also a contest 'between the soldier drilled to machine-like movements and the man with a rifle working on his own iniative. . . . War had been proclaimed between rigid formulas and untrammelled healthy common sense.'[4] When on 9th October 1899 – two days before the outbreak of hostilities – the British Government announced that it had decided to bring the army in South Africa up to 70,000 men strong, the editor of the London *Standard,* with considerable

[1] In his book *The Rough Riders*, p. 98, Theodore Roosevelt notes: 'As the Spaniards used smokeless powder, their artillery had an enormous advantage over ours.'

[2] *The Campaign of Santiago de Cuba* (1907), Vol. II, p. 135.

[3] See Sampson's dispatch No. 113 in *The Relations of the United States and Spain, etc.*, Rear-Admiral French Ensor Chadwick (1911), Vol. II, p. 345.

[4] *The War in South Africa, A German Official Account* (English edition, 1906), Vol. II, p. 336.

accuracy reflected public opinion when he stated: 'Against such an army of bayonets, sabres and cannon, what can General Joubert's half-trained mob of irregulars expect to accomplish?' He and his fellow countrymen never paused to consider how 70,000 men, mostly infantry, were going to subdue 90,000 mounted riflemen in an area of 430,000 square miles. over extensive stretches of which a horseman could ride in any direction for weeks on end.

In the small battles fought during the opening months of the war, it became apparent that, due to smokeless powder, the old terror of a visible foe had given way to the paralysing sensation of advancing on an invisible one. A universal terror, rather than a localized danger, now enveloped the attacker, while the defender, always ready to protect himself by some rough earth- or stone-work, was enabled, because of the rapidity of rifle fire, to use extensions unheard of in former battles, and in consequence overlap every frontal infantry attack. Thus, at the battle of the Modder River, the Boers extended 3,000 men on a frontage of 7,700 yards; at Magersfontein, 5,000 on 11,000; and at Colenso, 4,500 on 13,000. Yet in spite of this human thinness, these fronts could not be penetrated.

After the battle of Paardeberg, on 18th February 1900, the Boers took to guerrilla warfare, and the war proper may be said to have begun. It was to last until 31st May 1902; absorb in all 450,000 British soldiers, many of whom were mounted infantry, and was brought to a successful conclusion by an audacious scheme which struck at the enemy's mobility. A vast network of fenced block-house lines was woven over thousands of square miles of the theatre of war; these split it up into horse-proof areas. Next, one after another of them was cleared by mounted columns. It was a long process of attrition, but an eminently successful one.

The causes of the Russo-Japanese War were Russia's eastward expansion, which aimed at absorbing Korea, and the rise of Japanese imperialism. Because the Japanese realized that they would be no match against the Russians once the gap in the trans-Siberian railway at Lake Baikal had been filled, they determined to strike while strategy favoured them. As long as the gap existed, the reinforcement of the Russian troops in Manchuria would be slow, and as Vladivostok was ice-bound in the winter and Port Arthur ice-free, could the latter be secured before the next winter set in, not only would the Russian warships at Vladivostok be cut off from those at Port Arthur, but should the Russian Baltic fleet be sent east, without Port Arthur it would be denied an ice-free base of operations. Therefore the Japanese plan was to wrest Port Arthur from the Russians, and next concentrate the whole of their land forces in a great battle, the loss of which it was hoped would persuade the Russians to abandon the war.

Officially, the war was declared on 10th February 1904, and its operations may be listed under three headings: (1) The siege and fall of Port Arthur, which included the destruction of the Russian squadron in its harbour; (2) the series of Japanese victorious land battles, which culminated in the battle of Mukden, fought between 23rd February and 10th March 1905; and (3) the annihilation of the Russian Baltic fleet in the Strait of Tsushima on 27th May 1905. Nevertheless, the Russian army, although beaten in every battle, had not suffered a decisive defeat and was actually growing stronger daily, while Japan's war potential was approaching exhaustion. Therefore, from a purely strategical point of view, in spite of her tactical victories, the odds were against her winning the war.

That she did so was due to the collapse of the Russian inner front. Repression, corruption, and the disasters suffered in Manchuria, as early as 14th July 1904, led to the assassination of Plehve, the Russian Minister of the Interior. Outrages and strikes followed, and on 4th February 1905, the Grand-Duke Sergius was murdered. This and subsequent outrages persuaded the Tzar, Nicholas II (1894–1918), to conciliate the revolutionaries, and on 6th June he promised to convoke a National Assembly. But when it was discovered that he intended it to be a purely consultative body, furious agitation followed, and in September it culminated in a general strike, which for days brought Russia to a standstill. In October the Tzar gave way, and a parliamentary constitution was adopted.

Meanwhile, because Russia's inner front had become more

dangerous than her outer, when, on 10th June, the President of the United States offered to mediate between the belligerents, both parties willingly accepted his offer, and on 9th August peace negotiations were opened at Portsmouth, New Hampshire. By the terms of the treaty, signed on 23rd August, Russia agreed to evacuate Manchuria; cede to Japan the Liaotung peninsula, half of the island of Sakhalin, and recognize her preponderance in Korea. These were small items when compared with the consequences of the war. It made Japan the leading Power in Asia; it crippled Russia; and by liberating Germany from the fear of war on her eastern flank, it made her the dominant power in Europe, and thereby upset the balance of power. This caused Great Britain to abandon her traditional policy of isolation which, since 1815, had been the backbone of the *Pax Britannica.* Further, by challenging the supremacy of the white man over the coloured, the war awakened Asia and Africa and dealt a mortal blow to every European colonial empire.

Guns and earthworks were the two dominant factors in this war, and when the Japanese quick-firing artillery was well handled, victory was generally assured. The gun forced the enemy to entrench, and entrenched infantry compelled the gun to take cover behind the sky-line and adopt indirect laying. Defiladed fire demanded telephonic communications; trenches demanded wire entanglements, and for enfilading them the value of the machine gun became increasingly apparent; while cavalry faded out of the picture.

The outstanding tactical lessons of the war were:

(1) The failure of frontal attacks and the success of envelopments.
(2) The enormous defensive power of field entrenchments and wire entanglements.
(3) The increasing deadliness of the machine gun.
(4) And most marked of all, the power of quick-firing artillery.

In the reports of British officers attached to the Japanese army, Colonel W. H. H. Waters says: 'By the light of my own experiences I can see no reason why artillery should not often be the decisive factor, and it certainly was at Tellissu.'[1] And Major J. M. Home writes: 'The greatest impression made on me by all I saw is that artillery is now the decisive arm and that all other arms are auxiliary to it. The importance of artillery cannot be too strongly insisted upon, for other things being equal, the side which has the best artillery will always win. . . . So strongly am I convinced of the immense importance of artillery that it seems almost a question for deliberate consideration whether artillery should not be largely increased even at the expense of the other arms. . . .

'With the extraordinary development of artillery it begins to appear as though infantry fire action cannot usefully be employed at ranges beyond 600 yards, as beyond that distance the hostile guns ought to be able to prevent infantry from using their rifles.'[2]

4 · *Discords and Concords*

From the close of the Franco-Prussian War until his dismissal in March 1890, Bismarck's policy was to stabilize the peace Germany had won, and to assure it he set out to win the friendship of Russia, and, in order to isolate France, in 1879 he concluded with Austria a defensive treaty known as the Dual Alliance, which two years later was joined by Italy, which was outraged by the French occupation of Tunisia; the Dual Alliance then became the Triple Alliance. In 1888 William II succeeded to the German throne; two years later he dismissed Bismarck, and France alarmed by his capricious and bellicose behaviour entered into negotiations with Russia, which between 1893 and 1895 matured into a defensive agreement – the Dual Alliance.

Thus two opposing alliances came into being; nevertheless, as long as Great Britain was not party to either, the peace of Europe remained firm. Unfortunately this happy situation was not to last, because the rapid expansion of German overseas trade and the growth of her merchant service increasingly

[1] *The Russo-Japanese War: Reports from British Officers* (1908), Vol. III, p. 117.

[2] Ibid., Vol. III, pp. 209–10.

challenged British commerce.[1] Further, in order to protect German overseas trade and catch up with France's naval preponderance, in 1898 the Kaiser increased the size of the German Navy, and in 1900, when Britain was occupied in South Africa, he did so again. This led to an uproar in the British press.

In this challenge is revealed one of the root causes of war – the economic struggle for existence. Neither Germany nor Great Britain were in the wrong; it was not their respective cupidities or ambitions which brought them at loggerheads, it was the Industrial Revolution which made them competitors. It had so multiplied their populations that without foreign trade each would be beset by unemployment and eventually reduced to starvation level. When, in 1919, John Maynard Keynes looked back on the First World War, he wrote: 'The politics of power are inevitable, and there is nothing very new to learn about this war or the end it was fought for; England had destroyed, as in each preceding century a trade rival.'[2]

The isolation in which England had found herself during and after the South African War was broken by Edward VII (1901–1910) in 1903. In the spring of that year he visited Paris, and his personal charm as well as his antipathy for his nephew, the Kaiser, won over the Parisians. His visit was followed by negotiations which, in April 1904, led to the establishment of an Anglo-French entente, a treaty of friendship which was to

[1] In October 1902, Colonel William R. Robertson (later Field-Marshal Sir William), then head of the Foreign Intelligence Section of the War Office, wrote in a memorandum: '. . . the most potent cause is the rivalry in trade and colonial enterprise. . . .' (*Soldiers and Statesmen* (1926), Vol. I, p. 21). In 1880, German exports and imports totalled £290,500,000; in 1890, £384,100,000; in 1900, £539,800,000; in 1907, £804,900,000, which exceeded those of France (£605,200,000) and those of the United States (£683,900,000) and approached those of Great Britain (£1,163,800,000).

[2] *The Economic Consequences of the Peace* (1919), p. 30. On 11th September 1919, in an address given at St. Louis, President Woodrow Wilson laid bare the heart of the problem when he said: 'Why, my fellow citizens, is there any man here, or any woman – let me say, is there any child here – who does not know that the seed of war in the modern world is industrial and commercial rivalry? . . . This war, in its inception, was a commercial and industrial war. It was not a political war.'

grow into a secret military alliance. According to Sir William Robertson, plans for co-operation with France were discussed between the Director of Military Operations and the French military attaché in London in 1905. And 'From 1906 onwards the conversations grew more intimate and frequent, and were always conducted direct between the General Staffs of the two armies. . . . Not only was the Cabinet unaware of the conversations, but even the Foreign Secretary [Sir Edward Grey], who gave permission for them, knew nothing about the results. Writing to the Prime Minister on the subject in 1911 he said: "What they settled I never knew – the position being that the Government was quite free, but the military people knew what to do, if the word was given." '[1]

Sir William Robertson's comment is: 'It was of little use for the "military people" to "know what to do" unless adequate means were available for doing it, and this there could not be if the Cabinet knew nothing about what was taking place.'[2]

In accordance with the entente, the two governments settled their colonial differences; while Britain was given a free hand in Egypt, France was to be allowed a free hand in Morocco, as long as her integrity was respected. Nevertheless, in October 1904, a convention was drawn up between France and Spain for the partition of Morocco, and a copy of it sent to the British Foreign Secretary. This shady transaction was to prove to be a veritable Pandora's box.

Nor was trouble long delayed. In March 1905, although the Kaiser knew nothing of these secret treaties, he became suspicious that Morocco might become a second Tunis and visited Tangier. This led to a press campaign of such violence that, in order to avert the outbreak of war, President Theodore Roosevelt stepped into the international arena and suggested a conference. In January 1906, it met at Algeciras, and con-

[1] Cited from Grey's *Twenty-Five Years 1892–1926* (1925), p. 94.

[2] *Soldiers and Statesmen*, Vol. I., p. 49. Sir William Robertson also writes that, early in 1906, '. . . the Operations Directorate submitted a "Memorandum upon the Military Forces required for Overseas Warfare" . . . It did for the first time discuss a "war alliance with France against Germany", which was referred to as "an eventuality to be seriously considered". . . . The proposal was that a force of at least four cavalry brigades and three army corps' should be dispatched to France (Ibid., Vol. I, pp. 28–29).

firmed the pledges of the Powers to uphold the independence of Morocco.

Soon after this conference the British Government came to an understanding with Russia, which released the latter from perils in the Far East, and enabled her to turn her undivided attention to Europe. Thus a Triple Entente came into being to face the Triple Alliance; this meant that, in the event of hostilities, Germany would be faced with a war on two fronts.

While the Morocco crisis shocked international relations, in England a naval panic, engineered by a Mr Mulliner of the Coventry Ordnance Company, shocked the Government, the Opposition and the people, and so hysterical did the press become that Admiral Sir John Fisher, First Sea Lord of the Admiralty, decided to inform the King on the true situation. In a long letter to him he said:

'In March this year, 1907, it is an absolute fact that Germany has not laid down a single "Dreadnought", nor has she commenced building a single Battleship or Big Cruiser for eighteen months . . . half of the whole German Battle Fleet is only equal to the English Armoured Cruisers. . . .'[1]

Later, on 21st March 1909, in a letter to Lord Esher, Fisher said:

'The unswerving intention of 4 years has *now* culminated in *two* complete Fleets in Home Waters, each of which is incomparably superior to the whole German Fleet mobilized for war. . . . This can't alter for years. . . . *So sleep quiet in your beds*! . . .'[2]

Although Mr Arthur Balfour, leader of the Opposition, must have been aware of this, in the General Elections of January 1910, he let loose a cyclonic attack on Germany in order to terrify people into voting for the Conservative party, and was heavily counter-attacked by Mr Winston Churchill for 'trying to raise ill-wind between two great nations without cause.'

On 6th May 1910, Edward VII died, and was succeeded by his son George V (1910–1935), but before he was crowned on 22nd June 1911, another violent incident exploded in Morocco. The French Government, bent on complete control over

[1] *Memories*, Admiral of the Fleet Lord Fisher (1919), pp. 14–15.
[2] Ibid., pp. 189–90.

Morocco, occupied Fez, and the Kaiser, still in ignorance of the secret treaties, declared it to be a violation of the Treaty of Algeciras, which it was. When on 1st July he sent a gunboat, the *Panther*, to Agadir to protect German commercial interests and subjects in Morocco, Mr Lloyd George, the British Chancellor of the Exchequer, launched a violent attack on Germany, which nearly precipitated a general war. Fortunately, in November, a settlement was reached, and in accordance with it France obtained a free hand in Morocco and Germany a slice of the French Congo. This did not satisfy Italy, and fearful that France would next seize Tripoli, on the now normal pretext of securing trade and nationals, she declared war on Turkey, invaded Tripoli, and occupied Rhodes and other of the Dodecanese Islands.

Since Russia was now a member of the Triple Entente, her prospects of expansion in south-eastern Europe were more propitious than they had been in 1877. Her aim was a threefold one: To liquidate Turkey in Europe and gain Constantinople; morally to weaken Austria by undercutting her prestige in the Balkans, which simultaneously would weaken Germany. The instrument she intended to use was the Balkan States, particularly Serbia and Bulgaria. The former had gained her independence in 1878; the latter was still a tributary of the Sultan. This anomalous position had long rankled the Bulgarians, and on 5th October 1908, Prince Ferdinand proclaimed his country an independent kingdom and took the title of king. In reply, Austria annexed Bosnia and Herzegovina.

At once Russia seized the opportunity this offered her to unite the Balkan States by promoting among them the fear that, unless they dropped their respective antagonisms and combined in mutual defence, they would be swallowed piecemeal by Austria. The outcome was the formation of the Balkan League, and because at the time Turkey and Italy were at war, on 8th October 1912, Montenegro declared war on Turkey and was forthwith joined by Bulgaria, Serbia and Greece. The Turks were defeated, and on 3rd December an armistice was agreed, and peace was signed in London on 30th May 1913. No sooner was this done than the victors quarrelled over the spoils; the Bulgars fell upon the Serbs and Greeks;

the Rumanians entered the conflict, and the Turks regained Adrianople. Bulgaria was defeated, and when on 10th August the second Balkan War was ended by the Treaty of Bucharest, Turkey in Europe was reduced to Adrianople, Constantinople and the country around them, including the Gallipoli Peninsula.

The tension in Europe soon became so acute that, in the spring of 1914, Colonel E. H. House – President Woodrow Wilson's roving ambassador – at the time on a visit to Berlin, reported to the President: 'The whole of Germany is charged with electricity. Everybody's nerves are tense. . . . Whenever England consents, France and Russia will close in on Germany and Austria.'[1]

Russia was fearful that England's consent might be withdrawn. From London, Benckendorff, the Russian Ambassador, wrote to Sazonov, the Russian Foreign Minister: 'It is impossible for the Anglo-Russian entente to be maintained if the estrangement between Britain and Germany ceases.'[2] This was with reference to German attempts to dissipate it. The one thing Russia feared was delay; the Emperor Francis Joseph was eighty-four, and the Archduke Francis Ferdinand, the heir apparent, was opposed to the Greater Serbia movement. At all costs Russia was determined that the Yugoslavs should look to St. Petersburg and not to Vienna. Such was the situation when on 28th June 1914, the Archduke and his wife were assassinated by Serb terrorists at Sarajevo.

According to M. Bogitshevich, the Serbian Chargé d'Affaires in Germany, 'Serbia had already received the assurance of Russia that this time she would not desert Serbia.' Further, he writes:

'And what is more important still, *Serbia must have been assured that war against Germany and Austria had been resolved upon*, and the assassination of the Austrian heir to the throne furnished a favourable pretext for the war only because England and France had allowed themselves to be drawn into the conflict by Russia (which in and of itself was but a local conflict between Austria and Serbia). . . . If Sir Edward Grey had . . .

[1] *Intimate Papers of Colonel House* (1926), Vol. I, p. 249.
[2] Cited in *Uncovering the Forces of War*, Conrad K. Grieb (1947), p. 8.

simply declared to Russia and France (Germany need not have heard a word of it) *that England was uninterested in the conflict* – retaining entire freedom of action as regards what might subsequently arise – the European war would in that case certainly not have broken out. But all this is of course on the supposition that England had not already so bound herself that retreat was no longer possible.'[1]

Unfortunately, this is what had happened. Shrouded in secrecy, the Entente of 1904 had grown into an irrevocable secret military alliance, about which the British Parliament knew nothing.

On 23rd July, an Austrian ultimatum was presented to Belgrade with a time limit of forty-eight hours. Sazonov declared it to be an unparalleled act of aggression and that the only way to avert war with Germany was to let her know that she would be confronted by the united forced of the Entente. Russia then ordered partial mobilization, and Germany urged that the question should be settled by Austria and Serbia alone.

On 25th July Serbia replied to the Austrian ultimatum, and because the reply was incomplete Austria ordered full mobilization, and on the following day the German Chancellor sent for Sir Edward Goschen, the British Ambassador in Berlin, and told him that, if Great Britain remained neutral, in the event of a successful war against France, Germany would respect the integrity of France. This proposal was rejected by the British Government.

On 31st July, the German Ambassador in St. Petersburg was instructed to present an ultimatum to the Russian Government to demand the cessation of mobilization within twelve hours, failing which Germany would mobilize. As the demand was unanswered, on 1st August Germany and Russia were at war, and France ordered general mobilization.

On 2nd August, Italy declared her neutrality;[2] German cavalry patrols entered Luxemburg, and the German Minister in Brussels delivered a note to the Belgium Govern-

[1] *Causes of the War: An examination into the causes of the European War, with special reference to Russia and Serbia* (London, 1920), pp. 65 and 08.

[2] Austria did not declare war on Russia until 6th August.

ment in which a free passage of German troops through Belgium was demanded. It was rejected, and the next day the King of the Belgians made a personal appeal to the King of England to safeguard his country. At 6.45 p.m. Germany declared war on France, and a few hours later on Belgium. Lastly, at 3 p.m. on 4th August, Sir Edward Goschen was instructed by the British Foreign Office to obtain assurance from Germany that Belgian neutrality, which was guaranteed by treaty, would be respected. It was then that Bethman-Hollweg, the German Chancellor, said in reply: 'Just for a scrap of paper Great Britain is going to make war on a kindred race.'[1] At midnight on 4th August Britain declared war on Germany.

[1] If not a 'scrap of paper', the Treaty of 1839 was little more than a 'holy relic'. Under its terms British obligations were not defined, and there was no provision which necessitated England sending troops to Belgium to make war on any Power that should violate her territories.

CHAPTER IX

The Conduct of World War I

*

1 · Policy and War

When the twentieth century dawned, the frontiers of the British Empire had become the shores of the seas and the oceans; the United States of America had grown into a world power; Russia, although industrially backward, possessed immense potential strength; Germany and France had become prosperous empires, and though they and the other European nations were contentious, this they had been for a thousand years. Then, in 1914, came war, and when in 1918 it ended, except for the United States, the whole enormous edifice had crashed to earth. Britain was bankrupted and France bled white; Russia and Germany were in the throes of revolution; the Austro-Hungarian Empire had vanished; the Ottoman Empire had been dismembered; Italy was distraught; and every other country in Europe was scorched by the fiery blast – an epoch had gone up in flames.

Could statesmen and soldiers have foreseen to where their bickerings and chicaneries, their intrigues and alliances were to lead them, would they have precipitated the conflict? This is no idle question, for even were the problems too complex for them to unravel, even were they impelled by circumstances they could not avoid creating to cut the Gordian tangle with the sword, could they not have learned from the pages of history to wield it with some semblance of skill? Had not Polybius, some seventy generations earlier, written: 'For it is history, and history alone, which, without involving us in actual danger, will mature our judgement and prepare us to take right views, whatever may be the crisis or the posture of affairs.'[1]

Had they studied Clausewitz, they could not have failed to

[1] *The Histories of Polybius*, Bk. I, 35.

have understood that war belongs to policy, that it takes its character from policy, and that 'if policy is grand and powerful, so will also be the war.'

Had the war, as in 1870, been restricted to two nations, their respective problems would have been simple; but in 1914 they were complex, because the struggle was between two alliances, which together embraced the greater part of Europe. This meant that the war would affect the whole continent, and were its outcome – that is, the peace which followed it – to be profitable to the victor, then it was incumbent on the members of each alliance to decide on a common policy which would direct them toward that end. Were this not done, the war must inevitably be a chaotic one, and the peace which followed it none the less so.

Because the Entente alliance was more complex than that of the two Central Powers – Germany and Austria[1] –and because it was compelled to operate on exterior lines, it may be accepted as axiomatic that no common policy could have been agreed by *all* its members. But for its two major ones, France and Great Britain, this most certainly was not so, and from 1904 on there had been ample time for them to arrive at a common policy governed by a positive political aim – the nature of the peace it would be most profitable for them to establish. Clausewitz had written: 'The subordination of the political point of view to the military would be contrary to common sense', because 'policy is the intelligent faculty, war only the instrument.' But in August 1914, there was no Anglo-French political point of view,[2] therefore the military point of view was subordinated to a vacuum, which it at once filled to become the sole point of view: in other words, the means monopolized the end.

Throughout the war, this led to an intermittent wrangle over unity of command; a futile one,[3] because without unity

[1] Italy declared her neutrality on 2nd August, and thereby reduced the Triple Alliance to its original form of a dual one. Turkey did not join the Central Powers until 29th October; meanwhile Japan joined the Entente Powers on 15th August.

[2] See Sir Edward Grey's statement, *supra*, Chap. VIII, p. 145.

[3] The appointment of General Foch, on 26th March 1918, to co-ordinate the action of the Allied armies on the Western Front, which,

of policy there could be no workable unity of command. This was fully appreciated by Sir William Robertson when C.I.G.S. 'It is essential', he wrote, 'before trying to establish "unified command" that the Allied Governments should be agreed among themselves as to the general policy to be pursued, and be satisfied that the agreement will not be disturbed, since without unity of policy unity of command may lead to the operations being conducted in the interest of one ally rather than of the others; and so defeat its own ends.'[1]

Therefore, as things stood in August 1914, Lord Kitchener was undoubtedly right when he wrote to Sir John French, the British Commander-in-Chief: 'I wish you distinctly to understand that your command is an entirely independent one, and that you will in no case come in any sense under the orders of any Allied General.'[2] But his reason for this was gravely in error, because, according to Sir William Robertson, it was that Britain 'should aim at having the strongest army in Europe when the war came to an end, and so be able to ensure that suitable terms of peace were exacted.'[3] He also had failed to read his Clausewitz; had he done so, he could not have put the cart before the horse. In any case an exacted peace can be no more than an armistice, which actually happened.

As regards the aims of the two alliances, which their respective policies should have co-ordinated with the means at their disposal as well as with strategical and other conditions, they may be inferred from the causes which brought the two alliances into being. That of France was to cripple Germany, regain Alsace-Lorraine, and re-establish her leadership on the continent, which she had been deprived of by Sadowa and Sedan. That of Russia was to absorb the Balkans, and with them gain Constantinople and an outlet to the Mediterranean,

on 1st July, was extended to include all Allied aimies, in no way contradicts this, because his powers were so limited that he could expect no more from his subordinate commanders – Sir Douglas Haig, General Pétain, General Pershing and General Diaz – than optional execution of his instructions.

[1] *Soldiers and Statesmen, 1914–1918* (1926), Vol. II, pp. 296–7.

[2] British Official *History of the Great War*, 'France and Belgium' compiled by Brigadier-General J. E. Edmonds (1922), Vol. I, App. 8, p. 442.

[3] *Soldiers and Statesmen*, Vol. II, p. 296.

which meant the emasculation, if not the disintegration, of the Austro-Hungarian Empire. That of Germany was to prevent either of these contingencies, and maintain her supremacy. That of Great Britain was to destroy Germany as a trade rival, which she could only do with the aid of France and Russia. Her position was an anomalous one, as it had so often been in her coalition wars. Should the Central Powers be decisively defeated, the consequent supremacy of France in Western Europe, and the expansion of Russia in south-eastern Europe, would unhinge the balance of power on the continent, the maintenance of which had been Britain's traditional policy, as much so as were the Central Powers to win the war. In the past, she had more often than once overcome a similar difficulty by seeking a negotiated peace when her opponent had been sufficiently weakened, and before her most powerful ally could step into his shoes. Could she hope to do this again depended, not only on her statesmanship, but also on the statesmanship of her most powerful antagonist – Germany.

2 · *Fate of the War Plans*

On 4th August 1914, had an onlooker strolled round the gaming table of war and glanced at the hands of the players, he would have laid ten to one on Germany winning the game. Nevertheless, five weeks later, when the cards had been played, all the players were strategical bankrupts. How came this about? This is an important question, because out of it emerged the subsequent conduct of the war.

When the lethal gamble opened, Germany and Austria were centrally placed between Russia in the east, France, Britain and Belgium in the west, and Serbia in the south. Together they could put into the field 158 infantry and cavalry divisions to face 150 Russian, 87 French, British and Belgian, and 12 Serbian. Therefore, numerically, the dice of war were heavily loaded against them. But because they could operate on interior lines, while their opponents were compelled to operate on exterior, it was possible for them to concentrate the bulk of their forces against any one of their adversaries, as long as for the time being they succeeded in holding back the others.

This was the problem Count Alfred von Schlieffen set out to solve when, between 1891 and 1906, he was Chief of the German General Staff. Aware that the Russian mobilization would be considerably slower than the French, and correctly anticipating that the bulk of the French forces would assemble on the line Mézières-Epinal, he decided to oppose the Russians with an army of ten division and local troops (the Eighth Army) in East Prussia while the Austrian armies advanced into Galicia, and deploy seven armies against France on the line Krefeld-Mulhausen, five (First to Fifth) north of Metz, and two (Sixth and Seventh) south of it. The former – the right wing – was to consist of thirty-five and a half corps, seven cavalry divisions, sixteen brigades of Landwehr, and six Ersatz divisions; and the latter – the left wing – of five corps and three cavalry divisions. His idea was that, while the left wing gained contact with the French forces in Lorraine and Alsace, first held them and next fell back before them, the right wing, pivoted on Metz, would move forward through Luxemburg, Belgium, and the Dutch Maastricht appendix, then swing south-west with its head advancing west of Paris, and from there wheel eastward, fall on the rear of the French armies engaged with the left wing, and drive them pell-mell into Germany and Switzerland. It was to be a repetition of Frederick's battle of Leuthen (1757) on a gigantic scale.

In 1906 Schlieffen handed his plan over to General Helmuth von Moltke, nephew of the great Moltke, who – because of his name – had been selected by the Kaiser to succeed him. In 1914 he was sixty-eight years old, a sick man, and was soused in the staff ideas of his uncle, which he copied slavishly. Although as Chief of the General Staff he was Commander-in-Chief all but in name, once his armies had been deployed, he looked upon his role as no more than that of a starter of a race – all he had to do was to lower the flag, and then leave operations to his generals. He did not believe in executive control, worse still, he feared it, and 'actually drew some comfort from the Emperor's frequent declarations that in the event of war he would himself command in the west.'[1]

Although Moltke had in 1906 accepted Schlieffen's plan,

[1] *The German General Staff*, Walter Görlitz (1953), p. 144.

in 1912, at Schlieffen's suggestion, he changed it. On the French front he substituted for Schlieffen's original idea of a Leuthen the idea of a Cannae (216 B.C.). That is, victory through a double envelopment instead of a single one, and to effect this he increased the strength of the left wing.

In the Schlieffen plan, the numerical strength of the left wing was fifteen per cent. of the right wing, and this he intended to reduce to nine per cent. by shifting two corps from the left wing to the right wing directly the French in Alsace and Lorraine were engaged by the left wing. Not only would this strengthen the right wing, but – as important – it would necessitate the weakened left wing falling back, which, in its turn, would draw the French armies eastward, and the farther east they advanced the more decisive would his rear attack become. This move Moltke cancelled, and he brought the strength of the left wing up to forty-two per cent. of that of the right wing.

The French plan was a piece of back-stairs jobbery. In 1911, General Michel, at the time general-in-chief designate in the event of war, held that the Germans would advance through Belgium, and that therefore the most powerful French forces should be assembled on the left. The *Comité des Forges de France* disagreed, because this would not sufficiently protect the Lorraine iron-fields, and the General Staff supported the *Comité*, and by a shady trick persuaded the Minister of War to replace Michel by General Joffre.

The theory of 'mass plus velocity', then held by the General Staff, exactly fitted Joffre's bull-like temperament. The offensive was his one and only aim, as it was of his political master, President Fallières, who, in 1912, asserted: 'We are determined to march straight against the enemy without hesitation. . . . The offensive alone is suited to the temperament of our soldiers.'[1]

The plan of war agreed was one of pathetic simplicity, '*reposant*', as Jean de Pierrefeu says, '*tout entier sur l'idée mystique de l'offensive.*'[2] It was known as Plan XVII, and was based on two postulates: (1) That at first the Germans would

[1] *The Memoirs of Marshal Joffre* (English trans., 1932), Vol. I, p. 30.
[2] *Plutarque a menti* (1922), p. 55.

not bring into line reserve formations as well as active ones – which General Michel had said they would – therefore they would not be strong enough simultaneously to advance through Belgium as well as through Lorraine. And (2) that as the French soldier was irresistible in the attack, the sole thing necessary was to deploy the French armies between Mézières and Epinal, move straight forward, smash the German centre – or rather what was assumed to be the centre – and then paralyse the German communications in Lorraine.

The remaining belligerent plans can be given in brief. Great Britain's was to support France with an Expeditionary Force of four infantry and one cavalry divisions; but no blockade of Germany was resorted to other than the seizure of contraband cargoes allowed by maritime law, in accordance with the Declaration of London. Austria formed six armies; three strong ones to cut off Russian Poland in co-operation with eventual German forces, and three weak ones to operate against Serbia. Russia mobilized eight armies, under the Grand Duke Nicholas; two on the North-West Front to move against East Prussia; four on the South-West Front to advance against the Austrians; and the remaining two, in the first instance, were located to guard the flanks and coasts, with headquarters at St. Petersburg and Odessa. Both the Belgian and Serbian plans contemplated a strict defensive.

The five campaigns opened simultaneously, and their fate was as follows:

That of France was ruined at the first shock; yet, strange to relate, out of its débris emerged a second plan which put the finishing touch on the ruins of the German western plan, while the German eastern plan, which at the start appeared most hazardous, ended in an overwhelming tactical victory. That of Austria against Serbia was a muddled failure, and that of Russia against Austria was indecisive, although it went far to emasculate Austria for the rest of the war. Of these failures and successes, the one which had the most pronounced influence on the future conduct of the war was the ruin of the Moltke-Schlieffen plan.

When, on 14th August, the First German Army, under General von Kluck, was still battering its way through the

Liége fortifications, Joffre's immense battle of penetration, known to the French as the 'Battle of the Frontiers', was launched, to continue without intermission until 25th August, by when the French were everywhere defeated with crippling losses, which amounted to some 300,000 men killed, wounded and missing. Their defeat threw the French centre and left back to the west of Verdun, and so elated Moltke that he assumed the decisive battle in France had been won. Perturbed by the news he was receiving from the Eighth Army in East Prussia, he decided to reinforce it with two corps[1] and a cavalry division from the French front, and instead of taking them from the left wing, he took them from the Second and Third Armies of the right wing, which had already been deprived of three corps to observe the Belgian army in Antwerp and lay siege to Maubeuge.

This considerable reduction in the strength of the right wing, coupled with the independent actions of its army commanders, over whom Moltke by now had lost control, caused an inward shrinkage of the great wheel, which led to the First Army being drawn in a south-easterly direction *east* of Paris instead of advancing *west* of it; this left the French capital and railway hub uninvested.

On the day Moltke made his fatal decision, Joffre, perturbed by the approach of Kluck's army toward the left of the French line, in order to protect it, set out to build up a new army, the Sixth, under General Maunoury, in the vicinity of Amiens. Meanwhile Kluck pushed on, and although on the 29th he learnt of French detrainments at Amiens, he paid little attention to them. On 1st September, Joffre ordered Maunoury to fall back on Paris, and, on the 4th he instructed him to cross the river Ourcq and attack Kluck's exposed right flank, held by General von Gronau's IVth Corps. The next day the battle of the Ourcq – prelude to the battle of the Marne – opened, and by the 7th the fighting had become so precarious that Kluck, without consulting Bülow, in command of the

[1] At first he even thought of sending six corps. He persisted in sending two, although he was informed by the Eighth Army that they were not wanted, and if sent would arrive too late to take part in the battle of Tannenberg then being fought; it opened on 25th August.

Second Army on his immediate left, withdrew his IXth and IIIrd Corps from his left to support Gronau. This created a gap of some twenty miles wide between the First and Second Armies, and into it entered the British Army under Sir John French.

In the meantime Moltke, who had now established his G.H.Q. at Luxemburg, received just sufficient information to fill him with the gravest anxiety, and instead of going forward to co-ordinate the critical situation on the front of his First, Second and Third Armies, he selected as his emissary a junior staff officer, Lieutenant-Colonel Hentsch, and verbally empowered him, should he consider it necessary, to order the retreat of the right wing armies to the Aisne – surely one of the most extraordinary commissions ever entrusted to an inferior subordinate.

Hentsch set out on 8th September; he visited the Fifth, Fourth and Third Armies, and arrived at the headquarters of the Second at nightfall; there he found that Bülow had already decided to order his army to retreat on the following day. At 7 a.m. on the 9th Hentsch left for First Army headquarters; he found Kluck out, preoccupied with his battle with Maunoury, which was going against the latter, in spite of General Galliéni's[1] effort to save the situation by rushing the last reserves he could lay his hands on in Paris in taxi-cabs and 'buses to Maunoury's support. Instead of seeking out Kluck, Hentsch instructed General von Kuhl, Kluck's Chief of Staff, to order the First Army to retreat to Soissons, which, on his return, against his better judgement, Kluck complied with, and at the very moment when Maunoury was contemplating a withdrawal on Paris. Thus the Moltke-Schlieffen plan, created by the General Staff, was liquidated by the General Staff, because generalship was bankrupt.

On 13th September the Germans stood and faced their pursuers on the river Aisne – an almost stationary battle. Next, followed the race for the Channel, in which both sides attempted to outflank each other by bringing up corps from their respective eastern wings, but neither gained advantage over the other, and at length the sea was reached. In each move the

[1] Galliéni was Military Governor of Paris.

defender proved stronger than the attacker; the combination of bullet, spade and barbed wire, as Colonel Nickerson remarks, 'crushed every offensive on the Western Front so thoroughly that from October 1914 to March 1918 no attack or series of attacks was able to move the front line ten miles in either direction.'[1] Thus, as Bloch had predicted, the outcome was siege warfare, and Lord Kitchener exclaimed: 'I don't know what is to be done – this isn't war!'

3. *Strategy of Evasion*

The problem now became the reinstatment of mobility, and its solution depended on overcoming the defensive trinity of bullet, spade and wire. The soldiers set out to solve it in the conventional way, they turned to artillery and sought to blow a gap in their enemy's entrenched front. Had they considered the problem after the Russo-Japanese War, in which the power of the then recently introduced quick-firing gun had been demonstrated, they might have prevented the problem arising, as long as entrenchments were no more than shallow lines of field works – this will become apparent in the following Section. But as things stood in the autumn of 1914, they had neither sufficient guns nor sufficient shells to blast a gap, nor had they thought out the tactics of penetration.[2] They had failed to fathom the power of quick-firing artillery, and had overlooked that munition supply is based on industrial production.

As regards this latter oversight, the statesmen were even more to blame; for instance, in January 1914, Mr Lloyd George had publicly derided the possibility of war, and had urged that the season 'was the most favourable moment for twenty

[1] Op. cit. p. 280. 'The enemy', writes Private Frank Richards, 'rose up and started to advance. They were stopped at once: with the parapet as a rest for our rifles it was impossible to miss. The attack was over before it had hardly commenced . . . ten men holding a trench could easily stop fifty who were trying to take it' (*Old Soldiers Never Die* (1933), p. 36).

[2] Shortly before the outbreak of World War I, and when a student at the Camberley Staff College, the author discussed this problem in a paper entitled *The Tactics of Penetration*. Subsequently it was published in the November 1914 number of the *Journal of the Royal United Service Institution*.

years' to cut down expenditure on armaments.[1] So it came about that, before the war was a month old, because all belligerents had grossly underestimated the material demands of war, the supply of artillery ammunition began to fail, and the consequence was that all attempts to penetrate the Western Front ended in costly failure.

Exasperated by these unprofitable assaults, and ignorant of tactical considerations, the allied statesmen accused the soldiers of lack of imagination,[2] and set out to recapture mobility by a change of front, as if the locality itself was to blame for the stalemate. What they were unable to appreciate was, that should another locality be found in which the enemy's resistance was less formidable than on the Western Front, it would be only a matter of time before the same tactical conditions prevailed. It was the bullet, spade and wire which were the enemy on *every* front, and their geographical locations were purely incidental. Besides, as Napoleon had pointed out, to change one's line of operations is one of the most delicate of tasks; therefore it should never be undertaken 'light heartedly'.[3]

Should Clausewitz's statement be accepted, that in a war against an alliance the aim should be the defeat of the principal partner, because 'in that one we hit the common centre of gravity of the whole war', then, in 1914, the allied aim was to defeat Germany, since her defeat would carry with it the collapse of her allies. In what locality could Germany be most

[1] See *Soldiers and Statesmen*, Vol. I, p. 38. On 23rd July 1914, when he spoke on the Finance Bill in the House on Commons, Mr Lloyd George said: The movement against the expenditure on armaments 'is a cosmopolitan one and an international one. Whether it will bear fruit this year or next year, that I am not sure of, but I am certain that it will come. I can see signs, distinct signs, of reaction throughout the world' (*Parliamentary Debates*, 5th Series, Vol. LXV, col. 727). On the same day Austria presented Serbia with the ultimatum which detonated World War I!

[2] See *The World Crisis 1915*, Winston S. Churchill (1923), p. 20; and *War Memoirs of David Lloyd George* (1933), Vol. I, pp. 356 and 360. Churchill exclaimed: 'Confronted with this deadlock, military art remained dumb.' And Lloyd George said: 'The Allied generals were completely baffled by the decision of the Germans to dig in', and 'I can see no signs anywhere that our military leaders and guides are considering any plans for extricating us from our present unsatisfactory position.'

[3] *Corresp.*, XVII, No. 14343, and XXXII, p. 240.

profitably struck? The answer depended on the most practical allied line of operations, which, in its turn, was governed by the location of the allied main bases. They were France and Great Britain, and in no other area than France could the ponderous mass armies of this period be fully deployed and supplied in the field. The main bases and the main theatre of war were fixed by geography and logistics, and no juggling with fronts could alter this.

Because the allied governments had no common policy to direct them in the conduct of the war, and in spite of General Joffre's insistence that all available strength should be concentrated in France, once the stalemate set in a confusion of victory-winning plans was suggested by his British ally. In France, Sir John French proposed a joint military and naval operation to capture Ostend and Zeebrugge, in order to turn the German flank; Lord Fisher, First Sea Lord of the Admiralty, advocated a combined naval and military attack on the coast of Schleswig-Holstein; his master, Mr Churchill, First Lord of the Admiralty, pressed for an expedition against the Dardanelles; while, on 1st January 1915, Mr Lloyd George, Chancellor of the Exchequer, proposed that the B.E.F. in France, with the exception of a general reserve to be kept in England and Boulogne, should be withdrawn from France and sent to the Balkans.[1] Meanwhile, under the auspices of the Secretary of State for India, in October the Government of India dispatched a brigade to the Persian Gulf to protect the Persian Oil Company's refineries on the island of Abadan; and the Secretary of the Colonies was occupying himself with several small wars in Africa.

The masterful spirit among these would-be escapists from the stalemate was Mr Churchill, whose project to force the Dardanelles and occupy Constantinople and the Bosphorus began to dominate those of his competitors when, at the end of October, Turkey joined the Central Powers. Next, on 2nd January 1915, an unexpected call gave it the lead; that day

[1] See his 'Memorandum on War Strategy', which he placed before the War Council (*War Memoirs*, Vol. I, pp. 369-80). In it he suggested that an army of between 400,000 and 1,600,000 men, of which, hypothetically, 400,000 were Rumanians, Greek and Montenegrins, should be built up 'to attack Austria on her most vulnerable frontier.'

the Grand Duke Nicholas requested the British Military Mission attached to his headquarters to suggest to Lord Kitchener that if he could arrange for either a naval or military demonstration against Turkey it might ease the Russian situation on the Caucasian front. Without reference to the War Council or the Prime Minister, but with the approval of Mr Churchill, Kitchener telegraphed back that a demonstration would be made.[1] Thus was the fateful Dardanelles campaign initiated.

On 13th January, the forceful oratory of Mr Churchill persuaded the War Council to accept the project in the form of a local bombardment. Soon it grew into a major naval operation to force the Narrows, and finally it developed into a full scale combined operation, which comprised a battle fleet and an army of 75,000 men under General Sir Ian Hamilton. On 18th March, an abortive naval attack was made, in it three battleships were lost, and not until 25th April did the army set out to land on Cape Helles.

Although the Turkish forces opposing the invasion were insignificant, the invaders made so little headway that, before the day was out, General Sir William Birdwood, in command of the Australian and New Zealand Corps, suggested a complete withdrawal. To this counsel of despair Sir Ian Hamilton replied: 'You have got through the difficult business. Now you have only got to dig, dig, dig, until you are safe.'[2] Thus, within twelve hours of the first landings, bullet, spade and wire dominated the situation, and a minor Western Front was established, to endure until the final evacuation on 9th January 1916. In all, 410,000 British and French soldiers took part in the campaign, of whom 252,000 were killed, wounded, missing, prisoners, died of disease or evacuated sick.[3]

[1] Simultaneously Lord Kitchener asked Sir John French what views he held on the desirability of operating elsewhere than on the Western Front, to which Sir John replied: 'To attack Turkey would be to play the German game and to bring about the very end which Germany had in mind when she induced Turkey to join in the war, namely, to draw troops from the decisive spot, which is Germany itself' (*1914*, Field-Marshal Viscount French (1919), pp. 314–6).

[2] *Military Operations Gallipoli* (British Official History) Brig.-General G. F. Aspinall-Oglander (1929), Vol. I, p. 270.

[3] Ibid., Vol. II, p. 484.

As if the Gallipoli campaign was not a sufficient lesson to deter further experiments in escapist strategy, during the autumn of 1915 the French Government decided to send an expeditionary force to Serbia's assistance;[1] with this the British Government concurred, and British troops began to disembark at Salonika on 3rd October. This led to the Allied Macedonian campaign, or, as the Germans said: 'To the formation of the largest Allied "concentration camp", with "an enemy army prisoner of itself".'[2] For three years around Salonika, writes General Edmonds, 'a great Allied Force was locked up; in 1917 the average British strength was 202,265, besides French, Italians, Russians, Serbs, making a total of over 600,000 . . . and this force was guarded by half of the Bulgarian army with a little German stuffing.'[3] Once again the defensive trinity had proved invincible. The British bill for this escapade was a total of 481,262 sick admitted to hospital, and 26,750 casualties in action.

In the meantime the solitary brigade at Abadan, as a set-off for the Gallipoli failure and Salonika fiasco, had grown into an army, whose aim was to occupy Baghdad. Thus the costly Mesopotamian campaign came into being. On 7th December 1915, General Townshend and his army were invested by the Turks at Kut-al-Amara, where, on 29th April 1916, he surrendered with 10,061 British and Indian troops and 3,248 followers. 'From first to last the town had cost the Empire 40,000 casualties.'[4] By September 1917, the British ration strength had grown to about 340,000 and at the close of hostilities in 1918 it stood at over 414,000, of whom 217,000 were non-combatants. The total casualties were 93,500.

Besides these three large diversionary operations, a fourth emerged out of the protection of the Suez Canal. In January 1915, it was threatened by a medley of some 15,000 to 20,000 Turkish and Bedouin troops, who were easily dealt with, and

[1] This was the nominal reason; the actual one was to find a job for General Sarrail, who had great influence with the Left, which at the time threatened the downfall of the Government.

[2] *A Short History of World War I*, Sir James E. Edmonds (1951), p. 124.

[3] Ibid., p. 124.

[4] Ibid., p. 386.

up to December 1916, operations remained defensive in principle. Then, with the advent of Mr Lloyd George as Prime Minister, an offensive strategy was resorted to. All along he had held that Germany could best be defeated by destroying her allies – Clausewitz in reverse – and in search of a dazzling success which would consolidate his political position, he instructed his unwilling General Staff to consider an extension of the Canal operations to Palestine, with the capture of Jerusalem as the principal object. Thus another costly sideshow was born, which was to drag on until the end of the war. According to Sir William Robertson: 'The maximum number of troops employed in the Palestine campaign at one time amounted to 432,857, and the battle casualties to about 58,000. This figure, however, has little relation to the gross wastage, for the total number employed up to October, 1918, amounted in all ranks to 1,192,511.'[1]

All these peripheral endeavours to discover a penetrable front were a waste of effort, and in expenditure of man-power – the vital factor in mass-warfare – costly in the extreme. The stalemate laughed each to scorn.

4 · Strategy of Attrition

When, in the autumn of 1914, the Germans and British reached the English Channel near Nieuport, the Western Front assumed the shape of a huge salient which bulged westward between the sea and the Vosges with its apex near Compiègne. In 1915, Joffre's plan was to cut this salient off by a dual offensive: the British were to attack eastward in Artois and the French northward in Champagne. Throughout the war this plan remained the norm of French strategy, and in accordance with it a series of battles was fought in 1915, of which the most ambitious were the Third Battle of Artois – in it the British share was known as the Battle of Loos – (25th September–15th October), and the Second Battle of Champagne (25th September–6th October).

[1] *Soldiers and Statesmen*, Vol. II, p. 189. When casualties are omitted, the figures cited must include a large number of non-combatants. According to General Edmonds (op. cit., p. 376), the non-battle casualties (due to malaria, dysentry, etc.) numbered 503,377.

In all these battles, none of which did more than dent the salient, two things became apparent:

The first was the disproportion between losses and gains. For example, in the battle of Third Artois – Loos, the French and British respectively lost 48,200 and 48,267 men, and in the Second Battle of Champagne the French losses were 143,567. In both, no more than the German front line system of trenches, in places some 3,000 yards deep, was captured.

The second was that, in all the initial assaults of this year, mass artillery bombardments enabled the infantry to occupy parts of or all of the enemy's front line entrenchments. This went far to prove that, had a sufficiency of artillery existed during the mobile period of the war, it would have been possible to penetrate the unentrenched, or slightly entrenched, fronts of those days. This was one of the lessons Napoleon had taught his age, and he had said: 'It is only with artillery that one makes war.'[1] Now, when the opportunity had passed, and entrenched fronts were daily growing deeper and deeper, the French General Staff fondly imagined that they had discovered the secret of victory in the aphorism 'Artillery conquers, infantry occupies'. Tactics were reduced to a matter of push of pikes – actually push of shells – drill took the place of manoeuvre, method of surprise, and bombardments replaced leadership. Tactics, in fact, reverted to their level under the Spartans in the fifth century B.C., with one marked difference – the generals never went into battle.

It is understandable that the paltry gains and colossal losses of these artillery battles terrified the politicians and added fuel to their escapist policy. And there is this to be said for it: should attrition, as the generals urged, be accepted as the tactical norm, and should the Central Powers refuse to come to terms, there could be no end to the war except mutual extermination. On the other hand, because the war was a conflict between two alliances, no single member of either alliance was a free agent. Since the autumn of 1914 the Russians had suffered a series of disastrous defeats, therefore the Entente armies could not look idly on and leave their ally in the lurch. It was imperative to come to his aid, and only less so in order

[1] *Corresp.*, XIV, No. 11896.

to assure Italy who, in April 1915, had joined the Allies, that her partners were resolute.

The truth is, as Bloch had foreseen, that mass warfare, based on the magazine rifle and machine gun, if not impossible, as he declared it to be, was at best an unremunerative instrument of policy; nowhere could the bullet be escaped, and nowhere could a well-established entrenched system be decisively broken.

In the eastern theatre of the war, because of its vast spaces, fronts could frequently be turned, but in the western they stood inviolate. Nevertheless, it is strange that the soldiers so slowly fathomed the crucial difficulty in trench warfare. Experience had now taught them that with a sufficiency of artillery they could occupy their enemy's front line, and from this they concluded that, with more and more artillery, they would be able to take his second line, his third line, and so on until complete penetration was effected. What they failed to understand was, that the more shells they hurled at the enemy's entrenchments, the more would the surface of the ground be damaged, and from a normal battlefield it would grow into a crater area. Thus, in the removal of one obstacle they would create another, which would make forward movement so difficult that, even were the infantry to pass through the crater zone, they could not be supplied. Roads would have to be built through the chaos to enable the guns and supply vehicles to move forward, and by the time they were built, the enemy would be re-entrenched. Then another battle of penetration would have to be fought.

Undeterred by the holocausts of 1915, early in December, at an Allied conference, under the presidency of General Joffre, it was decided to prepare a 'maximum' offensive on the Western Front for the following spring. But before preparations were completed, the Germans struck at Verdun.

According to General Falkenhayn, who had succeeded Moltke as Chief of the German General Staff, the aim of the Verdun offensive was to weaken 'the enormous hold England still had on her allies', and because 'the strain on France had almost reached breaking-point', were Verdun wrested from her, 'that breaking-point would be reached and England's best sword knocked out of her hand.' Verdun was selected because its retention would compel the French General Staff 'to throw in every man they had. If they do so', writes Falkenhayn, 'the forces of France will bleed to death – as there can be no question of a voluntary withdrawal – whether we reach our goal or not.'[1] Verdun was, therefore, to be another battle of attrition.

On 21st February 1916, the battle was launched on a front of twenty miles, and although the French knew that it was impending, because its preliminary bombardment was limited to twenty-four hours, instead of the normal week or more, it came as a surprise to them. Fighting went on until 11th July, by when a penetration of five miles had been effected at a loss to the Germans of 281,000 men, and to the French of 315,000.

To relieve the pressure on Verdun, the long delayed Franco-British spring offensive, known as the Battle of the Somme, was launched on a twenty-five miles front on 1st July. It was preceded by a bombardment of eight days, in which 1,738,000 shells were poured onto the enemy's defences. Its tactical surprise was the introduction of the rolling barrage, under cover of which the infantry slowly moved forward from objective to objective. The battle continued until 14th November, by when a strip of ground some thirty miles long with a maximum depth of seven miles had been conquered at a cost of 419,654 British and 194,451 French casualties. The German losses were probably in the neighbourhood of half a million.

Although Sir Douglas Haig[2] was well pleased with the results of the battle, and in his *Dispatch* stated that it had 'placed beyond doubt the ability of the Allies' to achieve their aim; and although Sir William Robertson urged the government to prepare for 'harder and more protracted fighting and a much greater strain on resources than as yet experienced',[3] the enormous losses sustained had a violent repercussion on the political situation.

[1] *General Headquarters and its Critical Decision*, General Erich von Falkenhayn (English trans., 1919), p. 209 *et. seq.*

[2] He succeeded Sir John French as C. in C. on 15th December 1915, and eight days later Sir William Robertson, C.G.S. to Sir John French, was appointed C.I.G.S., and Lieut.-General Sir L. Kiggell replaced him. All three were ardent exponents of the strategy of attrition.

[3] *Soldiers and Statesmen*, Vol. I, p. 279.

With the Battle of the Somme the stalemate on all fronts became complete. The Italians had bled themselves white in eight Battles of the Isonzo, and on the Eastern Front, although the Brussilov offensive had succeeded in capturing an enormous number of Austrians, it had cost Russia a million men. Because there seemed to be no hope of forcing a decision in the field, the question of peace negotiations began to be considered in London, Berlin and Vienna. On 14th November, Lord Lansdowne, Minister without Portfolio in the Asquith coalition, suggested that the possibilities of peace should be examined; but on 7th December the Asquith administration fell, and Lloyd George, who was pledged to a more vigorous prosecution of the war, took over the government. Five days later Germany and her allies put forward notes in which they stated their willingness to consider peace proposals.

Although Austria's desire for peace was undoubtedly genuine, it may be questioned whether Germany's was. Russia was now tottering, and when she collapsed, Germany would be able to transfer a million men to the Western Front. Anyhow the outcome was that, on 31st January 1917, the Kaiser commanded that the U-boat campaign should be placed on an unrestricted footing. This so exasperated the United States that two days later diplomatic relations between Washington and Berlin were severed.

Meanwhile, on 15th November 1916, at an Allied conference assembled to consider the 1917 plan of campaign, the decision was to carry out a series of offensives on all fronts, with the Western Front as the principal one. A month later General Nivelle who, on 13th December had succeeded Joffre as French C.-in-C., accepted the decision, and it was agreed that the British should first attack on the Arras front to draw in and exhaust the enemy's reserves, after which the French would attack on the Aisne. The French aim was a decisive one, to break through the enemy's position; but should the rupture be found to be insufficient, the battle was to be broken off, and the offensive transferred to the Flanders front.

The first of these battles opened on 9th April, and was heralded by a bombardment of 2,700,000 shells. It was continued until 21st May, by when an advance of five miles had been made on a frontage of twenty miles, and up to 3rd May at a cost of 158,000 British casualties and an estimated 150,000 German. Eight days after it was launched, the French offensive on the Aisne opened and failed. It cost the French 187,000 casualties[1] and the Germans 163,000. Nivelle was replaced by General Pétain, and the demoralization of the French was such that, between 25th May and 10th June, fifty-four divisions mutinied.

In the meantime two events changed the entire aspect of the war. On 8th March riots broke out in Petrograd; on the 11th the Imperial Guard mutinied, and the next day revolution swept the city. On the 15th Tzar Nicholas II abdicated, and a provisional government was formed under Prince Lvov which, on the 22nd, was formally recognized by the Allied Powers. The second event was the declaration of war on Germany by the United States on 6th April.

What did these events portend? Two immense blood transfusions for the French theatre of war. Because a nation cannot hope to wage a successful major war when in the throes of revolution, Germany had every right to expect that, before the year was out, she would be able to reinforce the Western Front with at least a million men. Also Great Britain and France had every right to expect that, at some date in the not too distant future, they would be reinforced by at least a million Americans. So it came about that, because France was in a parlous condition, the Ribot administration, which in March had succeeded to the Briand, proposed that all offensive operations should be deferred until American assistance became available.

Haig, Robertson, Pétain and Nivelle thought otherwise. 'We are all of opinion', wrote Robertson in an official memorandum, 'that our object can be obtained by relentlessly attacking with limited objectives, while making the fullest use of our artillery. By this means we hope to gain our ends with the minimum loss possible.'[2] This policy was accepted by Mr Lloyd George, but soon after he recanted, and reverted to a

[1] The French Official History, based on Nivelle's returns, mentions 96,128, and another estimate 118,000 between 16th–30th April.

[2] *Soldiers and Statesmen*, Vol. II, p. 235.

plan he had advocated in January, to combine with Italy in an attack on Austria.

Actually, a limited offensive was not what Haig cherished. Ever since he became C.-in-C. in December 1915, he had set his heart on a decisive battle in Flanders, and so obsessed was he by it that he believed he could beat the Germans single-handed, and before the Americans came in.

The outcome was the costly Flanders campaign of the summer and autumn. On 7th June it was opened by the limited and successful Battle of Messines, which was preceded by a seventeen days' bombardment of 3,500,000 shells, and initiated by the explosion of nineteen mines packed with a million pounds of high explosives. It closed on 14th June, when the British casualties numbered 17,000 and the Germans 25,000, including 7,500 prisoners. According to Professor Cruttwell, 'it seems to have been the first considerable battle in which the British losses were less than those of the Germans.'[1]

On 31st July it was followed by the Third Battle of Ypres, for which the largest force of artillery ever seen in British history was assembled. In all, the preliminary bombardment lasted nineteen days, and during it 4,300,000 shells, some 107,000 tons in weight, were hurled onto the prospective low lying battlefield. Its entire surface was upheaved; all drains, dikes, culverts and roads were destroyed, and an almost uncrossable swamp created, in which the infantry wallowed for three and a half months. When, on 10th November, the battle ended, the Germans had been pushed back a maximum depth of five miles on a frontage of ten miles, at a cost of a little under 200,000 men to themselves, and, at the lowest estimate, of 300,000 to their enemy.[2]

Thus ended the last of the great artillery battles of attrition on the Western Front, and when in retrospect they are looked on, it becomes understandable why the politicians were so eager to escape them.

[1] *A History of the Great War, 1914–1918* (1934), p. 438.

[2] These are Captain B. H. Liddell Hart's estimates, see *Journal of the Royal United Service Institution*, November 1959. For purposes of propaganda, the British official historian's figures are cooked.

5 · *Rebirth of Mobility*

The reinstatement of mobility was at bottom a human problem. Without the rifleman, trenches were no more than ditches and entanglements fences. It was the man with the rifle or machine gun in the trench and behind the wire who gave tactical value to both; therefore the solution lay either in eliminating him or in disarming him. Could one or the other be done without months of preparation, which prohibited surprise, and without upheaving the surface of the battlefield, which impeded forward wheeled movement, the problem was solvable.

The first step toward the solution was taken by the Germans. In spite of being a party to the Hague Convention of 1899, which prohibited the use of poisons as weapons, they decided to adopt Dundonald's proposal of 1812 and 1855, and asphyxiate their enemy's trench garrisons with toxic gas. They selected chlorine, a common commercial product easily obtainable in quantity, and the method of discharge was to be from metal cylinders built into the front line parapet. Fortunately for the British and French, the Germans failed to realize that they had a battle winner, and instead of waiting until they had accumulated sufficient cylinders to asphyxiate a wide front, so it would appear, they looked upon their lethal gas attack as a minor experiment. The locality selected was a section of the north-eastern face of the Ypres salient, at the junction of the French and British lines, held by the Turcos and Canadians.

The attack was made at 5 p.m. on 22nd April 1915. It opened with a furious bombardment, and as it ceased a greenish-yellow gas rose from the German front line and drifted toward the enemy. Its effect was devastating; all men close to the front were choked to death, and those on the edges of the gas cloud broke to the rear in wild panic. Gas was again discharged on the 24th, and the outcome was that the Franco-British line was compelled to fall back three miles nearer in to Ypres. What the Germans had failed to reckon, was that a chlorine gas attack was unlikely to be repeated with equal success, because it could be countered by means of masks or cloth helmets impregnated with a suitable solution. These were immediately introduced by the Entente armies, and in 1916 were replaced by the box respirator.[1]

Gas cloud attack had many drawbacks; for effectiveness it depended wholly on the direction and velocity of the wind; the cylinders were cumbersome to transport and install, and when installed it was demoralizing for men to live alongside them, possible for weeks on end, during which enemy bombardment, or a casual shell, might detonate them. Also it was a purely static method of attack.

These disadvantages were overcome by the introduction of the gas shell,[2] which was largely independent of wind, which enabled sudden concentrations of gas to be landed on selected targets, which needed no special training, and which above all was a mobile method of attack. The sole disadvantage was that the shell was so small a container, but this was in part overcome by the introduction of more potent gases than chlorine, notably phosgene and mustard gas.

The latter, also called Yellow Cross and Yperite, is a remarkably persistent chemical and a powerful vesicant. It seldom kills, but men who come into contact with it, either as a liquid or a vapour, suffer severe blistering of the skin; the burns appear from four to twelve hours after exposure, and heal very slowly. Because one part of it in 4,000,000 of air will cause blisters, it is eminently suited for artillery shells, and a few are sufficient to cause many casualties hours or even days later, because its persistence is very slowly destroyed by earth.

Mustard gas was first used by the Germans in the Ypres Salient on 11th July 1917, and in the following six weeks it caused over 20,000 British casualties. From then on the British and French set out to manufacture it in large quantities.

The first skilful use of gas to effect a penetration was made in General von Hutier's attack on the Riga front on 1st September 1917. He selected a sector of the Russian lines of

[1] In 1854, the year before Lord Dundonald suggested to Lord Panmure the use of sulphur fumes as an asphyxiant, Dr J. Stenhouse invented the first charcoal respirator.

[2] Also, for short ranges, the mortar bomb and the Livens projector. The latter fired a cylinder which held 30 lb. of gas; it could rapidly be erected in a shallow trench, and fired in batteries of 100 to 500 at a time. On one occasion the British fired 2,500 into Lens.

no more than 4,600 yards in width; massed against it a powerful force of artillery – one gun to every eight yards – inundated it with gas shells, and then attacked. The whole operation was over in a few hours, and its success was due to his tactics, the aim of which was, not to demolish wire and trenches, but to incapacitate their defenders.

These tactics were consistently resorted to by the Germans in their great battles on the Western Front in March, April, May and June 1918. In them phosgene and mustard gas were used on a lavish scale before each was launched, with the aim of destroying the enemy's morale. Between 21st March and 5th April gas was one of the most important factors[1] that enabled the Germans to drive the British back on a front fifty miles between Arras and La Fère, and advance to a depth of nearly forty miles. And, in April, Armentières was inundated with mustard gas to such an extent that it is said to have run in the gutters of its streets. It enabled the Germans to take the town, without entering it, at practically no loss of life.

In the American attack on the St Mihiel Salient in September 1918, and in subsequent operations, severe casualties were inflicted by German gas shelling. And it is instructive to note that, out of the total American casualties suffered in the war – namely 258,338 – 70,752, or 27.4 per cent., were gas casualties.[2] Also, while 46,419 of the total casualties were fatal, only 1,400 due to gas resulted in death – that is, 2 per cent. compared with 24.85 per cent. Contrary to common belief, gas was the most humane weapon used in the war, and one of the most effective; even when the respirator gave 100 per cent. immunity, when worn it reduced the soldier to half a fighting man, and it gave little protection against mustard gas.

The second step toward solving the stalemate was, as we have said, to disarm the defender by rendering his rifles and machine guns ineffective. This could be done by protecting the attacker with a bullet-proof shield of sufficient size to cover

[1] In volume II, p. 597 of his memoirs General Ludendorff writes: '. . . our artillery relied on gas for its effect;' and on p. 579: that the artillery bombardment was to be powerful and short, 'to paralyse the enemy's artillery' and 'keep the infantry in their dug-outs.'

[2] See *Chemical Warfare*, Brigadier-General Amos A. Fries and Major Clarence J. West (1921), p. 388.

his body when in movement. As it would be too heavy for him to carry, it would have to be mounted on a self-propelled vehicle, which also would need to be armoured, and because this vehicle would have to move off the roads and over an entrenched battlefield, it would have to be provided with caterpillar tracks instead of wheels. These three requirements led to the introduction of the tank, a small mobile fort, or, as it was first called, 'a land ship'.

The idea was an exceedingly old one, but was impracticable until the invention of the internal combustion engine, and no sooner did the stalemate set in than independently in Britain and France a number of imaginative men put forward various suggestions on how armour could reinstate mobility.[1]

Tanks were first used on 15th September 1916, during the Battle of the Somme. Due to mechanical breakdowns and the difficulties of the cratered and entrenched battlefield few got into action, but those which did showed that, with improved machinery and increased numbers used in mass, instead of in driblets, the stalemate might be broken. This is borne out by the German account which said, 'that their men felt powerless to withstand the tanks'[2] – that is, felt themselves disarmed. Unfortunately this was not appreciated by the British High Command, with the result that, until the Battle of Cambrai, tanks continued to be used in driblets.

At Cambrai, the aim was to effect a surprise penetration of four lines of entrenchments in twelve hours without any kind of preliminary artillery preparation. Nine battalions of tanks, in all 378 fighting machines, were to lead two infantry corps over the Hindenburg (Siegfried) Line, the most formidable entrenched system on the Western Front. It was protected by immensely deep fields of wire, many on the reverse slopes, and to cut them would have required several weeks' bombardment and scores of thousands of tons of shells.

The assault was launched over undamaged ground at 6.20 a.m. on 20th November 1917. The enemy broke back in panic, and by 4 p.m., from a base of 13,000 yards, a penetration of

[1] See *The Tanks, the History of the Royal Tank Regiment and its Predecessors*, Captain B. H. Liddell Hart (1959), Vol. I, Chap. II.

[2] Ibid., Vol. I, p. 75.

10,000 yards had been effected. At the Third Battle of Ypres an equivalent advance without penetration took over three months. Eight thousand prisoners and one hundred guns were captured; the prisoners alone numbered nearly double the casualties sustained by the two attacking corps.

Although lack of reserves led to the battle ending in a severe repulse, there could no longer be any doubt that the re-introduction of armour on the battlefield, as mooted by Jomini nearly a century earlier, could solve the stalemate, and the decisive battle of Amiens, fought on 8th August 1918, proved this conclusively.

In it 462 fighting tanks, in co-operation with aircraft, led three corps of the British Fourth Army, under command of General Sir Henry Rawlinson, into battle.[1] Again surprise was complete, panic rampant, and the German front was penetrated.

'As the sun set on 8th August on the battlefield', writes the author of the German official monograph on the battle, 'the greatest defeat which the German Army suffered since the beginning of the war was an accomplished fact.'[2] It was the terror the tanks instilled, more so than their killing power, which led him to entitle his monograph *Die Katastrophe des* 8 *August, 1918*. It precipitated, not the final retirement after a ding-dong battle, but an initial rout without fighting – this was the unexpected novelty. Without the tank there would have been no surprise commensurate with the one achieved, and it was the suddenness of the assault which detonated the panic. Added to this, the feeling of utter powerlessness of the soldier on foot, when faced with an antagonist no rifle or machine gun bullet could halt, instinctively led him to exaggerate the danger in order to mitigate the ignominy of immediate surrender or flight – the tank was a psychological, more so than a material weapon.

Ludendorff made no mistake over the situation the tank created. 'Everything I had feared, and of which I had so often given warning', he writes, 'had here, in one place, become a

[1] On his right flank he was supported by the French First Army, which had no tanks.

[2] Cited in the *British Official History, 1918*, Vol. IV, p. 88.

reality. . . . The 8th of August put the decline of [our] fighting power beyond all doubt. . . . I became convinced that we were now without that safe foundation for the plans of G.H.Q., on which I had hitherto been able to build, at least so far as this is possible in war. Leadership now assumed, as I then stated, the character of an irresponsible game of chance, a thing I have always considered fatal. The fate of the German people was for me too high a stake. The war must be ended.'[1]

6 · *Collapse on the Inner Fronts*

Although concentrated gas bombardments and massed tank assaults proved that an enemy's entrenched front could be broken, they did no more than unlock the gate of the stalemate. To reinstate full mobility demanded that rapid penetration be followed by rapid exploitation, not by cavalry – the prevalent idea – but by tank forces, which could be supplied by cross-country transport – that is, by vehicles mounted on caterpillar tracks. In 1918 they did not exist; therefore full mobility could not be regained, and the result was, as Bloch had foreseen, the war was brought to an end, not by fighting, but by famine and revolution.

Besides the ever-increasing exhaustion due to the length of the war, the two most important factors accountable for the collapse of the Central Powers were the British blockade and the skilful use made by the British Government of propaganda: the one struck at the vitals of the enemy, and the other undermined his moral endurance.

Already by the spring of 1917 all belligerents were so war weary that the contagion of the March Revolution in Russia swept westward like wildfire. The mutinies in the French army were largely accountable to it;[2] German troops in Russia became infected; in Italy it contributed to the disaster of Caporetto, when 400,000 soldiers abandoned the battlefield; and, as early as 26th May, in a letter to Sir Douglas Haig, Sir William Robertson wrote: 'I am afraid there is no getting

[1] *My War Memoirs 1914–1918*, Vol. II, p. 684.

[2] Already, on 16th April, the Russian brigades which had been sent to France in 1916 – whose favourite paper was edited by Trotsky until he was expelled – had mutinied in their camp at La Courtine, and only surrendered after a three days' bombardment.

away from the fact that there is some unrest in the country now as a result, partly, of the Russian revolution. There have been some bad strikes recently, and there is still much discontent.'[1]

When the war opened, the blockade was hamstrung by the Declaration of London, and it only became effective when its restrictions had been progressively whittled away by a series of British Orders in Council. The second of these Orders, issued on 29th October 1914, severely curtailed supplies entering Germany and Austria, and, on 4th February 1915, the German reply was, that all waters surrounding Great Britain and Ireland would be blockaded by submarines. On 7th May this led to the sinking of the *Lusitania* and the loss of 128 American lives. It sent a thrill of horror through the United States and raised a clamour for war. Freed from American opposition to search at sea, on 15th May, by another Order in Council the British Government declared goods of all kinds entering or leaving Germany contraband. Thus full blockade was established, and the Kaiser, alarmed by the American outcry, ordered all attacks on passenger and neutral shipping to cease. So matters stood until 31st January 1917, when, as we have seen, he proclaimed an unrestricted submarine campaign, and in April the United States declared war on Germany.

The blockade struck at every man, woman and child, every factory and every farm in the enemy countries, and by the summer of 1918, had it not been for the wheat of Rumania and the Ukraine, the Central Powers would have been starved into capitulation. By then, cattle in Austria and Hungary had, since August 1914, decreased from 17,324,000 to 3,518,000, and pigs from 7,678,000 to 214,000.[2] Also it has been estimated that, during the last two years of the blockade, '800,000 noncombatants died in Germany from starvation or diseases directly attributed to under-nourishment – about fifty times more than were drowned by submarine attack on British shipping.'[3]

[1] *Soldiers and Statesmen*, Vol. I, p. 313.

[2] *Military Operations, Italy, 1915–1919* (British Official History, 1949), p. 379.

[3] *Unfinished Victory*, Arthur Bryant (1940), p. 3. See also pp. 9–10.

The strangle-hold of the blockade created a fertile soil for sowing the seeds of propaganda, and – not excepting the American Civil War – in no previous war was it so virulent and vile. In the Napoleonic and Franco-Prussian Wars, instead of fostering revolt in enemy countries, belligerents guarded against stimulating it. Napoleon could to his advantage have unleashed the 'pent-up animosity' of the Russian serfs and Ukrainians in 1812, and have stirred up a revolution in France during the Hundred Days, but he refrained to do so.[1] The Duke of Wellington, as he himself tells us, had a horror of fomenting revolution in any country; and, in 1871, Bismarck did not befriend the Paris Commune. The reason was that, in times past, war was waged to change the enemy's policy, and not to change his government – the policy maker. Its aim was to change the government's mind, and should the government be overthrown, there would be no stable authority to negotiate a peace with. The world was then still sane, and the idea of creating a social anarchy in an enemy's country would have been considered contrary to common sense.

War by propaganda is pre-eminently a democratic instrument, fashioned to dominate the mass-mind – Rousseau's 'general will'. Its purposes are: (1) to stimulate the mass-mind on the home front; (2) to win to one's support the mass-minds of neutral nations; and (3) to subvert the mass-mind on the enemy's inner front.

The first is accomplished by awakening the tribal instincts latent in man, and, in order to focus these instincts, to transform the enemy into a devil.

The aim of the second category is to bring neutral nations to accept and believe in the reality of this monstrosity, as British propaganda successfully did in the United States. Fired by notions, such as that German soldiers cut off the hands of Belgian children and crucified their prisoners[2] '. . . . the American people launched themselves into war with an emotional hysteria that can only be understood by realizing the power of propaganda in generating common action by a

[1] *Napoleon*, Eugene Tarle (1936), pp. 289 and 381.

[2] For a long list of these alleged atrocities see *Falsehood in War Time*, Arthur Ponsonby (1936).

nation under belligerent conditions. . . . The almost primitive ecstasy that could sometimes grip the American people has been recently summarized in unforgettable fashion:

' "We hated with a common hate that was exhilarating. The writer of this review remembers attending a great meeting in New England, held under the auspices of a Christian Church – God save the mark! A speaker demanded that the Kaiser, when captured, be boiled in oil, and the entire audience stood on chairs to scream its hysterical approval. This was the mood we were in. This was the kind of madness that had seized us." '[1]

'One of the most appalling revelations of the entire war', write Morison and Commager, 'was the ease with which modern technique and mass-suggestion enables a government to make even a reasonably intelligent people, with an individualistic, democratic background, believe anything it likes.'[2]

The aim of the third category was to rot the enemy pscyhologically by subverting the loyalty of his people and his armed forces – to disarm them morally. So insidious was this form of attack that in his memoirs Ludendorff again and again refers to it and the blockade as the most potent factors in Germany's defeat. He writes:

'The strangling hunger blockade and the enemy's propaganda, which went hand in hand in the fight against the German race and spirit, were a heavy burden – a burden that grew ever heavier as the war lasted. . . . Blockade and propaganda began gradually to undermine the moral resolution and shake the belief in ultimate victory. . . . All German sentiment, all patriotism, died in many breasts. Self came first. . . . We lost confidence in ourselves. . . . The idea of revolution, preached by enemy propaganda and Bolshevism, found the Germans in a receptive frame of mind. . . . Pernicious doctrines spread among the masses. The German people at home and the front, had received its death blow. . . . We were hypnotized by the enemy propaganda as a rabbit is by a snake. It worked by strong mass-suggestion, kept in close touch with the military

[1] *British Propaganda at Home and in the United States from 1914 to 1917*, James Duane Squires (1935), pp. 67–68. In the Appendix is listed 277 publications and books of British propaganda sent to the United States between the above dates.

[2] *The growth of the American Republic* (1942), Vol. II, p. 479.

situation, and was unscrupulous as to the means it used. . . . In the last stages of the war, and quite openly from the beginning of 1918 onwards, propaganda worked ever more clearly for the social revolution, side by side with the political revolution. The war was painted as being waged by the upper ten thousand at the expense of the workers, and the victory of Germany as the workers' misfortune. . . . In the neutral countries we were subjected to a sort of moral blockade. . . . We lost all credit, while that of the enemy rose immeasurably. . . . The express aim of the American and English propaganda became more and more the achievement of an internal revolution in Germany.'[1]

When Ludendorff mentions that from the beginning of 1918 Allied propaganda worked for a social revolution, clearly he had President Wilson's 'Fourteen Points' in mind, which were announced by him on 8th January.[2] A month later the President further declared: that there were to be no annexations, no contributions, and no punitive damages. Self-determination was to be accepted as an imperative principle, and every territorial settlement was to be made in the interest and for the benefit of the people concerned.

Although the Fourteen Points were not meant to be propaganda, actually they were propaganda of an astute kind. They caught the imagination of a war weary world, and presented Germany with the opportunity to end the war by a negotiated peace. Though, at the time, the Kaiser and his advisers refused to consider them, they sank deep into the hearts of the German people, and eventually brought the war to an ignominious end.

Overwhelmed by the battle of 8th August and the defeats which followed it, on 28th September Ludendorff entered Field-Marshal Hindenburg's room and suggested that an armistice could no longer be delayed. 'We did not consider any abandonment of territory in the East,' he writes, 'thinking that the Entente would be fully conscious of the danger threatening

[1] *My War Memoirs*, Vol. I, pp. 360–8. The German Government, he writes, did not 'understand the nature of propaganda. They were opposed to it on the ground that it was too blatant and vulgar' (Vol. I, p. 380). There was no Ministry of Propaganda in Germany (Vol. II, p. 701).

[2] See Appendix II.

them as well as ourselves from Bolshevism.'[1] In this he was mistaken.

On 3rd October the German Chancellor addressed a note to President Wilson in which he stated that the German Government accepted the 'Fourteen Points' and subsequent pronouncements as a basis for peace negotiations. Diplomatic exchanges followed until 23rd October, when the President, who should have realized that, because of the revolutionary conditions prevailing, the one thing needed to implement his programme was to salve what remained of European stability, instead of attempting, so far as it lay within his power, to add vigour to the existing enemy governments, and on no account weaken them, set out to destroy them. On that day he informed the German Government that, were he compelled to negotiate with the military rulers and monarchist autocrats in Germany, he would demand not peace negotiations but a general surrender. This meant the abdication of the existing German Government and its replacement by a revolutionary Socialist assembly. On 3rd November the German crews at Kiel mutinied and Berlin was swept by revolution; on the 9th the Kaiser abdicated, and on the 11th, at Rethondes Station in the forest of Compiègne an armistice was concluded between the Allied and Associated Powers and Germany.

Much the same happened to the Austro-Hungarian Empire, because Wilson insisted that the complete satisfaction of the Austrian and Hungarian Slavs should be a condition of the armistice. Thereupon autonomous governments were formed in Budapest, Prague, Laibach, Serajevo, Cracow and Lemberg, and a neutral government was set up in Vienna to liquidate the central administration. On 12th November the Emperor Karl renounced his share in it, after which a republic was proclaimed in Vienna and the ancient Austro-Hungarian monarchy ceased to exist.

Thus chaos was planted in Europe.

[1] Ibid., Vol. II, p. 721.

CHAPTER X

Lenin and the Russian Revolution

*

1 · Lenin and the March Revolution

The Petrograd revolution of March 1917 was a popular and not a revolutionary rising, brought about by war weariness and universal discontent. At the time there were three parties in the Duma, the Constitutional Democrats, or 'Cadets', who stood for a constitutional monarchy; the Social Democrats, who were Marxists, and the Social Revolutionaries, who represented the peasants. When on 15th March Nicholas II abdicated, it was the first of these parties which picked up his sceptre, and, on the 22nd, formed a Provisional Coalition Government under Prince Gregori Lvov.

In spite of the general outcry for peace, the Provisional Government determined to remain loyal to Russia's allies and to continue the war, a decision which was at once challenged by the Petrograd Soviet[1] which, on 27th March, issued a proclamation to the peoples of the world calling for an immediate cessation of hostilities.[2] Because it represented the most important elements of actual power – the soldiers, factory hands, railway workers, postal, telegraph and other services – and because it voiced the yearnings of the people, the authority of the Provisional Government was stillborn. This separation of responsibility and power unbarred the road to Lenin, and chaotically led to the October Revolution.[3]

Vladimir Ilyich Ulyanov (1870–1924), better known as

[1] Soviets were first formed in 1905. They originated as strike committees which developed into local popular parliaments elected by the workers, soldiers and peasants. Any group was free to form a Soviet.

[2] The minority states also had had enough of the war, and in succession, Finland, Estonia, Poland, Lithuania, the Ukraine, Caucasia and Siberia demanded either independence or autonomy.

[3] Until 1918 Russia adhered to the Julian Calendar, which was then thirteen days in arrears of the Gregorian, introduced in 1582. According to the former, Lenin's seizure of power occurred on 25th October, that is on 7th November according to the latter.

Lenin, was both an ardent and unorthodox Marxist. By rejecting the dogma that the new social order would only mature when Capitalism had reduced all but the capitalists themselves to a proletarian level, he knocked the bottom out of Marx's historical dialectics.[1]

When the March Revolution detonated in Petrograd, he was a penniless refugee in Switzerland; he lived in a single room in Zurich rented from a cobbler; of his small band of followers in Russia many were in prison, and to the outer world he was virtually unknown. He had been in Switzerland since the war began, and had spent his time inveighing against his opponents and stimulating his followers. For him, the war had but one purpose – the destruction of the capitalist system by converting it into a proletarian civil war. He called for the utilization of every means of subversion, the organization of strikes, street demonstrations, and propaganda in the trenches: 'Civil war, not civil peace – that is the slogan!'[2]

When the war opened, besides fighting the Russian army in the field, German policy included an attack on Russia's inner front by the promotion of independence movements in her minority countries and by the employment of emigrant Russian revolutionaries to stir up trouble in the Russian armies and factories.[3]

In March 1915, through an agent, the German Supreme Command first contacted Lenin in Zurich. But when they found that his aim was not the defeat of Russia for the benefit of Germany but instead to overthrow Tzardom, in order to precipitate a world-wide proletarian revolution, contact was broken off until the outbreak of the March Revolution, when it was resumed in the following circumstances.

On 16th March 1917, when Lenin's wife, Krupskaya, was washing the dishes after their midday meal, suddenly a Polish

[1] According to Marxist dialectics, it was contrary to the laws of history that a proletarian revolution could take place in a predominantly peasant country, in which the population was lost, as Marx had written, in 'the idiocy of rural life' (*Communist Manifesto*, p. 18). And nothing enraged him more than Slavophilism with its belief that it was the mission of Russia to regenerate the West. (R. N. Carew Hunt, *The Theory and Practice of Communism* (1950), p. 131).

[2] *Lenin's Collected Works* (English edition, 1930), Vol. XVIII, p. 478.

[3] Compare Clausewitz's *On War*, Vol. III, p. 159, see *supra* p. 75.

friend burst into the room and breathlessly exclaimed: 'Have you heard the news? – There is a revolution in Russia!' Although sceptical as to its value, since it was a purely bourgeois upheaval, Lenin decided to return to Russia, and wrote to a friend to obtain a passport for him. The request was forwarded to Baron Romberg, German Minister in Berne, who passed it on to Berlin and asked for instructions.

Meanwhile Lenin was engaged in writing his 'Letters from Afar' for *Pravda*, in which he likened all the belligerents to 'One bloody clot',[1] and made it plain that his aim was to promote civil war in Russia and overthrow the Provisional Government. Because the German Supreme Command was by now aware that the Provisional Government had no intention of abandoning the war, and because it was imperative to bring the war to a close, so that troops might be transferred from the Eastern to the Western Front, on receipt of Romberg's message they decided to accept the gamble and send Lenin back to Russia. Accordingly Romberg was instructed to arrange for the transport of Lenin and thirty-one other revolutionaires, including nineteen Bolsheviks, across Germany into Sweden. 'At the time', writes General Hoffmann, 'nobody could foresee the fatal consequences that the appearance of those men would have for Russia and for the whole of Europe.'[2] Nevertheless, the German General Staff was fully aware of Lenin's aim.

So it came about that the Rubicon of World Revolution was crossed; Lenin and his army of nineteen followers steamed out of Berne fully intent, not only to wreck the Provisional Government, but also to carry on a revolutionary struggle against the German bourgeoisie. Immediately before his departure he wrote to the Swiss workers: 'We will . . . carry on a revolutionary struggle against the Germans. . . . The German proletariat is the most trustworthy, the most reliable ally of the Russian and the world proletarian revolutions.'[3]

Lenin arrived in Petrograd on the night of 16th April, and

[1] See *Selected Works*, pp. 735–42 for the First Letter.
[2] *War Diaries and other Papers*, Major-General Max Hoffmann, (English edition, 1929), Vol. II, p. 177.
[3] *Collected Works*, Vol. XX, pp. 85. 87.

on the following day he addressed the All-Russian Conference of Soviets. He demanded widespread propaganda in the army, in order to convert the war from an imperialist into a proletarian one; the overthrow of the Provisonal Government and its replacement by 'A republic of Soviets of Workers', Agricultural Labourers' and Peasants' Deputies'. From then on, daily, almost hourly, he harangued the Petrograd crowds, fanned revolt, inveighed against the war, and promised all and sundry whatever they desired.

At length, on 1st July, in order to honour their word, the Provisional Government resumed the offensive against Germany. At first it met with success, but when, on the 19th, the Germans counter-attacked, by then Bolshevik agents, planted by Lenin in the Russian divisions, had so completely undermined the loyalty of the soldiers that regiment after regiment mutinied, murdered their officers and then disbanded. This and the simultaneous declaration of autonomy on the part of the Ukraine led to the fall of the Lvov administration, which, on 22nd July, was succeeded by one under Alexander Kerensky as Prime Minister with a Cabinet drawn from the representatives of all parties with the exception of the Monarchists and Bolsheviks – the extreme Right and Left. In the midst of the confusion the Bolshevik headquarters in Petrograd were suppressed; Trotsky and many Bolsheviks were arrested, and Lenin, disguised as an engine-driver, escaped to Finland, and there remained in hiding during the following three months.

2 · '*The State and the Revolution*'

In Finland, Lenin kept in touch with the situation in Petrograd, and spent his time writing one of his most noted pamphlets, *The State and the Revolution: The Marxist Doctrine of the State and the Tasks of the Proletariat in the Revolution.*[1]

It is a revealing document, because it shows that Lenin, who possessed a clear intellect and a will of iron was fundamentally a utopian. Although, time and again, when action demanded, he subordinated Marx's dogmas to the conditions of the moment, when not so engaged he was quite unable to see beyond the dreamland of *The Communist Manifesto.* Also, it

[1] *Selected Works,* Vol. II, pp. 143–225.

is extraordinary that, after more than twenty years of revolutionary activities, it was still necessary for him to instruct his followers in what he must have told them scores of times. Nevertheless, because the October Revolution was founded on this rehash of Marx, it is as well to cite a few of its more pertinent passages.

Because the State is an organ of class rule, the inevitable conclusion is 'that the proletariat cannot overthrow the bourgeoisie without first capturing political power' and 'without transforming the State into the "proletariat organized as the ruling class".' This leads 'to the conclusion that this proletarian state will begin to wither away immediately after its victory, because the state is unnecessary and cannot exist in a society in which there are no class antagonisms' (p. 159).

Therefore the revolution must '*concentrate all its forces of destruction* against the state power, and to regard the problem, not as one of perfecting the state machine, but one of *smashing* and destroying it' (p. 161).

'We are not utopians . . . we want the Socialist revolution with human nature as it is now, with human nature that cannot dispense with subordination, control and "foremen and clerks".

'But the subordination must be to the armed vanguard of all the exploited, of all the toilers, *i.e.*, to the proletariat. Measures can and must be taken at once, overnight, to substitute for the specific "official grandeur" of state officials the simple functions of "workmen and manager", functions which are already fully within the capacity of the average city dweller and can well be performed for "workmen's wages".

'*We ourselves*, the workers, will organize large-scale production on the basis of what capitalism has already created, relying on our own experience as workers, establishing strict, iron discipline supported by the state power of the armed workers. . . . This is *our* proletarian task, this is what we can and must *start* with in carrying out the proletarian revolution. Such a beginning, on the basis of large-scale production, will of itself lead to the gradual "withering away" of the bureaucracy, to the gradual creation of an order, an order without quotation marks, which will be different from wage-slavery, an order in which the functions of control and accounting – becoming more and more simple – will be performed by each in turn, will then become a habit and will finally die out as the *special* functions of a special section of the population' (p. 174).

'. . . it is constantly forgotten that the abolition of the state means also the abolition of democracy. . . .

'Democracy is a *state* which recognises the subordination of the minority to the majority, *i.e.*, an organization for the systematic use of *violence* by one class against the other, by one section of the population against another.

'We set ourselves the ultimate aim of abolishing the state, *i.e.*, all organized and systematic violence, all use of violence against man in general. We do not expect the advent of an order of society in which the principle of the subordination of the minority to the majority will not be observed. But in striving for Socialism we are convinced it will develop into Communism and, hence, that the need for violence against people in general, the need for the *subjection* of one man to another . . . will vanish, since people will *become accustomed* to observing the elementary conditions of social life *without force* and *without subordination*' (p. 197).

'Only in Communist society, when the resistance of the capitalists has been completely broken, when the capitalists have disappeared, when there are no classes (*i.e.*, when there is no difference between the members of society as regards their relation to the social means of production), *only* then does "the state . . . cease to exist", and it "*becomes possible to speak of freedom*". Only then will really complete democracy, democracy without any exceptions, be possible and be realised' (p. 201).

'Finally, only Communism makes the state absolutely unnecessary, for there is *nobody* to be suppressed. . . . We are not utopians' (p. 203).

'The economic basis for the complete withering away of the state is such a high state of development of Communism that the antithesis between mental and physical labour disappears. . . .

'. . . the expropriation of the capitalists will inevitably result in an enormous development of the productive forces of human society. But how rapidly this development will proceed, how soon it will reach the point of breaking away from the division of labour, or transforming labour into "the prime necessity of life" – we do not and *cannot* know' (p. 206).

'Accounting and control – that is the *main* thing required for the "setting up" and correct functioning of the *first phase* of Communist Society. *All* citizens are transformed into the salaried employees of the state, which consists of the armed workers. *All* citizens become employees and workers of a *single* national state "syndicate". *All* that is required is that they should work equally – do their proper share of work – and get paid equally. The accounting and control necessary for this have been *simplified* by capitalists to an extreme and reduced to the extraordinary simple operations – which any literate person can perform – of checking and recording, knowledge of the four rules of arithmetic and issuing receipts. . . .

'The whole of society will have become a single office and a single factory with equality of labour and equality of pay' (p. 210).

Like the Mandarin general in *The Golden Journey to Samarkand* –

Who never left his palace gates before,
But hath grown blind reading great books on war –

Lenin can never have left his garret in Zurich to stroll round one of its many factories; nor is it recorded that, like his master Marx, he ever did a hand's turn of manual labour in his life. Had he done either, he could not have written such undiluted nonsense. He was a man obsessed with a millennary illusion, and, as we shall see, the illusion tripped him up. His place in history is, that he is the first man on record who put the teachings of Marx into practice on the grand scale, and demonstrated to the world at large that they were the instruments of confusion and the tools of chaos.

3 · *Lenin and the October Revolution*

The failure of the summer offensive and the paralysis of the Provisional Government led to an increasing number of Bolshevik deputies being returned to the All-Russian Congress of Soviets, and their growing strength became apparent when, on 12th September, the Petrograd Soviet passed a Bolshevik resolution which demanded the immediate cessation of the war by 279 votes to 115. Encouraged by this, from Finland Lenin urged the Bolshevik Central Committee, established at the Smolny Institute in Petrograd, to put the utmost pressure upon Kerensky. This led to the release of Trotsky and other Bolshevik leaders from prison; a show of weakness which aggravated the situation, and all over the country local Soviets began to set themselves up and not only vote for Bolshevik resolutions but also demand a new meeting of the Second All-Russian Congress of Soviets.

But Lenin wanted action and not conferences, insurrection and not controversy, which between Russians is apt to be interminable; therefore he urged that the time for an armed uprising was 'fully ripe',[1] which in Petrograd was opposed by Kamenev and Zinoviev. Infuriated by this, and to prevent a split in the Party, Lenin decided to return to Petrograd. On 23rd October he secretly set out, and in disguise went into hiding at Lesnoye, close by the capital, and on the 25th, in preparation for the rising, the Petrograd Soviet created a Military Revolutionary Committee under Trotsky. On the following day Trotsky won over the garrison of the fortress of St. Peter and St. Paul, gained possession of the arsenal with 10,000 rifles, and at once distributed them anong the Red Guards, which since June had been organized in companies in the factories, and which the Provisional Government was either unwilling or unable to disarm.

Actually, this was the death-blow of the Provisonal Government, for although, on 5th November, Kerensky proclaimed a state of emergency, outlawed the Military Revolutionary Committee and ordered the arrest of Trotsky; deprived as he was of military power to enforce his commands, his orders were dead-letters.

At Lesnoye, Lenin had several meetings with his followers, and plans for revolt were discussed, but he was unable to persuade them to agree on a date. Convinced that, because the Second All-Russian Congress of Soviets was due to meet

[1] See *Selected Works*, Vol. II, p. 135.

on 7th November, and that it was essential to strike before it had time to organize itself, on the evening of 6th November he wrote to the Central Committee of the Party:

'We must not wait!! We may lose everything!! . . . under no circumstances must the power be left in the hands of Kerensky and Co. until the 25th [old style] – not under any circumstances; the matter must be decided without fail this very evening. . . . It would be a disaster, or a sheer formality to await the wavering vote of October 25th. . . . The government is wavering. It must be destroyed at all costs.'[1]

Late on the night of 6th November, in disguise, Lenin came from Lesnoye to Smolny to take personal control of the revolt, and very early in the following morning he and Trotsky sent out the Red Guards to seize the telephone exchange, the railway stations, telegraph office, power houses, state bank and other vital points. By 10 a.m. the whole edifice of government had so completely collapsed[2] that Lenin was able ironically to proclaim:

'The Second All-Russian Congress of Workers' and Soldiers' Deputies has begun. . . . Backed by the will of the vast majority of the workers, soldiers and peasants . . . the Congress takes the power into its own hands. . . . The Soviet government will propose an immediate democratic peace to all nations and an immediate armistice on all fronts . . . it will assure the convocation of the Constituent Assembly at the time appointed.'[3]

A Council of Peoples' Commissars, under the presidency of Lenin, was then elected by acclamation to rule Russia until elections for the Constituent Assembly were held.

In the meantime the whole of the civil service had gone on strike; nevertheless, in less than it takes minutes to relate, new ministers (commissars) were appointed, and the whole of the government departments housed in the Smolny Institute. Lenin, as President, occupied one room; Trotsky, in charge of of Foreign Affairs, another; the War Department, under Stalin, a third; the Home Office a fourth, and so on. 'In the Foreign Office the employees hid their books and refused to

[1] Ibid., Vol. II, pp. 139–40.
[2] Kerensky escaped from Petrograd on 7th November.
[3] Ibid., Vol. II, p. 226.

hand over their keys to Trotsky'; and 'in the banks half-literate volunteers were trying to make sense out of ledgers and cash books that were quite beyond them.'[1] One after another the newly appointed ministers would dash down the corridors and address frenzied crowds, and then hurry back to their rooms to transform the proletariat into the ruling class.

This was done by a series of frantic decrees, and between 8th November and the end of the year no less than 193 were promulgated. Private property was abolished; the land declared the property of the people; the factories were taken over by the workers; the banks nationalized; the stock market abolished; all state debts annulled; wages pegged at 500 roubles the month; the criminal courts replaced by workers' and peasants' tribunals; the workers were armed and became a militia; all secret treaties were annulled, etc., etc. Thus every institution was uprooted, and chaos, in the form of the proletariat, picked up the reins of government.

Because the Congress of Soviets was not a legislature, Lenin had no means of legalizing his decrees, and as the strikes in the government ministries continued, to enforce his authority he revived the old Tzarist Okhrana (secret police) in the form of the Tcheka which, under the fanatical Polish Bolshevik Dzerzhinsky, set out to exterminate opposition and compel the ruling class to work.

Next, Lenin took one of his famous backward steps. Because the vast majority of the people was now on the verge of revolt, and the Bolshevik party represented but a fraction of them, he decided to widen his base of operations by winning over the peasants, who numbered eighty per cent. of the population. To effect this in part, he invited the Left Social Revolutionaries, who so far he had anathematized, to enter into coalition with him. This they agreed to do, and it made his position more acceptable in the eyes of the masses. With the Left Wing peasants as his allies he was better placed to wipe out the bourgeoisie, and when they had been liquidated the peasants would be at his mercy.[2] To know when to halt and co-operate with his opponents in order to destroy them, or as he put it,

[1] *The Russian Revolution*, Alan Moorehead (1958), p. 284.

[2] For Lenin's outlook on the peasantry see Appendix I.

'One step back to gain two steps forward', was a leading principle in his revolutionary technique, which time and again paid a high dividend.

On 25th November, the final struggle for power opened with the elections for the Constituent Assembly, and for Lenin the results were startling. Out of the total of 41,700,000 votes cast only 9,800,000 were polled for the Bolsheviks, including the Left Social Revolutionaries, whereas the Right Social Revolutionaries polled 21,000,000. Directly the results were known, notwithstanding his proclamation, Lenin set out to wreck the Assembly; but in spite of his endeavours to prevent it meeting, it did so and passed a resolution that the Constituent Assembly should open at the Tauride Palace on 18th January 1918. When it did, Lenin surrounded the building and filled its corridors with his Lettish guards and Kronstadt sailors, broke up the meeting, and on the following day, while the doors of the palace were picketed by revolutionaries, the Executive Committee of the Congress of Soviets dissolved the Assembly. Thus Lenin established his autocracy, and became the unhallowed tzar of Petrograd.

From now on, the defeat of Russia ceased to be Lenin's aim, and Germany became his most dangerous enemy. Nevertheless, a Russian victory in concert with her allies was repugnant to him, because it would discredit the revolution in the eyes of the German proletariat, and Lenin's faith in world revolution was pinned on Germany. Further, he was convinced that diplomatic and psychological warfare could simultaneously be waged against the Central Powers and the Allies; therefore, on 9th November, he instructed Trotsky to invite the Allies and the Central Powers to conclude an immediate armistice. Next, he launched his initial psychological attack: he appealed over the head of their governments to the belligerent peoples to cease hostilities; he published the secret treaties of the Allies with Russia as proof of their imperialist designs, and, in the form of a slogan, he urged 'No annexations, no indemnities' as the basis of peace. 'Such conditions of peace', he wrote, 'will not be favourably received by the capitalists; but they will be greeted by all the nations with such tremendous sympathy, they will arouse such a great and historic outburst of enthusiasm and such universal indignation against the prolongation of this predatory war, that we shall at once obtain an armistice and consent to the opening of peace negotiations.'[1]

The results fell short of his expectations. Although Germany, eager to be quit of the war on her eastern front, entered into negotiations with Russia, and concluded with her an armistice on 5th December, the Allies remonstrated against a separate peace and grew increasingly hostile to the Bolsheviks. A prolonged wrangle with the Germans followed, during which Lenin turned the armistice into a public platform for the propagation of revolution within Germany. While the wrangling went on, the full blast of Bolshevik propaganda was directed against the German army; hundreds of thousands of revolutionary leaflets and over a million copies of President Wilson's Fourteen Points were surreptitiously distributed among its men, and German prisoners of war were so effectively indoctrinated with revolutionary ideas that, on their return to Germany, they had to be confined in 'political quarantine camps'. 'Our victorious army on the Eastern Front', wrote General Hoffmann, 'became rotten with Bolshevism. We got to the point where we did not dare to transfer certain of our eastern divisions to the West.'[2]

To put a stop to this and the delays, on 17th February 1918, the German Supreme Command broke off negotiations and set out to advance on Petrograd. Thereupon Lenin, who had no army to speak of to support him, against the violent opposition of many of his followers, at once came to terms, and a peace treaty was signed at Brest-Litovsk on 3rd March. For him, the all-important lesson of the negotiations was that, without adequate armed force to back them, no more can be expected from psychological warfare than an ephemeral success. Therefore, on 23rd February, he ordered Trotsky to recruit a Red Army.

By the terms of the treaty, the Germans occupied Estonia

[1] 'The Tasks of the Revolution', *Selected Works*, Vol. II, p. 128.

[2] Cited by John W. Wheeler-Bennet in *Brest-Litovsk the Forgotten Peace* (1938), p. 352. See also Ludendorff's *My War Memoirs*, Vol. II, p. 683.

and part of Latvia, and the Russians were compelled to withdraw from Finland and the Ukraine, and cede Kars, Ardahan and Batum to Turkey. In all Russia lost 26 per cent. of her population, 27 per cent. of her agricultural land, 26 per cent of her railways, and three-quarters of her coal and iron.[1] So crippling and degrading were these losses that the Left Socialist Revolutionaries resigned from the Government; peasant risings followed and were ruthlessly suppressed.

No sooner was the treaty signed than the Soviet regime was confronted with intervention on the part of Russia's allies,[2] as well as with civil war from the Baltic to the Black Sea and from Murmansk to Vladivostok. In April the Japanese landed troops at the latter, and in July Allied troops were disembarked at the former, while the White Russian generals, Kolchak from Omsk, Kornilov (later Denikin) from the Black Sea, Wrangel from the Crimea, and Yudenich from Estonia advanced on Moscow, to where the seat of Soviet government had moved on 15th March. As in the French Revolution, foreign intervention led to a wholsesale terror, during which, on 16th July, Nicholas II and his family were butchered at Ekaterinburg.

The civil war reached its climax in the autumn of 1919 and the winter of 1920; one by one the White Russian generals were defeated, in part by Bolshevik propaganda, in part by the Red Army, but in the main because their aim was to restore the old regime, and this lost to them the support of the peasants, who feared that their recently gained lands would be restored to their former owners. As the civil war petered out, the interventionist forces were withdrawn, but Russia's troubles were not ended. On 25th April 1920, the Poles, under Marshal Joseph Pilsudski, advanced on Kiev; were driven back to Warsaw where, between 16th and 25th August, the Bolshevik general Mikail Tukhachevski was routed, and central

[1] See *The Communist Party of the Soviet Union*, Leonard Schapiro, (1960), p. 186.

[2] By the close of 1918 the interventionist forces had reached a total of nearly 300,000 men: French, British, American, Italian, Japanese, German Balts, Poles, Greeks, Finns, Czechs, Slovaks, Estonians and Latvians, in Archangel, Murmansk, Finland, Estonia, Latvia and Poland, as well as on the Black Sea, on the trans-Siberian railway, and at Vladivostok.

Europe saved from a Soviet invasion.[1] Lord D'Abernon, British ambassador to Germany between 1920–1926, entitled his history of the campaign *The Eighteenth Decisive Battle of the World*, which in no way exaggerates its importance, for had Poland succumbed, there was nothing to prevent Tukhachevski's horde from penetrating into Germany. Lenin's comment clearly shows that this was his ultimate aim, he says:

'By attacking Poland, we are attacking the Allies; by destroying the Polish Army, we are destroying the Versailles Peace upon which rests the whole system of present international relations.

'Had Poland become sovietized . . . the Versailles Peace would have been terminated, and the system built on victory over Germany would have been destroyed likewise.'[2]

On 12th October 1920, an armistice was agreed between Poland and Russia, and on 18th March, the following year, peace was signed at Riga, and the hoped for proletarian world revolution was put into cold storage.

4 · The End of Utopianism

There is nothing illogical in the desire of the 'have-nots' to appropriate the wealth of the 'haves'; in fact, it is part and parcel of the law of animal life. The bear robs the hive and the wolf the fold, and when 'nature red in tooth and claw' is stretched into its human dimension, there is nothing irrational in Marx's theory that, granted the power, one social class should devour another. But what is irrational is, to assume that by robbing the hive the bear will assume the industry of the bee, or by robbing the fold the wolf will become as pacific as the sheep. It is astonishing that a man of Marx's high intelligence could have believed in ritualistic cannibalism on the social plane; that by wresting the forces of production from the bourgeoisie and centralizing them in the hands of the proletariat, the proletariat would automatically acquire

[1] For Tukhachevski's estimate of this battle see Pilsudski's *L'Année 1920* (1929), p. 255.

[2] Cited by T. A. Taracouzio in *War and Peace in Soviet Diplomacy* (1940), p. 101. It is of interest to note that the Treaty of Versailles was branded by Lenin as a 'hundred times more humiliating and rapacious than our Brest Peace' (ibid., p. 179).

the skills of the ruling class. And it is equally astonishing that a man of Lenin's mental calibre could have attempted to put this magic into practice.

As we have seen, after twenty years of profound study of Marx, Lenin came to the conclusion that it was possible 'overnight' to substitute for what he called 'the official grandeur of state officials' the simple functions of workmen and managers; functions 'fully within the capacity of the city dweller', and 'operations which any literate person can perform.'

' "The proletariat organized as the governing class",' writes V. L. Borin, 'is just an irresponsible phrase, a piece of nonsense uttered by Marx . . . an illusionary future lacking a single grain of reality.'[1] Not only is the proletariat in every land a minority class, which means that, as the governing class, it has to enforce its will on the majority of the people as well as on the comparatively small class of capitalists, but its individual members, like those of all classes, are governed by human nature – the ineradicable instincts which have shaped man's history since he became man.

The peasants took over the land not merely to work it, but to work it at a profit, and they cultivated only sufficient of it to meet their own needs, because the industrial workers had nothing to offer in exchange for their produce. 'In the factories', writes Borin, 'the workers were busy electing their soviets and carrying on discussions. They were now the governing class and nobody could give them orders. . . . Above all they took things easy. When their shoes needed re-soling they cut up the driving belts from their machines; after all it was their property. Thus instead of developing rapidly, industrial production came rapidly to a standstill.'[2] And as the industrial workers had little or nothing to exchange with the peasants for food, famine swept the cities, and the workers began to desert the factories and flock to the land in search of sustenance.

Exactly three months after the proletariat had been transformed into the governing class, in his pamphlet 'How to Organize Competition', Lenin wrote:

'The workers and peasants are still "shy", they have not

[1] *Civilization at Bay* (1951), p. 74.
[2] Ibid., pp. 78–79.

yet become accustomed to the idea that *they* are the *ruling* class. . . . Accounting and control – this is the *main* economic task . . . of every factory committee or organ of workers' control. . . . The land, the banks, the factories and works now belong to the whole of the people! You *yourselves* must set to work to take account and control the production and distribution of products – this is the *only* road to the victory of Socialism . . . to organize this accounting and control, which is *fully within the power* of every honest, intelligent and efficient worker and peasant, we must rouse their organizing talent, the talent which is in their midst.'[1]

Four months later the tune began to change. On 28th April 1918, in 'The Chief Task of our Day' Lenin declared:

'Without the guidance of specialists in the various fields of knowledge, technology and experience, the transition to Socialism will be impossible . . . the specialists are, in the main, bourgeois. . . . Had our proletariat . . . quickly solved the problem of accounting, control and organization . . . we . . . would have completely subordinated these bourgeois specialists to ourselves by means of universal accounting and control. . . . Now we have to resort to the old bourgeois method and agree to pay a very high price for the "services" of the biggest bourgeois specialists . . . assuming that we have to enlist several hundred . . . exacting foreign specialists, the question is, would the expenditure of fifty or a hundred million roubles per annum . . . for the purpose of reorganizing the labour of the people according to the last word in science or technology be excessive or too heavy? Of course not . . . every thinking and honest worker and poor peasant will agree . . . that we cannot immediately rid ourselves of the bad heritage of capitalism [except] by purging our ranks . . . of loafers, idlers and embezzlers of state funds (now all the land, all the factories and all the railways are the "state funds" of the Soviet Republic).'[2]

A month later, when the civil war was in its initial stage, in Lenin's pamphlet 'The Famine', a harrowing picture of conditions in Petrograd and the industrial provinces is painted,

[1] *Selected Works*, Vol. II, pp. 259–60.
[2] Ibid., Vol. II, pp. 319–21.

and is attributed to 'an orgy of profiteering in grain and other food products' by the bourgeoisie and the kulaks (wealthy peasants), and not to the experiment in Socialism. When the civil war ended and intervention ceased, hundreds of thousands of people had starved to death, and out of Petrograd's 2,000,000 inhabitants only 700,000 remained.

At length, in the spring of 1921, Lenin saw daylight, and in order to obtain bread, on 8th March, he convoked the Tenth Congress of the Party, at which all decrees affecting agriculture were rescinded, and the peasants freed to return to private enterprise, hire wage-labour, and dispose of their produce at whatever price it would fetch. This was called his New Economic Policy (NEP) – a retreat from Socialism.

In a pamphlet dated 5th November 1921,[1] Lenin explains that the revolutionary approach, namely, 'to proceed at once to break up the old social and economic system completely' was an error, and that, since the spring 'a reformist type of method' had replaced it, the aim of which was 'to *revive* trade, small proprietorship, capitalism. . . . while cautiously and gradually getting the upper hand over it.' That 'Genuine revolutionaries have come a cropper most often when they begin to write "revolution" with a capital R, to elevate "revolution" to something almost divine.' That the proletariat state must grasp 'with all its might' that 'Trade is the only possible economic link between the scores of millions of small farmers and large-scale industry.'

A year later, in a soul-searching pamphlet, 'Five Years of the Russian Revolution and the Prospects of the World Revolution',[2] he equates NEP with State Capitalism, a 'non-Socialist element' he calls it, and asks whether it should not be rated higher than Socialism? His answer is: 'Although it is not a Socialist form, state capitalism would be for us, and for Russia, a more favourable form than the existing one', and 'to a certain degree . . . it would be better if we first arrived at state capitalism and then at Socialism.' He asks next: 'What is the position now . . . after we have granted the peasants freedom to trade? The answer is evident to everyone: in the

[1] 'The Importance of Gold, etc.', *Selected Works*, Vol. II, pp. 754–60.
[2] Ibid., Vol. II, pp. 811–21.

course of one year the peasants have not only overcome the famine, but have paid the tax in kind on such a scale that we have now received hundreds of millions of poods [a pood is a little over 36 lb.] of grain, and that is almost without employing any means of coercion . . . I think it is a great achievement . . . light industry is undoubtedly on the upgrade, and the conditions of the workers in Petrograd and Moscow have undoubtedly improved.' But the conditions of heavy industry remained grave – it continued to be a state monopoly.

Notwithstanding this improvement, in the last article he wrote, dated 2nd March 1923, and entitled 'Better Fewer, but Better',[1] Lenin is a disillusioned man.

'Our experience of the first five years', he says, 'has fairly crammed our heads with disbelief and scepticism. These qualities assert themselves involuntarily when, for example, we hear people dilating at too great length and too flippantly on "proletarian" culture. We would be satisfied with real bourgeois culture for a start. . . . The situation as regards our machinery of state is so deplorable, not to say disgusting, that we must first of all think very carefully as to how to eliminate its defects. . . . We must come to our senses in time. . . . We must think of testing the steps forward which we proclaim to the world every hour, which we take every minute, and which later on we find, every second, to be flimsy, superficial and not understood. . . . We have been bustling for five years trying to improve our state apparatus, but it has been mere bustle; and these five years have proved that bustle is useless, even futile, even harmful. This bustle created the impression that we were doing something; as a matter of fact, it only clogged up our institutions and our brains. It is high time things were changed. We must follow the rule: "Little, but good". We must follow the rule: "Better get a good staff in two or even three years, than work in haste without getting any at all. . . ." Everybody knows that a more badly organized institution than our Workers' and Peasants' Inspection does not exist, and that under present conditions nothing can be expected from the People's Commissariat. . . . If we cannot arm ourselves with patience, if we are not prepared to devote

[1] Ibid., Vol. II, pp. 844–55.

several years to this task, we had better not start on it at all.'

The dreamer had awakened to find that the alluring vision of the Marxian Beatitude, which he so fanatically had believed in and so frantically had quested, was an illusion; a will-o'-the-wisp which had led him, not to the Workers' but to the Bankers' Paradise – total capitalism.

From this un-Marxian consummation, his successor, Joseph Stalin (1879–1953), set out to concentrate all power into his own hands; this necessitated the abrogation of local governments, which meant the abolition of the political, cultural and economic autonomy of the Soviet Republics. To achieve this took him nine years, and during them industrialization and collectivization were accomplished at a cost of millions of human lives, accompanied by ferocious purges of the Party in which the bulk of Lenin's old associates perished. Thus, instead of the State withering away, as Marx had predicted and Lenin had fanatically believed, it reverted to an autocracy – the only form of government the Russians had ever known.

'*Qui veut faire l'ange, fait la bête*', such is the uninscribed epitaph on Lenin's tomb.

CHAPTER XI

Soviet Revolutionary Warfare

*

1 · Politics and War

Soviet political relations, both internal and external, are analogous with those within and between primitive tribes, as discussed in Section 4 of Chapter II. To survive, the in-group (Communist) must possess cohesion and submit to authority, so that it may exercise the fullest attainable force against the out-group (Capitalist). To both the tribesman and the revolutionary 'to destroy or be destroyed' is the governing slogan, and as in the animal world there is no distinction between war and peace. Because of this, as Mr Byron Dexter has pointed out: 'The distinguishing characteristic' in Soviet warfare 'is the interchangeability of political and military weapons. A "peace offensive" in Moscow, a cultural conference in Warsaw, a strike in France, an armed insurrection in Czechoslovakia, the invasion of Greece and Korea by fully equipped troops – all are instruments of one war, turned on and turned off from a central tap.'[1] To the Marxist, the bloodiest of wars and the most serene periods of peace are, as is laid down on the opening page of *The Communist Manifesto*, in themselves but phases in a constant and uninterrupted class struggle, 'now hidden, now open fight', which ends 'either in a revolutionary reconstruction of society at large, or in the common ruin of the contending classes.'

This theory of unified war – a war in all dimensions – directed by a supreme central intelligence, agrees with Clausewitz's remark that 'War belongs to the province of social life'; which means 'that it is not an act performed by military men only, but is an expression of the conflict of ideas, objectives and way of life of an entire society with those of some other society.'[2] This was further elaborated by Clausewitz when he wrote:

[1] 'Clausewitz and Soviet Strategy', *Foreign Affairs*, October 1950, Vol. 29, No. 1, p. 41. [2] Ibid., p. 41.

'We see, therefore, in the first place, that under all circumstances War is to be regarded not as an independent thing, but as a political instrument [that is, an instrument related to both peace and war]; and it is only by taking this point of view that we can avoid finding ourselves in opposition to all military history. This is the only means of unlocking the great book and making it intelligible. Secondly, this view shows us how Wars must differ in character according to the nature of the motives and circumstances from which they proceed.'[1]

It would not be a surprise to learn that Lenin had these observations in mind when, at the Sixth Congress of the Communist International, he said:

'The proletariat must carefully analyse the historical and political class significance of each given war, and must evaluate with particular care, from the standpoint of world revolution, the role of the dominating classes of all the countries partaking in the war.'[2]

Nevertheless, there is a major difference between the two, for whereas Clausewitz never questioned that morality, as understood by civilized peoples, was a factor in social life, Lenin eschewed it, and thereby reduced war to a purely animal struggle in which no punches were barred. He said:

'We repudiate all morality derived from non-human and non-class concepts. We say that it is a deception, a fraud in the interests of the landlords and capitalists. We say that our morality is entirely subordinated to the interests of the class struggle of the proletariat [the in-group] . . . We say: morality is what serves to destroy the old exploiting society [the out-group] and to unite all toilers around the proletariat, which is creating a new Communist society. . . . We do not believe in an eternal morality.'[3]

Therefore, as in tribal warfare, Soviet morality is expediency, and because ethical considerations are excluded, cunning takes precedence over valour, and the indirect psychological attack

[1] See *Supra*, chap IV, p. 63.

[2] Cited by Taracouzio in *War and Peace in Soviet Diplomacy* (1940), p. 24.

[3] Cited by Carew Hunt, op. cit., pp. 79–80. In Trotsky's opinion: 'The highest form of the class struggle is civil war which explodes in mid-air all moral ties between the hostile classes' (ibid., p. 81).

over the direct physical attack, because, as long as the enemy adheres to the moral code, he is placed at a serious disadvantage to his amoral, or animal, opponent.

War, in all its dimensions, is absolute, and will only cease when Capitalism (the out-group) is exterminated. Therefore, according to Lenin:

'Socialists cannot be opposed to any kind of wars without ceasing to be Socialists. We are struggling against the very root of wars – capitalism. But in as much as capitalism has not yet been exterminated, we are struggling not against wars in general, but against reactionary wars, and [at the same time] for revolutionary wars.'[1]

And again:

'We are living not merely in a state, but in a *system of states*, and the existence of the Soviet Republic side by side with imperialist states for a long time is unthinkable. One or other must triumph in the end. And before that end comes, a series of frightful collisions between the Soviet Republic and the bourgeois states will be inevitable.'[2]

Because, in accordance with Marxian theory, war and revolution are interchangeable terms, the highest economy of force is to be sought in transforming an international or imperialist conflict into a civil war – that is, into a war in which the enemy destroys himself. The aim in these conflicts is to make them the 'midwife' of revolution, by unceasing political and psychological attack: by systematic propaganda, the fomenting of strikes, mass fraternisation, and by stimulating mutiny and desertion. A point to bear in mind is that, while in a purely military conflict the reserves are to be found in the armed population of the belligerent countries, in a revolutionary war they are to be sought in the class antagonisms within the enemy's country: in his discontented proletariat, in the liberation movements of his colonies and minorities, and in the conflicts between his non-proletarian factions.

It was for these purposes that from its inception the Red Army was organized and trained not only as a military but also as a revolutionary instrument. According to Pierre Fer-

1 Cited by Taracouzio, op. cit., p. 28.

2 Cited by Stalin in *Problems of Leninism* (edit. 1954), p. 193.

vacque, in 1920, when Tukhachevski invaded Poland, his army of 200,000 men was followed by a horde of 800,000 politicians, police and pillagers, whose duty was to bolshevize the conquered territories, exterminate the wealthy and shoot all bourgeois and aristocrats.[1] Although 800,000 is a tall figure to swallow, large numbers were undoubtedly employed, because Tukhachevski himself informs us that his army was preceded by an advance guard of propagandists, and Lord D'Abernon writes:

'Moscow disposed of a host of spies, propagandists, secret emissaries, and secret friends, who penetrated into Polish territory and undermined the resistance of certain elements of the Polish population . . . the services rendered by the unarmed were not less effective than those brought about by military pressure. The system adopted was to avoid frontal attack whenever possible and to turn positions by flank marches, infiltration and propaganda.'[2]

Finally, according to Lenin:

War must be evaluated 'not by the number of its casualties but by its political consequences. Above the interests of the individuals perishing and the suffering from war must stand the interests of the class. And if the war serves the interests of the proletariat, as a class and *in toto*, and secures for it liberation from the [capitalist] yoke, and freedom for struggle and development – such a war is progress, irrespective of the victims and the suffering it entails.'[3]

2 · *Lenin and Clausewitz*

Like Engels and Marx, Lenin was fascinated by Clausewitz's *On War*; he not only studied it with insight, but annotated it extensively;[4] the whole of the chapter on 'War as an Instru-

[1] *Le chef de l'armée rouge, Mikail Tukhachevski* (1928), p. 124.

[2] *The Eighteenth Decisive Battle of the World* (1920), p. 28.

[3] Cited by Taracouzio, op. cit., p. 53.

[4] His marginal comments were first published in *Pravda* in 1923, and subsequently have been republished several times (see Raymond L. Garthoff's *How Russia Makes War* (1959), p. 54). There is a French translation of them by Berholdt C. Friedl, 'Cahier de Lénine No. 18674 des Archives de l'Institut Lénine a Moscow', *Les Fondements Théoriques de la Guerre et de la Paix en U.S.S.R.* (Paris; Editions Medicis, 1945), pp. 47–90.

ment of Policy'[1] was heavily underlined by him, and inscribed 'the most important chapter', which it undoubtedly is. The following citations show how deeply he was indebted to Clausewitz:

Under the heading 'War is Politics continued by Other (*i.e.* Forcible) Means', Lenin wrote: 'This famous dictum belongs to one of the profoundest writers on military questions, Clausewitz. Rightly, the Marxists have always considered this axiom as the theoretical foundation for their understanding of the meaning of every war.'[2] On another occasion, he termed Clausewitz 'one of the most notable writers on the philosophy of wars and on the history of wars . . . a writer, whose basic thoughts have at present become the indisputable acquisitions of every thinking person.'[3]

The influence of Clausewitz on him is to be found scattered among his many pamphlets. For instance, in 'The Impending Catastrophe and How to Combat it', written in September 1917, he bade his followers remember that 'The character of war is determined by the *policy* of which the war is a continuation ("war is the continuation of politics"), by the *class* that is waging the war, and by the aims for which it is being waged.'[4] And that war 'itself does not change the direction in which the politics were developing before the war; it only accelerates this development.'[5]

In his 'Advice of an Onlooker', written on 21st October 1917, in preparation for the October Revolution, Lenin outlined the technique of insurrection to be employed. 'Armed insurrection', he said, 'is a *special* form of the political struggle'; a truth expressed by Marx 'with remarkable clarity when he wrote that armed "*insurrection is an art quite as much as war*".' He then went on to say: 'Of the principal rules of the art, Marx noted the following' – they are closely akin to Clausewitz's principles of war,[6] but related to an armed insurrection:

[1] See English edition of *On War*, Vol. III, pp. 118–30, and *supra* Chapter IV, Section 4.

[2] Lenin's *Collected Works* (English edition), Vol. XVIII, p. 224.

[3] Cited by Garthoff, op. cit., p. 55.

[4] *Selected Works*, Vol. II, p. 116.

[5] Cited by Taracouzio, op. cit., p. 275.

[6] See *supra*, Chapter IV, Section 6.

'(1) Never *play* with insurrection, but when beginning it firmly realize that you must *go to the end.*

'(2) You must concentrate *a great superiority of forces* at the decisive point, at the decisive moment, otherwise the enemy, who has the advantage of better preparation and organization, will destroy the insurgents.

'(3) Once the insurrection has begun, you must act with the greatest *determination*, and by all means, without fail, take *the offensive.* "The defensive is the death of every armed rising."

'(4) You must try to take the enemy by surprise and seize the moment when his forces are scattered.

'(5) You must strive for *daily* successes, even if small (one might say, hourly, if it is the case of one town), and at all costs retain "*moral ascendancy.*"

'Marx summarized the lessons of all revolutions in respect to armed insurrection in the words of Danton, "the greatest master of revolutionary tactics yet known": "audacity, audacity, and once again audacity". '[1]

Stalin quotes these instructions in his *Problems of Leninism*, and adds to them:

'The decisive battle, says Lenin, may be deemed to have fully matured *if* "(1) all the class forces hostile to us have become sufficiently entangled, are sufficiently at loggerheads, have sufficiently weakened themselves in a struggle which is beyond their strength"; *if* "(2) all the vacillating, wavering, unstable, elements – the petty-bourgeoisie, the petty-bourgeois democrats as distinct from the bourgeoisie – have sufficiently exposed themselves in the eyes of the people, have sufficiently disgraced themselves through their practical bankruptcy"; *if* "(3) among the proletariat a mass sentiment in favour of supporting the most determined, supremely bold, revolutionary action against the bourgeoisie has arisen and begun vigorously to grow. Then revolution is indeed ripe; then, indeed, if we have correctly gauged all the conditions indicated above . . . and if we have chosen the moment rightly, our victory is assured".'[2]

[1] *Selected Works*, Vol. II, pp. 100–4.

[2] *Problems of Leninism*, pp. 86–87.

In spite of the defensive being, in Lenin's opinion, the death of every armed rising, he paid close attention to Clausewitz's theory of defensive and counter-offensive. After the revolutionary parties have learned to attack, he wrote: 'they have to realize that this knowledge must be supplemented with knowledge how to retreat', and 'that victory is impossible unless they have learned how to attack and retreat properly.'[1]

In other words, the aim in strategy is not only to win battles but also to gain time wherein to accumulate forces which can win them. This he said he did during the Brest-Litovsk negotiations, in order to prepare the offensives against Kolchak and Denikin. Three years after the signing of the Brest-Litovsk peace he wrote: 'Now the biggest fool can see that the "Brest Peace" was a concession that strengthened us and broke up the forces of international imperialism.'[2]

That Engels, Marx and Lenin,[3] the three most noted revolutionary exponents since the French Revolution, none of whom was a soldier, were so deeply indebted to Clausewitz is surely the highest compliment ever paid to his insight on the nature of war.

3 · *The Third (Communist) International*

Because the October Revolution gave the workers of the world a fatherland to fight for, Lenin had expected that world-wide revolution would follow on its heels. With high expectations, on 20th January 1918, he wrote: 'That the Socialist revolution in Europe must come, and will come, is beyond doubt. All our hopes for the *final* victory of Socialism are founded on this certainty and on this scientific prognosis.'[4] And again on 7th March, four days after the signing of the Peace of Brest-

[1] Ibid., p. 88. [2] Ibid., p. 88.

[3] In his article 'Clausewitz, Lenin, and Communist Military Attitudes Today' (*Journal of the Royal United Service Institution*, May, 1960), Prof. Werner Hahlweg writes: '*On War* was also known to other Communist leaders, such as Trotsky, Stalin, Radek, and Frunze, as well as to such Russian marshals as Zaposnikov and Zhukov. . . . When the Russo-German war broke out in 1941, five Russian translations of *On War* existed in the Soviet Union . . . his theories have become so mingled with Russian military practice that it is no exaggeration to claim that the latter cannot be understood without the former.'

[4] *Selected Works*, Vol. II, p. 270.

Litovsk: '... it is indisputable that all the difficulties of our revolution will be overcome only when the world Socialist revolution matures, and it is maturing everywhere.'[1]

But after the Armistice of 11th November 1918, notwithstanding his prognosis, no revolution matured, and when in the following year the civil war was hammering at the gates of the Soviet Union, it became apparent to Lenin that no world revolution would be achieved without a world-wide revolutionary instrument, and at the moment such an instrument was doubly necessary, not to destroy capitalism, but to prevent capitalism from destroying the Mecca of the revolution. Therefore, on 4th March 1919, he brought into being the Third (Communist) International, or Comintern, an organization of Communist Parties of all nations, nominally independent of Moscow, and designed to replace the Second International, which had collapsed in 1914.[2]

The instructions issued by the First Congress of the Comintern clearly show the danger the Soviet Union was then in; they urged the workers of the world to demand of their respective governments: The termination of intervention in Russia; non-interference in Russia's domestic affairs; resumption of diplomatic relations with Russia; the invitation of Russia to the Peace Conference; the lifting of the economic blockade, and the resumption of trade with Russia. But nothing came of this, in part because the Communist Parties, engaged in their factional squabbles, were as impotent to foment revolution as the proletariat in Russia had been to rule.

Disillusioned by the incompetence of the proletriat, once the civil war had ended, Lenin shifted his faith to the Party, and in April–May 1920, wrote a thesis entitled 'Left Wing Communism, an Infantile Disorder'. It was addressed to all the Communist Parties affiliated to the Third International, and its aim was to convert them into an operative revolutionary instrument. In it he pointed out that, 'unless the strictest,

[1] Ibid., Vol. II, p. 297.

[2] The Second International accepted the philosophy of the Liberal State combined with Marx's economic policy, and believed in the peaceful evolution of Socialism. On the outbreak of war in 1914, it split into two groups, 'Social Patriots' who supported the war, and 'Social Pacifists' who opposed it; neither was pledged to international revolution.

truly iron discipline' is inculcated in the Parties, victory over the bourgeoisie is impossible. Next, he asked: How is discipline to be enforced? And his answer was:

'First, by the class consciousness of the proletarian vanguard [*i.e.*, the Party], and by its devotion to the revolution, by its perseverance, self-sacrifice and heroism. Secondly, by its ability to link itself with ... to merge with the broadest masses of the toilers – primarily with the proletariat, *but also with the non-proletarian* toiling masses. Thirdly, by the correctness of the political leadership exercised by this vanguard, by the correctness of its political strategy and tactics. . . . Without these conditions, discipline in a revolutionary party that is really capable of being a party of the advanced class, whose mission it is to overthrow the bourgeoisie and transform the whole of society, cannot be achieved.'[1]

He attacked the narrow sectarianism of the Communist Parties, whose attitude was that of uncompromising hostility towards all non-Communists. This, instead of subverting, only stiffened the ranks of the bourgeoisie. He called it 'treachery to the revolution', and held that to shun all compromise on principle was childish. To reinforce his argument, he singled out Comrade Sylvia Pankhurst, the notorious British sufragette, who held that:

'The Communist Party must not enter into compromise. . . . The Communist Party must keep its doctrine pure ... its mission is to lead the way, without stopping or turning, by the direct road to the Communist revolution.'

' "To lead the way without compromise, without stopping or turning",' he declared, 'if said by an obviously impotent minority of workers ... is obviously mistaken. It is just as if 10,000 soldiers were to fling themselves into battle against 50,000 enemy soldiers, when it would have been wiser to "stop", to "turn", or even to effect a "compromise" pending the arrival of 100,000 reinforcements which were on their way but could not go into action immediately. That is intellectual childishness and not the serious tactics of a revolutionary class.'[2]

[1] *Selected Works*, Vol. II, pp. 574–5.
[2] Ibid., Vol. II, pp. 620–1.

The policy outlined in this thesis was adopted at the Second Comintern Congress, held in July–August 1920, and it was agreed that, in order to capture the bourgeois governments, it was essential to create a proletarian class of politicians to distract, corrupt, and pervert them by Trojan-horse tactics. The Congress also confirmed the policy in vogue of Communist workers infiltrating the trade unions, with the object of gaining control of them. The tactics to be adopted by the cells were, first to gain the confidence of the workers by improving their lot, and, when it had been won, to create confusion by aggravating existent grievances and fomenting new ones. These agents were to be instructed to attach no importance to collective agreements between employers and employed, to work in the dark like wood worms, and gradually eat away the fabric of factory discipline.

In addition, and of equal importance, crypto-Communist units, composed of non-party members, were to be recruited to infiltrate every kind of bourgeois organization as well as create associations, clubs, debating societies, etc., and gradually saturate them with Marxism. Today – forty years after the Second Congress was held – these organisms of conspiritorial corruption proliferate in every country in the world, and in Great Britain alone the Labour Party has proscribed over forty of them. Their slogans are liberty, free speech, peace, disarmament, colonialism, the colour-bar, world-brotherhood, and anything which will stir up popular emotionalism and undermine national discipline and social order.

With the establishment of the Third International, Lenin completed his revolutionary organization.

4 · *Peace as an Instrument of Revolution*

A fundamental principle in Marxian dialectics is verbal inversion. When the accepted meaning of a word or an idea is turned upside down, not only are Communist intentions obscured, but the mind of the non-Communist is misled, and mental confusion leads to a semantic nightmare in which things appear to be firmly planted on their feet, but actually are standing on their heads.

This process of mental contortion is to be seen at most conferences between non-Communist and Communist Powers. Disarmament to one means one thing, to the other another thing; so also does peace. While to the non-Communist peace is a state of international harmony, to the Communist it is a state of international discord. To misquote Milton, for the latter 'Peace hath her victories no less renown'd than war', because Communists hold that peace and war are reciprocal terms for a conflict which can only end when the Marxian Beatitude is established; since their final aim is pacific, they are peace lovers.

Were this key process of 'double talk' more fully appreciated, there would be no need for Western Presidents, Prime Ministers, and superannuated Field-Marshals to rush to Moscow to discover what is in the mind of the Kremlin, any more than there is for them to race to Mecca to discover what is in the mind of Islam. To ask the Kremlin's present tenant, Mr Khrushchev, to abandon *The Communist Manifesto* is equivalent to requesting the Archbishop of Canterbury to abandon *The New Testament.*

Communism is a religion, and none the less potent for being a secular one. It is an *idée fixe*, a faith held by a vast number of Russians to be beyond criticism. Further, a point of world-wide significance in the Communist peace offensive – one which almost universally is overlooked – is its appeal to many Western Christian Socialists. Nearly thirty years ago, Oscar Levy, the translator of Nietzsche's collected works into English, pointed out that, in spite of its atheism, Bolshevism is a Christian heresy.[1] It is an international and a cosmopolitan faith; it looks back upon a Garden of Eden in which strife was non-existent, because property was shared in common, and therefore there was nothing to fight about,[2] and it looks forward to a heaven in which, once the devil of capitalism has

[1] *The Idiocy of Idealism*, Oscar Levy (1940), p. 14.

[2] Marx overlooked that men are as prone to fight over ideas as they are over things, and should the entire world become Communist, there would inevitably arise as many antagonistic warring Communist sects as there have been antagonistic warring Christian ones. In Lenin's day the quarrels over the correct interpretation of Marx's doctrines were violent and incessant, and Stalin liquidated everyone who disagreed with him, including nearly all Lenin's surviving adherents.

been exorcised, man will return to his pristine state of innocence. Therefore it is millennary; also it is messianic – the proletariat is its messiah. It stands up for the poor, the weak and the downtrodden, and it pours forth its wrath on the rich, the cultured and the learned. *The Communist Manifesto* is its *Sermon on the Mount.*

Oscar Levy records that: '. . . at least one Russian did not overlook the connexion between Bolshevism and Christianity. This was Mr Lunacharski, the first Soviet Minister of Education who, in the hey-day of the Revolution, gave out the memorable saying: "Christ, if He would ever come back to earth, would immediately join the Communist party".'[1]

This suggests that Christians should do so, which discloses yet another relationship between the two religions. Both are proselytizing creeds, and both hold that the war of the word is more potent than the war of the sword. Therefore, since Western statesmen and politicians are so ignorant of the technique of Marxian warfare, it bears repetition to point out that to Marxists peace is an instrument of subversion – that is, of conquest – as well as a breathing space in which to prepare for war. Should peace be concluded between a Communist and a Capitalist power, it is not in order to end hostilities, but instead to shift them from the battlefield of armies to the battlefield of classes. Peace is, therefore, no more than a manoeuvre in an unbroken struggle, and should it concede anything to the non-proletarian classes, it is in order to disintegrate them.

When he gained power, Lenin's first decree, or declaration, was an appeal for immediate peace negotiations. Not made, as we have seen, to bring the war to an end, but to transform it into a series of revolutionary civil wars – that is, internecine instead of international struggles – in which the newborn Bolshevik State could gain a breathing spell. Or, as Taracouzio writes: 'Pragmatically to the Marxist, peace must be a provisional *status quo* in which the class war between the proletariat and capitalism must go on, while to the Soviet Union, it must connote outward international tranquillity.'[2]

After the Peace of Riga, in March 1921, and until the signing

[1] Op. cit., p. 64.
[2] Op. cit., p. 58.

of the Soviet-German Pact of Non-Aggression in Moscow on 23rd August 1939, because the Soviet Union was not powerful enough to wage war, peace became its formal foreign policy, under cover of which military preparations were advanced and war continued on its psychological level. This policy was agreed at the First Enlarged Plenary Session of the Communist International in March 1922, at which it was resolved that 'the proletarian revolution, by overthrowing capitalism' was 'the only effective means to prevent the danger of war';[1] and during this long period of seventeen years the constantly repeated assurances of the peaceful intentions of the Kremlin had a powerful influence on winning over the sympathy and admiration of the proletarian masses in capitalist countries.

This policy of a camouflaged war was strengthened by the advocacy of 'Socialism in a Single Country', which led the capitalist powers to assume that the aim of world revolution had been abandoned. It was advanced by Lenin in 1922, in order to develop economic relations with the outside world, and it was finally adopted by Stalin in 1925. It was a long-term policy aimed at building up the strength of the Soviet Union, so that eventually it could direct the world revolution instead of being dependent upon it.

Closely related to Soviet peace policy was the call for total disarmament, first proposed by Litvinov at the Fourth Session of the Preparatory Disarmament Commission of 30th November 1927, and advanced on numerous occasions between then and April 1932, when the General Disarmament Conference resumed its work. At it, Litvinov demanded: The disbandment of all armed land, naval and air forces; the destruction of all weapons, warships, fortresses and arsenals; the abolition of compulsory military service; the suppression of all defence budgets, and the liquidation of all military and naval organizations, for which were to be substituted national police forces of sufficient strength to maintain internal law and order.

Litvinov was, of course, well aware that these utopian proposals would be rejected, and when they were he immediately substituted for them another draft convention, in which partial and gradual disarmament were proposed. This led to

[1] Cited by Taracouzio, op. cit., p. 58.

a prolonged academic wrangle over air warfare, poison gas, and the difference between offensive weapons – large guns and heavy tanks – and defensive weapons – guns and tanks of lesser size! Eventually, after weeks of futile argument the Disarmament Conference broke up. Nothing was achieved, other than that the Soviet delegates retired from the semantic contest crowned with pacific laurels.

In any case the proceedings were a hoax, because, had Litvinov's proposals been accepted, they would have violated Marxian theory, according to which war is a preordained necessity until all class distinctions are extinguished. Had not Lenin said:

'We cannot indeed forget, without becoming bourgeois pacifists or opportunists, that we live in a class society and that there is no other way of escaping from it but through class struggle and the overthrow of the ruling class. . . . Our watchword must be armament of the proletariat for the purpose of defeating, suppressing, and disarming the bourgeoisie.'[1]

Further, the whole theory of class war was based on violence, which Lenin declared: '. . . in the twentieth century, as throughout civilization in general, rests not merely upon fists and clubs, but upon the *army*.'[2] And, as already noted, the Red Army was organized and trained, not only to protect the U.S.S.R., but as a revolutionary gendarmerie – a police force standing on its head, because its aim was to foment revolts instead of suppressing them.

It was not armaments and numbers of armed men which secured victory for the Soviets between 1918 and 1922. Instead, as Lenin said:

'We were able to survive and to defeat the powerful coalition of the Entente Powers which was supported by White armies only because there was no unity among these Powers. Up to this time we have been victorious not only because of the serious conflicts among these imperialist powers but precisely because these conflicts were not incidental domestic disagreements but deeply rooted fundamental economic struggles of the imperialist powers among themselves.'[3]

All Soviet peace proposals are aimed at creating or accentu-

[1] Ibid., p. 268. [2] Ibid., p. 270. [3] Ibid., p. 137.

ating confusion in the enemy's ranks. On the face of it 'peaceful coexistence' seems to be eminently pacific; but in the Soviet jargon it means living alongside a leaky carboy of acid, and assures progressive corrosion.[1] One and all, these peace proposals are apples of discord, which within and between nations give rise to dissensions and lack of unity. *Divide et impera* is as formidable a weapon in Soviet peace policy as it was in the days of the Romans.

[1] When accepted at their dictionary meaning, the words 'peaceful coexistence' are the exact opposite of what Marx meant by 'the class struggle.' Time and again this should have been pointed out to the Soviet 'double-talkers'.

CHAPTER XII

The Twenty Years Armistice

*

1 · The Carthaginian Peace

In 1930, with twelve years of chaos to look back upon, Ferrero remarked in a lecture that 'Our civilization can make war well enough, but it has forgotten how to make peace.'[1] Actually, it was unable to make peace, because it had forgotten how to make war. War had lost its significance, and when the cease-fire sounded, its means monopolized its end. All that happened was, the conflict continued in another form; therefore there could be no peace.

This was true, not only for Lenin who, as we have seen, looked upon peace as an instrument of subversion, but also for the victors of the war who, as we shall now see, converted peace into an instrument of domination. To both the end was the same – the subjection of their respective antagonists; to both the means were akin – compulsion. The one undermined his victim's resistance by psychological attack, the other by economic attack in the form of the blockade, which was maintained till July 1919, and like a pistol was pressed against the victim's back until he put his signature to a dictated peace treaty.[2] This was an act of profound stupidity, because, as Vattel had pointed out 160 years earlier, an unsupportable peace is an oppression a nation will only endure as long as it

[1] *Peace and War* (1933), p. 148.

[2] During the last two years of the war, over one million non-combatants in Germany and Austria died of starvation. On 13th December 1918, when the Germans pleaded to be allowed to import wheat, fats, condensed milk, medical stores, etc., their plea was rejected. In Bohemia, in February 1919, 20 per cent. of the babies were born dead, and 40 per cent. died within the first month of birth. Only in March 1919, when Lord Plumer, G.O.C. British Army of the Rhine, informed the British Government that his soldiers were 'unable to endure the spectacle of starving children', was the blockade partially relaxed (*Unfinished Victory*, Arthur Bryant (1940), pp. 4, 16, 10, 18).

lacks the means to annul it, 'and against which men of spirit rise on the first favourable opportunity.'[1]

On 5th November 1918, President Wilson transmitted to Germany the terms of the armistice agreed by the Allied Governments, and declared their willingness 'to make peace with the Government of Germany on the terms of peace laid down in the President's Address to Congress of January 8, 1918, and the principles of settlement enunciated in his subsequent Addresses.'[2]

'The nature of the Contract between Germany and the Allies', writes Keynes, '. . . is plain and unequivocal. The terms of the peace are to be in accordance with the Addresses of the President, and the purpose of the Peace Conference is "to discuss the details of their application". The circumstances of the Contract were of an unusually solemn and binding character; for one of the conditions of it was that the Germans should agree to Armistice Terms which were to be such as would leave her helpless. Germany having rendered herself helpless in reliance on the Contract, the honour of the Allies was peculiarly involved in fulfilling their part and, if there were ambiguities, in not using their position to take advantage of them.'[3]

The Contract was accepted by Germany because her people were starving, and at 5 a.m. on 11th November 1918, the terms of the Armistice were signed by her delegates. Nevertheless, when on 28th June 1919, the Treaty of Versailles was dictated, according to Harold Nicolson, 'nineteen out of President Wilson's twenty-three "Terms of Peace" were flagrantly violated.'[4] How came this about? It was the precipitate of high ideals compounded with the lowest morals; the product of the variant temperaments of the three chief artists of the Treaty – Woodrow Wilson, Georges Clemenceau, and David Lloyd George – lopped or stretched to fit the procrustean bed of emotional mass democracy.

[1] See *supra*, Chapter I, p. 20.

[2] Cited by John Maynard Keynes (later Lord Keynes) in *The Economic Consequences of the Peace* (1919), p. 54. Keynes was the official representative of the British Treasury at the Paris Peace Conference. For Wilson's Addresses see Appendix II.

[3] Ibid., p. 55. [4] *Peacemaking 1919* (1933), p. 13.

President Wilson had a theocratic and one-track mind; he had a complete faith in democracy, and believed that the voice of the people was identical with the judgment of God. He identified himself with his mystic Charter and was convinced that were it included in the Peace Treaties, 'it mattered little what inconsistencies, what injustices, what flagrant violations of his own principles those Treaties might contain',[1] because in time its magic must by the will of the peoples of the world rectify all errors. Before Congress, on 11th February 1918, he had declared: 'There shall be no annexations, no contributions, no punitive damages . . . self-determination is not a mere phrase. It is an imperative principle of action which statesmen will henceforth ignore at their peril.'[2] Nevertheless, Keynes says: 'He had no plan, no scheme, no constructive ideas whatever for clothing with the flesh of life the commandments he had thundered from the White House.'[3]

In 1918, Clemenceau was a disillusioned old man of seventy-seven. When he heard that Germany had accepted the terms of the Armistice, he exultantly exclaimed: '*Enfin! Il est arrivé ce jour que j'attends depuis un demi-siècle! Il est arriveé le jour de la revanche!*'[4] He was the apotheosis of French tribalism, but no hypcrite. His policy was to put back the clock and undo all that Germany had accomplished since 1870. He 'stood throughout the Peace Conference', writes C. Howard Ellis, 'for nothing but hatred and fear, and a cynically frank desire to cripple and fetter [Germany] for ever.'[5] It was he and not the President who dominated the Conference, and to him the President's Charter was sentimental humbug: '*Quatorze commandements!*' he contemptuously exclaimed, '*c'est un peu raide! Le bon Dieu n'en avait que dix!*' And to the misfortune of France, out of his slogan '*La guerre est finie, la guerre continue*'[6] emanated the catastrophe of 1940.

[1] Ibid., p. 53.

[2] Half a century earlier, his predecessor, Abraham Lincoln, had fought one of the most terrible of wars to save his country from this 'imperative principle'.

[3] Keynes, op. cit., p. 39.

[4] Cited in *Fürst Bülow Denkwürdigkeiten* (1931), Vol. III, p. 302.

[5] *The Origin, Structure and Working of the League of Nations* (1928), p. 43.

[6] Cited by Arthur Bryant, op. cit., p. 45.

Lloyd George was firstly an artist of power, and secondly an artisan of peace. He knew what peace demanded, but because of the enthusiasm awakened by the ending of the war, he placed power first, and decided to appeal to the country, and on the tidal wave of popular emotionalism seek an unassailable mandate.

On the day following the Armistice, in an address to his Liberal supporters he said: 'No settlement which contravenes the principles of eternal justice will be a permanent one. . . . We must not allow any sense of revenge, any spirit of greed, any grasping desire, to over-rule the fundamental principle of righteousness.'[1] Ten days later, in modified form, these sentiments inspired his election manifesto. Because they met with scant popular response, on 29th November, in order to arouse more enthusiasm, the Prime Minister declared that 'Germany must pay for the costs of the war up to the limits of her capacity.' But before this sop could be digested, Mr George Barnes, the Labour member of the War Cabinet, who was more familiar with the sentiments of the people than Lloyd George, shouted from his platform: 'I am for hanging the Kaiser.' Here was the smell of blood, and British democracy eagerly gave tongue. On 11th December, three days before the elections, Lloyd George capitulated to the 'general will', and in his final manifesto he promised the demented electorate: 'trial of the Kaiser; punishment of those responsible for atrocities; and fullest indemnities for Germany.' They reaped a political grand slam. When, on 28th December, the results of the polls were declared, the Coalition Government was returned to power with a majority of 262 over all independent parties.

Why did Lloyd George turn this political somersault? Howard Ellis's answer is almost certainly the right one. 'He generally saw the better course', he says, 'and always adopted the worse when that seemed necessary in order not to endanger his lease of power. . . . He won his General Election by an overwhelming majority on hanging the Kaiser and making Germany pay for the war.' And, during the Conference, 'on the rare occasions when he did try to rise above the blood-lust

[1] Cited by Nicolson, op. cit., p. 21.

of the people he was faced with the imminent risk of losing his job, and promptly retracted.'[1]

Thus it came about that the primeval code of enmity dominated the Peace Conference, and in Clemenceau the war-crazed democracies found their Cato.[2]

The Conference formally assembled on 18th January 1919, and because its task was to draft a treaty of peace, its aim should have been to eliminate the causes which had precipitated the war. According to Keynes, 'the most serious of the problems which claimed its attention were not political or territorial but financial and economic, and that the perils of the future lay not in frontiers or sovereignties but in food, coal and transport.'[3] Nevertheless instead of alleviating them the bulk of its decision aggravated them. The more important were:

TERRITORIAL: Alsace-Lorraine to be returned to France; the greater part of the province of Posen (the Polish Corridor) with its 600,000 German inhabitants to be ceded to Poland; Danzig, a predominantly German city, to be made a free city under the protection of the League; Memel to be ceded to Lithuania, and Eupen-Malmédy to Belgium. These changes involved the transfer of 28,000 square miles of German territory, inhabited by 7,000,000 German nationals. In addition, Germany was deprived of her entire colonial empire, the third largest in the world.

INDUSTRIAL: The Saar Basin to be ceded to France for fifteen years,[4] and the Upper Silesian coalfields to be surrendered to Poland. These mutilations, coupled with the loss of Alsace-Lorraine, deprived Germany of 60,800,000 tons of coal annually, and in addition to this loss she was compelled to deliver yearly over a period of ten years 40,000,000 tons of coal to France, Italy, Belgium and Luxemburg.

[1] Howard-Ellis, op. cit., pp. 42, 44.

[2] The dominance of France is to be seen in the names of the peace treaties, all are French: Versailles with Germany, 28th June 1919; Neuilly with Bulgaria, 27th November 1919; Trianon with Hungary, 4th June, 1920; St. Germain with Austria, 16th July 1920; and Sèvres with Turkey, 10th August 1920.

[3] Op. cit., p. 134.

[4] The Saar Basin was exclusively inhabited by Germans, and had been part of Germany for 1,000 years. Its coal mines were placed at the disposal of France in compensation for damage done to her own.

COMMERCIAL: All vessels of her mercantile marine exceeding 1,600 tons gross; half her vessels between 1,000 and 1,600 tons; one quarter of her trawlers and fishing boats, and 20 per cent. of her inland navigation tonnage to be surrendered to the Allied Powers, as well as 5,000 locomotives and 150,000 railway wagons in good order.

FINANCIAL: All German foreign investments and property, national or private, to be confiscated, and a Reparations Commission appointed to assess Germany's indebtedness to the Allies. In 1921 it was fixed at 132 milliard gold marks (£6,600,000,000) – that is thirty-three times the indemnity Germany had exacted from France in 1871.

MILITARY: The Rhineland to be declared a demilitarized zone; the fleet to be forbidden to possess battleships and submarines; the army to be restricted to a long service force of 100,000 officers and men. As it was prohibited to have tanks, heavy guns, military aircraft and anti-aircraft artillery, it was to be little more than a gendarmerie.

MORAL: Her leading men, including most of her princes and generals, to stand trial as 'war criminals', and as the crowning insult, the Treaty demanded that Germany admitted her guilt for the whole war.

These terms are examined by Keynes, and he states that he is mainly concerned, 'not with the justice of the Treaty . . . but with its wisdom and with its consequences.'[1] 'My purpose in this book', he writes, 'is to show that the Carthaginian Peace is not *practically* right or possible.'[2]

Years later, in 1946, his forecasts were challenged in a book entitled *The Carthaginian Peace or the Economic Consequences of Mr. Keynes*; it was the work of a brilliant young Frenchman, Etienne Mantoux, who tragically was killed in action eight days before Germany unconditionally surrendered on 7th May 1945. In opposition to Keynes he held that justice demanded that Germany should pay for the whole damage caused by the war,[3] and he set out to prove that many of Keynes's forecasts were not verified by subsequent events. In this he was right;

[1] Op. cit., p. 60. [2] Ibid., p. 33.

[3] Compare with Vattel's remarks on peace-making, see *supra* Chapter I, pp. 18–19.

but the validity of his criticism rests, not on the terms of the Treaty upon which Keynes based his forecasts, instead on the failure of the victors to implement them. This was due, not only to German intransigeance, but also to the chaos which resulted from the victors' attempts to implement them. Soon it was discovered that, in order to revive their international trade, it was more profitable for them to restore Germany's economy than to shackle it. Failure to do so, Keynes had predicted would inevitably lead to another European explosion.

'If we aim deliberately', he wrote, 'at the impoverishment of Central Europe, vengeance, I dare predict, will not limp. Nothing can then delay for very long that final civil war between the forces of Reaction and the despairing convulsions of Revolution, before which the horrors of the late German war will fade into nothing, and which will destroy, whoever is victor.'[1]

Further he forecast that the only way full reparations could be exacted was to nurse the trade and industry of Germany for a period of five to ten years; supply her with large loans, and make her the greatest industrial nation in Europe.[2] In a blind and confused way the course of events forced the victors into this direction.

In December 1922, Germany defaulted on her reparation payments, and to enforce them, on 11th January 1923, French and Belgian troops occupied the Ruhr. Thereupon the mark crashed, and in the following November stood at the fantastic figure of 4,200,000,000,000 to the dollar. The currency was then stabilized at 1,000,000,000,000 paper marks for one *retenmark*, and in April 1924, the Dawes Committee recommended that a loan of 800 million gold marks be granted to Germany in order to place her currency on a new basis. No sooner was this agreed than foreign capital began to pour into Germany, and during the period of the Dawes Plan – that is up to 1929 – its net importation was more than twice the amount of reparation payments. As Mantoux admits: 'Reparations were being paid, literally, with the money of foreign investors, not with the savings and taxes of the German people.'[3] Also he writes: 'Mr. Keynes had predicted that the Reparation clauses could

[1] Op. cit., p. 251. [2] Ibid., p. 189. [3] Op. cit., p. 147.

never be carried out. They never were. This outcome has earned him the glory of a prophet.'[1] Not alone so, because he also predicted that:

'When Germany has recovered her strength and pride, as in due time she will, many years must pass before she again casts her eyes Westward. Germany's future now lies in the East, and in that direction her hopes and ambitions, when they revive, will certainly turn.'[2]

The crux of the whole problem has concisely been stated by Professor E. H. Carr: 'The victors of 1918 "lost the peace" in Central Europe because they continued to pursue a principle of political and economic disintegration in an age which called for larger and larger units.'[3] In other words, the Treaty should have aimed at the integration of Europe, if only in order to eliminate the economic causes of war.

On 28th June 1919, the Treaty of Versailles was signed by the German plenipotentiaries at the pistol point of the blockade, and therefore was morally invalid. The other treaties were as bad, notably those of Trianon and St. Germain, which organized chaos in Central Europe.[4] In one and all, instead of there being no annexations, no contributions, no punitive damages, these three malignant viruses of war were implanted, and as to the self-determination of peoples, instead of the peacemakers regarding it as 'an imperative principle of action', they ignored it as 'a mere phrase'.

Colonel Hoffman Nickerson has written that he suspects '. . . that the worst bunch of autocrats known in history – say Nero, Heliogabalus, Caesar Borgia and Louis XV – given the Europe of 1919, would have mustered up enough collective intelligence and good will to make something of it.' Nevertheless, in the final reckoning, it was not Wilson, nor Clemenceau,

[1] Ibid., p. 155.

[2] *A Revision of the Treaty*, John Maynard Keynes (1922), p. 186.

[3] *The Twenty Years of Crisis* (1940), p. 294.

[4] By the terms of the Treaty of Trianon, Hungary was deprived of 71 per cent. of her territory, and 3,000,000 ethnic Hungarians were incorporated in Czechoslovakia, Rumania and Yugoslavia. By those of St. Germain, Austria was reduced to some two-thirds of her German-speaking territory, was prohibited to unite with Germany, and 3,500,000 of her German subjects were assigned to Czechoslovakia, and 230,000 to Italy.

nor Lloyd George who compounded the betrayal, it was, as Colonel Nickerson points out, hysterical and irresponsible mass democracy, which came into full bloom during the war. 'Without democracy', he writes, 'although a certain amount of war will always be inevitable, nevertheless its ferocity and destruction might be kept within bounds by setting up government independent of election and therefore not compelled alternately to rouse popular passion and to cringe before it.'[1]

Obscured even from the would-be destroyers of democracy, from now on 'independence of election' became a hidden tendency in the *Weltanschauung* which emanated from out the war. Blindly human events began to swing toward a new political lodestar which, although invisible, would seem to be guiding the world bark of mutinous nations toward a new international order, whether better or worse was impossible to say.

2 · *Adolf Hitler*

During the war, the Allied nations had been told that it was being fought to make the world safe for democracy; but when it was won they found that the opposite was true. Instead of being safe, democracy was left so rickety that one dictator after the other emerged from out of the chaos, to establish autocracies of various kinds in Poland, Turkey, Italy, Spain, Portugal, Austria and Germany. These dictators held one thing in common – abhorrence of Bolshevism; therefore they stood in opposition, not only to the old democratic order, but also to the new Marxist order, which had taken root in Russia and which during the final lap of the war and throughout its aftermath threatened every non-Communist country.

Of the dictators, the one who attained the highest historical significance was Adolf Hitler (1889–1945): one of the most extraordinary men in history. He was born at Braunau-am-Inn on 20th April 1889. In the war he had risen to the rank of corporal, and after it he became the seventh member of an obscure political group in Munich, which called itself the 'German Workers' Party'. In 1923, when the French were in occupation of the Ruhr, and were fostering a Communist

[1] *Can we limit War* (1934), p. 112.

separatist movement in the Rhineland and a Catholic separatist movement in Bavaria, he sprang to fame. On 9th November, he and Ludendorff attempted a *coup d'état* in Munich, and although it failed, his trial was a political triumph, because it made him one of the most talked of men in Germany. During his imprisonment in the fortress of Landsberg am Lech, he wrote the first volume of his *Mein Kampf*.

Hitler was the living personification of Dr Jekyll and Mr Hyde. As the one he raised Germany from out of the slough of degradation into which the Treaty of Versailles and the inflation which followed the French occupation of the Ruhr had engulfed her, and restored her national dignity and economy. As the other, he brutalized vast numbers of her people and made her name stink in the nostrils of the world.

He was a consummate psychologist and probably the world's greatest demagogue, a man who could plumb to its deepest depths the irrational in human nature, and distil from the emotions of the masses potent political intoxicants. Above all, he had absolute faith in himself and a super-rational belief in his invicibility, which endowed him with an irresistible personal magnetism. As a statesman, his ability to sense and grasp the psychological moment for action was his outstanding gift. Once he said to Hermann Rauschning:

'No matter what you attempt, if an idea is not yet mature, you will not be able to realise it. I know that as an artist, and I know it as a statesman. Then there is only one thing to do: have patience, wait, try again, wait again. In the subconscious, the work goes on. It matures, sometimes it dies. Unless I have the inner, incorruptible conviction: *this is the solution*, I do nothing. Not even if the whole party tries to drive me to action. I will not act; I will wait, no matter what happens. But if the voice speaks, then I know the time has come to act.'[1]

When that moment arrives, 'When a decision has to be taken', Goering once said to Sir Nevile Henderson, 'none of us count more than the stones on which we were standing. It is the Fuehrer alone who decides.'[2]

Rauschning, no flatterer of Hitler, writes:

[1] *Hitler Speaks*, Hermann Rauschning (1939), p. 181.
[2] *Failure of a Mission*, Sir Nevile Henderson (1940), p. 282.

'I have often had the opportunity of examining my own experience, and I must admit that in Hitler's company I have again and again come under a spell which I was only later able to shake off, a sort of hypnosis. He is, indeed, a remarkable man. It leads nowhere to depreciate him and speak mockingly of him. He is simply a sort of great medicine-man. He is literally that, in the full sense of the term. We have gone back so far toward the savage state that the medicine-man has become king amongst us.'[1]

This rings true. Hitler was the product of the savagery of his age; he fitted it like a glove the hand. In this lay that inescapable power which made him the enchanter of the German people.

3 · *Hitler's Foreign Policy*

The principles of National Socialism are chaotically scattered throughout *Mein Kampf*; a work of no literary merit, nor the empty babblings of a lunatic, as it has frequently been called. It is an apocalypse, a book of revelations, in which Hitler's conscious and sub-conscious aspirations are poured forth. Although in his subsequent speeches[2] he modified it in places, when it is borne in mind that it was dictated in the mid-twenties, at a time when few could see further than one move ahead, notwithstanding it is a blueprint not only of what he intended to do years before he attained power, but what, in spite of the chaos of the times, he actually did.

While in Marxism the fundamental principle is economic determinism through the struggle of classes, in National Socialism it is biological determinism through the struggle of races. Hitler was a Darwinian, to him 'the eternal laws of life . . . are and will remain those of a ceaseless struggle for existence' (p. 554).[3] 'He who would live must fight. He who does not wish to fight in this world, where permanent struggle is the law of life, has not the right to exist' (p. 242).

[1] *Hitler Speaks*, p. 254.

[2] See *Speeches of Adolf Hitler 1922–1939*, edited by Norman H. Baynes (1942), and *Hitler's Words*, (*Speeches, 1922–1943*), edited by Gordon W. Prange (1944).

[3] Page references are to James Murphy's English translation of *Mein Kampf* (1939).

On the question of race, he said to Rauschning:

'The conception of the nation has become meaningless. . . . The "nation" is a political expedient of democracy and Liberalism. We have to . . . set in its place the conception of race. . . . The new order cannot be conceived in terms of the national boundaries of the peoples with an historic past, but in terms of race that transcends those boundaries. . . . I know perfectly well . . . that in a scientific sense there is no such thing as race . . . [but] I as a politician need a conception which enables the order which has hitherto existed on historic bases to be abolished and an entirely new and anti-historic order enforced and given an intellectual basis. . . . And for this purpose the conception of races serves me well. . . . France carried her great Revolution beyond her borders with the conception of the nation. With the conception of race, National Socialism will carry its revolution abroad and recast the world.

'I shall bring into operation throughout all Europe and the whole world this process of selection which we have carried out through National Socialism in Germany. . . . The active section in the nations, the militant Nordic section,[1] will rise again and become the ruling element over these shopkeepers and pacifists, these puritans and speculators and busybodies.'[2]

Hitler's foreign policy derived from his concept of the biological struggle: might is right, not only in the jungle but also in international affairs. The stronger nation masters the weaker, and therefore is the fitter to survive. The future, as Hitler saw it, would be dominated by the *Herrenvolk*, not by the proletariat as Marx conceived, nor by the bourgeoisie, but by his master race – a type of Nietzschean superman. And it was because his racial ideology transcended all classes and nations that it was so violently opposed by both Communists and Democrats; they saw in it a common enemy.

Out of this concept emanated Hitler's Napoleonic dream – his vision of the future – which was very similar to the great French Emperor's as recorded by Las Cases.[3] To bring the

[1] By 'Nordic section' he means men of Nordic type rather than men of Nordic blood, men of National Socialist culture and faith: 'heroic man' in contradistinction to 'economic man'.

[2] *Hitler Speaks*, pp. 229–30.

[3] See *supra* Chapter III, p. 56.

continent of Europe under the aegis of Germany (instead of France) by unifying it, by eliminating the causes of war, by eradicating the threat of Bolshevism, and by putting an end to 'plutocratic exploitation' by liberating Europe from the shackles of international loan-capitalism.

To achieve this, the steps he decided on were: (1) To abrogate the Treaty of Versailles; (2) to bring Austria and all German minorities bordering on Germany within the Reich; (3) to dominate Europe economically; and (4) to establish a *Lebensraum* (living space) in Eastern Europe – that is, to occupy and colonize a vast stretch of it.

The first three and their repercussions led to the outbreak of the Second World War, and will be examined in the next Section; the fourth, which was discussed at length in *Mein Kampf*, forms the subject of the present one.

In the mid-twenties, Hitler rightly saw that, although France was 'the implacable enemy of Germany' (p. 505), England was the centre of gravity of his problem. For 300 years, he declared, England's policy had been to keep the European States 'opposed to one another in an equilibrium of forces', so as to protect 'her own rear while she pursued the great aims of British world-policy' (p. 500). Therefore it was not to her advantage to see Germany disappear as a great European Power.

While England, he said, has always desired 'to prevent any one Continental Power in Europe from attaining a position of world importance. . . . What France has always desired . . . is to prevent Germany from being a homogeneous Power', and thereby secure 'her hegemony in Europe.' Therefore 'The final aims of French diplomacy must be in perpetual opposition to the final tendencies of British statesmanship' (p. 504). How, then, could Germany profit from these divergent policies?

His answer is: 'Only by alliance with England was it possible to safeguard the rear of the new German crusade' – that is, the eastern expansion of Germany. Therefore 'no sacrifice should be considered too great in gaining England's friendship' (p. 128). 'The British nation will therefore be considered as the most valuable ally in the world as long as it can be counted upon to show that brutality and tenacity in its government . . .

which enables it to carry through to victory any struggle that it once enters upon' (p. 279).[1] The sole alternative was an alliance with Russia, and it should be remembered that Germany and Russia had but recently (16th April 1922) signed a treaty of mutual friendship at Rapallo.

Hitler was violently opposed to an alliance with Russia. 'An alliance', he exclaimed, 'which is not for the purpose of waging war has no meaning and no value' (p. 537). Not only were the Russians not to be trusted, but a military coalition with them 'would be the signal for a new war. And the result would be the end of Germany' (p. 538). Further: 'How can we', he asked, 'teach the German worker that Bolshevism is an infamous crime against humanity if we ally ourselves with this infernal abortion. . . . The struggle against the Jewish Bolshevization of the world demands that we should declare our position towards Soviet Russia' (p. 539).

He did so in no uncertain terms.

'The foreign policy of a People's State', he said, 'must first of all bear in mind the duty of securing the existence of the race which is incorporated in this State. And this must be done by establishing a healthy and natural proportion between the number and growth of the population on the one hand and the extent and resources of the territory they inhabit on the other. . . . What I call *healthy* proportion is that in which the support of a people is guaranteed by the resources of its own soil and subsoil (p. 523).

'Our Movement must seek to abolish the present disastrous proportion between our population and the area of our national territory, considering national territory as the source of our maintenance and as a basis of political power' (p. 526).

"The confines of the Reich as they existed in 1914 were thoroughly illogical; because they were not really complete, in the sense of including all the members of the German nation. Nor were they reasonable, in view of the geographical exigencies of military defence' (p. 529). . . . 'For the future of the German nation the 1914 frontiers are of no significance' (p. 530).

This being so, Hitler continues:

[1] In 1935 he made use of almost identical words in a conversation with the writer.

'We National Socialists, must stick firmly to the aim that we have set for our foreign policy; namely that the German people must be assured the territorial area which is necessary for it to exist on this earth.[1] And only for such action as is undertaken to secure those ends can it be lawful in the eyes of God and our German posterity to allow the blood of our people to be shed once again. . . . For no nation on earth possesses a square yard of ground and soil by decree of a higher Will and in virtue of a higher Right. The German frontiers are the outcome of chance and are only temporary frontiers that have been established as the result of political struggles which took place at various times' (p. 531).

Then comes the *dénouement* which was to startle the world in 1941:

'To-day we are all convinced of the necessity of regulating our situation in regard to France; but our success here will be ineffective in its broad results if the general aims of our foreign policy will have to stop at that. It can have significance only if it serves to cover our flank in the struggle for the extension of territory which is necessary for the existence of our people in Europe' (p. 532).

'Therefore we National Socialists have purposely drawn the line through the line of conduct followed by pre-War Germany in foreign policy. We put an end to the perpetual Germanic march towards the South and West of Europc and turn our eyes towards the lands of the East. We finally put a stop to the colonial and trade policy of pre-War times, and pass over to the territorial policy of the future.'

'But when we speak of new territory in Europe to-day we must principally think of Russia and the border States subject to her' (p. 533).

'For centuries Russia owed the source of its livelihood as a State to the Germanic nucleus of its governing classes. . . . The Jew has taken its place[2] . . . it is impossible for the Jew to keep this formidable State in existence for any long period of

[1] Earlier in *Mein Kampf* (pp. 126–8) Hitler has much to say on the biological right to occupy another nation's land, should the pressure of population demand it.

[2] In Lenin's day the Jews formed a high proportion of the Bolshevik Party.

time. He himself is by no means an organizing element, but rather a ferment of decomposition. This colossal Empire in the East is ripe for dissolution. . . . We are chosen by Destiny to be the witnesses of a catastrophe which will afford the strongest confirmation of the nationalist theory of race' (p. 533).

4 · The Road to War

Between 1924, when Hitler was a prisoner at Landsberg, and 1929, thanks to the influx of some £750,000,000 in foreign loans, conditions in Germany began rapidly to improve. Yet, in spite of her reviving prosperity, when Hitler was freed, he persistently predicted impending disaster. In 1929 it came and with a vengeance. A crash on the American Stock Exchange precipitated a world-wide monetary depression, which was to last until 1932.

For Germany's artificial prosperity it was catastrophic. In 1930, 17,500,000 Germans had to be supported by the State and in 1931 15,000,000 were practically starving. The Communist vote rose from 3,265,000 in 1928 to 4,592,000 in 1930, and the votes of the National Socialists from 810,000 to 6,409,000. Meanwhile unemployment soared from 1,320,000 in September 1929, to over 6,000,000[1] in 1932. On 31st July 1932, in the Reichstag elections, the National Socialists polled 13,745,000 votes, and became by far the largest party.[2] In consequence, on 30th January 1933, President Hindenburg called upon Hitler to fill the office of Chancellor and form a government.[3] When, on 2nd August 1934, Hindenburg died, the office of President was merged with that of the Chancellor, and Hitler became Fuehrer of the German people as well as Supreme Commander of the armed forces of the Reich, who swore allegiance to him personally.

Soon after he became Chancellor, Hitler opened his attack on the Treaty of Versailles. On 17th May 1933, before the

[1] These were registered unemployed, beside whom there were vast numbers of unregistered and semi-employed.

[2] The Social Democrats polled 8,000,000, the Communists 5,250,000 and the Centre 4,500,000.

[3] In a speech at Munich, on 24th February 1933, Hitler said: 'We are the result of the distress for which the others were responsible.' (Baynes, Vol. I, p. 252.)

Reichstag he declared that Germany alone was disarmed and that no other Power had fulfilled its obligation under the Treaty to do the same. Five months later he returned to the charge, and on 14th October, in another speech he announced that, because Germany was denied equal rights, and because 'No war can become humanity's permanent state; no peace can be the perpetuation of war',[1] Germany withdrew from the Disarmament Conference and the League of Nations.[2]

Next, on 26th January 1934, in order to secure Germany's eastern flank, Hitler entered on a ten-year peace pact with Poland, and when a year later the Saar Plebiscite was held, and a 95 per cent. vote supported a return to Germany, he was so encouraged that, on 16th March 1935, he announced his intention to reintroduce conscription, raise a peacetime army of thirty-six divisions and recreate the German Air Force. The response to this violation of the Treaty was the Franco-Soviet treaty of mutual assistance in Eastern Europe, signed on 2nd May, and a fortnight later a similar treaty was signed between France, the Soviet Union and Czechoslovakia. Next, on 18th June, Britain signed a unilateral agreement with Germany, according to which Germany was allowed to bring her naval strength up to 35 per cent. of the British. And when in October Mussolini invaded Abyssinia, on 18th November the League, headed by Britain, enforced economic sanctions against Italy, which drove the unwilling Duce into Hitler's arms.

On 27th February 1936 the Franco-Soviet treaty was ratified. Thereupon Hitler, although the German army was still in an embryonic stage, declared that the Locarno Treaty of 1925[3] had been violated, and, on 7th March, he occupied the demilitarized Rhineland. Eight days later, in a speech at Munich, he said: 'I go with the assurance of a sleepwalker in the way Providence dictates':[4] he had intuitively sensed that his military impotence was more than offset by Franco-British disunity.

[1] Baynes, Vol. II, p. 1094.

[2] Admitted as a member on 8th September 1926.

[3] A Treaty of Mutual Guarantee Between Britain, France, Germany, Italy and Belgium to keep the peace among themselves in all circumstances.

[4] Baynes, Vol. II, p. 1307.

In May, Léon Blum formed his left-wing Popular Front Government in France, and although the Communists were not formal members of it, they attained great strength and influence. This, coupled with the Franco-Soviet treaty, split the continent into two ideological camps when on 17th July civil war broke out in Spain. Russia intervened on the part of the Republicans, largely composed of Communists and Anarchists, and Germany and Italy intervened on the part of the Nationalists under General Francisco Franco; while the Blum Government assisted the Republicans with arms, and British popular opinion sided with them. In October, Germany and Italy signed a pact which laid the foundation of the Berlin-Rome Axis, and, on 25th November, an Anti-Comintern Pact was concluded between Germany and Japan.

While these events were distracting Europe, Great Britain sank deeper and deeper into the slough of pacifism. By the spring of 1935 she was so embogged that in the notorious Peace Ballot, fostered by the League of Nations Union, 11,000,000 people proclaimed their unswerving faith in the League as an instrument of peace. On all questions of defence, this completely shackled the government.'[1]

Besides Hitler's steady evasion of the Versailles treaty, in order to make Germany independent of international loan-capitalism, he resorted to a system of finance which antagonized the great trading nations, particularly the United States and Great Britain, who between them represented the Money Power of the world. In *Mein Kampf* he recognizes two forms of capitalism, the one based on the product of creative labour, and the other on usury (p. 180). Of the latter he wrote:

'. . . that international stock-exchange capital was not only the chief instigating factor in bringing on the War but now when war is over it turns the peace into a hell. The struggle

[1] Although many supporters of the League believed that collective security should be backed by force of arms, the vast bulk of the electorate did not. This is borne out by Mr Stanley Baldwin who, on 12th November 1936, said in the House of Commons: 'Supposing I had gone to the country and said that we must rearm, does anyone think that this pacific democracy would have rallied to that cry at that moment? I cannot think of anything that would have made the loss of the election from my point of view more certain' (*Parliamentary Debates*, 5th Series, Vol. 317, col. 1144).

against international finance capital and loan capital has become one of the most important points in the programme on which the German nation has based its fight for economic freedom and independence' (p. 184).

He held that, as long as the international monetary system was based on gold, a nation which cornered gold could impose its will on those which lacked it. This could be done by drying up the sources of exchange, and thereby compelling other countries to accept loans on interest in order to distribute their production.

Therefore he decided: (1) To refuse foreign interest-bearing loans, and base German currency on production instead of on gold; (2) to obtain imports by direct exchange of goods – barter – and subsidize exports when necessary; (3) to put a stop to what was called 'freedom of the exchanges' – that is, license to gamble in currencies and shift fortunes from one country to another according to the political situation; and (4) to create money when men and materials were available for work instead of running into debt by borrowing.

Because the life of loan capitalism depended upon the issue of interest-bearing loans, were Hitler allowed to succeed,[1] other nations would certainly follow his example, and a time might come when all non-gold-holding governments would exchange goods for goods and gold would lose its power. To smash Hitler's financial system, therefore became the aim of loan capitalism.

In September 1937, a new American depression set in, and it developed with such rapidity that, on 19th October, the stock market collapsed, and in the following month the census of unemployment registered 11,000,000 totally unemployed and 5,500,000 partially so. This, coupled with Hitler's barter system, intensified the economic war, and so fierce did it become that in April 1939, the acting military attaché at the American embassy at Berlin reported: 'The present situation when viewed in the light of an active war which Germany is

[1] *The Times* (London) of 11th and 12th October 1940, pointed out that under Hitler's system: 'Germany ceased to experience any serious financial difficulty'; and 'Nothing is ever heard of the necessity of increasing taxation, compulsory savings, or the issue of enormous public war loans. Quite the contrary.'

now in the process of waging becomes clear. It is an economic war in which Germany is fighting for her very existence, Germany must have markets for her goods or die and Germany will not die.'[1]

When the depression struck the United States, Hitler had completed the first half of his anti-Versailles campaign. He had wiped out unemployment in Germany, had revived her prosperity, had remilitarized the Rhineland, had won over Italy and Japan, was in the process of raising a powerful army and air force, and most important of all had firmly established his rule throughout the Reich. Therefore he was free to turn to the second half.

Thirteen years before he had written in *Mein Kampf:* 'As a State, the German Reich shall include all Germans' (p. 334). This meant Austria and the Sudeten Germans in Czechoslovakia, the return of Danzig, and the elimination of the Polish Corridor. Then, and only then, would the Treaty of Versailles be annulled, and Germany, instead of being the pariah of the continent, would become its potential master.

With the dissolution of the Habsburg monarchy in 1918, Austria became an economic derelict, and many of her people believed that the only hope of her revival lay in a union with Germany, a yearning exploited by the growth of a powerful and vocal Austrian National Socialist Party in Vienna, which demanded self-determination.

On 11th February 1938, Hitler invited the Austrian Chancellor, Kurt von Schuschnigg, to Berchtesgaden, and on arrival Schuschnigg was forthwith presented with an ultimatum which, under threat of military invasion, he was compelled to sign. As it meant the surrender of Austria to Germany, early in March, Schuschnigg decided on the desperate expedient of holding a plebiscite on 13th March, in order to ascertain the will of the Austrian people. When, on 9th March, Hitler learnt of this, in a fury he ordered the army to cross the Austrian frontier, which it did on the 12th. Thus, and to the rejoicings of large numbers of Austrians, Austria was swallowed by the Reich; Czechoslovakia was outflanked, and the German frontier

[1] *The White House Papers of Harry L. Hopkins* (English edition, 1948), Robert E. Sherwood, Vol. I, p. 114.

brought into contact with Italy. All that the Western Powers did was to protest, which in no way discouraged Hitler from taking the next step – the liberation of the Sudeten Germans.

Unlike Austria, Czechoslovakia was a multinational State, and of her minorities the 3,500,000 Sudeten Germans, under the leadership of Konrad Henlein, was the largest and most important. In 1919 the Wilsonian magical wand of self-determination had been waved in the name of democracy to create Czechoslovakia; now, in 1938, Hitler resolved to wave it in the name of National Socialism and destroy her by transforming Henlein into his Trojan horse. On 28th March he summoned him to Berlin.

On 20th May, the Czech Government, alarmed by rumours of German troop concentrations near the frontier, ordered partial mobilization, and to Hitler's surprise France, supported by Russia, reaffirmed her promise to come to Czechoslovakia's aid. Because Hitler was not ready to face a general war, he soft-pedalled his project until 12th September, when, as the signal for a rising in Sudetenland, in a violent speech he attacked the Czech Government. Faced with the revolt, which meant a general war should France intervene, the French Prime Minister, Edouard Daladier, took fright and appealed to the British Prime Minister, Neville Chamberlain, but his hands were tied by the total unreadiness of his country to go to war, and Hitler knew it. On the 15th Chamberlain flew to Berchtesgaden to bargain with him. He made a second trip on the 22nd and a third on the 28th. The last resulted in a conference attended by Hitler, Mussolini, Chamberlain and Daladier; the Soviet Union was not invited, nor was Czechoslovakia consulted. It resulted in a decisive victory for Hitler – within ten days of 1st October the Sudetenland was to be surrendered to Germany. On the 30th, the Czech Government, under Eduard Beneš, capitulated, and Hitler's prestige soared to new heights.

In spite of his success, Hitler had no intention of calling a halt, and between 21st October and 17th December he issued a series of directives in which he ordered his army to prepare for the occupation of Czechoslovakia, Memel and Danzig, and as this was being done fortune played in his hands.

Between 6th and 9th March 1939, in order to suppress

separatists' intrigues in Slovakia and Ruthenia, the Czech President, Emil Hacha, dismissed their governments. Thereupon the deposed Slovak Premier, Josef Tiso, appealed to Hitler, and on his arrival in Berlin on 13th March, Hitler at once guaranteed the independence of Slovakia. The new Slovak President, Karol Sidor, was immediately informed of this, and under the now normal threat of military invasion was compelled to accept the ultimatum.

While Tiso was in Berlin, President Hacha also appealed to Hitler, and on 14th March was summoned to Berlin. There he received his ultimatum. The submission of Czechoslovakia was demanded, and should no resistance be offered, it would be granted autonomy within the Reich; the alternative was conquest. A draft communiqué was then prepared for Hacha's signature, in which it was stated that the President 'confidently placed the fate of the Czech people in the hands of the Fuehrer.'[1]

Two hours later the German troops crossed the Czech frontier, and when the British and French ambassadors protested, they were informed that the Fuehrer had done no more than comply with the President's request.

Intoxicated by his successes, and holding his opponents in profound contempt, Hitler took his last and this time fatal step. Instead of waiting a year or two until the political storm he had raised had subsided, on 23rd March 1939, he claimed the return of Memel, and immediately occupied it. Simultaneously he put forward proposals to Poland for the return of Danzig and the construction of an extra-territorial railway and road across the Polish Corridor. Then, on 31st March, to his consternation, the British Prime Minister announced in the House of Commons:

'... in the event of any action which clearly threatened Polish independence and which the Polish Government accordingly considered it vital to resist with their national forces, His Majesty's Government would feel themselves bound at once to lend the Polish Government all support in their power. They have given the Polish Government an assurance to this effect.'[2]

[1] Cited by Alan Bullock in *Hitler a Study in Tyranny* (1952), p. 445.
[2] *Parliamentary Debates*, Fifth Series, Vol. 345, col. 2415.

France associated herself with Great Britain, and, on 13th April, the unconditional guarantee to Poland was extended to Rumania and Greece.

Although Hitler may have held that these guarantees were no more than bluffs, the one thing he had to avoid was a war on two fronts. Therefore, in spite of the view he had expressed in *Mein Kampf* that a military coalition with Russia 'would be the signal for a new war, and the result would be the end of Germany', he decided to woo her. He did so, and on 21st August, in the words of Sir Winston Churchill, 'The sinister news broke upon the world like an explosion':[1] the Soviet Tass Agency announced that Hitler's envoy was flying to Moscow to sign a Non-Aggression Pact with the Soviet Union. It was signed on 23rd August, and Stalin gained what he wanted: war in Western Europe and peace in the U.S.S.R.

On the receipt of the news, the British Government announced that they were determined to fulfil their obligations to Poland, and on the 25th a formal treaty with Poland was proclaimed. Thus it came about that the unconditional decree of 31st March detonated war which, six years later, was to lead to the unconditional surrender of Germany. On 1st September German troops crossed the Polish frontier, and the Twenty Years Armistice ended.

5 · *Tactical Theories and Fallacies*

Tactically, World War I differed from previous wars in that three novel weapons were introduced – lethal gas, the aeroplane, and the tank. In spite of its undoubted powers, the first need not detain us, because after the war its development was dropped,[2] and it was not used as a weapon in World War II. Had the war lasted another year, what was as yet seen by a few would have become generally apparent: tank and aero-

[1] *The Second World War* (1948), Vol. I, p. 307.

[2] This was due to popular emotionalism, which is nearly always irrational. As long ago as 1864, a Mr R. W. Richardson, in the *Popular Science Review*, pictured an army put to sleep and anaesthetized by means of non-lethal gas (cited by Amos A. Fries and Clarence J. West in *Chemical Warfare* (1921), pp. 4–5).

plane had added so vastly to mobility that startling new tactics could be developed which would radically influence the art of war. By neutralizing the bullet, the tank added hitherto unattainable security to superficial movements, and by transcending the battlefield and converting the skies into a universal road, the aeroplane added a new dimension to war. Both favoured the offensive.

The leading exponent of the offensive use of aircraft was the Italian General Guilio Douhet, whose theories, elaborated in his book *The Command of the Air*,[1] had a profound influence on war, and tallied closely with those held by General William Mitchell in the United States and General Sir Hugh Trenchard in England.

Douhet was looked upon as a futurist; but actually he was a tactical reactionary, because he harked back to the great artillery bombardments of World War I, which were purely destructive operations, and tilted them from an horizontal into a vertical position. He compared the aeroplane 'to a special gun capable of firing shells a distance equal to its flying range'; therefore an air force was no more than 'a large battery of guns' (p. 162). He held that, 'Because of independence of surface limitations and its superior speed . . . the aeroplane is the offensive weapon *par excellence*' (p. 18). 'What determines victory in aerial warfare', he writes, 'is fire power. Speed serves only to come to grips with the foe. . . . A slower, heavily armed plane, able to clear its way with its own armament, can always get the best of the fastest pursuit plane' (p. 41).[2] Therefore in air warfare there is no need to consider the defensive, whether in the air or on the ground, and, in consequence, air power should act independently of armies and fleets. 'All possible resources must be used to strengthen the Independent Air Force so that it can operate and defend itself in the air solely by means of intensive and violent offensives. . . .' This 'statement is fundamental and admits no exceptions' (p. 95).

[1] The first edition was published in Italy in 1921, and the second edition in 1927. The English edition (1943) is a translation of the latter, and references are to it.

[2] This contradicts what he had written on p. 34: 'An Independent Air Force should be organically composed of bombing units and combat units . . . the second to protect the bombers.'

'. . . auxiliary aviation[1] is worthless, superfluous, harmful' (p. 85). '. . . the use of anti-aircraft guns is a mere waste of energy and resources' (p. 49).

The first task in the air offensive is to gain command of the air. 'To have command of the air means to be in a position to prevent the enemy from flying while retaining the ability to fly oneself' (p. 26). 'To achieve command of the air means victory; to be beaten in the air means defeat. . . . Any diversion from this primary purpose is an error. . . . It can . . . be accomplished only by aerial means, to the exclusion of army and navy weapons. . . . *An adequate national defence cannot be assured except by an aerial force capable . . . of achieving command of the air*' (p. 29). This is repeated time and again, and, granted a superior air force, Douhet light-heartedly assumes that command of the air can be gained within a few days of the outbreak of war.

Once command of the air is gained, the second phase opens; its aim is to obliterate the enemy. The targets should be 'industrial and commercial establishments; important buildings . . . transportation arteries and centres; and . . . areas of civilian population' (p. 22). Further, 'in the future, war will be waged essentially *against the unarmed populations of the cities and great industrial centres*' (p. 223). 'The guiding principle of bombing action should be this: the objective must be destroyed completely in one attack' (p. 22). This would appear to be easy, because it cannot be denied 'that 1,000 tons of explosive, incendiary, and poison-gas bombs dropped on Paris or London could destroy these cities' (p. 150).

'A complete breakdown of the social structure', he writes, 'cannot but take place in a country subjected to this kind of merciless pounding from the air. The time would soon come when, to put an end to the horror and suffering, the peoples themselves, driven by the instinct of self-preservation, would rise up and demand an end to the war – this before their army and navy had time to mobilize at all!' (p. 52). His conclusion is, that '. . . the nation which, once it has conquered the air, can maintain in operation, not 100, but 50 or even 20 such planes [of 6,000 horse-power], will have won decisively, because

[1] Aircraft detached to co-operate with the army etc.

it will be in a position to break up the whole social structure of the enemy in less than a week, *no matter what his army and navy may do*' (p. 118).

In his opinion, 'aerial war will be short' (p. 160). 'Mercifully, the decision will be quick . . . since the decisive blows will be directed at civilians, that element of the countries at war least able to sustain them' (p. 54).

Of the future of land warfare, he takes no notice whatsoever of motorization; 'it will take on', he writes, 'a static character very similar to that of the World War . . . continuous fronts will be set up in the future war as in the World War. . . . All theories and concepts of a war of movement will fail against these continuous fronts' (pp. 142–143). This went far to reinforce his argument that air power alone could win a war.

The exponents of the future role of the tank were almost entirely restricted to the members of the General Staffs of the French and British Tank Corps; but whereas the former adhered to close co-operation between tanks and infantry – as illustrated in the Cambrai tactics – from the earliest days the latter had considered the independent use of tanks and the future development of tank armies including all arms. These ideas were founded on the traditional conception of battle as a clinch and struggle between armed forces, and although tactically sound, they excluded the use of a very different tactical idea, which the tank rendered practical. This idea first occurred to the writer in the summer of 1917, and reached maturity in March the following year, when the Germans broke through the British Fifth Army.

In the débâcle which followed he saw tens of thousands of men pulled back by their panic-stricken headquarters. He saw Army Headquarters retire, then Corps, next Divisional, and lastly Brigade, or *vice versa*. He saw the intimate connection between will and action; that action without will loses co-ordination; that without a directing brain an army is reduced to a mob. Then it became fully apparent to him that by means of the tank a new tactics could be evolved, which would enable a comparatively small tank army to fight battles like Issus and Arbela over again. What was their tactical secret? It was that, while Alexander's phalanx held the Persian battle-body in a clinch, he and his Companion Cavalry struck at the enemy's will, concentrated as it was in the person of Darius. Once this will was paralysed, the body became inarticulate.

In May 1918, this idea was elaborated in a long memorandum entitled 'Strategical Paralysis as the Object of the Decisive Attack', later changed to 'Plan 1919'.[1] Its salient points were:

The fighting power of an army lies in its organization, which can be destroyed either by wearing it down or by rendering it inoperative. The first comprises killing, wounding, and capturing the enemy's soldiers – body warfare; the second in rendering inoperative his power of command – brain warfare. To take a single man as an example; the first method may be compared with a succession of wounds which will eventually result in his bleeding to death; the second – a shot through the brain.

The brains of an army are its Staff – Army, Corps and Divisional Headquarters. Could they suddenly be removed from an extensive sector of the German front, the collapse of the personnel they control will be little more than a matter of hours.

As our present theory is to destroy personnel, our new theory should be to destroy command. Not after the enemy's personnel has been disorganized, but before it has been attacked, so that it may be found in a state of disorganization when attacked.

The means proposed were a sudden eruption of squadrons of fast-moving tanks,[2] which unheralded would proceed to the various enemy headquarters,[3] and either round them up or scatter them. Meanwhile every available bombing machine was to concentrate on the supply and road centres. Only after these operations had been given time to mature was the enemy's front to be attacked in the normal way, and directly penetration was effected, pursuit was to follow.

[1] For the plan in full, see *Memoirs of an Unconventional Soldier*, Major-General J. F. C. Fuller (1936), pp. 321–36.

[2] The specifications of this tank were: maximum speed 20 miles an hour; circuit 150 to 200 miles; and ability to span a 14-foot gap. Later it was built and known as the Medium D Tank. The first model was produced in 1919, but failed to come up to specifications.

[3] At the time there were nine German Army Headquarters on the Western Front, on an average distance of eighteen miles from the front line. Corps and Divisional Headquarters were, of course, much closer.

The memorandum dealt with the duties of all arms; those of the R.A.F. were as follows:

(1) To act as an advanced guard to the tanks; (2) to guide tanks on to their objectives; (3) to protect tanks from hostile gun fire; (4) to assist tanks in disorganizing the enemy's headquarters; (5) to supply advanced squadrons of tanks with petrol, ammunition, etc.; (6) to act as messengers between tank squadrons and their bases; and (7) to carry tank brigade commanders above their sectors, so that they might follow operations and handle their reserves accordingly.

In modified form, this tactical theory was first put to the test in 1939, and became known as *Blitzkrieg*.

Both Douhet's theory and the writer's were based on the offensive, and demanded an offensive strategy to implement them, which, in its turn, demanded an aggressive political aim. Therefore the key to their acceptance, rejection or modification is to be sought in the peace policies of the future belligerents.

Those of France and Great Britain were to maintain the *status quo* under the aegis of the League; they had nothing to gain from another war, and as their peoples were pacific democracies so also were their governments. On the other hand, as may be gauged by any reader of *Mein Kampf*, Hitler's policy was ultra aggressive, and his government was autocratic, it mattered little whether the German people were pacific or not. These divergent aims shaped the tactical policies of the three main belligerents of 1939.

As a tactical theorist, Hitler was as clairvoyant as he was astute as a politician. He had watched the last war closely and had absorbed its tactical lessons – a remarkable thing for a corporal to do. But what was more remarkable, he projected them into the future and built his military power on them. In 1939, the superiority of the German Army over all other armies did not lie in numerical superiority, nor in superiority of arms and equipment, but in its tactics, which, if not devised by Hitler himself, were forced by him upon his reluctant General Staff.

In *Mein Kampf* he had written that in the next war motorization 'will make its appearance in an overwhelming and decisive form' (p. 537). He had a passion for high-speed motor cars, express motorways (*Reichsautobahnen*) and aircraft; therefore warfare based on high mobility and striking power appealed to him. Both the German Air Force (*Luftwaffe*) and Army were organized to develop speed; but the task of the former was not to win a war single-handed, as Douhet insisted, but primarily to co-operate with the Army. Its bombers were to prepare the advance of the ground forces; and its dive bombers were to act as flying field artillery and cover the assault of the cutting-edge of the army – its armoured divisions. Only secondarily was the *Luftwaffe* to operate as an independent air force.

Force alone was not accepted by Hitler as the sole effective means. To Hermann Rauschning he said: 'I have learnt from the Bolsheviks. . . . One always learns most from one's enemies.' Further:

'The place of artillery preparation for frontal attack by the infantry in trench warfare will in future be taken by revolutionary propaganda, to break down the enemy psychologically before the armies begin to function at all. . . . How to achieve the moral break-down of the enemy before the war has started – that is the problem that interests me. Whoever has experienced war at the front will want to refrain from all avoidable bloodshed. . . . Mental confusion, contradiction of feeling, indecisiveness, panic: those are our weapons. . . . The lessons of revolution, these are the secret of the new strategy. . . . To me all means will be right. . . . My motto is: "Destroy [the enemy] by all and any means".'[1]

French tactical theory was purely defensive; it was based on building an immensely powerful system of fortifications, known as the Maginot Line, from Basle to Wissembourg, and thence to Longwy – that is, along the common Franco-German frontier – in order to cover Alsace and Lorraine. From it, bomber aircraft were to operate like long-range artillery.

There is little to criticize in this, because French man-power was half the German; therefore by blocking the Alsace-Lorraine front, the French were able to concentrate the bulk of their potentially inferior army on the Belgian frontier. Frequently the criticism has been raised that, in order to render

[1] *Hitler Speaks*, pp. 19, 21.

France impregnable, the Maginot Line should have been continued from Longwy to the Channel. But had this been done, its defence would have absorbed practically the whole of the French field army, and any form of offensive would have become impossible. As Napoleon had said in *Le Souper de Beaucaire:* 'He who remains behind his entrenchments is beaten; experience and theory are at one on this.'

The error was that the French failed to concentrate their armoured forces on the Belgian frontier; they had ample means to do so, because their tanks, both numerically and technically, were superior to the German. But instead of concentrating them in armoured divisions, they distributed them as infantry support units. This was a crucial tactical error, and alone is sufficient to account for the French débâcle.

In Great Britain, tactical theory was even more Rip-Van-Winkle-like than in France. Secure behind their natural Maginot Wall – the English Channel – the British Government and General Staff went to sleep for twenty years, and not until Hitler was thundering against Poland, did they wake up, and on 26th April 1939, reintroduce conscription. The tactical theory was that the first phase of World War I would repeat itself; therefore there would be ample time for a blockade of Germany to become effective. Meanwhile the Air Force would bomb German industrial cities and her civil population. For some unknown reason this was called 'Strategic Bombing'; it was based on Douhet's theory. Of armoured divisions there was only one available, part of which was in England when the Germans invaded France.

Although the Russians carefully studied Douhet's and the writer's tactical theories, they neither adopted the former nor understood the latter. In May 1937, a month before he was liquidated in Stalin's enormous purge of 1937–1938, which gutted the Russian Army,[1] Marshal Tukhachevski wrote in the *Bol'shevik:*

[1] The total number of victims was 35,000, or about half the officer corps: 3 out of 5 marshals; 13 out of 15 army commanders; 57 out of 85 corps commanders; 110 out of 195 division commanders; 220 out of 406 brigade commanders, and 30,000 officers below the rank of colonel (See *The Communist Party of the Soviet Union*; Leonard Schapiro (1960), p. 420).

'The swift growth of our aviation, tanks and mechanized formations at first also provoked some of the theoretical twist of the Fuller type. This was manifested as a new "manoeuver" theory which considered that the great speed of the tank did not permit of its use productively in combined operations with the infantry. From this grew an attempt to claim the complete independence of tank formations . . . and non-understanding of the requirement that tanks, like infantry, cannot successfully act in combined troop combat without mighty artillery support.'[1]

Another criticism ran:

'Western military thinkers, like Fuller and Liddell Hart, are said, in Russia, to be afraid of using the masses in the next war. Their desire to limit the size of armies, supplementing man-power by a highly developed technical equipment, is merely a rationalization of the bourgeois fear of masses.'[2]

Such Marxian silliness was to cost the Russians dear. In 1941, their tactics remained what they had always been, slow forward and backward movements of masses of unthinking men: droves of military kine, an inviting prey for the German armoured tigers.

[1] Cited by Raymond L. Garthoff in *How Russia Makes War*, p. 85.

[2] *Political Science Quarterly*, Vol. 51, No. 3 (1936), 'Soviet Philosophy of War', D. Fedotoff White, p. 349.

CHAPTER XIII

The Conduct of World War II

*

1 · Character of World War II

For war to be an effective instrument of policy, policy must be grounded on actual military conditions, and in 1914 they may be said to have been normal. The war opened on long-established frontiers and on the traditional lines of a struggle between similarly equipped armies that recognized the customary methods of waging war. But in its last lap, and still more so during its aftermath, very different conditions came into being. On the military side they were due to the introduction of novel weapons, and on the political to a sequence of catastrophic revolutions which challenged nineteenth-century civilization and profoundly changed the character of war.

As we have seen, of these revolutions by far the most important were those which disrupted Russia and Germany; the one founded on the ideology of Marx as interpreted by Lenin and Stalin, and the other on that of Hitler as formulated in the National Socialist creed. Both were totalitarian, embraced all forms of war, and their aims in war were not, as hitherto, only to compel their antagonists by force of arms to accept a policy repugnant to them, but also to change their national structures, ideologically, economically, and socially. This meant that the next war would be a struggle between variant ideologies – the Democratic, the Marxian, and the National Socialist, as well as between fighting forces. And because the ideology of the Democratic Powers expressed the sovereignty of individual nations and the free and unfettered will of their inhabitants, their potential foes were neither the German nor the Russian peoples; instead they were, on the one hand the National Socialist claim to racial superiority, which involved peoples outside the frontiers of the Reich, and on the other hand the Marxian materialistic philosophy of Soviet Russia, which embraced all the nations of the world. In short, ideas took precedence over populations and armies, and to be fully effective the destruction of an idea must bc total, which means that it can only be killed by a more acceptable idea.

These antagonistic ideologies led to three variant outlooks on war: that of the Democracies was either to free enslaved peoples or to prevent their enslavement; that of the National Socialists – to expand the Reich racially and territorially; and that of Soviet Russia – to foster world revolution through an ever-increasing extension of the class struggle. To the Democracies peace was an end in itself – the cessation of war; to the National Socialists it was a time wherein to incubate war; and to the Russian Marxists it was but another form of war. Of the Russian and German outlooks on war, the former was the more all-embracing, because its ideology was global and its warfare continuous, therefore it was the more threatening to the Democracies. What mattered was not whether Hitler was more evil than Stalin, or Stalin more so than Hitler, but which of their aims was the more dangerous to the democratic way of life.

In 1914, to all intents and purposes, the belligerents were firmly united nations, whose peoples staunchly supported their respective governments. But in 1939, and particularly in those countries in which revolutionary governments had been established, there existed extensive reactionary inner fronts, and in many other countries Communist, Fascist and National Socialist movements had taken root, all of which challenged Democracy. These fronts and movements enabled an enemy, who co-operated with them, to attack his antagonist internally, as important an operation in the ideological struggle as the overthrow of the enemy armies was in the physical struggle. War remained war, but it had become more complex; nevertheless, in spite of its complexities, Clausewitz's dictum that 'War is only a continuation of State policy by other means' remained constant.

2 · *Allied War Policy 1939–1940*

When, on 28th May 1937, Mr Neville Chamberlain became Prime Minister, he believed more firmly than any of his predecessors had that the fate of Europe depended on Anglo-

German collaboration. Between 1925 and 1930 Herr Stresemann, Field-Marshal Hindenburg's Foreign Minister, had vainly attempted to bring it about, and since then each succeeding British administration had failed to consider it, and what was as unfortunate, after Hitler's rise to power, the Baldwin administration paid no more than lip-service to defence. So it came about that, when Chamberlain took office, he had no military backing to his diplomacy, hence his policy of appeasing Hitler. The alternative, urged by Mr Churchill, then a private member of Parliament, was an alliance with Russia.[1] This was repugnant to Chamberlain, as may be gathered from a letter he wrote on 26th March 1939:

'I must confess to the most profound distrust of Russia. I have no belief whatever in her ability to maintain an effective offensive, even if she wanted to. And I distrust her motives, which seem to me to have little connection with our ideas of liberty, and to be concerned only with getting everyone by the ears. Moreover, she is both hated and suspected by many of the smaller States, notably by Poland, Roumania and Finland.'[2]

Could Russia have been relied on, there might have been sense in Churchill's alternative; but Chamberlain had gauged Stalin's intentions far more clearly than he had. Nevertheless, it is difficult to understand why Chamberlain decided to give his pledge to Poland, for it could be no other than a thinly disguised bluff. Feiling's explanation is, that his resolve to do so was based on news that a surprise attack on Poland was imminent.

Unable to base their war policy on the balance of power, on 3rd September 1939 – two days after Hitler invaded Poland – Britain and France proclaimed an ideological crusade against Hitler and Hitlerism. In the House of Commons Churchill

[1] In March 1938: 'I had been urging the prospects of a Franco-British-Russian alliance' (*The Second World War*, Vol. I, p. 213). In September 1938: 'I had for some time had friendly relations with M. Maisky', Soviet Ambassador in London (ibid., p. 229). On 4th May 1939: 'Not only must the full co-operation of Russia be accepted, but the three Baltic States . . . must also be brought into association' (ibid., p. 285). On 19th May 1939, in the House of Commons: '. . . why should you shrink from becoming the ally of Russia now? (ibid., p. 293).

[2] *Life of Neville Chamberlain*, Keith Feiling (1946), p. 403.

defined the war aim in no uncertain terms: 'This is not a question of fighting for Danzig or fighting for Poland', he declared. 'We are fighting to save the whole world from the pestilence of Nazi tyranny and in defence of all that is most sacred to man.'[1] Therefore the war was to be a Manichean contest between Good and Evil.[2]

This crusade of righteousness foreboded no happy end, unless the anti-Hitler Opposition in Germany became powerful enough to overthrow the National Socialist regime. Chamberlain was aware of this, and that the Opposition was supported by a number of Hitler's generals. In August and again in September 1938,[3] through its agents, the Opposition had contacted the British Foreign Office; therefore, on 4th September 1939, Chamberlain opened the ideological attack in a broadcast to the German people. He said: 'In this war we are not fighting against you, the German people, for whom we have no bitter feeling, but against a tyrannous and foresworn régime.'[4] Clearly his aim was to stimulate the Opposition, and from now on to divide the German people became a main plank in his policy.

After the defeat of Poland, in reply to Hitler's peace proposals – which were rejected by the British and French Governments – Chamberlain declared:

'We have no intention of depriving of her rightful place in Europe, a Germany which will live in friendship and confidence with other nations.' We look forward to the solutions 'through negotiation and agreement when time for that came. . . . We did not enter this war from revengeful motives, but only to defend freedom. We seek no material advantage for ourselves. We desire nothing from the German people which would wound their self-respect.'[5]

In mid-February 1940, two British Foreign Office repre-

[1] *Parliamentary Debates*, 5th Series, Vol. 351, col. 295.

[2] Compare with Vattel's first rule of 'the voluntary law of nations'; see *supra* Chapter I, p. 17.

[3] See *The German Resistance*, Gerhard Ritter (English edition, 1958), pp. 95 and 101.

[4] *Documents concerning German Polish Relations*, Cmd. 6106 (1939), No. 144, p. 195.

[5] Cited by Ritter, op. cit., p. 142.

sentatives met a member of the Opposition at Ouchy in Switzerland, and brought with them a tentative offer of five points in writing, the translation of which reads:

'(1) Assurance will be given that the British Government will not by attacking in the West use to Germany's military disadvantage any passing crisis which may be connected with the action taken by the German Opposition.

'(2) The British Government declares itself ready to work with a new German Government which has its confidence to get a lasting peace and will give Germany the necessary financial aid.

'(3) Further assurances it cannot give without previous agreement with the French Government. If France's confidence is obtained then further assurances are possible.

'(4) In the case of French participation in the negotiations it would be desirable that the approximate date for the carrying out of this action inside Germany be communicated.

'(5) If the German Opposition should wish their action made easier through a diversion by the Western Powers, the British Government is ready within the bounds of possibility to meet that wish.'[1]

'It is only legend,' Ritter writes, 'which asserts that from the outset Britain left the German Opposition in the lurch; that is not true of the "phony war" period, nor of the Chamberlain Government.'[2]

On 3rd September 1939, Mr Churchill became First Lord of the Admiralty, with a seat in the War Cabinet, and he was soon engaged at his old game of devising diversionary sideshows. On the 7th he instructed the Naval Staff to prepare a plan 'for forcing a passage into the Baltic'; he christened it 'Catherine', after Catherine the Great, because, as he says, 'Russia lay in the background of my thought.'[3] Ten days later, the Russians, not having been granted the privilege of reading the Baltic plan, invaded Poland and swallowed up half of her;[4] whereupon, on 1st October, in a broadcast

[1] Ibid., p. 158. [2] Ibid., p. 163.

[3] *The Second World War*, Vol. I, p. 364 and Appendix G.

[4] Of this event, he writes: 'I had never any illusion about them [the Russians]. I knew that they accepted no moral code and studied their own interest only' (Ibid., Vol. I, p. 351). Why then had he so ardently courted them?

Churchill said: 'I cannot forecast to you the action of Russia. It is a riddle wrapped in a mystery inside an enigma.'[1] Reference to any work on Soviet foreign policy would have informed him that it had remained constant for over twenty years – it was peace at home and trouble abroad.

His next diversionary side show he calls 'my pet', and he threw himself with 'increasing confidence into this daring adventure.'[2] It was the Narvik expedition of April 1940; it ended in a fiasco, tumbled the Chamberlain administration, and, on 10th May 1940, Churchill became Prime Minister and Minister of Defence. In this dual capacity the conduct of Britain's part in the war passed into his hands.

Churchill was a man cast in the heroic mould, a berserker ever ready to lead a forlorn hope or storm a breach, and at his best when things were at their worst. His glamorous rhetoric, his pugnacity, and his insistence on annihilating the enemy appealed to human instincts, and made him an outstanding war leader, which was the greatest of his contributions to his country. Nevertheless, as Napoleon once said:

'The first quality in a general in chief is to have a cool head, which receives exact impressions, which never gets excited or dazzled by good or bad news. . . . There are men who, due to their physical and moral constitution, create a picture out of everything . . . nature has not intended them either to command armies or to direct the grand operations of war.'[3]

How far Churchill fulfilled these requirements may be judged from what his closest collaborators had to say of him:

'You cannot judge the P.M. by ordinary standards', writes General Lord Ismay, 'he is not in the least like anyone that you or I have ever met. He is a mass of contradictions. He is either on the crest of a wave, or in the trough: either highly laudatory, or bitterly condemnatory: either in an angelic temper, or a hell of a rage: when he isn't fast asleep he's a volcano. There are no half-measures in his make-up. He is a child of nature with moods as variable as an April day. . . .'[4]

[1] Ibid., Vol. I, p. 353.
[2] Ibid., Vol. I, p. 493.
[3] *Corresp.*, Vol. XXXII, pp. 182–3.
[4] Cited in *Auchinleck*, John Connell (1959), pp. 472–473. From May 1940, to July 1945, Ismay was Churchill's Chief of Staff in his capacity as Minister of Defence.

'Winston', writes Field-Marshal Viscount Alanbrooke, 'never had the slightest doubt that he had inherited all the military genius of his great ancestor, Marlborough. His military plans and ideas varied from the most brilliant conceptions at the one end to the wildest and most dangerous at the other' . . . 'Frequently in his oration he worked himself into such a state from the woeful picture he had painted that tears streamed down his face' . . . 'Perhaps the most remarkable failing of his is that he can never see a whole strategical problem at once. His gaze always settles on some definite part of the canvas and the rest of the picture is lost. . . . This failing is accentuated by the fact that often he does not want to see the whole picture especially if the wider vision should in any way interfere with the operation he may have temporarily set his heart on.'[1]

'He is extraordinarily obstinate', writes Major-General Sir John Kennedy. 'He is like a child that has set his mind on some forbidden toy. It is no good explaining that it will cut his fingers or burn him. The more you explain, the more fixed he becomes in his idea' . . . 'Whenever an idea, however wild, was thrown up, he ordered detailed examinations, or plans, or both, to be made at high speed. . . . To cope with the situation adequately, it would almost have been worth while to have two staffs: one to deal with the Prime Minister, the other with the war' . . . 'Everybody realized and appreciated Churchill's great qualities. But there were few who did not sometimes doubt whether these were adequate compensation for his methods of handling the war machine. . . .'[2]

Three days after assuming the premiership, Churchill summoned the House of Commons for a vote of confidence in the new administration, and after offering its members 'blood, toil, sweat and tears', he declared his policy.

'You ask', he said, 'What is our policy? I will say: It is to wage war, by sea, land and air, with all our might and with all the strength that God can give us: to wage war against a

[1] *The Turn of the Tide*, Arthur Bryant (1957), pp. 415, 502 & 723. Alanbrooke was C.I.G.S. from December 1941, to the end of the war.

[2] *The Business of War*, Sir John Kennedy (1957), pp. 275, 173 & 61. Kennedy was Director of Operations at the War Office from October 1940, to the end of 1944.

monstrous tyranny, never surpassed in the dark, lamentable catalogue of human crime. That is our policy. You ask, What is our aim? I can answer in one word: Victory – victory at all costs, victory in spite of all terror, victory, however long and hard the road may be. . . . Come, then, let us go forward together with our united strength.'[1]

In war, victory is never more than a means toward the end, and to the true statesman, the end of war is peace. This Churchill failed to understand until the eleventh hour had struck, when it was too late to make good the damage done. From 13th May onward, for him the war was to be 'the defeat, ruin, and slaughter of Hitler, to the exclusion of all other purposes, loyalties, or aim.'[2] So it came about that, when in March 1948, he wrote the Preface of his great history, with remarkable honesty he describes to where 'Victory at all costs' had led a demented world:

'The human tragedy reaches its climax in the fact that after all the exertions and sacrifices of hundreds of millions of people and of the victories of the Righteous Cause, we have still not found Peace and Security, and that we live in the grip of even worse perils than those we have surmounted.'

3 · Blitzkrieg 1940

The theory of strategical paralysis found its practical exponent in General Heinz Guderian, born in 1888. After the First World War, through reading English books and articles on tanks and their tactics, as well as General de Gaulle's, he became deeply interested in armoured warfare. Since the conception of paralysing the enemy's command was formulated in 1918, tank and aircraft developments and the introduction of various types of anti-tank weapons demanded its modification. Unless tanks could travel under cover of night rapidly and with assurance, which they could not do and still cannot do,[3] it was no longer practical to attempt to blot out the enemy headquarters in advance of the main attack. Guderian's contribu-

[1] *The Second World War*, Vol. II, p. 24.

[2] Ibid., Vol. III, p. 21.

[3] A means to effect this was devised during World War II, but never used. See Appendix to the writer's *The Second World War* (1948) pp. 413–5.

tion to the theory lay in his realization that the enemy's command could be as fully paralysed by a sudden and swift blow which shattered his front. In brief, his conception was based on what Captain B. H. Liddell Hart calls 'the indirect approach' instead of a direct one – the aim remained constant, the method varied.

When, in February 1940, a conference, presided over by Hitler, was assembled to discuss the forthcoming invasion of France, after the army group and the army commanders had spoken, Guderian, who commanded the XIX Armoured Corps, strongly backed by General Manstein, explained to Hitler how he intended to advance his corps to the Meuse by the fourth day, and cross the river on the fifth day. Hitler then asked him: 'And then what are you going to do?' and Guderian comments: 'He was the first person who had thought to ask me this vital question.' His reply was:

'Unless I receive orders to the contrary, I intend on the next day to continue my advance westwards. The supreme leadership must decide whether my objective is to be Amiens or Paris. In my opinion the correct course is to drive past Amiens to the English Channel. Hitler nodded and said nothing more. Only General Busch, who commanded the Sixteenth Army on my left, cried out: "Well, I don't think you'll cross the river in the first place!" Hitler, the tension visible in his face, looked at me to see what I would reply. I said: "There's no need for you to do so, in any case.' 'Hitler made no comment.'[1]

The English Channel as Guderian's next objective! – as the crow flies, 160 miles west of the Meuse at Sedan. No wonder General Busch was astonished, because no conventional general would have placed it more than a dozen miles west of that river. So distant an objective discloses the secret of Guderian's *Blitzkrieg*.

It was to employ mobility as a psychological weapon: not to kill but to move; not to move to kill but to move to terrify, to bewilder, to perplex, to cause consternation, doubt and confusion in the rear of the enemy, which rumour would magnify until panic became monstrous. In short, its aim was to paralyse

[1] *Panzer Leader*, General Heinz Guderian (English edition, 1952), p. 92.

not only the enemy's command but also his government, and paralysation would be in direct proportion to velocity. To paraphrase Danton: 'Speed, and still more speed, and always speed' was the secret, and that demanded '*de l'audace, et encore de l'audace, et toujours de l'audace.*'

In May 1940, the German forces which invaded France were organized into three Army Groups – A, B and C. C was deployed to contain the Maginot Line, with A and B north of it. The frontage of B extended between Winterswijk, on the Dutch frontier, and Aachen, and from Aachen A's extended to C's right flank. A comprised three armies, the Fourth on the right, the Twelfth in the centre, and the Sixteenth on the left. Out of a total of ten armoured divisions, the 5th and 7th were allotted to the Fourth Army; the 6th and 8th were formed into the XLIst Armoured Corps, under General Reinhardt, and the 1st, 2nd and 10th into the XIXth Armoured Corps, commanded by Guderian. Together they were grouped under General von Kleist, and were assembled in the Twelfth Army area. This group, with the 7th Armoured Division, under General Rommel, on its right, constituted the striking force.

Its task was to advance through the Ardennes, cross the Meuse between Dinant and Sedan, and smash through the enemy front. In illustration of *Blitzkrieg in excelsis*, it is sufficient to follow Guderian's corps.

On 10th May, the attack was launched; on the 11th the French advanced troops in the Ardennes were hounded westward; on the 12th Guderian stormed and took Bouillon, and before nightfall two of his divisions occupied the eastern bank of the Meuse at Sedan, while Reinhardt's corps closed in on Monthermé, and Rommel's division was at Houx. On the 13th, under cover of dive-bomber attacks, the Meuse was crossed and bridged, and by nightfall the village of Chémery, eight miles south of Sedan, was in German hands. On the night of the 14th–15th, against Guderian's violent protests, the advance was halted by Kleist. Early on the 16th it was resumed, to be halted again on the 17th. From then on it became a race for the English Channel. On the 18th St. Quentin was reached; on the 19th the Canal de Nord, between Douai and Péronne, was crossed, and on the 20th Montreuil,

Doullens, Amiens and Abbeville were occupied. The whole stretch of country between the Scarpe and Somme rivers was now in German hands; the British lines of communication were cut, and the way to the Channel ports opened. In eleven days the Germans had advanced 220 miles: such was *Blitzkrieg*, and what was its dividends in terms of demoralization?

One of the best short summaries on what happened on the other side of the hill is to be found in an anonymous booklet entitled *The Diary of a Staff Officer*, published in 1941. It was written by an air intelligence liaison officer on the Staff of the Commander-in-Chief of the British Air Force in France. The following are a few citations from it:

MAY 14: 'The Germans have walked through 5 miles of fortifications in depth with a loss of probably 500 men. . . . When the dive-bombers came down on them [the French] they stood the noise – there were hardly any casualties – for only two hours, and then bolted out with their hands over their ears.'

MAY 15: 'Sedan fell as the result of air bombardment. . . . It was a superb example of the military precept known as surprise.'

MAY 16: 'The whole development of the southern front in these 7 days has been so fast and has been conducted on such unorthodox principles – principles of neck or nothing to the *n*th degree – that it is hard to believe the situation is so precarious as it is in fact.'

MAY 17: 'It is Poland over again.' [The French General Staff did not consider that the *blitz* tactics resorted to in Poland could be applied in the more broken terrain of France.]

MAY 18: 'They would have us believe that the Battle of the Marne will be fought again, but do they believe it themselves? . . . The pace is too fast and the battle of movement has come into its own again. . . . It is the co-operation between the dive-bombers and the armoured divisions that is winning the war for Germany.'

MAY 19: 'News that the *Panzers* are in Amiens [probably a reconnaissance group]. This is like some ridiculous nightmare. . . . The Germans have taken every risk – criminally foolish risks – and they have got away with it. . . . The French General Staff have been paralysed by this unorthodox war of movement. The fluid conditions prevailing are not dealt with in the textbooks and the 1914 brains of the French Generals responsible for formulating the plans of the allied armies are incapable of functioning in this new and astonishing lay-out.'[1]

MAY 22: 'Our one and only armoured division was landed in France yesterday. . . . Where are the German infantry? Where are the main bodies of the armies? Are we right in estimating them to be 100 miles behind this thunderbolt of 5,000 tanks?' [The actual number was less than half this figure.]

Rumour is a swift traveller, and panic grows with distance. At 7.30 a.m. on 15th May Churchill was awakened by the ring of his bedside telephone; the voice was Reynaud's. 'We have been defeated', it said. 'The front is broken near Sedan; they are pouring through in great numbers with tanks and armoured cars.' Dumbfounded, Churchill replied: 'All experience shows that the offensive will come to an end after a while. I remember the 21st of March, 1918. After five or six days they had to halt for supplies, and the opportunity for counter-attack is presented.' But in March 1918, the Germans had no tanks, this had skipped Churchill's memory, and he excuses himself by writing: 'Not having had access to official information for so many years, I did not comprehend the violence of the revolution effected since the last war by the incursion of a mass of fast-moving heavy armour.'[2] He might have found all he needed in his remarkable memorandum 'Variants of the Offensive' of World War I; but the last place to seek it was in official sources.

On 16th May, he felt it imperative for him to go to Paris, and when, at 4 p.m. he landed at Le Bourget, the officer who met him told him that 'the Germans were expected in Paris in a few days at most.' He drove to the Quai d'Orsay to meet Reynaud, Daladier and Gamelin, and when the latter had

[1] It is of interest to note that, during the German advance, broadcasts in French were sent out in a continuous stream by the German Director of Radio. They caused panic and confusion among the French civil population, and led to roads being blocked by streams of refugees, which made troop movements behind the broken French front almost impossible. (Cited from the *Schellenberg Memoirs* by Desmond Flower and James Reeves in *The War* (1960), p. 74.)

[2] *The Second World War*, Vol. II, pp. 38–39.

briefly explained the situation, Churchill asked him: 'Where is the strategic reserve . . . ? *'où est la masse de manoeuvre?* General Gamelin turned to me and, with a shake of the head and a shrug, said: "*Aucune*". . . . Outside in the garden of the Quai d'Orsay clouds of smoke arose from large bonfires, and I saw from the window venerable officials pushing wheelbarrows of archives on to them. Already therefore the evacuation of Paris was being prepared.'[1]

Another account of this panic-stricken day is given by Paul Baudouin, Secretary of the French Cabinet.

'Crowned like a volcano by the smoke of his cigars', he writes, Churchill 'told his French colleague [Reynaud] that even if France was invaded and vanquished England would go on fighting. . . . Until one in the morning he conjured up an apocalyptic vision of the war. He saw himself in the heart of Canada directing, over an England razed to the ground . . . and over a France whose ruins were already cold, the air war of the New World against the Old dominated by Germany.'[2]

Although in England, the masses of the people, secure behind their sea wall, were not greatly perturbed by the German advance, the Government lost its head, and the country was thrown into confusion by a host of ill-considered panic measures. Crazy obstructions were erected across the roads; signposts were uprooted, and the names of railway stations, inns, villages and towns were obliterated. Further, on 18th May, Churchill instructed his Chief of Staff that 'Actions should . . . be taken against Communists and Fascists, and very considerable numbers should be put in protective . . . internment.'[3] This led to wholesale arrests; hundreds of people, whose sole 'crime' was that they considered the war a blunder,[4]

[1] Ibid., Vol. II, pp. 41–42.

[2] *The Private Diaries of Paul Baudouin* (English edition, 1948), p. 33.

[3] *The Second World War*, Vol. II, p. 49.

[4] Mr P. C. Loftus told the House of Commons of one man who was arrested because he was a member of Sir Oswald Mosley's British Union of Fascists. His story was: 'He happened to own a motor-boat and was on the Thames at the time of Dunkirk when the wireless appeal came over. He volunteered to go, and rescued about 450 men, his motor-boat being fairly well plastered with machine-gun bullets. On his return to England he was arrested.' (*Parliamentary Debates*, 5th Series, Vol. 373, col. 983.)

were held in custody without charge or trial, and in conditions which can only be described as barbarous. One internee, a German-Jew refugee, who previously had been interned at Dachau, stated that conditions were so much worse at the Ascot Concentration Camp than in Germany, he would rather spend six months in Dachau than one at Ascot.[1]

On 13th June, four days before Marshal Pétain announced that France had asked for an armistice, Churchill despatched a 'message of good cheer' to the French Government, in which he proposed a fraternal and indissoluble union of the peoples of the British and French Empires.[2] Three weeks later he instructed Admiral Sir James Somerville to sink the French warships at Oran and Mers-el-Kebir.[3] With this 'mournful episode', as Churchill calls it, the panic started by the *Blitzkrieg* fizzled out.

4 · *The Russian and German Inner Fronts*

The German invasion of France was based on a strategical gamble – Hitler's anticipation that, once France had been defeated, England would accept a negotiated peace. He had made no preparations to invade her, either because he had so hurriedly precipitated the outbreak of war, or, what would seem as probable, he considered a full-scale invasion an impracticable undertaking. Therefore, instead of the Western Front having been liquidated before he turned against Russia, all he had done was to render it negative for the time being. Also, by now he was fully aware that President Roosevelt – who throughout had been assisting Britain – was strenuously preparing to bring the United States into the war; of this there could be no doubt whatsoever, when, on 11th March 1941, the Lend-Lease Bill was passed by Congress. It was as fateful an event in world history as the American declaration of war on 6th April 1917. Without it, Great Britain could not for long have continued at war.

[1] Cited in a leaflet of The 18 B Publicity Council.

[2] For this fantastic scheme see *The Second World War*, Vol. II, pp. 183–4.

[3] Somerville called it a 'beastly operation' and 'a lousy job'; also 'the biggest political blunder of modern times' (*Sunday Times*, London, 7th August 1960).

Vis-à-vis Russia, Hitler's problem was one of time: could he defeat her and establish his *Lebensraum* before the United States intervened in the war? If he could not, then of a certainty the Western negative front would once again become a positive front, and he would be caught between two fronts, the thing he dreaded most. The solution lay in the correct choice of the Russian strategical centre of gravity, and reference to Clausewitz would have told him where it lay. Had not the latter pointed out that Russia could only be subdued 'by effects of internal dissension'?[1] Later, had not Theodor Mommsen compared the Russian Empire with a dust-bin held together by the rusty hoop of Tsardom; and later still had not Lenin declared:

'Nowhere in the world is there such oppression of the majority of the country's population as there is in Russia: The Great Russians form only 43 per cent. of the population, i.e. less than half; the rest have no rights as belonging to other nationalities. Out of 170,000,000 of the population of Russia, about 100,000,000 are oppressed and without rights.'[2]

In 1941, Stalin's oppression was incalculably worse than any Tsar's, and the Ukrainians, White Russians, Balts, Cossacks, Caucasians, and many others had not forgotten the horrors of his ten years of collectivization (1929–1938), during which some 10,000,000 people had been massacred, transported and starved to death. In 1941, in the Ukraine, White Russia and the Baltic States alone, some 40,000,000 people yearned for liberation; therefore, in order to disintegrate the colossus, all Hitler had to do was to cross the Russian frontier as a liberator, and terminate collectivization. It would have won over to him, not only the minorities, but it would also have dissolved Stalin's armies, because they so largely consisted of collectivized serfs. This is why Stalin dreaded a German invasion, and he did not believe that the Germans would be so foolish as to conduct the war 'with arms alone.'[3]

'Had the Germans', writes Reitlinger, 'brought with them

[1] See *supra* Chapter IV, p. 75.

[2] *Collected Works* (English edition, n.d.), Vol. XVIII, pp. 225–6.

[3] So General Vlasov told Himmler, see *The House Built on Sand*, Gerald Reitlinger (1960), p. 361.

to Russia something like President Wilson's Fourteen Points of 1918, Russia would have disintegrated just as Germany had done then.' And following the argument, he adds, 'Hitler need never have diverted his armies from Moscow in order to secure the Ukraine, since the Ukrainians would have offered it to him.'[1] Instead he proclaimed the inhabitants of the U.S.S.R. to be *Untermenschen* (sub-humans), and decided on a war of extermination.[2]

The invasion was launched on 22nd June 1941, and in the battles up to 26th September, when the great battle of Kiev ended, no less than 1,500,000 prisoners were captured, and by Christmas nearly another million were in the bag. The reason for these vast numbers is given by General Anders: 'Many soldiers', he writes, 'seeing the war as an opportunity for a change of order in Russia, wished for German victory and therefore surrendered in great masses . . . many high Soviet officers went over to the enemy offering to fight against the Soviets.'[3]

Everywhere the Germans were welcomed as liberators by the common people: the Ukrainians looked upon Hitler as the 'saviour of Europe',[4] and the White Russians were eager to fight on the German side. Guderian tells us that 'women came out of their villages on to the very battlefield bringing wooden platters of bread and butter and eggs and, in my case at least, refused to let me move on before I had eaten.'[5] And at Rostov, writes Erich Kern, 'all over the city there were people waiting on the streets ready to cheer and welcome us in. . . . Never before had I seem such a sudden transformation. Of Bolshevism, there was no more. The enemy had gone. . . . Wherever we went we met laughing and waving people. . . . The Soviet Empire was creaking at the joints.'[6]

Then came Himmler with his infamous Security Service

[1] Ibid., p. 22.

[2] For his policy and how it was carried out see Alan Bullock's *Hitler a Study of Tyranny*, pp. 633–44.

[3] *Hitler's Defeat in Russia* (1953), p. 168. Anders was C.-in-C. of the Free Polish Army.

[4] *The Goebbels Diaries*, p. 135.

[5] *Panzer Leader*, p. 193.

[6] *Dance of Death* (English edition, 1948), pp. 102, 94, 86. Kern was an n.c.o. in the *Leibstandarte Hitler*.

(*Sichereitsdienst*), and early in 1942, Dr Berthold, a leading official of the German Administration in Poland, told von Hassell that the brutal treatment of the Russians and Ukrainians 'exceeds anything yet known.'[1] Erich Kern corroborates this, he points out that at the time that Bolshevism was politically bankrupt, it was saved by Himmler and his assassins. 'By rousing the Russian people to a Napoleonic fervour', he writes, 'we enabled the Bolsheviks to achieve a political consolidation beyond their wildest dreams and provided their cause with the halo of "a patriotic war".'[2] And Görlitz writes: 'The fact that the destruction of Bolshevism began soon to mean simply an effort to decimate and enslave the Slav people was the most fatal of all the flaws in the whole campaign."[3]

Because Bolshevism and National Socialism were equally repugnant to the Democracies, and because Hitler's aim was to establish a *Lebensraum* in Eastern Europe, which would inevitably entangle him with Russia, there can be no doubt whatsoever that in 1939 the best policy for France and Great Britain would have been to keep out of the war, let the two great dictatorial Powers cripple each other, and in the meantime have re-armed at top speed. Had they done so, a time would have come when they could profitably intervene. Should Russia then be winning, Hitler would be discredited, and support could be given to Germany, and should the reverse be the case, Germany could be invaded from the west under favourable conditions. This, however was rendered impractible by Chamberlain's pledge to Poland.

Now that Germany had invaded Russia, the opportunity to win a profitable peace again presented itself; therefore British and American policy should have been, as Hanson W. Baldwin suggests: Not to elevate 'one totalitarianism at the expense of another *and of the democracies*', but instead to aid

[1] *The Von Hassell Diaries*, 1938–1944 (1948), p. 219.

[2] *Dance of Death*, p. 108.

[3] *The German General Staff*, p. 397. 'Do you know where we lost the war in Russia?' a German officer asked an American journalist. 'In Stalingrad' was the prompt reply, 'No,' said the officer, 'we lost it long before that – in Kiev, when we hoisted the swastika instead of the Ukrainian flag!' Cited by Eugene Lyons in *Our Secret Allies: the Peoples of Russia* (1954), p. 232.

Russia only sufficiently to keep her in the war, and not damage Germany sufficiently to drive her out of it.[1]

This favourable opportunity was missed through the pugnacity of Mr Churchill. On the evening of 21st June 1941, a few hours before the Germans crossed the Russian frontier, when at dinner with Mr Winant, the American Ambassador, Churchill remarked to him that a German attack on Russia was imminent, and that he would go all out to help Russia. And when Winant asked him, 'whether for him, the arch anti-Communist, this was [not] bowing down in the House of Rimmon?' Churchill replied: 'Not at all, I have only one purpose, the destruction of Hitler, and my life is much simplified thereby. If Hitler invaded Hell I would make at least a favourable reference to the Devil in the House of Commons.'[2] Apparently, it never occurred to him that the war was being fought, not to simplify his life, but to win a profitable peace.

Next day, in a lurid broadcast to the British people, he said: 'We have but one aim and one single, irrevocable purpose. We are resolved to destroy Hitler and every vestige of the Nazi régime. From this nothing will turn us – nothing. We will never parley, we will never negotiate with Hitler or any of his gang. . . . Any man or state who fights against Nazidom will have our aid. Any man or state who marches with Hitler is our foe. . . . That is our policy and that is our declaration. It follows therefore that we shall give whatever help we can to Russia and the Russian people.'[3]

On 7th July, in a message to 'Monsieur Stalin', Churchill tendered all possible help, and five days later a treaty was agreed between Britain and the Soviet Union which pledged mutual help 'without any precision as to the quantity or quality', and affirmed that neither would conclude a separate peace. On 18th July, Stalin's reply to Churchill's offer was to ask him to open a front 'in the West (Northern France) and in the North (the Arctic)', adding that 'the best time to open this front is now.'[4]

[1] *Great Mistakes of the War* (1950) p. 10.

[2] *The Second World War*, Vol. III, p. 331.

[3] Ibid., Vol. III, p. 332.

[4] *Stalin's Correspondence with Churchill, Attlee, Roosevelt and Truman 1941–1945* (1957), Vol. I, p. 12.

Eventually this collaboration led, on 26th May 1942, to an Anglo-Soviet treaty of alliance, 'omitting all reference to frontiers.' 'This', writes Churchill, 'was a great relief to me, and a far better solution than I had dared to hope.'[1] Time was to prove that it was an even greater blunder than the Anglo-French guarantee to Poland of 31st March 1939.

Comment, though platitudinous, is devastating:

Firstly, because in his broadcast Churchill had declared that any man or state who fought against Hitler would be aided by Britain, like his predecessor he should have done his utmost to stimulate the anti-Hitler Opposition in Germany. From 1940 onward innumerable attempts were made by its members to gain British support, yet on each occasion they were either ignored or repulsed.[2] Blinded by his hatred of Hitler, he looked upon all Germans as beasts of prey, and thereby committed the same blunder Hitler had when he failed to distinguish between pro- and anti-Stalinist peoples in the U.S.S.R. Instead of wooing the Opposition, he attempted to break the morale of the German nation by resorting to strategic bombing on Douhet's lines.[3]

Secondly, bound to Poland as the British Government was by the Anglo-Polish treaty, and faced with Poland's partition, in which Stalin was as guilty as Hitler, Churchill should not have impulsively thrown his country into the arms of the Soviet Union, but should have paused until Stalin had sought his aid, and only have proffered it on the understanding that the Soviet-German Pact of 23rd August 1939 was first annulled, and that all Polish prisoners and deported Poles in Russian hands were released.

Thirdly, he should have realized that there could be neither moral nor political advantage in substituting Stalin for Hitler, and were this to happen, not only would the war be politically lost, but the balance of power in Europe would pass into Soviet hands.

His partner in this negation of statesmanship was the American President.

[1] *The Second World War*, Vol. IV, p. 300.
[2] See Ritter, p. 212.
[3] See *infra* Section 7.

5 · *President Roosevelt's anti-Japanese and pro-Russian Policies*

On 18th October 1939, an American historian, who for long had contemplated the ways of the world, noted in his war diary:

'So far as England is concerned, the war is not now a naval affair! So far as France is concerned, it is not now a military affair! It has become a war of systems. It is Stalinism versus Europeanism, and the sooner the directors of the war forces of the Western Allies realize it, the better it will be for them. There is now taking place in Europe something that is more sinister than war.'[1]

This remarkable prevision, that the war so recently unleashed transcended the physical struggle and was a contest between two antagonistic cultures, the free Western way of life and Asiatic despotism, was unseen by Mr Churchill and President Roosevelt. But while in the last lap of the war, when it was no longer possible for him to change the course he had steered, the former became aware of it, the latter never did: this was the tragedy of Europe. What manner of man was the American President?

Robert E. Sherwood, one of his close collaborators and the writer of many of his speeches, depicts him as follows:

'Frances Perkins has written of Roosevelt that he was "the most complicated human being I ever knew". Henry Morgenthau, Jr., has written: "Roosevelt is an extraordinary person to describe. . . . Weary as well as buoyant, frivolous as well as grave, evasive as well as frank . . . a man of bewildering complexity of moods and motives." Miss Perkins and Morgenthau were members of Roosevelt's Cabinet and knew him far longer and better than I did. But I saw enough of him, particularly in hours when he was off parade and relaxed, to be able to say "Amen!" to their statements on his complexity. Being a writer by trade, I tried continually to study him, to try to look beyond his charming and amusing and warmly affectionate surface into his heavily forested interior. But I could never

[1] *The Tragedy of Europe: A Day by Day Commentary on the Second World War* (in five volumes), Francis Neilson (1940), Vol. I, p. 156.

really understand what was going on in there. His character was not only multiplex; it was contradictory to a bewildering degree. He was hard and he was soft. At times he displayed a capacity for vindictiveness which could be described as petty, and at other times he demonstrated the Christian spirit of forgiveness and charity in its purest form. He could be a ruthless politician, but he was the champion of friends and associates who for him were political liabilities, conspicuously Harry Hopkins, and of causes which apparently competent advisers assured him would constitute political suicide. He could appear to be utterly cynical, worldly, illusionless, and yet his religious faith was the strongest and most mysterious force that was in him.... He liked to fancy himself as a practical, down-to-earth, horse-sense realist – he often used to say "Winston and Uncle Joe and I get along well together because we're all *realists*" – and yet his idealism was actually no less empyrean than Woodrow Wilson's.'[1]

Should this description be a just one, it would appear that the American President possessed none of the qualities demanded by Napoleon to direct the grand operations of war.

During the days of the New Deal many Communists saw in it an instrument which would assist them, and Roosevelt collaborated with them because, through their control of the American Labour Party, they held the balance of power in New York State, and also were a major factor in the industrial states of Ohio, Illinois and Pennsylvania. Although it paid him handsomely when, in 1940, he was elected to a third term, it gathered around him some strange characters, among whom was Harry Hopkins.[2] He was a moribund ex-social worker, vain, ambitious and gullible, who on 10th May 1940, was invited to take up his residence in the White House, and a year later was appointed by the President to administer Lend-Lease, a duty which endowed him with the authority of *de facto* Deputy President.[3] The President, writes General Albert

[1] *The White House Papers of Harry L. Hopkins*, Robert E. Sherwood (English edition, 1948), Vol. I, p. 10. The American edition is entitled *Roosevelt and Hopkins: An Intimate History*.

[2] Churchill rated him 'high among the Paladins', and Representative Dewey Short of Missouri called him 'the White House Rasputin'.

[3] See Sherwood, Vol. I, p. 267.

C. Wedemeyer, was 'surrounded by intriguers and soft-on-communism eggheads who enjoyed his wife's patronage and were given formidable power by Harry Hopkins and others in the President's confidence.' Another dupe was General George C. Marshall, Chief of Staff of the U.S. Army, an honest and simple man who, Wedemeyer says: 'became an easy prey to crypto-Communists, or Communist-sympathizing sycophants, who played on his vanity.'[1] Thus it came about that Stalin and his henchmen 'were all along well informed of American attitudes and intentions by Communist stooges in Washington . . . some government bureaus[2] were infiltrated both by Communist sympathizers and Soviet agents and . . . U.S. policies, plans, and official attitudes were not only influenced by these infiltrators but also promptly reported back to Moscow.'[3]

This does not seem in any way to have perturbed the President, because, as Sherwood writes: 'The Roosevelt doctrine was that if we were to get into the war we should fight it as far from our own shores as possible and with the greatest number of allies, regardless of ideology.'[4] This may account for General Wedemeyer's remark that, when as late as March 1945, he informed Roosevelt that he felt certain the Communists would cause trouble in China as soon as the war was ended, 'He did not seem to understand what I was talking about.'[5]

All his hatred was focused on Hitler. 'So far as he was concerned', said Hopkins, 'there is absolutely nothing important in the world but to beat Hitler.'[6]

But it was not until the collapse of France that the President became convinced that, were Britain to meet with disaster, Hitler would attack the Western Hemisphere, and

[1] *Wedemeyer Reports!* (1958), p. 370.

[2] 'They held influential positions in the White House, the State Department, the Treasury Department, the War Department, the Office of Strategic Services, the War Production Board, the Board of Economic Warfare, the Office of Price Administration, the Office of War Information, and many other government agencies.' (*The Twenty-Year Revolution from Roosevelt to Eisenhower*, Chesley Manly (1954), p. 42.)

[3] Wedemeyer, p. 348. See also *Masters of Deceit*, J. Edgar Hoover (1958).

[4] Sherwood, Vol. I, p. 133.

[5] Wedemeyer, p. 341.

[6] Sherwood, Vol. I, p. 183.

'his greatest fear then and subsequently was of a negotiated peace.'[1] A year later, when Hitler invaded Russia, at Hopkins' own request he sent him on a mission to Moscow. At the same time Roosevelt announced the freezing of Japanese assets and credits in the U.S.A., and placed an embargo on the export of aviation fuel and machine tools to Japan. This was a declaration of economic war.

Hopkins arrived in Moscow on 31st July 1941, and was enthralled by Stalin.[2] Like Churchill, he blindly espoused the Soviet cause, and forthwith, without any reservations, started the flow of lend-lease goods to Russia. General John R. Deane, head of the U.S. Military Mission in Moscow, writes that Hopkins carried out the Russian aid programme 'with a zeal which approached fanaticism.'[3] His mission fulfilled, he left Moscow to join the President and Churchill at the Atlantic Conference, held in Placentia Bay, Newfoundland, between 8th and 13th August.

At it, with reference to Japan, Churchill states: 'I told his circle [the President's] that I would rather have an American declaration of war now and no supplies for six months than double the supplies and no declaration. When this was repeated to him [to Roosevelt] . . . he went so far as to say to me, "I may never declare war; I may make war. If I were to ask Congress to declare war they might argue about it for three months".'[4] Further, he promised Churchill that 'the United States, even if not herself attacked, would come into the war in the Far East and thus make final victory sure.'[5] Also he promised that on his return to Washington he would send a strongly worded note to the Japanese ambassador accredited to the White House. This he did on 17th August.

In addition to these secret commitments, on the President's suggestion, a joint declaration setting forth 'certain common

[1] Ibid., Vol. I, p. 127.

[2] As late as 1943 Roosevelt remarked to the Polish Ambassador, Ciechanowski: 'Harry gets on like a house afire with Stalin – in fact, they seem to have become buddies' (*Defeat in Victory*, Jan Ciechanowski (English edition, 1948), p. 244.

[3] *The Strange Alliance* (1947), p. 90.

[4] Churchill, *The Second World War*, Vol. III, p. 528. In a letter to General Smuts, dated 9th November 1941.

[5] *Parliamentary Debates*, 5th Series, Vol. 377, col. 607.

principles' in the national policies of the United States and United Kingdom was drafted by Churchill, amended, and issued under the title of 'The Atlantic Charter'.[1] It was a highly idealistic document, and had it been adhered to, it would have been impossible to implement. Nevertheless, until it was scrapped at the Teheran Conference in November 1943, it was first-class propaganda.

From then on negotiations were shuttled between Tokyo and Washington, each side playing for time. On 5th November Churchill wrote to Roosevelt: 'The Japanese have as yet taken no final decision, and the Emperor appears to be exercising restraint. When we talked about this at Placentia you spoke of gaining time, and this policy has been brilliantly successful so far. But our joint embargo is steadily forcing the Japanese to decisions for peace or war.'[2]

A fortnight later the Japanese Government made up its mind, and a proposal for a general settlement was received in Washington on 20th November. Its basis was:

The withdrawal of Japanese troops from French Indo-China upon an equitable peace in the Pacific Area; the mutual restoration of commercial relations between Japan and the United States; the willingness of the United States to supply Japan with oil; and the undertaking of the United States to refrain from such measures and actions as might be prejudicial to the restoration of peace between Japan and China.

On Monday 25th November, these proposals were considered by the President and his War Cabinet, and an account of this meeting is given by Henry L. Simson, Secretary of War, in his *Diary*. It reads:

'. . . at 12 o'clock we (*viz.*, General Marshall and I) went to the White House. . . . There the President brought up . . . the relations with the Japanese. He brought up the event that we were likely to be attacked perhaps (as soon as) next Monday. . . . The question was what should we do. The question was

[1] See Appendix III. At an inter-allied meeting, held in London on 24th September 1941, the Charter was formally adopted by the governments of Belgium, Czechoslovakia, Greece, Luxemburg, the Netherlands, Norway, Poland, Russia, Yugoslavia, and the Free French (*Defeat in Victory*, Jan Ciechanowski, pp. 61–62).

[2] *The Second World War*, Vol. III, pp. 526–7.

how we should manoeuver them into the position of firing the first shot without allowing too much danger to ourselves.'[1]

Although it was known from intercepted secret Japanese messages[2] that the proposals of 20th November were final, a ten point memorandum was prepared by Cordell Hull, Secretary of State, and on 26th November it was handed to the two Japanese ambassadors in Washington. Its purport was:

In exchange for a new trade agreement and the unfreezing of each other's credits, Japan was required to conclude a mutual non-aggression treaty with Washington, Moscow, the Netherlands, Chungking, and Bangkok; withdraw her forces from China and French Indo-China, and undertake to support no regime in China other than that of Chiang Kai-shek.

It was accepted by the Japanese Government as an ultimatum, and on 7th December the answer was the surprise attacks on Cold Harbor, Malaya, Thailand and Hongkong. Thus war was extended from a European conflict into one of world-wide dimensions. Of his reception of the news Churchill writes:

'So we had won after all.... Hitler's fate was sealed. Mussolini's fate was sealed. As for the Japanese, they would be ground to powder.... Being saturated and satiated with emotion and sensation, I went to bed and slept the sleep of the saved and thankful.'[3]

Because the United States was the greatest industrial power in the world, from the moment she entered the war she became potentially – and soon actually – the dominant belligerent. Unfortunately for the world, because her leaders lacked historic sense and looked upon the war as a lethal game rather than an instrument of policy, battles began to lose their political value. So much was this so that, during the latter half of the war, their results were as often as not neutralized by political decisions. Thus it came about that conferences were far more decisive than the battles fought.

[1] U.S. Congress, *Hearings before the Joint Committee on the Pearl Harbor Attack* (1946), Pt. II, p. 5433.

[2] The Japanese code had been broken by the U.S. Army & Navy Intelligence, and throughout the negotiations all messages between Tokyo and Washington were at once translated and sent to the White House. It remained broken throughout the war.

[3] *The Second World War*, Vol. III, pp. 539–40.

The first of these decisive conferences assembled at Washington in late December 1941; it was code-named 'Arcadia'. To attend it, Churchill left England on the 12th, and while at sea he received a report from his Foreign Secretary, Mr Anthony Eden, then in Moscow, on his first conversation with Stalin, a statesman who never fell into the error of looking upon war as anything other than an instrument of policy.

From Eden's report Churchill learnt that Stalin had broached to him what he considered should be the shape of post-war Europe. He proposed that Germany should be split into a number of small independent states; that the Baltic States, Finland and Bessarabia, as they were before Hitler invaded Russia, should be restored to the Soviet Union; and that the 'Curzon Line' should be accepted as the Soviet-Polish frontier.[1]

The main problems discussed at the Conference were the conduct of the war and its aim. To direct strategy, the British Chiefs of Staff, or their representatives, were combined with the American Joint Chiefs of Staff in a committee known as the Combined Chiefs of Staff, with its headquarters in Washington. This was an eminently sound decision; but throughout the war unanimity was frequently impeded by the systems of control adopted by the two heads of state. While Churchill looked upon his Chiefs of Staff as the instruments of his will, Roosevelt treated his as free agents. The result was that, while much of the time of the British Chiefs of Staff was occupied in wrangles with Churchill, the Americans were given so free a hand that unity between them was normally at a discount; they acted more like heads of services than as a joint staff.

Further, it was reaffirmed that the offensive against Germany should take precedence over the war in the Pacific;[2] that during 1942 Germany should be subjected to an ever-increasing air bombardment, and that all available assistance should be given to Russia.

The all important question of what the aim of the war

[1] For the report in full see Churchill's *The Second World War*, Vol. III, pp. 558–9.

[2] First affirmed at the Anglo-American Staff Conversations of 27th March 1941.

should be, without which its grand strategy would be purposeless, was sidetracked by the President. Instead of setting before the members of the Conference a realistic, attainable political aim and a policy which could achieve it, he announced what he called his 'Great Design' – a utopian vision of a new world order. In idea it was a reversion to Woodrow Wilson's messianic dream without his Fourteen Points – another millennium in Hades.

He proposed that, once the war was won, the peace-loving nations[1] should be united in a grand brotherhood for peace. He suggested that this association of sovereign powers should be modelled on the American inter-state system and be based on the principles of the Atlantic Charter. It was to be known as the United Nations Organization.

This new Holy Alliance was accepted by the Conference as the war aim of the Allied Powers, and on 1st January 1942, a joint declaration embodying the pact[2] was signed by the United States, the United Kingdom and twenty-six other nations including the U.S.S.R.

Because, in accordance with the terms of the pact, the complete defeat of Germany and Japan was deemed to be essential, victory at all costs became the political aim. And because this demanded the full co-operation of Russia, it meant that, unless Stalin could be converted to American republicansim before the war ended, Stalinism would replace Hitlerism in post-war Europe.

That Roosevelt believed he was capable of effecting this magical transmutation is borne out by William C. Bullitt, at one time American Ambassador to the Soviet Union and to France. In an article entitled 'How we Won the War and Lost the Peace', which appeared in the magazine *Life* of 30th August 1948, he asserts that Roosevelt, acting on the advice of Harry Hopkins, hoped to convert Stalin by giving him without stint or limit everything he asked for; by asking nothing in return; by prevailing on him to adhere to the aims of the Atlantic Charter; and by meeting him face to face and

[1] At the Yalta Conference, in April 1945, a peace-loving nation was defined as one which by a certain date had declared war against Germany!

[2] See Appendix IV.

persuading him to accept 'Christian ways and democratic principles.'[1]

At the President's request, Bullitt prepared a memorandum in which he set out his reasons for believing that this policy would fail, and after he had discussed it with him for three hours, Roosevelt turned to him and said:

'Bill, I don't dispute your facts; they are accurate. I don't dispute the logic of your reasoning. I just have a hunch that Stalin is not that kind of man. Harry says he's not, and that he doesn't want anything but security for his country. And I think if I give him everything I possible can and ask for nothing from him in return, noblesse oblige, he won't try to annex anything and will work with me for a world of democracy and peace.'

This 'hunch' was the linch-pin in the President's pro-Russian policy, and it was to render abortive every victory won by the two great Western Allies; bring the Slavs to the Elbe, and replace Hitler by Stalin.

6 · The Strategical Grand Climacteric

The grand climacteric of the war was reached in the second half of 1942. Between 4th and 6th June, in the decisive naval battle of Midway Island, Japanese aircraft-carrier power was permanently crippled, and with it the initiative in the Pacific passed to America. On 30th June, in Egypt, General Rommel's exhausted army advanced to within sixty miles of Alexandria, and between 23rd October and 4th November was decisively beaten at El Alamein. This British victory, when coupled with the Allied invasion of North-West Africa, on 7th November, spelt the ruin of Italy. Lastly, on 28th June, the German summer offensive in Russia opened, and by mid-September the Sixth German Army, under General Friedrich von Paulus, reached the outskirts of Stalingrad on the Volga. Two months of abortive assaults followed, and, on 19th November, the Russians launched a dual counter-offensive against the Third Rumanian, Eighth Italian, and Second Hungarian Armies, which held the river Don north-west of Stalingrad, and against the Fourth Rumanian Army south of Stalingrad. Its success

[1] See also *The Great Globe Itself*, William C. Bullitt (1947), p. 17.

placed the Sixth Army in so critical a position that it should at once have withdrawn; but Hitler forbade it, and Paulus was not man enough to disobey him. The result was that his army was surrounded, and on 2nd February 1943, its remnants capitulated. The initiative then passed to the Russians, and was never again wrested from them.

Because of their failure to look upon war as a political instrument, the significance of Stalingrad was missed by the Western Powers. One man, however, saw it clearly, and he was General Franco. He held that two separate wars were in progress; one in the east against Communism and the other in the west against Hitlerism, and to win the latter and lose the former would be political folly. To convince him that the two wars were one, on 19th February 1943, Sir Samuel Hoare, British Ambassador in Spain, entered into correspondence with Count Jordana, the Spanish Foreign Minister. He pointed out to him that, on 6th November 1942, Stalin had declared: 'That it was not the future policy of Russia to interfere in the international affairs of other countries', and that therefore the final victory would be an Allied one. To this, Jordana replied:

'If events develop in the future as they have done up to now, it would be Russia which will penetrate deeply into German territory. And we ask the question: if this should occur, which is the greater danger not only for the continent but for England herself, a Germany not totally defeated and with sufficient strength to serve as a rampart against Communism . . . or a Sovietized Germany which would certainly furnish Russia with the added strength of her war preparations . . . which would enable Russia to extend herself with an empire without precedent from the Atlantic to the Pacific . . . ?

'And we ask a second question: is there anybody in the centre of Europe, in that mosaic of countries without consistency or unity, bled moreover by war and foreign domination, who could contain the ambitions of Stalin? There is certainly no one. . . . We may be sure that after the German domination, the only domination which could live in these countries is Communism. For this reason we consider the situation as extremely grave and think that the people in England should reflect calmly on the matter, since should

Russia succeed in conquering Germany, there will be no one who can contain her. . . . If Germany did not exist, Europeans would have to invent her and it would be ridiculous to think that her place could be taken by a confederation of Lithuanians, Poles, Czechs, and Roumanians who would rapidly be converted into so many more states of the Soviet confederation. . . .'[1]

Very different was the policy adopted by President Roosevelt and Mr Churchill when, in mid-January 1943, they met in conference at Casablanca, and at the very moment when the German Sixth Army was in its death throes. They agreed to prepare for the invasion of Sicily, and press on with preparations for the invasion of Northern France – later to be code-named 'Overlord'. As regards Germany, they decided to prepare for the 'heaviest possible air offensive against German war effort'[2] – her industrial system and the morale of her people – and to issue 'a declaration of the firm intention of the United States and the British Empire to continue the war relentlessly until we have brought about the "unconditional surrender" of Germany and Japan. The omission of Italy', adds Churchill, 'would be to encourage a break-up there. The President liked this idea, and it would stimulate our friends in every country.'[3] If so, then 'unconditional surrender' would discourage the break-up of Germany and dispirit the anti-Hitler Opposition, and, in consequence, prolong the war.

According to Elliott Roosevelt, the President's son, his father first used the phrase 'unconditional surrender' at a luncheon attended by the President, Churchill, Hopkins and himself, and Churchill pronounced it to be 'Perfect! I can just see how Goebbels and the rest of 'em'll squeal!' Further, Elliott writes that his father commented: 'Of course it's just the thing for the Russians. They couldn't want anything

[1] *Ambassador on Special Mission*, Rt. Hon. Sir Samuel Hoare (1946), pp. 184–5. At the Adana Conference, 30th January 1943, the Turkish Prime Minister had told Mr Churchill much the same, namely: 'All the defeated countries would become Bolshevik and Slav if Germany was beaten' (*The Second World War*, Vol. IV, p. 635).

[2] *The Second World War*, Vol. IV, p. 620.

[3] Ibid., Vol. IV, p. 613. In the final draft of the Declaration Italy was included.

better. Unconditional surrender! Uncle Joe might have made it up himself.'[1]

The President's version differs widely; he says the words just 'popped into my mind',[2] and Churchill's is more than vague.[3] Actually, there was nothing new in the term; it is no more than a paraphrase of Churchill's 'Victory at all costs!' And as far as the President is concerned, he might have acted more wisely, had he remembered that, in a Fireside Chat on 29th December 1940, he had said: 'A nation can have peace with the Nazis only at the price of total surrender. . . . Such a dictated peace would be no peace at all. It would be only another armistice, leading to the most gigantic armament race and the most devastating trade war in history.'[4] Nevertheless, he adopted this hypothetical Nazi policy, and, as we shall see, its results were identical to those he foretold.

Should Elliott Roosevelt be correct, then Goebbels, instead of squealing, must have been overjoyed. On 27th March 1942, he had entered in his diary: 'If I were on the enemy side, I should from the very first day have adopted the slogan of fighting against Nazism, but not against the German people. That is how Chamberlain began on the first day of the war, but, thank God, the English didn't pursue this line.'[5] And on 12th April 1943: 'But, after all, the English are making the same mistake, no doubt at Churchill's instigation. They refrain in every way from saying anything tangible about their war aims. I can only add, thank God; for if they were to put up a peace programme on the lines of Wilson's Fourteen Points they would undoubtedly create difficulties for us.'[6] As to 'Uncle Joe', though he never had any intention other than the destruction of Germany, he was not such a simpleton as to

[1] *As He Saw It*, Elliott Roosevelt (1946), p. 117.

[2] *The White House Papers*, Vol. II, p. 693.

[3] See *The Second World War*, Vol. IV, p. 614. Nevertheless, on 11th February 1943, he told the House of Commons that: 'It was only after full, cold, sober and mature consideration of these facts, on which our lives and liberties certainly depend, that the President, with my full concurrence as agent of the War Cabinet, decided that the note of the Casablanca Conference should be the unconditional surrender of all our foes.' (*Parliamentary Debates*, 5th Series, Vol. 368, col. 1473.)

[4] *The White House Papers*, Vol. I, p. 225.

[5] *The Goebbels' Diaries*, p. 102.

[6] Ibid., p. 251.

inform his enemy of it. A true disciple of Lenin, on 23rd February 1943, he publically stated: 'It would be ridiculous to identify Hitler's clique with the German people. . . . History shows that the Hitlers come and go, but the German people and the German State remain.'[1]

The Stalingrad disaster, writes Ritter, roused the anti-Hitler Opposition 'to frantic activity.'[2] On 22nd January the two main rebel factions met in Berlin to square their differences. Then, on the following day, before they had arrived at a decision whether or not to assassinate Hitler, Roosevelt's and Churchill's proclamation of unconditional surrender came over the air; 'a formula which' Görlitz declares, 'gave the death blow to any hope that may have been entertained either by the "Shadow Government" or by the oppositional elements in the General Staff, that their enemies would negotiate with a "respectable" government.'[3] And Ritter adds that, as the sole peace terms were to be unconditional surrender, 'not only did most of the generals, but even many of the Opposition . . . refuse to relieve the tyrant by revolution from the responsibility for such a disaster.'[4] Thus a promising gamble, which might have brought the war to an end before the Russians could capitalize their Stalingrad victory, was missed.

7 · *The Strategic Bombing of Germany*

In a Memorandum, dated 21st October 1917, Mr Churchill described the role of aircraft in war accurately. He wrote:

'All attacks on communications or bases should have their relation to the main battle. It is not reasonable to speak of an air offenisve as if it were going to finish the war by itself. It is improbable that any terrorization of the civil population which could be achieved by air attack could compel the Government of a great nation to surrender. Familiarity with bombardment, a good system of dug-outs and shelters, a strong control by police and military authorities, should be sufficient to preserve the national fighting power unimpaired.

[1] Cited by Chamberlin, op. cit., p. 289.
[2] *The German Resistance*, p. 192.
[3] *The German General Staff*, p. 434.
[4] *The German Resistance*, p. 212.

In our case we have seen the combative spirit of the people aroused, and not quelled, by the German raids. Nothing we have learned of the capacity of the German population to endure suffering justifies us in assuming that they could be cowed into submission by such methods, or, indeed, that they would not be rendered more desperately resolved by them. Therefore our air offensive should consistently be directed at striking at the bases and communications upon whose structure the fighting power of his armies and his fleets of the sea and of the air depends. Any injury which comes to the civil population from the process of attack must be regarded as incidental and inevitable.'[1]

Although on 2nd September 1939, the day after Germany invaded Poland, in reply to an appeal made by President Roosevelt, a declaration was made by the British, French and German Governments that they would restrict bombing to military objectives; and although on 15th February 1940, Mr Chamberlain told the House of Commons that: 'Whatever be the length to which others might go, the Government will never resort to blackguardly attacks on women and other civilians for purposes of mere terrorism',[2] on the day following his assumption of the premiership, Churchill initiated what previously he had called 'The hideous process of bombing open cities from the air';[3] he authorized the bombing of the city of Freiburg im Breisgau. Thus, according to Mr J. M. Spaight: 'We [the British] began to bomb objectives on the German mainland before the Germans began to bomb objectives on the British mainland. That is a historical fact.'[4] Thus was strategic, or rather unstrategic, bombing initiated, because the strategic gain in bombing an ancient university city is exactly – nil.

On 3rd September 1940, Churchill wrote another memorandum, in content very different from the one dated 21st October 1917. 'The Fighters are our salvation', he said, 'but

[1] *The War in the Air, Appendices*, H. A. Jones (1937), Appendix IV, p. 19.

[2] *Parliamentary Debates*, 5th Series, Vol. 357, col. 924.

[3] *The Second World War*, Vol. I, p. 14.

[4] *Bombing Vindicated* (1944), p. 68. This refers to civil targets. Mr Spaight was Principal Assistant Secretary, Air Ministry.

the Bombers alone provide the means of victory. We must therefore develop the power to carry an ever-increasing volume of explosives to Germany, so as to pulverise the entire industry and scientific structure on which the war effort and economic life of the enemy depend. . . .'[1]

From then on, Bomber Command, which came directly under the Ministry of Defence, became Churchill's private army.

He was strongly supported by Lord Trenchard, a fanatical Douhetist who, on 29th August 1942, 'wrote a powerful paper . . . advocating a concentration of bombing *in excelsis.*' In it he said: 'If we decide to use it [air power] with determination and concentration we can not only save millions of lives, but we can shorten the war by months, perhaps years. . . . As the enemy conquered Poland and France by their "tank blitz", so can we smash the German machine by the "bomber blitz." '[2]

Hypothetical though this was, there is nothing unstrategic about it; but where Churchill, Trenchard, and so many other exponents of strategic bombing were at fault was that, even should the Douhet theory be accepted as practicable, at no time before the advent of the atomic bomb was bombing sufficiently destructive to bring the war to a rapid end, unless it was concentrated against the most vital targets. There were five main groups:

(1) The Military Group, which need not detain us, because in the main it comes under the heading of tactical bombing.

(2) The Industrial Group, factories of various kinds scattered throughout the Reich, which were estimated to cover an area of about 130 miles square. To destroy so vast and scattered a target and keep it destroyed would certainly be no *blitz.* It would take years to effect, and would demand an astronomical number of aircraft.

(3) The Urban Group, the cities and their inhabitants, in order to demoralize the latter and cause them to revolt.

(4) The Sources of Energy Group, coal and oil. Upon the first the German economy was powered, and without the

[1] *The Second World War*, Vol. II, pp. 405–6.
[2] Ibid., Vol. IV, pp. 494–5.

second the fighting forces could not function. Although coalfields are difficult to destroy by air attack, all that is needed in order to paralyse them is to keep the railways leading to and from them under bombardment.

(5) The Transportation Group, mainly railways which, if rendered inoperative, would paralyse Germany as a whole.

Of these groups the last two were by far the most important; nevertheless, it was only during the final twelve months of the war that they became the dominant targets. Instead of concentrating on them, between May 1940 and May 1944, they were seldom bombed, and urban bombing with increasing violence was continued to the close of the war.

In spite of innumerable attacks on the war industries, instead of their output declining it steadily increased. This, graphically, is shown in the two charts reproduced from *The United States Strategic Bombing Survey, Overall Report* (*European War*), published in 1945. One reason for this was that:

'The destruction of buildings . . . did not involve a proportionate destruction of vital machine tools and, as it turned out, the enemy was able to salvage such tools and to resume production at a far more rapid rate then had been anticipated.' (p. 18.)[1]

The attacks on urban targets resulted in enormous physical damage. 'During the period from October 1939 to May 1945 the Allied Air Forces, primarily the R.A.F., dropped over one-half million tons of high explosives, incendiaries, and fragmentation bombs . . . on 61 cities. . . . These cities included 25,000,000 people . . . attacks are estimated to have totally destroyed or heavily damaged 3,600,000 dwelling units, accounting for 20 per cent. of Germany's total residential units, and to have rendered homeless 7,500,000 people. They killed about 300,000 people and injured some 780,000.' (p. 72.) Berlin was estimated to be 60 to 70 per cent. destroyed . . . three-fourths of the damage was caused by fire' (p. 93). Although decline in morale was considerable, it had practically no effect on armament production (p. 97), and the mental reaction of the people to air attack is thus described in the *Survey:*

[1] References are to the *Strategic Bombing Survey.*

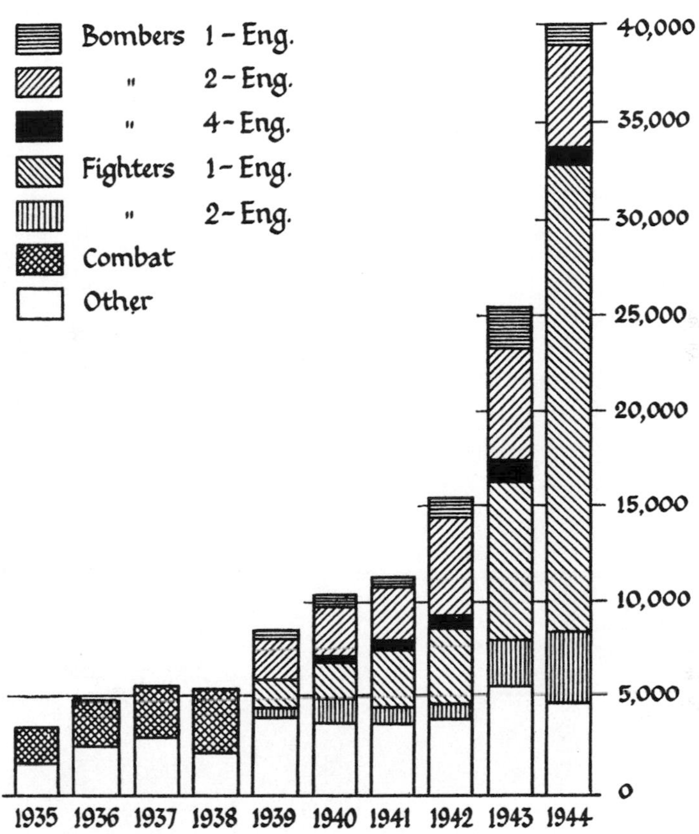

GERMAN AIRCRAFT PRODUCTION

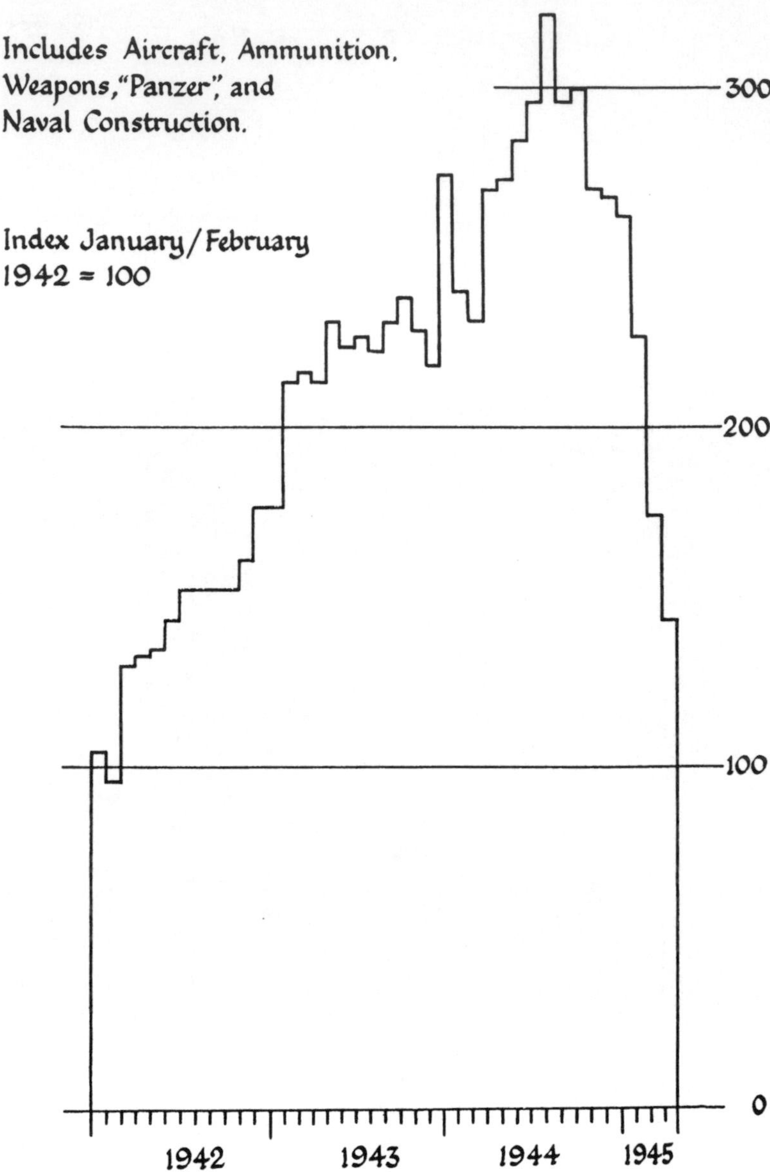

GERMAN COMBAT MUNITIONS OUTPUT

'Under ruthless Nazi control they showed surprising resistance to the terror and hardships of repeated air attack, to the destruction of their homes and belongings, and to the conditions under which they were reduced to live. Their morale, their belief in ultimate victory . . . and their confidence in their leaders declined, but they continued to work efficiently as long as the physical means of production remained. The power of a police state over its people cannot be underestimated' (p. 108).

Early in 1944, when preparations to invade Normandy were in progress, the question arose as to which were the most profitable targets for Bomber Command R.A.F. and the U.S. Strategic Air Force to strike at. The decision arrived at was that priority should be given to transportation and synthetic oil plants. Thus, at long last, strategic bombing became truly strategic, and the requirements Churchill had laid down in his Memorandum of 21st October 1917, were met.

During the preparatory period of the invasion, the main air object was to disrupt all rail traffic between Germany and Normandy; and later, as the front moved eastward, to attack the railways and canals extending into Germany. By October 1944, Western German traffic was almost paralysed. This had a catastrophic effect on the distribution of coal. We read in the *Survey:*

'Essen Division car replacements of coal which had been 21,400 daily in January 1944 declined to 12,000 in September. . . . By November deliveries of coal to factories in Bavaria had been reduced by nearly 50 percent. . . . By January 1945 coal placements in the Ruhr district were down to 9,000 cars per day. Finally in February well-nigh complete interdiction in the Ruhr district was obtained. Such coal as was loaded was subject to confiscation by the railroad to supply locomotive fuel coal. . . . Contemporaneously, as mining continued at a higher level than transport, coal stocks at Ruhr collieries rose from 415,000 tons to 2,217,000 and coke stocks increased from 630,000 tons to 3,069,000 in the same 6 months' (pp. 63–64).

In May 1944, preliminary attacks were made on the larger synthetic oil plants, but it was not until after the Normandy landings in June that the main blow was struck. By July every major plant had been hit. In May these plants had been producing 316,000 tons a month; in June their output fell to 107,000 tons, and in September to 17,000, and aviation petrol dropped from 175,000 tons to 5,000. These attacks also dealt a crippling blow to the munitions and explosives industries, and reduced the supply of synthetic rubber, which fell to about one-sixth of its war time peak of 12,000 tons a month.

From the above it will be seen that the air attack on Germany only became a true strategical operation when it was directed against the sources of energy and the means of distribution. From the first, had bombing been restricted to them, vast economies would have been effected, and the savings could have been invested in the production of landing-craft, anti-submarine and transport aircraft, which throughout the war were in constant short supply.

According to the *Survey*, the total tonnage of bombs dropped in the European war by British and American aircraft was 2,700,000 tons; of which 30.5 per cent. fell on military targets, 13.5 per cent. on industrial, 24 per cent. on urban, and 32 per cent. on railways, canals, and synthetic oil plants (p. 71). Therefore, when military targets are excluded, it will be seen that a greater tonnage of bombs was dropped on secondary targets (industrial and urban) than on primary (railways and synthetic oil). This, in no small part, was due to Churchill's insensate itch to kill Germans, or, as he is reported to have said: 'To make the enemy burn and bleed in every way.'[1]

According to the *Survey*, England devoted 40 to 50 per cent. of her war production to her air forces, and the United States 35 per cent. Therefore, no more than 50 to 60 per cent. was allotted to British sea and land power combined. In agreement with this, when on 2nd March 1944, Sir James Grigg, Secretary of State for War, introduced the Army Estimates, he informed the House of Commons that 'The R.A.F. programme is already employing more workpeople than the Army programme, and I daresay that there are, in fact, as many engaged on making heavy bombers as on the whole Army programme.'[2]

[1] *The Times* (London), 2nd February 1943.
[2] *Parliamentary Debates*, 5th Series, Vol. 397, col. 1602.

Whatever the numbers may have been, they were largely wasted on an operation which Churchill once had called 'an 'experimental horror.'[1]

8 · *The Architects of Disaster*

The débâcle of the Axis forces in the battle of Tunis, 6th–12th May 1943, was only second in importance to the German disaster at Stalingrad; it brought the war in North Africa to an end, and it opened the road to Sicily, which was invaded by Anglo-American forces on 10th July. Fifteen days later a palace revolt in Rome led to the fall of Mussolini, and from then on until 2nd September a wrangle between his successor, Marshal Pietro Badoglio, and the Western Allies over the meaning of 'unconditional surrender' gained for Hitler time sufficient to pour thirteen divisions into Italy, and convert, what Churchill had called the Axial 'soft under-belly' into a crocodile's back.[2]

On 17th August, when the wrangle was at its height, the First Quebec Conference assembled. It gave priority to 'Overlord', and agreed on 1st May 1944 as the date of the invasion of Northern France. Also, in face of British opposition, an American proposal was provisionally accepted; it was that the landing in Northern France should be supplemented by a landing on the French Riviera, the forces needed for it to be withdrawn from the Army of Italy. This operation was code-named 'Anvil'.

An item, mentioned neither by Churchill nor by Field-Marshal Alanbrooke, which figures prominently in Sherwood's account of the conference, 'is a document headed "Russia's Position", which was quoted from "a very high level United States military strategic estimate".' It was produced at the conference by Hopkins, and whatever may have been its

[1] *The Second World War*, Vol. I, p. 168.

[2] At Casablanca Churchill had acclaimed 'unconditional surrender' to be 'perfect'; but on 9th August he changed his mind, in a cable to his Foreign Secretary he urged: 'Merely harping on "unconditional surrender" with no prospect of mercy . . . may well lead to no surrender at all' (*The Second World War*, Vol. V, p. 91).

origin,[1] its concepts, as Sherwood points out, indicate 'the policy which guided the making of decisions at Teheran and . . . at Yalta.'

The following are the paragraphs cited by Sherwood:

'Russia's post-war position in Europe will be a dominant one. With Germany crushed, there is no power in Europe to oppose her tremendous military forces. It is true that Great Britain is building up a position in the Mediterranean *vis-à-vis* Russia that she may find useful in balancing power in Europe. However, even here she may not be able to oppose Russia unless she is otherwise supported.

'The conclusions from the foregoing are obvious. Since Russia is the decisive factor in the war, she must be given every assistance and every effort must be made to obtain her friendship. Likewise, since without question she will dominate Europe on the defeat of the Axis, it is even more essential to develop and maintain the most friendly relations with Russia.

'*Finally, the most important factor the United States has to consider in relation to Russia is the prosecution of the war in The Pacific.* With Russia as an ally in the war against Japan, the war can be terminated in less time and at less expense in life and resources than if the reverse were the case. Should the war in the Pacific have to be carried on with an unfriendly or a negative attitude on the part of Russia, the difficulties will be immeasurably increased and operations might become abortive.'[2]

Wherever these ideas came from, they closely agreed with the President's 'hunch'. They suggest a policy of ultra-appeasement. Not of two ill-prepared Powers faced with a better prepared one, as at Munich, but of the two greatest industrial powers in the world, at the time rapidly approaching full rearmament, faced with an unreliable partner crippled by over two years of ferocious warfare, and almost entirely

[1] The ideas expressed in it bear a marked similarity to those in an earlier memorandum prepared by General James H. Burns for Hopkins. Sherwood observes that this memorandum 'was an excellent statement of Hopkins' own views on the subject of relations with the Soviet Union' (*The White House Papers*, Vol. II, pp. 639–42). If so, then it looks as if the document, if not written by Hopkins, was inspired by him.

[2] Ibid., Vol. II, pp. 744–5.

dependent on their assistance to maintain his armies in the field. Actually, in August 1943, the position of Russia was diametrically opposite to the one posited in the Hopkins document.

That the President blindly accepted this submissive policy is understandable, but that Churchill did not reject it out-of-hand is inexplicable. On 21st October 1942, he had told his Foreign Secretary: 'It would be a measureless disaster if Russian barbarism overlaid the culture and independence of the ancient States of Europe.'[1] Yet, three months later, he flew from Casablanca to Adana to induce Mr Saracoglu, the Turkish Prime Minister, to join in the war on the grounds that Russia's intentions were both peaceful and friendly, and that he would not be a friend of Russia if he thought she would imitate Germany.[2]

Immediately after the Quebec Conference, the Balkans begin to bulk largely in Churchill's mind. He says that it was never his wish to send an army into them,[3] nor can his intention have been to forestall an eventual Russian occupation, because when in September he sent a mission under Mr. Fitzroy Maclean, M.P., to Yugoslavia, he told him: 'So long as the whole of Western civilization was threatened by the Nazi menace, we could not afford to let our attention be diverted from the immediate issue by considerations of long-term policy. We were as loyal to our Soviet Allies as we hoped they were to us. . . . Politics must be a secondary consideration.'[4] Nevertheless, his constant reference to the Balkans frightened the American Chiefs of Staff, and, according to Sherwood, before the first of the Big Three Conferences met at Teheran toward the end of November 1943, 'they prepared themselves for battles . . . in which the Americans and the Russians would form a united front.'[5] Therefore the greater share of the betrayal of Europe must be debited to the President and his advisers.[6]

[1] *The Second World War*, Vol. IV, p. 504.
[2] Ibid., Vol. IV, pp. 635–6. [3] Ibid., Vol. V, pp. 114, 187 and 324.
[4] *Eastern Approaches*, Fitzroy Maclean (1950), p. 281.
[5] *The White House Papers*, Vol. II, p. 770.
[6] Although Cordell Hull was Secretary of State, because he was considered to be anti-Russian, Hopkins acted, in effect, as such, and was present at Teheran.

The more important subjects discussed were:

(1) 'Overlord' and 'Anvil'. Stalin declared that of all the military problems 'Overlord' was the most important and decisive; that 'Anvil' should either precede or coincide with it, and that he was adamant against Churchill's suggestion to move on Vienna by way of the Ljubljana Gap, or any Balkan or Turkish venture.

(2) Poland. 'Nothing was more important', Churchill declared, 'than the security of the Russian Western frontier', therefore Poland should relinquish all her territory east of the Curzon Line and move westward into Germany. 'If Poland trod on some German toes, that could not be helped.'[1] Also, he was not going to break his heart over the cession of part of Germany, although it meant shifting nine to ten million people. These proposals abrogated the Atlantic Charter and the Anglo-Polish guarantee of 1939.

(3) The Balkans. Churchill emphasized the importance of the Balkans, and urged that support should be given to Tito's partisans in Yugoslavia, and withdrawn from those under Mihailovich, who were anti-Bolshevik. This was agreed and done early in December.[2]

(4) Finland. Churchill urged that 'Russia must have security for Leningrad and its approaches', and that 'The position of the Soviet Union as a permanent naval and air Power in the Baltic must be assured.'[3] As with Poland, no mention was made of Russia's unprovoked attack on Finland in 1939; and Stalin demanded the restoration of the 1940 treaty, the cession of Hangö and Petsamo, and compensation in kind for 50 per cent. of war damage.

(5) Germany. The problem of Germany was examined at considerable length. Stalin wanted her split up, to which the President warmly agreed, and suggested her division into five

[1] *The Second World War*, Vol. V, p. 319.

[2] Four months later in a letter to the Foreign Secretary Churchill wrote: 'Since we discussed these matters in Cairo [4th December 1943] we have seen the entry of a grandiose Russian Mission to Tito's headquarters, and there is little doubt that the Russians will drive straight ahead for a Communist Tito-governed Yugoslavia, and will denounce everything done to the contrary as "undemocratic." ' (*The Second World War*, Vol. V, p. 422.)

[3] Ibid., Vol. V, p. 352.

parts, each self-governed; but that Kiel, the Kiel Canal, Hamburg, the Ruhr and the Saar should be administered by the United Nations. Churchill considered that the root evil lay in Prussia, the Prussian Army, and the General Staff. He would seem to have been oblivious of the fact that, throughout, the General Staff had been antagonistic to the Hitler regime. He wanted to see Prussia isolated, Bavaria, Württemberg, the Palatinate, Saxony and Baden detached, and Bavaria, Austria and Hungary formed into a non-aggressive confederation. Stalin disagreed with the Danubian combination, and the President fully agreed with Stalin.

(6) Japan. Stalin assured the President that the United States need have no fear about the Pacific, since the Soviet Union would declare war on Japan once Hitler had been defeated. This so pleased the President and his Chiefs of Staff that, in gratitude and without Churchill's knowledge the former discussed with Stalin the question of a common front against the British, and proposed that he and Stalin should back Chiang Kai-shek against Churchill on the question of Hong Kong and Shanghai. Further, he mentioned to Stalin 'the possibility that Russia might have access to the port of Dairen in Manchuria',[1] which, incidentally, was Chinese territory.

In the end little was formally agreed; nevertheless, the seeds of Europe's ruin were sown.

'Pushed by the Russians and pulled by the Americans', writes Chester Wilmot, 'the overall strategy of the Western Powers had been diverted away from the area of Soviet aspirations. Even before Teheran it was inevitable that the enforcement of "Unconditional Surrender" upon Germany would leave the U.S.S.R. the dominant power in Eastern Europe, but it was by no means inevitable that the Russian influence would extend deep into Central Europe and the Balkans. After Teheran, it became almost a certainty that this would happen. Thus the Teheran Conference not only determined the military strategy for 1944, but adjusted the political balance of post-war Europe in favour of the Soviet Union.'[2]

[1] Sherwood, Vol. II, p. 786.
[2] *The Struggle for Europe* (1952), pp. 141–2.

9 · *Surrender to Russia*

From 3rd September 1943, when the Allies landed on the toe of Italy, progress up the peninsula was so slow that Rome was not occupied until two days before the invasion of Normandy on 6th June 1944. For lack of landing-craft, the invasion of Southern France (Operation 'Anvil) had to be postponed until 15th August, when it was of no assistance to the main operation ('Overlord'); at the time the Germans in Normandy were being decisively beaten in the battle of Falaise. Although this diversion of force wrecked Sir Harold Alexander's campaign in Italy, Eisenhower and the American Chiefs of Staff had insisted on it, and had been supported by the President who, when Churchill and his generals in Italy expostulated, had, on 29th June 1944, declared:

'Since the agreement was made at Teheran to mount an "Anvil", I cannot accept, without consultation with Stalin, any course of action which abandons this operation. . . . Finally, for purely political considerations over here [the Presidential Elections], I should never survive even a slight setback in "Overlord" if it were known that fairly large forces had been diverted to the Balkans.'[1]

Thus Churchill's suggestion – which had nothing directly to do with the Balkans – that it was more profitable to employ the Army of Italy in a 'thrust against Vienna through the Ljubljana Gap'[2] than to divert a large part of it to Southern France came to naught, and with it the last chance of a German defeat before the Russians could cross the German eastern frontier.

'By the first of September', writes General Bradley, 'the enemy's June strength on the Western front had been cut down to a disorganized corporal's guard.'[3] Notwithstanding, pursuit was out of the question, not because Eisenhower lacked troops, but because he had not sufficient petrol to keep mobile the vast number he had. Instead of contracting his battle front, as Montgomery urged, he decided to slow down his advance and prepare for another major battle on his entire

[1] *The Second World War*, Vol. VI, p. 57, and Appendix D.

[2] Ibid., Vol. VI, p. 57.

[3] *A Soldier's Story*, Omar Bradley (English edition, 1951), p. 411.

front. This delay provided the Germans with a breathing space in which to reorganize.

Further to cripple allied strategy, during the Second Quebec Conference, which assembled on 10th September, Mr Henry Morgenthau, Secretary of the United States Treasury, brought forward a plan to prevent rearmament of Germany after the war. It was largely drafted by Harry Dexter White, Morgenthau's Assistant Secretary, who in August 1951 was cited before the Senate Security Sub-Committee, and found to be a Soviet agent.[1] The aim of the plan was to dismantle or destroy all industrial plants left undamaged by military action; wreck the Ruhr and Saar mines, and convert Germany from an industrial into an agricultural and pastoral country. The plan was accepted by the President and Mr Churchill, and made public on 24th September.[2] As it appeared to define in detail what unconditional surrender meant, it convinced the millions of Germans who were opposed to the Nazi regime that it was better to go down fighting under Hitler than accept a Carthaginian peace.

This gratuitous spiritual blood transfusion, coupled with Eisenhower's broad-front strategy, led to a series of desperate engagements along the 350-mile front from Nijmegen to Colmar, when suddenly in mid-December Hitler's counter-offensive in the Ardennes clearly revealed the poverty of Eisenhower's generalship. Though the counter-offensive failed, it cost the Allies 77,000 men and a slump in prestige, which so impressed Stalin that he seized the opportunity, while the Americans and British were embarrassed, to agree to another Big Three meeting, for which the President had pressed since his re-election. Also, because Hitler had committed his entire strategic reserve in the Ardennes offensive, Stalin decided to open the Russian winter campaign in mid-January; he hoped

[1] *The Twenty-Year Revolution*, Chesly Manly, pp. 102–3.

[2] It was heavily criticized and later modified. When Stimson, U.S. Secretary of War, read to the President the words about converting Germany into a pastoral country, Stimson records that: 'He was frankly staggered by this and said he had no idea he could have initialled this; that he had evidently done it without much thought' (*On Active Service in Peace and War*, Henry L. Stimson and McGeorge Bundy (English edition, 1949, p. 336)). Churchill says much the same of himself (*The Second World War*, Vol. VI, p. 138).

that by the time the Big Three met his armies would have overrun the whole of Poland, and that he would be in a position to present his allies with a *fait accompli.* This came about, because on 4th February 1945, the day the Big Three met at Yalta in the Crimea, the Russian marshals had carried their armies to the Oder.

The President left America for the Crimea with high hopes and little preparations;[1] the war was nearing its end and the time had come to assure himself of Stalin's full-hearted collaboration in U.N.O. This appeared easy, because he could see no fundamental clash of interests between the Soviet Union and the United States. Also, although Churchill was a full-blooded imperialist, Stalin, so he fondly held, was nothing of the kind, and, in order to liquidate the British, French and Dutch Asiatic empires, he needed his support. He also needed Stalin's aid to finish off the Japanese, because his Chiefs of Staff had warned him that without Russia it might cost the United States 'over a million casualties' to conquer Japan.[2] Therefore, before the conference assembled, he made up his mind to allow Stalin a free hand in Europe as a *quid pro quo.*

Because of Stalin's realism and the President's idealism – he was advised by Harry Hopkins, and among others by Algar Hiss of the State Department and a Soviet underground agent – the Yalta Conference led to a super-Munich.

It was agreed that Germany should be partitioned into zones, and each zone occupied by an allied army;[3] that unconditional surrender would be enforced; that forced labour would be imposed; and that twenty billion dollars in reparations, of which Russia was to receive half, should be considered.

When Stalin had agreed to take part in the United Nations

[1] See *Speaking Frankly,* James F. Byrnes (English edition, n.d.), p. 23.

[2] *On Active Serice in Peace and War,* p. 365.

[3] Berlin, which was deep within the Soviet Zone, was 'to be governed jointly by a Komendatura consisting of commandants appointed by the respective zone Commanders-in-Chief.' Therefore the Americans, British and French would need adequate and unhampered access to the city. 'But . . . the War Department (or at least a branch of it) . . . thought it unnecessary to define. . . . [and] That it could be done better . . . by the zone commanders when more was known of the state of the roads, railways, and the like. The subject . . . remained in abeyance' (*Churchill, Roosevelt and Stalin,* Herbert Feis (1957), p. 533).

San Francisco Conference in April, Poland, for whose integrity Great Britain had entered the war, was thrown to the Russian wolves. Her eastern frontier was approximately fixed on the Curzon Line; her western provisionally pushed out to the rivers Oder and Western Neisse; and the Lublin Committee of Soviet stooges, which at the instigation of the Kremlin had, on 31st December 1944, proclaimed itself the 'Provisional Government of Liberated Democratic Poland', was, when diluted with a few members of the *emigré* government, to be accepted, on condition that free elections were held; but these were not to be supervised by neutral observers, as this might insult the Poles!

Next, at a secret meeting, from which Churchill was excluded, the President secured Stalin's aid against Japan. In exchange he agreed to acknowledge the *status quo* in Outer Mongolia; the restoration to Russia of all territories lost in 1904–1905, Southern Sakhalin and the Kurile Islands. Also he agreed to Russia's joint control with China of the eastern and southern Manchurian railways. As much of these territories was Chinese, it would appear that the President had forgotten about imperialism and the Atlantic Charter.

During the conference the allied armies under Eisenhower advanced on the Rhine; but it was not until 23rd March that the Third U.S. Army, under General George S. Patton, crossed it at Oppenheim, and on the following day the British Twenty-First Army Group and the Ninth U.S. Army, both under Field-Marshal Montgomery, did so at Wesel.

When, on 13th April, Field-Marshal Model and 325,000 officers and men capitulated in the Ruhr, the road to Berlin was unbarred; Marshals Zhukov and Koniev were still on the Oder and Neisse, but Vienna had fallen to Marshal Malinovsky. It was imperative for Eisenhower to push on at top speed, because the Russians had broken or disregarded every important item of the Yalta Agreement which by then had been put to the test, and with Berlin and Prague in Anglo-American hands, the United States and Great Britain would be in a strong position to insist that the Russians honoured their agreements. 'If we did not get things right', says Churchill, 'the world would soon see that Mr. Roosevelt and I had underwritten a fraudulent prospectus when we put our signatures to the Crimea settlements.'[1]

Eisenhower, the complete non-Clausewitzian soldier, thought otherwise. 'Military factors, when the enemy was on the brink of final defeat', he writes in his report, 'were more important in my eyes than the political considerations involved in an allied capture of the capital. The function of our forces must be to crush the German armies rather than dissipate our strength in the occupation of empty ruined cities.'[2] The outcome was that on 14th April, two days after President Roosevelt's death, Mr Harry S. Truman, who had succeeded him, instructed Eisenhower to halt his troops on the Elbe, and abandon Berlin and Prague to the Russians. The former was occupied by them on 2nd May, and the latter on the day following the cessation of hostilities at midnight 8th–9th May.

'For the United States and Great Britain, the fruits of the battle of Normandy were apples of Sodom, which turned to ashes as soon as they were plucked. Hitler and his legions were destroyed, and in their stead stood Stalin and his Asiatic hordes. Because "Victory – victory at all costs" had been the Western Allies aim, and because of their insistence that "it was to be the defeat, ruin, and slaughter of Hitler, to the exclusion of all other purposes, loyalties and aims", Stalin, the supreme realist, whose strategy had throughout kept in step with his policy, had been able to impose his messianic cult upon Estonia, Latvia, Lithuania, part of Finland, Poland, eastern and central Germany, a third of Austria, Yugoslavia, Hungary, Rumania, and Bulgaria. Vienna, Prague and Berlin, the vertebrae of Europe, were his, and, except for Athens, so was every capital city in eastern Europe. The western frontier of Russia had been advanced from the Pripet Marshes to the Thuringerwald, a distance of 750 miles, and, as in the days of Charlemange, the Slavs stood on the Elbe and the Böhmerwald. A thousand years of European history had been rolled back.'[3]

[1] *The Second World War*, Vol. VI, p. 370.

[2] *Report of the Supreme Commander to the Combined Chiefs of Staff on the Operations in Europe of the Allied Expeditionary Force, 6 June 1944 to 8 May 1945* (1946), p. 131.

[3] Cited from the author's *The Decisive Battles of the Western World* (1956), Vol. III, p. 589.

10 · The Tactical Grand Climacteric

The great naval battle of Leyte Gulf, fought and won by the American Third and Seventh Fleets between 23rd–26th October 1944, sealed the fate of Japan. Except for a few odd warships, her navy ceased to exist, and Admiral Mitsumasa Yonai, Navy Minister of the Koiso Cabinet, declared 'that he realized that the defeat "was tantamount to the loss of the Philippines." As for the larger significance of the battle, he said, "I felt that that was the end." '[1]

The 'larger significance' was missed by President Roosevelt and his advisers. It was no longer how to defeat Japan, but how to extract the highest political profit from her defeat. It was a far simpler problem than the one that had faced them in Europe. There they had to consider their allies; but the war with Japan was 95 per cent. an American war, and, in order to avoid complications, it was essential that the United States should win it single-handed. Had this been understood, it would have been seen that, as Russia was the only Power who could complicate the issue, it was highly desirable for the United States to bring her war with Japan to an end before or immediately after Germany collapsed – that is, while Russia was still engaged in Europe. Was this possible? The answer is an unqualified 'yes', provided that the strategical and political centres of gravity of the problem were kept in mind.

From the first, the position of Japan had been one of extreme strategical fragility, because her economic potential was approximately only 10 per cent. of that of the United States, and her acreage of arable land no more than 3 per cent., yet it had to support a population over half as large. Because Japan depended on Manchuria and Korea for most of her raw materials and much of her grain, which had to cross the Sea of Japan and the Yellow Sea, her merchant navy was the centre of gravity of her strategy. The attack on Japanese shipping was the main task of the American submarines, and the part they played in bringing about the defeat of Japan would be difficult to overestimate; out of the total of 8,900,000

[1] Cited by C. Vann Woodward in *The Battle of Leyte Gulf* (1947), p. 231.

tons of Japanese shipping sunk, no less than 54.7 per cent. is attributed to submarines.[1]

Instead of concentrating against Japan's shipping and forcing her surrender through economic collapse, the strategy adopted by the Joint Chiefs of Staff was based on invasion of the Japanese homeland, and in preparation, long-range bombing offensives from the Mariana Islands were initiated shortly after the battle of Leyte Gulf. In the aggregate 104,000 tons of bombs were dropped on sixty-six cities, and 42,900 tons on industrial areas.[2] Although this bombing reduced production, loss of shipping remained the dominant factor in Japan's economic decline, because it was the interdiction of coal, oil, other raw materials as well as grain, and not the destruction of factories and urban centres that struck the deadliest blow at her economy.

The *Survey* points out that much of this bombing was duplicative, because most of the Japanese factories, oil refineries, steel mills, and munition plants lacked raw materials, and in consequence Japan's economy was in a large measure being destroyed twice over, once by cutting off imports, and secondly by air attack. Further, that attack of Japan's extremely vulnerable railroad network would have greatly extended and cumulated the effects of the shipping attack already made. 'The Survey', we read, 'believes that such an attack [on a stated number of rail ferries, tunnels and bridges] had it been well-planned in advance, might have been initiated . . . in August, 1944. . . . The Survey has estimated that the force requirements to effect complete interdiction of the railroad system would have been 650 B-29 visual sorties carrying 5,200 tons of high explosive bombs.'[3]

When these requirements are deducted from the 15,000 sorties flown and the 104,000 tons of bombs dropped on the sixty-six cities, the residue is a fair comment of the strategic error committed by the Joint Chiefs of Staff.

The political centre of gravity also eluded the President and

[1] *United States Strategic Bombing Survey, Summary Report,* (Pacific War), p. 11.

[2] Ibid., p. 17.

[3] Ibid., p. 19.

his advisers; it lay in the person of the Japanese Emperor, because he was the godhead of the armed forces, and in the eyes of his people a divinity. But the one thing he could not do was to order his people to surrender unconditionally, and thereby acquiesce in becoming a war criminal, to be placed on trial, or shot at sight.[1]

Early in 1944, Rear-Admiral Sokichi Takagi, of the Japanese Naval General Staff, came to the conclusion that, in order to end the war, Japan should seek a compromise peace, and although on 15th April 1945, Admiral Kantaro Suzuki succeeded General Kuniaki Koiso to implement one, he was unwilling to do so as long as the status of the Emperor was jeopardized by unconditional surrender. At length in June, the Emperor, who since January had increasingly become convinced that the war must be ended, decided to send Prince Fumimaro Konoye on a mission to Moscow to seek Soviet mediation. At the same time Naotake Sato, the Japanese Ambassador in Moscow, was instructed to inform the Soviet Government that under no circumstances could Japan accept unconditional surrender; he was to persuade the Kremlin to bring about a peace on terms.

Meanwhile Washington also considered ways and means to end the war, and although the War Department urged invasion and the Air Force mass bombing, others were of opinion that were 'a rational version' of unconditional surrender adopted, the Japanese might give in, and that 'the only doubt which still forestalled a decision was the future status of the Emperor.'[2] One opinion, based on interrogations of prisoners of high rank, was 'that the Japanese were on the point of giving up but were held back by a fear that the imperial institution would be abolished and the emperor himself punished as a war criminal.'[3]

While these proposals were under review, progress on the

[1] In accordance with the Morgenthau Plan, when captured all listed as arch criminals were to be shot, and the President 'had expressed himself as definitely in favour of execution without trial' (*On Active Service in Peace and War*, pp. 338–9).

[2] See *United States Army in World War II*, Ray S. Cline (1951), pp. 333–47.

[3] *Secretary Stimson: A Study in Statecraft*, N. Current (1954), p. 224.

atomic bomb had advanced to a point at which its success was almost certain.[1] In April 1945, Stimson appointed a committee to advise him on its use, and on 2nd June he set down his views in a memorandum to President Truman. He proposed as an alternative to an invasion of Japan the use of the atomic bomb, if its final trial, then in preparation, was successful. He suggested that its use be preceded by a warning, which should point out 'the varied and overwhelming character of the force we are about to bring to bear on the islands', and 'the inevitability and completeness of the destruction which the full application of this force will entail.' Further, he personally thought, 'if we should add that we do not exclude a constitutional monarchy under her present dynasty, it would substantially add to the chance of acceptance.'[2]

On 17th July, the Potsdam Conference assembled, and on the same day Stimson informed the President of the momentous news that, on the previous day, the final test of the bomb had proved an unqualified success. Thereupon Truman and Churchill, in order to obviate the casualties an invasion of Japan would entail, decided to use the bomb. 'Now all this nightmare picture', writes Churchill, 'had vanished. In its place was the vision – fair and bright it seemed – of the end of the whole war in one or two violent shocks. . . . Moreover, we should not need the Russians.'[3]

He was mistaken, for Mr Stettinius informs us: 'Even as late as the Potsdam Conference, after the first atomic bomb had been exploded . . . the military insisted that the Soviet Union had to be brought into the Far Eastern War. At both Yalta and Potsdam the military staffs were particularly concerned with the Japanese troops in Manchuria. Described as the cream of the Japanese Army, this self-contained force . . . was believed capable of prolonging the war even after the

[1] Mr Churchill first mentions the bomb on 30th August 1941 (*The Second World War*, Vol. III, p. 730), and Dr Goebbels on 21st March 1942 (*The Goebbels Diaries*, p. 96).

[2] *On Active Service in Peace and War*, p. 368.

[3] *The Second World War*, Vol. VI, pp. 552–3. On p. 553 Churchill states the he has never doubted that Truman was right to use the bomb, and six pages on he writes: Japan's 'defeat was certain before the first bomb fell.'

islands of Japan had been surrendered, unless Russia should enter the war.'[1]

Before the conference assembled, all the messages between Tokyo and Sato in Moscow were deciphered in Washington,[2] and on 13th July the following dispatch from the Japanese Foreign Minister to Sato came through: 'See Molotov before departure for Potsdam. . . . Convey his Majesty's strong desire to secure a termination of the war. . . . Unconditional surrender is the only obstacle to peace. . . .'[3] Although this made Japan's desperate position crystal clear and opened the road to an immediate end of the war, on 26th July the following ultimatum was presented to Japan: 'We call upon the Government of Japan to proclaim now the unconditional surrender of all the Japanese armed forces. . . . The alternative for Japan is complete and utter destruction.'[4] Not a word was said about the Emperor.

Two days later Suzuki rejected the ultimatum; he announced that it was 'unworthy of public notice'.[5] It was then decided, in order to cover Russia's entrance into the war, which had been fixed for 8th August, to drop two atomic bombs, one on Hiroshima on 6th August, and the other on Nagasaki on 9th August. So it came about that, at 8.15 a.m. on Monday, 6th August, a ball of fire appeared over the north-western centre of Hiroshima. Its explosive force was equivalent to 20,000 tons of T.N.T.; at its centre its temperature was about 150,000,000°C. – about ten times greater than the temperature at the solar centre',[6] and the pressure exerted was estimated at hundreds of thousands of tons to the square inch. A 'fire-storm' resulted in which hundreds of fires were simultaneously started; the most distant was 4,600 yards from

[1] *Roosevelt and the Russians: The Yalta Conference*, Edward R. Stettinius (English edition, 1950), p. 96. At the time the 'cream' consisted of skimmed milk. Its trained men had long been removed, and it had no petrol.

[2] The Japanese cipher had been broken prior to Pearl Harbour and remained so throughout the war.

[3] *Japan's Decision to Surrender*, Robert J. C. Butow (1954), p. 130.

[4] For the 'Potsdam Proclamation' in full see ibid., Appendix C, pp. 243–4.

[5] *On Active Service in Peace and War*, p. 369.

[6] *The Nature of the Universe*, Fred Hoyle (1960), p. 36.

the centre of the explosion. Four and a half square miles of the city were completely burnt, and from 70,000 to 80,000 people were killed and 50,000 injured. Nevertheless, the factories on the periphery of the city 'were almost completely undamaged', and 'it is estimated that they could have resumed substantially normal production within 30 days of the bombing, had the war continued.'[1]

On 9th August, the Japanese Supreme Direction Council agreed to refer the issue of unconditional surrender to the Emperor. He decided for peace, and on the 10th a broadcast from Tokyo announced that the Japanese Government was ready to accept the terms of the Allied Potsdam Declaration of 26th July, 'with the understanding that the said declaration does not comprise any demand which prejudices the prerogatives of His Majesty as a Sovereign Ruler.'[2]

To avoid the rounding up of the many scattered Japanese armies, which would own no authority but that of the Emperor, the Allied reply of 11th August contained this paragraph: 'From the moment of surrender the authority of the Emperor and the Japanese Government to rule the state shall be subject to the Supreme Commander of the Allied powers.'[3] On the 14th this was accepted by the Emperor; the cease fire was sounded, and on 2nd September the Japanese envoys signed the instrument of surrender.

Stimson's comments on this are illuminating:

'The true question, as he saw it, was not whether surrender could have been achieved without the use of the bomb, but whether a different diplomatic and military course would have led to an earlier surrender. Here the question of intelligence became significant. Interviews after the war indicated clearly that a large element of the Japanese Cabinet was ready in the spring to accept substantially the same terms as those finally agreed on. Information of this general attitude was available to the American Government. . . . It is possible, in the light of the final surrender, that a clearer and earlier exposition of American willingness to retain the Emperor would have pro-

[1] *U.S. Strategic Bombing Survey* (Pacific War), p. 24.
[2] For reply in full see Butow, Appendix D, p. 244.
[3] Ibid., Appendix E, p. 245.

duced an earlier ending of the war; this course was earnestly advocated by Grew and his immediate associates during May, 1945.'[1]

There can be little doubt, had it not been for the political and strategical myopia induced by the policy of unconditional surrender, that the war could have been ended in May 1945, and it was vital that it should end in May, were a profitable allied peace in the Far East to be won. Had it so ended, Russia could not have intervened, and all the disastrous consequences of her intervention would have been avoided. Had it done so, there would have been no need to drop the two atomic bombs which, as Hanson W. Baldwin rightly says were used for one purpose only: 'not to secure a more equable peace, but to hasten victory.'[2]

Yet the fact remains that they were dropped and to the consternation and bewilderment of mankind. The very source of creative power had been tapped and transmuted into a catastrophic agent; the ultimate military expression of the Industrial Revolution had been reached, nuclear energy in the form of an explosive had led to the tactical grand climacteric in human conflict – it had eliminated physical warfare as a profitable instrument of policy.

11 · Defeat Through Victory

When after the First Quebec Conference Churchill became more and more aware of the Russian menace to Europe, by then the growing power of the United States, coupled with the dependence of British economy on Lend-Lease, so shackled him that by the date of the invasion of Normandy the conduct of the war had passed almost entirely into the hands of the American President and his Joint Chiefs of Staff. At length came the German surrender, and with it 'to my eyes', Churchill writes, 'the Soviet menace . . . had already replaced the Nazi foe . . . I could only feel the vast manifestation of Soviet and Russian imperialism rolling forward over helpless lands.'[3] Four days later, on 12th May 1945, he cabled President Truman:

[1] *On Active Service in Peace and War*, pp. 371–2. Joseph C. Grew was Acting Secretary of State.

[2] *Great Mistakes of the War* (1950), p. 101.

[3] *The Second World War*, Vol. VI, pp. 495–6.

'The general effect of the plan', we read, 'is a reduction in the level of industry as a whole to a figure of about 50 or 55 per cent. the pre-war level in 1938.'[1]

This meant starvation for millions of Germans, and America, the most generous of countries, should have foreseen that the civilized world would not tolerate this indefinitely.

'Occupation Directive (JCS 1067/6)': It outlined the policy to be followed by General Eisenhower, and as a member of the Council of Control he was to urge its adoption by the other occupying Powers. The political and administrative structure of Germany was to be decentralized. Fraternization was forbidden. All members of the Nazi Party and supporters of Nazism were to be excluded from public office and private enterprise. All military organizations, including the German Officers Corps, were to be dissolved. All officials of the Nazi Party, members of the political police, the Waffen S.S., the General Staff, leading officials, urban and rural burgomasters, and Nazi sympathizers were to be arrested. No political activities were to be allowed. All criminal and civil courts were to be closed, as well as all educational institutions. The payment of military and private pensions was prohibited. All gold, silver, currencies and securities were to be impounded. No steps were to be taken toward the economic rehabilitation of Germany. And no action that would tend to support the basic living standard in Germany on a higher level than that existing in any one of the neighbouring countries was to be taken.[2] In short, Germany was to be converted into a super-concentration camp.

All this was finally agreed, signed and sealed at the Potsdam Conference, which assembled in the Cecilienhof on 17th July, by when Stalin was so firmly seated in the saddle that the delegates did little more than acclaim his victory.

The two main items on the agenda were Germany and Poland. As regards the former, the decisions of the Yalta Conference were confirmed, so were the instructions laid down in the above two directives. Reparations were apportioned,

[1] For the plan in full see *German Realities*, Gustav Stolper (1948), Appendix D, pp. 294–99.

[2] See ibid., Appendix C, pp. 273–93.

mainly to the benefit of Russia, and the methods of trial of the major war criminals were agreed. Further, it was agreed that Königsberg and the area adjacent to it should be transferred to the Soviet Union.

As regards Poland, agreement was reached on her western frontier, the final delimination of which should await the peace settlement. Pending this, the German territories east of the Oder and Western Neisse rivers, as well as the bulk of East Prussia and the former Polish Corridor were placed under the administration of the Polish State.[1]

Further to this, the Conference agreed on the removal of Germans from Poland, Czechoslovakia and Hungary and their transference to Western Germany 'in an orderly and humane manner.'[2] For nearly two years, and to the high profit of the Soviet Union, Europe floundered in chaos, and the situation became so threatening that President Truman entrusted ex-President Herbert Hoover with an economic mission to report on what should be done. This he did on 18th March 1947.

'At the present time', we read, 'the taxpayers of the United States and Britain are contributing nearly $600,000,000 a year to prevent starvation of the Germans in the American and British zones alone. . . . There is only one path to recovery in Europe. That is production. The whole of Europe is interlinked with German economy. . . . The productivity of Europe cannot be restored without the restoration of Germany as a contributor to that productivity. . . . There is the illusion that the New Germany left under the annexations can be reduced to a "pastoral state". It cannot be done unless we exterminate or move 25,000,000 people out of it. . . . There is an illusion in "war potential". Almost every industry on earth is a "war potential" in modern war. . . . The overall illusion is that Ger-

[1] Commenting on these annexations, Mr Churchill writes: 'For the future peace of Europe here was a wrong beside which Alsace-Lorraine and the Danzig corridor were trifles' (Vol. VI, p. 561). At the Teheran Conference he had said: 'If Poland trod on some German toes that could not be helped', and that he was not going to break his heart about the cession of part of Germany to Poland (Vol. V, pp. 319, 351).

[2] This entailed the expulsion of some 15,000,000 people, and even at the time of the Conference they were being hounded out. It was carried out in so ruthless a way that, according to Stolper (p. 26), roughly 6,000,000 were eventually unaccounted for.

many can ever become self-supporting under the "level of industry" plan within the borders envisioned at present for Germany. A still further illusion is that Europe as a whole can recover without the economic recovery of Germany. . . . We can keep Germany in these economic chains but it will also keep Europe in rags.'[1]

This was the authentic voice of America; but the greatest illusion of all was President Roosevelt's 'hunch'.

When the tragedy of Europe is viewed in retrospect, without fear of contradiction it may be said that it was indeed the black day in Europe's history when, on 6th April 1917, the United States became involved in the first of the world wars. It led to the dictated Peace of Versailles, a veritable Pandora's box, out of which emerged yet another world war. The second intervention was even more disastrous, it led to no peace at all, instead to a perpetual state of 'wardom' – of Hobbesian fear.

The reason for this has nothing to do with cupidity, which has precipitated so many European wars, because the Americans have never coveted an acre of Europe's land. Instead it was due to their failure to understand that war is an instrument of policy. They did not know how to wage war, and in consequence they did not know how to make peace. They looked upon war as a lethal game in which the trophy was victory.

The first fatal step was taken at the Arcadia Conference, at which the cloud-cuckoo land of President Roosevelt's 'Great Design' was substituted for a well-reasoned grand strategical policy. Yet, strange to relate, at about the same time a Yale professor, Nicholas J. Spykman, set down in black and white what that policy should be:

'If the foreign policy of a state is to be practical', he pointed out, 'it should be designed not in terms of some dream world but in terms of the realities of international relations in terms of power politics.' He urged that the two objectives of United States policy should be predominance in the New World, and a balance of power in the Old, and because this balance had been upset on the opposite shores of the Atlantic and Pacific,

[1] For the report in full see Stolper, Appendix E, pp. 300–11.

the war aim of the United States should be to restore it. This, he wrote, did not demand the annihilation of Germany and Japan, lest Europe and the Far East be opened to domination by Russia. 'A Russian State from the Urals to the North Sea', he said, 'can be no great improvement over a German State from the North Sea to the Urals.' The same reasoning applied to the Far East, and he wrote: 'The danger of another Japanese conquest of Asia must be removed, but does not inevitably mean the elimination of the military strength of Japan and the surrender of the Western Pacific to China or Russia.'[1]

The crucial British twin errors were of timing and aim. In their turn, they have been made crystal clear by a Cambridge professor, Herbert Butterfield.

'There is a very good historical precedent', he writes, 'for a thesis, which belongs to the cream of diplomatic tradition in better times. . . . It is the thesis that if two rival giants are offering an alternate threat to the existing order of things on the continent, and if you are unwilling to let the rascals fight it out by themselves, choose carefully the time of your intervention in their struggle and see that you intervene only in order to save which-ever of the two it may be from being destroyed by the other. For so long as there are two of these giants on the continent the whole world can breathe; but if you devote a war of righteousness to the purpose of destroying one of them you are using your blood and treasure to build up the other one into a greater monster than ever, and you will infallibly have to face it at the next stage of the story. In other words the policy of ridding the world of aggression by the method of total war – of the war for righteousness – is like using the devil to cast out the devil: it does not even have the merit of being practical politics.'[2]

It would appear that, had the statesmen known as much about war as an instrument of policy as the professors, we might today be living in a very different world.

[1] *America's Strategy in World Politics: The United States and the Balance of Power* (1942), pp. 446 and 460.
[2] *Christianity and History* (1950), p. 141.

CHAPTER XIV

The Problem of Peace

*

1 · Retrospect

Before the aftermath of the Second World War is discussed, it may assist the reader to focus his thoughts if first we glance back on some of the salient features of the period so far reviewed.

To begin with we see the emergence of a new form of civilization, the child of the mating of Rousseau's idea of the 'general will' and the energy begotten by Watt's steam engine. Its institutions are still those of the old agricultural order of society, and its activities blindly grope towards those of a new industrial one. The tensions between the two set up violent oscillations; within the nations they lead to social upheavals, and between the nations to increasing animosities. In embryo it is to be seen in the Napoleonic Wars, and its future is predicted in two absolute theories, the one on war as expounded by Clausewitz, and the other on economics as expounded by Marx. Both are utopians, and although their premises are right, their conclusions are at fault. Clausewitz's insistence that war is a political instrument is the first principle of all military statecraft, but his equal insistence on the complete overthrow of the enemy vitiates the end of grand strategy, which is that a profitable peace demands not the annihilation of one's opponent, but the elimination or modification of the causes of the war. Marx was profoundly right when he insisted that, because man is a tool-using animal, the implements he fashions must necessarily influence the evolution of society, and the forms that society takes; but he was in error when he drew from this the conclusion that the forms could only be changed by means of the class struggle. While Clausewitz failed to see that peace was the ultimate aim in war, Marx failed to see that in the steam age the ultimate economic and social aims were to create an industrial society through an evolutionary and not a revolutionary process, because employers (directors, managers, etc.) and workers are complementary and not antagonistic agents in production – male and female as it were. Both set too much store on violence, which can enforce but cannot create.

The first of the wars of the evolving industrial civilization was the American Civil War. In greater part, as we have seen, its origins were due to economic causes, and its progress revealed the increasing dependence of armaments on industry, and a decline in morality, because the old cultural ties were loosened by the amorality of advancing materialism. The war began as an urban-rural contest of factory versus plantation, and it ended by proclaiming Big Business the winner.

The years which span the close of the American Civil War and the end of the century witnessed vast industrial developments both in the United States and Western Europe. Nation after nation became industrialized, and ever-increasing competition between them led to colonization on an unprecedented scale, and with it to violent international contentions. Nevertheless, to the detriment of internal tranquillity, changes in social institutions lagged behind industrial progress, and, in spite of the increased deadliness of weapons fashioned by industry, military theory remained much as it had been in the days of the muzzle-loader. Statesmen and soldiers continued to think in terms of bayonets and sabres, and it did not occur to them that in an industrial age the factory had become the powerhouse of the barrack, as in the agricultural age the peasantry was the main source of fighting power. When toward the close of the century, oil as a new motive power and developments in the electrical sciences heralded in the second phase of the Industrial Revolution, little attention was paid to the radical changes they portended in the techniques of war.

Thus it came about that, although the causes of the First World War were largely industrial and commercial, in 1914 the armies of all belligerents set out to fight the war with no clear idea of the sort of conflict they were called upon to wage, and only after complete stalemate had set in did they appeal to industry and science to haul them out of the quagmire of their trenches. Nevertheless, when due to the attrition of German industrial power and agricultural production by the blockade the war collapsed, instead of the victors seeking a peace in which its economic causes might be eliminated, they ignored them and got back to Big Business on 1913 lines, and, as a corollary, they returned in greater part to the military organizations which had led to the initial stalemate.

With the return to Big Business, the oscillations which had precipitated the war began to repeat themselves. While in Europe the nations were in revolutionary turmoil, in America industrial concentration developed so rapidly that half the wealth of the United States passed into the hands of some 200 giant corporations. This centralization of wealth, which on the one hand increased productivity and on the other failed to build up the people's purchasing power to consume it, toppled over in the financial crash of 1929, and out of its debris Big Business began to pass into Big Government.

In Russia this had already occurred when Lenin's experimentations in Marxism, which ruined production, forced him to introduce State capitalism and his N.E.P. policy, and in Italy Mussolini had striven to build up the people's purchasing power in his Corporate State. Then, in 1933, both Roosevelt in America and Hitler in Germany set out to solve the selfsame problem, the one by means of his New Deal and the other by means of his New Order. But as none of these would-be economic messiahs could discover how to equilibrate consumption with production, they were impelled toward war, because, as Lewis Mumford points out: 'An army is a body of pure consumers . . . it tends to reduce toward zero the gap in time between profitable production and profitable replacement. . . . Quantity production must rely for its success upon quantity consumption; and nothing ensures replacement like organized destruction.'[1]

Lastly, in 1939, came the Second World War; there were many dead but no unemployed; consumption put the strain on production, and the urge to destroy led to a cataract of lethal inventions. The most outstanding were the development of atomic energy as a new source of power, and the intro-

[1] *Technics and Civilization*, pp. 93–94.

duction of electronically controlled devices out of which emerged the techniques of automation. The purpose of the latter is progressively to substitute machinery for the human brain, as the purpose of Watt's steam engine and Daimler's internal combustion motor was to substitute machinery for human and animal muscle. With automation and nuclear energy the Industrial Revolution entered its third phase.

Nevertheless, when in 1945 the fighting ended with the explosion of the first atomic bomb, the problem of peace remained unsolved, and the state of wardom continued. Therefore the question arises, will the industrial war society of today lead to an industrial peace society tomorrow?

2 · *Impact of Nuclear Energy on War*

The conversion of nuclear energy into an explosive has been compared with the discovery of gunpowder, and the conclusion drawn is that, although in its day the latter was as violently anathematized as the former is now, it was not rejected; therefore nuclear explosives have come to stay. Although this is logical, because the 'know-how' of a new scientific process cannot be deleted, it should be accepted with an important reservation. It is that, directly the political factor is introduced, in all wars, except those of the most primitive kind, the destructive means employed to achieve a profitable end must be limited. For example, when in feudal times the aim of a king was to bring his truculent barons to heel, the primitive artillery of that period was found invaluable to deprive them of their power of resistance – their castles. But had its destructive effect been such that, not only their castles, but their retainers, serfs, orchards and cattle within a radius of several miles would be obliterated, nothing would have been left to bring to heel – the means would have swallowed the end.

The same applies to all civilzed warfare, because there is always a relationship between force and aim. The first must be sufficient to attain the second, but not so excessive that it cancels it out. This is the crux in nuclear warfare.

Since the Hiroshima atomic-bomb, which had an explosive equivalent of 20,000 tons of TNT (20 kilotons), was dropped, thermo-nuclear devices, such as the hydrogen bomb, have been developed with an explosive equivalent of 20,000,000 tons of TNT (20 megatons), and there is no upward limit to their increase in power. Further, so-called 'tactical' nuclear projectiles have been devised with an explosive equivalent as small as 100 tons of TNT,[1] which confuse the issue; for where is the line to be drawn between high and low scale nuclear missiles? Common sense replies, in apportioning the means to the aim; but, unfortunately, common sense is the rarest of the senses in war, and directly a nuclear weapon, even of the lowest explosive equivalent, is introduced, no check can be relied on to prevent it growing in destructive power until megaton size is reached, when, it has been estimated that, in an attack with hydrogen bombs 'lasting perhaps thirty hours, 30 per cent. of the population of the United States would be dead or seriously injured.'[2] From the point of view of any sane political aim, all-out nuclear warfare is nonsense.

Notwithstanding, the basic assumption in American strategy is that the next war will start with a Pearl Harbour nuclear attack; therefore the United States must be in a position to wipe out the Soviet Union before the Soviet Union can wipe out the United States. This would be logical, were the aim of American policy to resort to a nuclear surprise attack; but the reverse is the case, because it has been publicly advertised that the American Government will never be the first to make use of all-out nuclear weapons. The error in this strategical outlook is to postulate that war today is absolute, that to win a war the enemy must be annihilated politically, which to be effective demands the occupation of his country. The whole conception is reactionary, it is nothing other than a return to the great artillery battles of the First World War, in which at the price of removing one obstacle another was created. Not a cratered zone which had to be crossed before the enemy's position could be occupied, but to occupy the enemy's entire country and administer it when it is in a state

[1] *Nuclear Weapons and Foreign Policy*, Henry A. Kissinger (1957) p. 13.

[2] *The Military and Industrial Revolution of our Time*, Fritz Sternberg (1959), p. 6.

of unimaginable confusion. As bad, because this archaic strategy excludes all political, social, economic and moral considerations, it leaves the door wide open to the Soviet Union to exploit them. Yet, in Mr Isaac Deutscher's opinion: 'Probably no nation lives in greater horror of nuclear war than do the Russians',[1] which is undoubtedly true, if for no other reason than it deprives war of its political meaning, which is the soul of Russian strategy.

This does not mean that Khrushchev and his colleagues fear that an all-out nuclear war would annul the final consummation of Communism, because with Marx they hold that no technical discovery, however powerful, can abrogate the laws of history. What they fear is, that it would for the time being delay its advent by crippling the industrial foundations upon which the entire conception of the Communist earthly paradise is built. Nuclear war or no nuclear war, it is the certainty of the Marxian revolution that Khrushchev had in mind when, in 1955, at the height of the 'peace offensive', he said: '. . . if anyone thinks that we shall forget about Marx, Engels, and Lenin, he is mistaken. This will happen when shrimps learn to whistle.'[2] This must also have been in his mind when at a reception at the Polish Embassy in Moscow, in 1956, with reference to the Democracies, he said: 'We will bury you.' [3]His frequent rocket rattlings should delude no one, they are no more than the brandishings of fire extinguishers, and his 'brinkmanship' is both bluff and political blackmail. Deutscher is certainly right, no man fears an all-out nuclear war more so than he.

So it comes about that the two great camps into which the world of wardom is now divided are, as in trench warfare of former days, separated by a no-man's-land which neither dares to cross, and we arrive at a stalemate which both fear to break, and which, through fear that the other may dare to break it, leads to both sides frantically multiplying their nuclear armaments in order indefinitely to postpone the Crack of Doom.

[1] *The Great Contest: Russia and the West* (1960), p. 43.

[2] 'When Shrimps Learn to Whistle', Denis Healey, *International Affairs* (January 1956), Vol. 32, p. 2. [3] Cited by Kissinger, op. cit., p. 6.

Because an all-out nuclear war is highly improbable, will a return be made to conventional wars – that is, to wars in which nuclear weapons are excluded? If so, it would be no great exchange should warfare remain unlimited, as it was in the last world conflict. Therefore the heart of the problem is not to be sought in types of weapons, but in the aim which governs their use. Once again, to repeat what has been insisted on throughout this book, be it borne in mind that a limited war is a war fought for a clearly defined limited political object, in which expenditure of force is proportioned to the aim; therefore strategy must be subordinated to policy. For the benefit of his American kinsmen, Dr Kissinger has written:

'The prerequisite for a policy of limited war is to re-introduce the political element into our concept of warfare and to discard the notion that policy ends when war begins or that war can have goals distinct from those of national policy.'[1]

This is pure Clausewitz.

Earlier in this Section, the danger of introducing nuclear weapons into the tactical field has been touched upon; yet this is what has actually happened in the NATO forces, in order to compensate for Russia's vastly superior conventional military strength, and General Sir John Cowley mentions that the tactical weapons already introduced 'can have warheads of far greater power than the bombs that destroyed Hiroshima or Nagasaki.'[2] Therefore, whatever may be their ulterior motives, the Russians are logical when they insist that there is no such thing as a limited nuclear war, and that the employment of tactical nuclear weapons will inevitably lead to an all-out nuclear attack.[3] Therefore it follows, when both sides are equipped with them, that they will become deterrents on the tactical level, which reduces the idea of fighting a limited nuclear war to an absurdity. Thus it comes about that the stalemate is doubly assured, and except for wars other than

[1] Op. cit., p. 141.

[2] 'Future Trends in Warfare', *Journal of the Royal United Service Institution* (February 1960), Vol. CV, p. 8.

[3] Kissinger (op. cit., p. 176) points out, there are certain nuclear weapons which are difficult to discard, such as atomic warheads for anti-aircraft missiles.

those which directly involve the two great nuclear camps, such as wars by proxy or police operations, it looks as if physical warfare, either as an instrument of policy or of annihilation, is speeding toward the dustbin of obsolete things, to keep company with witchcraft, cannibalism, and other outgrown social institutions.

In Chapter VII we have seen that, as long ago as the end of the last century, Bloch, the Warsaw banker, glimpsed this. He predicted that, because of its deadliness, the then recently introduced magazine rifle would make wars so unprofitable as to be impossible to contemplate. This might have become true had man not been an irrational creature. Now the introduction of nuclear weapons is coaxing him into a rational frame of mind,[1] and if he must continue to fight, he will have to seek his battlefields in spheres of conflict other than in the physical. With reference to this, the reader is asked to bear in mind that the stalemate problem of the First World War was not ultimately solved by physical means but by economic – the blockade of the Central Powers.

3 · *Policies and the Cold War*

What do we mean by 'cold war'? The answer was given as long ago as 1651 by Thomas Hobbes in Chapter XIII of his *Leviathan*:

'Warre consisteth not in Battell onely', he wrote, 'or the act of fighting; but in a tract of time, wherein the Will to contend by Battell is sufficiently known: and therefore the notion of *Time*, is to be considered in the nature of Warre; as it is in the nature of Weather. For as the nature of Foule weather, lyeth not in a showre or two of rain; but in an inclination thereto of many dayes together; So the nature of War, consisteth not in actuall fighting; but in the known disposition thereto, during all the time there is no assurance to the contrary. All other time is PEACE.'

Today, the only difference is that, since his day, the disposition to fight has been extended more deeply into the moral

[1] The most notable exception is the pacifist, whose irrational faith in the elimination of war by the simple process of renouncing it has been rationalized by the introduction of nuclear weapons. Of all people he should welcome these deterrents; instead he fanatically opposes them.

and economic fields of strife, which, as Hobbes must have been aware, have always been the foundations of the physical conflict. Although in cold war the physical struggle is restricted rather than excluded, its main aim is to undermine its foundations, and the more they are undermined the less the need to batter down the edifice they support. In this there is nothing new, as a simple example will make clear. A walled city can be physically attacked by battering down its walls; economically attacked by starving out its garrison, and morally attacked by subverting it. When, before the age of gunpowder, walls were difficult to breach, the second and third were frequently resorted to. Today, in the age of nuclear explosives, because the process of breaching is mutually destructive, they are being relied upon again.

Lenin, as we have seen, appreciated this at the time of the Brest-Litovsk peace negotiations, when his people were starving, his followers divided, and his army impotent. Since then, although the Soviet Union has become the second greatest industrial and the greatest military Power in the world, because of the physical stalemate created by nuclear weapons cold war is likely to continue as long as the spell of foul political weather lasts. The conclusion is that, because the essence of the clash between East and West is between two ideologies akin to those which detonated the American Civil War, Lincoln's famous warning to his fellow-countrymen may in the present age be extended to the world in general. Today, it may be said: 'A world divided against itself cannot stand, it cannot endure permanently half-slave and half-free. We do not expect the world to fall; but we do expect it will cease to be divided. It will become all one thing, or all the other.' Which is it to be? The answer depends on the policies of the contestants.

The basic difference between the policies of the Democracies and Soviet Russia is their respective outlooks on peace. To the one peace begins when war ends, to the other it is a continuation of war by every means short of actual fighting. To the one international differences in peacetime are settled by argument, to the other they are accentuated by it. While in democratic countries government is based on collectivism, the votes and opinions of the masses, Soviet government is based on individualism, the authority of one man or a small oligarchy. The consequence is that it is easy for the latter to be on a permanent war footing, in which leadership is paramount, policy but little influenced by public opinion, discipline rigid, and secrecy assured, while, other than in wartime, these things are almost impossible for the former; like a mob confronted by a force of disciplined soldiers, the Democracies recoil before Soviet power, and fear to exploit Soviet difficulties. They act as did the democratic Athenians when threatened by the autocratic Philip of Macedon.

'So you', thundered Demosthenes, 'if you hear of Philip in the Chersonese, vote an expedition there, if at Thermopylae, you vote one there; if somewhere else, you keep pace with him to and fro. You take your marching orders from him; you have never formed any plan of campaign for yourselves, never foreseen any event, until you learn that something has happened or is happening. . . . Our business is not to speculate on what the future may bring forth, but to be certain that it will bring disaster, unless you face the facts and consent to do your duty.'[1]

As Kissinger so rightly says: '. . . . it is futile to seek to deal with a revolutionary power by "ordinary" diplomatic methods.'[2] And the Democracies should be aware, as Clausewitz insisted, that the most decisive act of judgment a statesman can exercise 'is rightly to understand . . . the war in which he engages.' Because the age we are living in is one of permanent emergency, this is equally applicable to peace. He should not, Clausewitz continues, 'take it for something, or wish to make of it something, which by the nature of its relations it is impossible for it to be.'[3] Unfortunately for the Free World, this is what its statesmen have consistently been doing since 1945.

They should realize that no compromise with the Soviets is possible as long as they continue to hold that world revolution is preordained by history. Therefore they should avoid

[1] *First Philippic*, 41, 47 and 50.
[2] Op. cit., p. 007.
[3] See *supra*, Chapter IV, p. 67.

all conferences like the plague; not only do they invariably provide a platform for Communist propaganda, but as Señor Salvador de Madariaga has pointed out: when 'we consent to talk with those who are opposing freedom . . . we are betraying our first front line, the peoples of Eastern Europe, in exchange for a "peace" which is no peace.'[1]

It is this inner front – rather than first line – which is the Achilles heel of the Soviet Imperium. Not only are half of the inhabitants of the U.S.S.R. non-Russian, and many of them are nationally-minded and antagonistic to Muscovite rule; but it has also been estimated that less than five per cent. of the peoples behind the Iron Curtain are in sympathy with their draconic Communist regimes. As we have seen, whenever a crisis has occurred within the Russian Empire, whether in Tzarist or Communist times, the minority nations have revolted, and whenever oppression has appeared to weaken in the countries behind the Iron Curtain, disturbances or revolts have followed. In the Hungarian rising of 1956 it should not be forgotten that the only non-Hungarian people who fought on the side of the rebels were deserters from the Russian army.

Therefore, in the cold war, the psychological centre of gravity of the Soviet Empire is to be sought in the hearts of the subjugated peoples within the U.S.S.R. and behind the Iron Curtain. Further, it should be borne in mind, and it seldom is, that this psychological 'bomb' is as great a deterrent to the Soviets resorting to actual war as the hydrogen bomb itself. Russia's weakness is our strength, and her strength is our ignorance; no man realizes this more fully than Nikita Khrushchev – what, then, is his cold war policy?

It is to break away from Lenin's concept of the inevitability of war between the Communist and Capitalist countries, and to substitute the economic attack for the military attack. This change in tactics dominated the principal speakers of the Twentieth Party Congress, which was assembled in February 1956. They all agreed that, while the economy of the Soviet Union and the People's Democracies was progressively advancing, the economy of the capitalist countries was not keeping pace with it; therefore it was no longer

[1] *The Blowing up of the Parthenon* (1960), pp. 91–92.

necessary to rely upon war as the main instrument of policy. 'As Khrushchev said, "armed interference" was unnecessary, since the "certainty of the victory of communism" was based on the conviction that "the socialist mode of production possesses decisive advantages over the capitalist mode of production." ' And A. I. Mikoyan pointed out that, since there could be no victory in a future war, war could no longer benefit the Soviet Union, and that ' "the interests of successful communist construction" and "the struggle to raise the standard of living" were "in direct contradiction with the policy of the arms drive and of expending human and material forces for war purposes. . . ." In short, the policy of coexistence, which was now officially proclaimed as the central principle of Soviet foreign relations, fitted in both with the internal needs, and with the existing world situation, as well as with the long term requirements of the struggle against capitalism.'[1]

Therefore, because Khrushchev and his colleagues held that Capitalism was doomed through its inherent inefficiency, it was more profitable to besiege its garrison and starve it into surrender by economic competition than to assault it by military force. In the words of Bloch: 'The soldier is going down and the economist is going up. There is no doubt of it. Humanity has progressed beyond the stage in which war can any longer be regarded as a possible Court of Appeal.'[2]

4 · *The Third World War*

Based on this policy, in November 1958, Khrushchev drafted a Seven Year Plan for the Soviet economy in the years 1959–1965, and he called it 'a decisive step towards implementing the task of the U.S.S.R. – to catch up with and overtake in the historically shortest period of time the most highly developed capitalist countries in per caput output of goods.'[3] In January 1959, it was adopted by the Twenty-First Party Congress, and in November 1960, confirmed by eighty-one communist and workers parties in conference at Moscow.[4] At the former

[1] *Survey of International Affairs 1955-1956*, Geoffrey Barraclough and Rachel F. Wall (1960), p. 226.

[2] See *supra*, Chapter VII, p. 129.

[3] Cited in *The Soviet Seven Year Plan*, anonymous (1960), p. 110.

[4] See Appendix V.

Khrushchev affirmed that the next seven years would be decisive, and that by 1965 the U.S.S.R. would produce more industrial goods per head of the population than the United Kingdom and Western Germany, and that by 1970, or even before, the output per head of the United States would be surpassed.[1]

This was a declaration of war, a war in which the economic offensive was to become the positive instrument of Soviet policy, and under cover of the terror induced by the threat of all-out nuclear war, armies were to give way to factories, weapons to goods, and markets were to become the battlefields of the future. In a different form it was to be a return to the bloodless warfare of the absolute kings, whose aim had been to bankrupt each other's exchequers rather than ruin each other's armies. If the reader will turn back to Chapter V, p. 80, and re-read what, in 1835, Andrew Ure had to say on the rivalries between the factory owners of the first phase of the Industrial Revolution to capture foreign markets – which he called 'the new belligerent system' – he will obtain some idea of the type of warfare the Soviet Union intends to wage.

Since 1939, the industrialization of the U.S.S.R. has bordered on the fabulous. In recent years its productivity has advanced at a rate roughly twice that of the United States, and in 1959 it was estimated to have reached 45 per cent. of it. To a large extent this has been due to the same cause which led to the rapid increase in productivity in Great Britain during the first phase of the Industrial Revolution – namely, to the ploughing back of profits into the capital equipment industries instead of sharing them with the workers. While in the first phase the poverty of the British workers was an incidental concomitant of the competition between the factory owners,[2] in the Soviet Union it is planned, and may be described as 'organized poverty'. Therefore consumer goods are restricted, as there is but a limited market for them, and, as we shall see in the next Section, this planned poverty, which in its incidental form was the disease of the early

[1] This claim is based on the assumption that production in the West would remain at its 1958 level.

[2] See *supra*, Chapter V, p. 80.

capitalist-industrial scramble, is not likely to last indefinitely.

In spite of the rapid growth of Soviet productivity, the position of the Western Economic Bloc is unlikely to become critical until China is far more industrialized than she is at present, and even then she may form an Asiatic Economic Bloc of her own, apart from the U.S.S.R. When China is omitted, the main danger is not so much Soviet competition as its own lack of economic integration.

Its material resources are very great, and in population – one of the main elements in industrial production – it considerably outdistances its antagonist, as may be seen from the following population figures. Western Bloc: United States – 177,399,000; Western Europe – 319,225,000, and Canada, Australia and New Zealand – 29,708,000. Soviet Bloc: U.S.S.R. – 208,826,000, and its Satellites – 86,079,000. A total of 536,332,000 compared with 294,905,000 – that is, a superiority of 231,427,000.[1]

At present, the superiority of the Soviet Bloc over the Western resides in its organization, which is para-military. The Presidium is its Chiefs of Staff, the Party its corps of officers, and its industrial and other workers its economic soldiers. As in an army, the first can plan without reference to the third, and can rely on its orders being implicitly obeyed by the second. This is the key difference between the opposed economic systems.

As in actual war, the economic offensive demands the concentration of the means of attack, that is the integration of the economies of the Soviet Bloc. This subject also figured prominently in the programme of the Twentieth Party Congress, and was outlined by Khrushchev as follows:

'Close economic co-operation gives exceptional opportunities for the best possible utilisation of productive and raw-material resources, and successfully combines the interests of each country with those of the socialist camp as a whole. . . . Today it is no longer necessary for each socialist country to

[1] Compiled from the population figures given in *The World Almanac* 1960. Turkey is included in the Western Bloc, and Yugoslavia excluded from both.

develop all branches of heavy industry, as had to be done by the Soviet Union.... Now, when there is a powerful community of socialist countries... each European people's democracy can specialize in developing those industries and producing those goods for which it has the most favourable natural and economic conditions. This at the same time creates the necessary prerequisites for releasing considerable resources to develop agriculture and the light industries, and on this basis to satisfy more and more fully the material and cultural requirements of the peoples.'[1]

This means that the economies of the Satellite countries are to be organized so as not to overlap the economy of the Soviet Union, and that they are progressively to be converted into departments of one gigantic workshop. Because virtually no tariffs are allowed, the whole is aimed to constitute a common power-house as well as a common market, and all production not absorbed by the latter will become 'ammunition' wherewith to bombard the West. Should China be included in this economic bloc, Isaac Deutscher estimates that eventually a single economic entity will come into being with a common market four or five times larger than the North American, and at least twice as large as the North American and Western European markets combined.[2]

That this change in policy is aimed to undermine the economy of the Capitalist countries is beyond doubt, because, even before it was finally decided, the advance guard of the attack had taken the field. In November 1955, at a reception in Moscow, Khrushchev told a British press reporter: 'Your system will collapse through economic competition with Communism';[3] and that same year, writes Mr Welton, '... goods from Russia, Poland, Hungary, Rumania, Bulgaria, Czechoslovakia, East Germany and China were entering the Middle East on terms beyond the competitive power of the West.' These countries, he adds, 'were not only prepared to take Middle East products whether they needed them or not, but also to grant credit facilities which no democratic government

[1] Cited in *Survey of International Affairs 1955–1956*, pp. 243–4.
[2] *The Great Contest*, p. 51.
[3] Cited in *The Third World War*, Harry Welton (1959), p. 6.

answerable to the taxpayer and the free trade unions could possibly match.'[1]

Further, he cites what Mr John Diefenbaker, Prime Minister of Canada, had to say on this question at an Anglo-Canadian rally in London on 4th November 1958:

'Trade has become a major weapon in the Communist world offensive. First it was the U.S.S.R., and now Red China has joined in an Asian trade onslaught, intended to capture markets and, with and through them, the minds of free men. The Communist drive is designed to undermine the economy and strength of the free world.'[2]

The paradox in this offensive is, that the alleged contradiction in the capitalist system, which Marx affirmed would destroy it from within, has, in the form of 'organized poverty', been adopted as its basis in order to destroy it from without by depriving the capitalist countries of their markets.

Should this economic offensive progressively gain ground, the Western Powers will become less and less able to maintain an effective front against Soviet expansion, either ideological or physical, and Lenin's aim to unite Germany and the Soviet Union, and thereby create a gigantic agrarian and industrial combination, will be brought a long step nearer to fulfilment.[3]

To accomplish this is the linch-pin in Khrushchev's German policy, and should he succeed in creating this monster, what remains of Free Europe will be at the mercy of the Soviet

[1] Ibid., p. 171. Between 1955 and 1958 trade with countries outside the Soviet Bloc increased by nearly 70 per cent. (*The Soviet Seven Years Plan*, p. 93).

[2] Ibid., p. 313.

[3] Lenin's war aims, laid down by him at the time of the Brest-Litovsk peace treaty, were in 1924 in condensed form published by Karl Radek in No. 3 of the *Communist International.* They read: 'The proletariat of industrial Germany, Austria and Czechoslovakia, in uniting with the proletariat of Russia will create a mighty agrarian and industrial combination from Vladivostok to the Rhine . . . capable of feeding itself and of confronting the reactionary capitalism of Britain with a revolutionary giant, which with one hand would disturb the senile tranquillity of the East and with the other beat back the private capitalism of Anglo-Saxon countries. If there were anything that could compel the English whale to dance, it would be the union of revolutionary Russia with a revolutionary Central Europe' (cited by Vladimir L. Borin in *This Terrorism and You* (1948), pp. 45–46).

Union, and the dream of World Communism will become a potential reality.

At the time when this was written, the Defence Ministry of the Federal Republic claimed that Western Germany was the main battlefield of the cold war. According to the Ministry,

'Propaganda in west Germany is directed by an office of the east German central committee with 16,000 agents in the Federal Republic, among them hundreds of instructors. The number of pamphlets coming across the frontier each month has risen from 320,000 in 1957 to 12 million. There are now 45 east German wireless transmitters, and its television programme reaches a west German audience larger than the east German population. Numerous illegal communist papers are printed in west Germany, including 11 *Land* papers, more than 100 works papers, and 25 magazines.'[1]

Further, the Ministry states that 8,400,000,000 marks (about £700,000,000) are yearly spent on the propaganda campaign against the West; that there are sixty-three Communist Parties in Western and neutral countries, each an active fifth column, and that there are hundreds of front groups directed by fifteen pro-Communist world organizations, controlled by a central committee in Prague, which may be regarded as a successor to the Comintern.[2] Such is the reverse of Khrushchev's 'peaceful coexistence'.

To meet the Soviet challenge, the democratic nations must realize that the problem they are called upon to respond to is very different from the international trade rivalries of former times,[3] the aims of which were purely economic. Today they are faced with economic war on military lines, the aim of which is a revolutionary one, and in which trade represents armed force. As the situation now stands they are economically at sixes and sevens, unintegrated and un-cooperative, separated by tariffs and quotas, and daily wrestling for each others' markets. In the economic wardom which faces them, these rivalries and discords are nothing other than economic civil war.

[1] See Appendix VI.

[2] *The Times*, London, 7th October 1960.

[3] With the exception of Hitler's, which was one of the causes that precipitated the Second World War (see *supra* Chapter XII, pp. 234–5).

The integration of their respective economies, however, would seem to be impossible unless they adopt a system of exchange freed from trade booms and slumps, hard and soft currencies, and periodic worsening balances of payment, which can only be effected by the demonetization of gold and the basing of wealth on its true source – production. This, as we have seen, was appreciated by Hitler in the mid-thirties, when he put a stop to the debauchment of the German currency by resorting to a system of unilateral barter.

In his day, Lenin also appreciated it. According to Lord Keynes, he 'is said to have declared that the best way to destroy the Capitalist System was to debauch the currency'; and his comment is: 'Lenin was certainly right. There is no subtler, no surer means of overturning the existing basis of society than to debauch the currency. The process engages all the hidden forces of economic law on the side of destruction, and does it in a manner which not one man in a million is able to diagnose.'[1]

Lenin resorted to state capitalism which is immune from the machinations of financiers and is virtually uninfluenced by the fluctuations of the foreign exchanges. The unquestionable contradiction in the capitalist system is, not that it makes the rich richer and the poor poorer, but that it carries within itself the germs of its own debauchment, which periodically throw one nation after the other into the fever of a financial crisis which wrecks their economies. Until these germs are eliminated there can be no stable integration of the economies of the Capitalist Powers, and in consequence no firm political unity between them. Should this be a correct diagnosis, the salvation of the West lies in its own hands, and should it fail to save itself, it may well be that by 1970, as Khrushchev predicts, it will unwittingly have signed its own death warrant.

5 · *Impact of Technology on Social Life*

Marx's contribution to social history, that 'productive relations' change with changes in the 'productive forces', is only another way of saying that society is changed by changes

[1] *The Economic Consequences of the Peace*, pp. 220–1.

in technology. When they occur, the struggle which arises is not so much, as Marx postulated, between social classes, as between the evolving institutions of the new society and the established institutions of the old.

When the first impact of the Industrial Revolution on social life occurred, the social institutions of all Western peoples, related as they were to a mature agricultural civilization, were much alike; but today they are no longer so. In the West we see a society which is socially free, and in the East a society which is under rigid state control. While in the West, the impact of industrialism has followed an evolutionary path, and increase in productivity has progressively led to a rise in the standard of living, in the Soviet Union, in spite of its remarkable productivity, because its revolutionary economic policy is based on organized poverty, the living standard of the vast majority of its peoples has been artificially restricted. Added to this, the problem is further complicated by the impact of Communism on China, which today is in the same stage the Soviet Union was in a generation ago.

Since the opening of the present century, and never more so than today, industrial progress in the United States, and to a lesser extent in Great Britain and Western Europe, instead of making the rich richer and poor poorer, as Marx predicted, has proceeded in the opposite direction. The incomes of the working masses have steadily increased, and those of the rich have declined. In America the earnings of the workers have in many cases reached those of middle class standards, and there are no signs of the distribution of wealth halting. Within the foreseeable future poverty will be abolished, first in the United States and later in Western Europe, and with it will vanish Marx's concept of the proletariat, on which he so largely built his hypothetical economic order.

Coincidentally with this non-Marxian evolution, the growth of state enterprise, which in the United States became apparent during the period of the New Deal, has been accelerated not only in the United States but also in Western Europe. This has been due to the increased activity of the State in industrial undertakings which are beyond the capacity of private enterprise to finance, and to the Western governments being compelled to maintain enormous peacetime military establishments as well as most of the scientific research apparatus upon which they depend. The tendency today is, therefore, toward increasing state enterprise and decreasing private enterprise. These two evolutionary changes, the elimination of poverty on the one hand, and the growth of state control on the other, are progressively being speeded up by the almost daily advances in technology.

A very different permutation is to be seen in the Soviet Union. It is neither an evolutionary nor a revolutionary development of Marxism; instead it is its perceptible withering away.

When Khrushchev stepped into Stalin's shoes, he was aware that terror was defeating its own end. During the despot's rule, not only had he and his colleagues lived in constant dread of sudden liquidation, but terror was paralysing the initiative industrialism required in order to maintain its vigour and health. It was not that he and his comrades contemplated a modification, let alone an abandonment of Marxism – their religion – but that the advances in technology were forcing them to liberalize the existing tyranny by giving more freedom to the Russian peoples.

By the turn of the mid-century, through force of its inherent requirements, industrialization in Russia had brought into being a middle class of scientists, technicians, managers, etc., whose skills, as in capitalist countries, are most effectively stimulated by the prospect of high salaries. Today some of these people are earning as much as a million roubles (say, £20,000) a year, and considerable numbers several thousand pounds. These new rich form an administrative and technological plutocracy, and inevitably act as fugelmen to the rising generation of educated Russian youth.

These young people are penned in by Marxism, and unlike the youth of the West can find no outlet for their ambitions through democratic institutions. Trained to think in terms of the *Communist Manifesto*, they are beginning to think in terms of their own pockets, and the more roubles they are paid the more they will want. What does this point to? Not to a revolt against Communism, which in a police state is virtually impossible, but to a revulsion from 'organized poverty', and with it to the withering away of the concept that the proletariat can develop into the ruling class. Instead, now that the Russians are being educated, human nature reasserts itself, and the more highly educated section of the masses will become the seed-bed of a new bourgeoisie which eventually will turn Marxism upside down.

This is corroborated by both Mr Averell Harriman and Sir Fitzroy Maclean. The first found that academicians, professors and teachers were beginning 'to express doubts about some of the alleged scientific dogmas of Marxism.' That in the universities and higher technical schools 'there is a wide indifference to Communist ideology', and 'Even in matters of foreign affairs, Marxist dogma on the inevitable decay of capitalism is becoming more difficult to reconcile with conditions abroad. As Soviet students learn more and more about life beyond the Communist frontier their scepticism is inevitably increasing.'[1]

In his turn, Fitzroy Maclean compares the present state of the Soviet Union with Victorian England during the first phase of the Industrial Revolution: its rapid industrialization, its sudden economic expansion, its sacrifice of the workers, and the emergence of a wealthy bourgeois class attached to its vested interests.

'But', he writes, 'the reader will say, are not these worthy people all Communists? Do not they all believe in world revolution? Of course they do. They are Communists just as the Victorians were Christians. They attend Communist Party meetings and lectures on Marxism-Leninism at regular intervals in exactly the same way the Victorians attended church on Sunday. They believe in world revolution just as implicitly as the Victorians believed in the Second Coming. And they apply the principles of Marxism in their private lives to just about the same extent as the Victorians applied the principles of the Sermon on the Mount to theirs.'[2]

Should these appreciations be correct, and there is no reason to doubt them, then it is apparent that technology is

[1] *Peace with Soviet Russia?* (1960), pp. 130–1.
[2] *Back to Bokhara* (1959), pp. 62–63.

transforming revolutionary Marxism into a bourgeois revival. While the Western nations are moving away from private enterprise toward state enterprise, the Soviet Union is moving away from state control to a freer social order. Will these two movements converge, or will they fight each other to the death?

6 · The Problem of China

The answer is probably to be sought in China's future relations with the U.S.S.R.

China is not a Russian satellite, she is an ideological partner of the Soviet Union – but with a difference. While the Soviet Union is moving away from the forced industrialization of the Stalin period, China is still in the throes of an identical period and is therefore militantly minded. Because at present she is hopelessly at a loss in an economic war, Mao Tse-tung – the Stalin of the Chinese Revolution – has already come to loggerheads with his partner Khrushchev over his policy of peaceful coexistence, which excludes war. He has poured scorn on it by stating that China is in no way terrified by the dangers of an all-out nuclear war, and can well afford to expend a 100,000,000 of her people in one. Though at present, because of her lack of nuclear weapons, this may be an idle boast, it nevertheless reveals a terrifying biological necessity which arises out of a fundamental difference between China and Russia.

While Russia has never suffered from a shortage of land for her growing population, demographically China is a saturated country, and must either expand or explode. The one has a population of 210,000,000 in about 8,600,000 square miles of territory, and the other some 680,000,000 in 3,760,000 square miles. Further, the population of China is increasing at an annual rate of 12,000,000, or about four times that of the U.S.S.R.

This fundamental biological difference, coupled with the development of Chinese economy, must be giving Khrushchev and his henchmen a severe headache; for they see looming over their eastern frontier the form of a young giant, who before he is fully grown may seek his promised land in the sparsely populated spaces of Asiatic Russia.

This is corroborated by Mr Adlai Stevenson who, on his return from a visit to the Soviet Union, wrote in the *New York Times* of 2nd October, 1958:

'One day I asked a high official . . . "how about the production of babies in China?" adding that if the population of China continued to expand at the present rate the Soviet Union would one day look to its neighbor like the largest emptiest land in the world. – "Ah, that's the trouble", he replied unhesitatingly. . . . And whenever I remarked, as I often did, that a United Nations' commission estimated the population of China in the year 2000 at 1,600,000,000, the look of consternation was invariable. Nor was I surprised when on a couple of occasions Soviet officials quickly raised their vodka glasses and replied: "Which is another reason for better Soviet-American relations." '

Wedged in as the Soviet Union is between two fronts, should it find itself threatened by an overwhelmingly powerful China, will it not be compelled through self-preservation to substitute for its corrosive policy of peaceful coexistence a defensive alliance with the West? Such an alliance will of course depend on how far the Western Powers feel themselves threatened by the Yellow Peril should the Soviet Union succumb. But there is nothing irrational in assuming that they may agree to an alliance on terms, say, the liberation of Eastern Europe and the reunification of Germany. Such seemingly incompatible alliances and somersaults are not unknown to history.

There is an alternative possibility, which would avoid involving Russia as an enemy.

Instead of expanding into Asiatic Russia, the Chinese could move into South-East Asia and Indonesia, which are far less thickly populated than China. Thence into New Guinea, Australia and New Zealand, together approximately the size of China and inhabited by 13,600,000 people – one fiftieth of China's present population!

Should over-population (the biological cause of war) in China become insupportable, when she is in possession of nuclear weapons, as one day she undoubtedly will be, she may find it more expedient to expand than to explode by detonating a conventional war in South-East Asia. This would draw in the Western Powers and compel Russia to intervene on her behalf. Next, she could put Mao Tse-tung's boast to the gamble by resorting to nuclear warfare.

This possibility must also be giving Khrushchev a headache, for although China may be able to afford the loss of 100,000,000 of her miserable people, a loss which for her would actually be a biological asset, anything approaching it would biologically be catastrophic for the Soviet Union.

APPENDIX I

Lenin and the Peasantry

Lenin's outlook on the peasantry closely followed that of Marx, who despised them as 'rural idiots'. It is made clear in his 'Two Tactics of Social-Democracy', a long pamphlet written in 1905, and in an article entitled 'The Attitude of Social-Democracy toward the Peasant Movement', published in the same year. The following extracts are from the latter:

'... Let us assume that the peasant uprising has been victorious. The revolutionary peasant committees ... can proceed to the confiscation of any big property. We are in favour of confiscation.... But to whom shall we recommend that the confiscated land be given? On this question we have not tied our hands nor shall we ever do so.... There will always be reactionary admixtures in the peasant movement, and we declare war on them in advance ... to whom shall the confiscated lands be given, and how? We do not gloss over that question, nor do we promise equal distribution, "socialization", etc. What we do say is that this is a question we shall fight out later on, fight again on a new field and with other allies. Then, we shall certainly be with the rural proletariat, with the entire working class *against* the peasant bourgeoisie....'

'At first we support the peasantry in general against the landlords ... but at the same time we support the proletariat against the peasantry in general ... we can and do say *only one thing:* we shall put every effort into assisting the entire peasantry to make the democratic revolution, *in order thereby to make it easier* for us, the Party of the proletariat, to pass on, as quickly as possible, to the new and higher task – the Socialist revolution....'

'... The urban and industrial proletariat will inevitably be the basic nucleus of our Social-Democratic Labour Party, but we must attract to it, enlighten and organize all toilers and all the exploited – all without exception: handicraftsmen, paupers, beggars, servants, tramps, prostitutes – of course, subject to the necessary and obligatory condition that they join the Social-Democratic movement and not that the Social-Democratic movement joins them, that they adopt the standpoint of the proletariat and not that the proletariat adopts theirs' (*Selected Works*, Vol. I, pp. 441–3).

APPENDIX II

President Wilson's Fourteen Points, Four Principles and Five Particulars

The Fourteen Points, 8th January 1918

(1) 'Open covenants of peace openly arrived at, after which there shall be no private undertakings of any kind, but diplomacy shall proceed always frankly and in the public view.'

(2) 'Absolute freedom of navigation upon the seas outside territorial waters alike in peace and war. . . .'

(3) 'The removal, as far as possible, of all economic barriers. . . .'

(4) 'Adequate guarantees given and taken that national armaments will be reduced to the lowest point consistent with domestic safety.'

(5) 'A free, open-minded and absolute impartial adjustment of colonial claims based upon a strict observance of the principle that in determining all such questions of sovereignty the interest of the populations concerned must have equal weight with the equitable claims of the Government whose title is to be determined.'

(6) 'The evacuation of all Russian territory . . . Russia to be given unhampered and unembarrassed opportunity for the independent determination of her own political development and national policy.' Russia to be welcome in the League of Nations and to be given all possible assistance.

(7) Belgium to be evacuated and restored.

(8) France to be evacuated, the invaded portions restored and Alsace-Lorraine returned to her.

(9) 'A readjustment of the frontiers of Italy should be effected along clearly recognisable lines of nationality.'

(10) 'The peoples of Austria Hungary . . . to be accorded the freest opportunity for autonomous development.' (Subsequently modified to complete independence.)

(11) Rumania, Serbia and Montenegro to be evacuated,

occupied territories to be restored. Serbia to be given free access to the sea.

(12) The Turkish portions of the Ottoman Empire to be assured a secure sovereignty. Subject nationalities to be assured security and unmolested opportunity of autonomous development. Freedom of the Straits to be guaranteed.

(13) An independent Polish State to be erected 'which should include the territories inhabited by indisputably Polish populations, which should be assured a free and secure access to the sea.'

(14) A general association of nations to be formed under specific covenants 'for the purpose of affording mutual guarantees of political independence and territorial integrity to great and small States alike.'

The Four Principles, 11th February 1918

(1) 'Each part of the final settlement must be based upon the essential justice of that particular case.'

(2) 'Peoples and provinces must not be bartered about from sovereignty to sovereignty as if they were chattels or pawns in a game.'

(3) 'Every territorial settlement must be in the interests of the populations concerned; and not as a part of any mere adjustment or compromise of claims among rival states.'

(4) 'All well-defined national elements shall be accorded the utmost satisfaction that can be accorded them without introducing new, or perpetuating old, elements of discord and antagonism.'

The Five Particulars, 27th September 1918

1) The first insisted on justice to friends and enemy alike.
2) The second denounced all separate interests.
3) The third provided that there should be no alliances within the body of the League.
4) The fourth forbade all economic combinations between League members.
5) The fifth reaffirmed the prohibition against secret Treaties.

APPENDIX III

The Atlantic Charter

Joint Declaration by the President and the Prime Minister, 12th August 1941

The President of the United States of America and the Prime Minister, Mr Churchill, representing His Majesty's Government in the United Kingdom, being met together, deem it right to make known certain common principles in the national policies of their respective countries on which they base their hopes for a better future for the world.

First, their countries seek no aggrandisement, territorial or other.

Second, they desire to see no territorial changes that do not accord with the freely expressed wishes of the peoples concerned.

Third, they respect the rights of all peoples to choose the form of government under which they will live, and they wish to see sovereign rights and self-government restored to those who have been forcibly deprived of them.

Fourth, they will endeavour, with due respect to their existing obligations, to further the enjoyment by all States, great or small, victor or vanquished, of access, on equal terms, to the trade and to the raw materials of the world which are needed for their economic prosperity.

Fifth, they desire to bring about the fullest collaboration between all nations in the economic field, with the object of securing for all improved labour standards, economic advancement, and social security.

Sixth, after the final destruction of the Nazi tyranny they hope to see established a peace which will afford to all nations the means of dwelling in safety within their own boundaries, and which will afford assurance that all the men in all the lands may live out their lives in freedom from fear and want.

Seventh, such a peace should enable all men to traverse the high seas and oceans without hindrance.

Eighth, they believe that all the nations of the world, for

realistic as well as spiritual reasons, must come to the abandonment of the use of force. Since no future peace can be maintained if land, sea, or air armaments continue to be employed by nations which threaten, or may threaten, aggression outside of their frontiers, they believe, pending the establishment of a wider and more permanent system of general security, that the disarmament of such nations is essential. They will likewise aid and encourage all other practicable measures which will lighten for peace-loving peoples the crushing burden of armaments.

APPENDIX IV

The United Nations Pact

A joint Declaration by the United States of America, the United Kingdom of Great Britain and Northern Ireland, the Union of Soviet Socialist Republics, China, Australia, Belgium, Canada, Costa Rica, Cuba, Czechoslovakia, the Dominican Republic, El Salvador, Greece, Guatemala, Haiti, Honduras, India, Luxembourg, the Netherlands, New Zealand, Nicaragua, Norway, Panama, Poland, South Africa and Yugoslavia.

The Governments signatory hereto,

Having subscribed to a common programme of purposes and principles embodied in the Joint Declaration of the President of the United States of America and the Prime Minister of the United Kingdom of Great Britain and Northern Ireland, dated August 14, 1941, known as the Atlantic Charter,

Being convinced that complete victory over their enemies is essential to defend life, liberty, independence, and religious freedom, and to preserve human rights and justice in their own lands as well as in other lands, and that they are now engaged in a common struggle against savage and brutal forces seeking to subjugate the world, DECLARE:

(1) Each Government pledges itself to employ its full resources, military or economic, against those members of the Tripartite Pact and its adherents with which such Government is at war.

(2) Each Government pledges itself to co-operate with the Governments signatory hereto, and not to make a separate armistice or peace with the enemies.

The foregoing declaration may be adhered to by other nations which are, or which may be, rendering material assistance and contributions in the struggle for victory over Hitlerism.

APPENDIX V

The Moscow Communist Conference of November 1960

The following citations are from the statement issued by eighty-one communist and worker parties on the conclusion of their conference at Moscow in November 1960, as summarized in *The Times* (London) of 6th December 1960.

'The complete triumph of socialism is inevitable.'

'The course of social development proves right Lenin's prediction that the countries of victorious socialism would influence the development of world revolution chiefly by their economic construction.'

'The time is not far off when socialism's share of world production will be greater than that of capitalism. Capitalism will be defeated in the decisive sphere of human endeavour, the sphere of material production.'

'The world capitalist system is going through an intense process of disintegration and decay.'

'Never has the conflict between the productive forces and relations of production in the capitalist countries been so acute. Capitalism impedes more and more the use of achievements of modern science and technology.'

'The anarchcial nature of capitalist production is becoming more marked.'

'The uneven course of development of capitalism is continually changing the balance of forces between the imperialist countries. . . . The problem of markets has become more acute than ever.'

'United States monopoly capital is clearly unable to use all the productive forces at its command. The richest of the developed countries of the world has become a land of especially chronic unemployment.'

'The success of the policy of socialist industrialization has led to a great economic upsurge in the socialist countries, which are developing their economy much faster than the capitalist countries.'

'The Soviet Union will become the leading industrial power in the world. China will become a mighty industrial state.

The socialist system will be turning out more than half the world industrial product.'

'Peaceful coexistence of countries with different systems or destructive war – this is the alternative today.'

'Peaceful coexistence of states does not imply renunciation of the class struggle.... The coexistence of states with different social systems is a form of class struggle between socialism and capitalism.'

'Peaceful coexistence of countries with different social systems does not mean conciliation of the socialist and bourgeois ideologies. On the contrary, it implies intensification of the struggle of the working class of all communist parties for the triumph of socialist ideas. But ideological and political disputes between states must not be settled through war.'

APPENDIX VI

Communist Propaganda in West Germany

The main organs of propaganda are the Soviet Zone German 'Freedom Sender 904', and the 'Autonomous Department' (*Selbständige Abteilung*) of the East Berlin Ministry of War.

Nightly the former broadcasts a programme directed especially against the West German defence forces inciting desertion and disobedience jazzed up with hot music to attract listeners, while the task of the latter is to produce and circulate subversive publications. Among these are:

The *Soldatenfreund* (Soldier's Friend) for enlisted men and n.c.o.'s. It carries fictitious letters to the editor, invents abuses and exaggerates actual complaints, stirs up trouble and makes extensive use of obscene photographs and crude eroticism.

The *Wehrpolitik* (Defence Policy) for officers and intellectuals. It is of higher calibre, and publishes articles written by former Nazi officers based on objective sources and given a communist slant.

The *Kaserne* (The Barracks) for pacifists and anti-militarists. It specializes in pictures of graves, crosses, corpses, coffins and grotesque untruths not lacking in pornography.

The *Tabu* is a more cleverly written magazine designed for young people. It is artistically produced, and contains illustrated articles on popular science, anti-religious topics, etc., as well as suggestive photographs of nudes.

Besides these organs of propaganda, extensive use is made of anonymous letters and false official communications, such as posting to the wives of officers and men of the defence forces scented notes written in a female hand implicating their husbands in some extra-maritial intrigue, or of faked official notices to the relatives of soldiers informing them that their husbands and sons have met with a fatal accident or are suspected of some crime, etc.

The extent of these subversive activities may be judged from the fact that every month between one and two million of the above publications fall into the hands of the West German postal authorities. Their influence is largely discounted by their crudeness and baseness. Dirt is poor propaganda.

Index